Johannesburg

A Public Culture BOOK

Johannesburg

The Elusive Metropolis

Edited by

SARAH NUTTALL AND ACHILLE MBEMBE

With an afterword by Arjun Appadurai and Carol A. Breckenridge

Duke University Press   Durham and London   2008

© 2008 DUKE UNIVERSITY PRESS

All rights reserved

Printed in the United States of America on acid-free paper ∞

Designed by C. H. Westmoreland

Typeset in Minion by Achorn International, Inc.

Library of Congress Cataloging-in-Publication Data
Johannesburg : the elusive metropolis / Sarah Nuttall and
Achille Mbembe, eds. ; with an afterword by Arjun Appadurai
and Carol A. Breckenridge.
p. cm.
Includes bibliographical references and index.
ISBN 978-0-8223-4262-5 (cloth : alk. paper) —
ISBN 978-0-8223-4284-7 (pbk. : alk. paper)
1. Johannesburg (South Africa)—Social conditions.
2. Johannesburg (South Africa)—Civilization. 3. Sociology,
Urban—South Africa—Johannesburg. I. Nuttall, Sarah.
II. Mbembé, J.-A., 1957–
HN801.J64J64 2008
306.096822'1—dc22   2008019636

Contents

Acknowledgments

In the early 1990s, Carol Breckenridge, then editor of *Public Culture,* suggested that the journal run a special issue on Africa. When we were asked to edit it, it quickly became clear to us that producing such an issue without a profound reinterrogation of Africa as a sign in modern formations of knowledge would have little value, both for *Public Culture*'s readers and for us as editors. Instead, we thought that what was needed was a gesture of defamiliarization capable of providing the reader with a sense of the worldliness of contemporary African life forms. To undertake this gesture of defamiliarization, there was no better scene or site than a late modern African metropolis. We believed that a critical rereading of Johannesburg could help to shift, if only partially, the center of gravity of traditional forms of analysis and interpretations of Africa in global scholarship. We also hoped to show that when it comes to "things African," it is possible to move away from the fascination with the horrors of a seemingly static world and to rehabilitate our curiosity while also insisting on this virtue as a necessary hallmark of a truly global academic project.

Beth Povinelli and Dilip Gaonkar not only vigorously endorsed the project but also helped in shaping it intellectually. In particular, discussions with Beth Povinelli in Johannesburg and New York enriched the overall rationale of what has now come to be a full-length book. To the original articles published in *Public Culture* have been added new contributions and an afterword by Arjun Appadurai and Carol Breckenridge. *Public Culture*'s editorial committee provided challenging comments on and criticisms about the original essays, to which we have now added previously unpublished chapters. Kaylin Goldstein was a superb interlocutor and manager of the production process. Ken Wissoker at Duke University Press has been a pleasure to work with and an extremely valuable commentator on the manuscript. The Witwatersrand Institute for Social and Economic Research (WISER) has been an extraordinarily conducive environment from which to produce this book. We owe a great intellectual debt to all of our colleagues, specifically Deborah Posel, Jon Hyslop, Liz Walker, Ivor Chipkin, Graeme Reid, Irma Du Plessis, Tom Odhiambo, and Robert Muponde. We would also like to thank Arjun Appadurai, Carol Breckenridge, Paul Gilroy, Dominique Malaquais, Vyjayanthi Rao, and Vron Ware for their intellectual companionship during a semester spent at Yale University. Isabel Hofmeyr, Jon Hyslop, and Lindsay Bremner all commented on the introduction. David Goldberg read the entire manuscript, and we are enormously indebted to him. Part of the funding for the research and images in this book has come from a grant from AIRE-Développement, a program of the French Institute for Research in Development, based in Paris. William Kentridge generously granted permission for the reproduction of some of his Johannesburg drawings, which add immeasurably to the visual life of the book.

There is a manner about
Johannesburg, it makes the impression of a metropolis.
SARAH G. MILLIN, *The South Africans*

Introduction: Afropolis

ACHILLE MBEMBE AND SARAH NUTTALL

Johannesburg is the premier African metropolis, the symbol par excellence of
the "African modern." It has been, over the last hundred years, along with São
Paulo, Mumbai, Kuala Lumpur, Shanghai, Seoul, and Sydney, one of the critical nodes of Southern Hemispheric capitalism and globalization. The African
modern is a specific way of being in the world. As elsewhere in the global
South, it has been shaped in the crucible of colonialism and by the labor of
race. Worldliness, in this context, has had to do not only with the capacity to
generate one's own cultural forms, institutions, and lifeways, but also with the
ability to foreground, translate, fragment, and disrupt realities and imaginaries
originating elsewhere, and in the process place these forms and processes in
the service of one's own making. This is why modernity and worldliness, here,
have been so intrinsically connected to various forms of circulation—of people, capital, finance, and images—and to overlapping spaces and times.

This book is therefore, above all, an exercise in writing the worldliness of a contemporary African city. To write an African metropolis into the world is a complex and compelling task. On the one hand, it requires a profound reinterrogation
of Africa in general as a sign in modern formations of knowledge. On the other
hand, it calls for a critical examination of some of the ways in which cities in general and African cities in particular have been read in recent global scholarship.

Over the last quarter of the twentieth century, the paradigm of "the global
city" has dominated the study of the urban form. It has also been one of the
cornerstones of studies of globalization. The starting point of the global city

1 View of inner city, Johannesburg, 2007. Courtesy of Constitution Hill

paradigm is the largely shared assumption that contemporary life paths and social structures are profoundly shaped by the global circuits of capital.[1] Most of the literature on the global city understands the city form to be the spatial expression of the shifts in the geography and structure of the international economy since the 1970s.

These shifts have been the object of many detailed and sometimes contradictory studies. In spite of their heterogeneity, these studies generally agree that in the countries of the global North, the passage from an industrial to an informational economy has led to a dramatic decentralization of production and the increased mobility of capital, as well as to an internationalization and expansion of the financial industry. Coupled with the geographical dispersal of manufacturing processes and sites has been the rising dominance of service production and various processes of immaterial labor that involve the manipulation of knowledge and information. Communication and control can now be exercised efficiently at a distance.

The territorial dispersal of economic activity has resulted, though, in a growing need for expanded central control, management, and planning. The global city is, to a large extent, the result of this dialectic between the globalization of the economy and the need for the agglomeration of central functions of coordination, control, and management in a few leading financial centers. In Saskia Sassen's model, global cities are nodal points for the coordination of processes of production, innovation, and accumulation on a world scale. They are mainly defined by a number of key functions. First, they operate as highly concentrated command points in the organization of the world economy. Second, they are key locations for finance and for specialized service firms. Third, they are critical sites of production, including the production of innovation. Finally, they are major markets for the products and innovations produced. As Sassen (1991: 3–13) argues, a global city is therefore not simply a global marketplace for finance. It is a city that has developed a capability to produce and practice global control.

The global city paradigm is not simply a thick description of the changing functions of a few major northern cities in the context of new international, spatially dispersed, yet globally integrated forms of economic activity. It is also a highly functionalist theory of the city. It fails to consider that to declare a city to be truly global (including in its purely economistic sense), the latter has to be read against a complex, overlapping, disjunctive order of multiple centers, peripheries, and scapes of various scales, moving at various speeds (Appadurai 1996: 32). A truly global city, moreover, is composed not only of flows of money, skills, knowledge, security, machinery, and technology, but also of ideas, people, images, and imaginaries—a cultural economy. Many analysts have argued that the global city paradigm is a universalizing category that overlooks experiences of urban life in the South. The result has been belatedly to extend the category of the global city to incorporate what are now called the cities of the South (Sassen 2002). In this context, the repertory of sites has been expanded to include cities ranking "in the mid-range of the global hierarchy," where secondary networks of global economic flows can be identified (Krause and Petro 2003: 23). It has been argued, for instance, that major cities of the South share many of the characteristics of the global cities of the North, including cultural and ethnic heterogeneity, transnational flows of labor and capital, and uneven spatial and social development.

Noting that "it is futile to cling to the obsessive difference between here and there," others, such as Edward LiPuma and Thomas Koelbe (2004: 177), have tried to define global cities "through other lenses," such as "the cultures of global circulation" (Larkin 2004: 91–112). According to Ashley Dawson

(2004: 18), "like their counterparts in the North, the global cities of the South have also become increasingly connected with one another, transforming the exclusive links with the imperial metropolis that characterized colonial culture into a series of lateral connections with other sites in an emerging transnational urban system of the South." While some of these cities are operational hubs for the exchange of commodities and services, others are part of various transurban archipelagoes in highly pluralized spaces of connectivity. But it is not only the multiscalar, multitemporal, and multicentric nature of the global that critics are highlighting. With populations swelling above 20 million, Dawson claims, "the global cities of the South literally embody the future of humanity" (19).

Even more important than defining global cities through other lenses have been attempts at provincializing the global city model (Dawson and Edwards 2004; Bishop, Phillipps, and Yeo 2003). For instance, the contention is that with the shift of production to the South following the crisis in social reproduction of the 1970s, "a new urban order has begun to emerge," and megacities of the South are displacing the old urban centers of the North not only in terms of numbers, but "as the cutting edge of globalization." Ryan Bishop and his colleagues argue that many Southeast Asian cities can be read as perfect sites for an archeology of the future. These cities operate as a testing ground for techniques later applied to the global cities behind which they supposedly lag. Rem Koolhaas writes in his "Lagos: How It Works" (n.d.: 138), "We are resisting the notion that Lagos, Accra, and Abidjan represent African cities en route to becoming modern. Or, in the more politically correct idiom, that they are becoming modern through a valid, African way. Rather, we think it possible to argue that they represent a crystallized, extreme, paradigmatic set of case studies of cities at the forefront of globalizing modernity." He adds: "Many of the much-touted values of contemporary global capital and its prophetic organizational models of dispersal and discontinuity, federalism and flexibility, have been realized and perfected in West Africa. This is to say that Lagos is not catching up with us. Rather, we may be catching up with Lagos" (Koolhaus n.d.: 138, 85).[2]

Uncertainty, Spectrality, and Informality

This way of writing African cities into theory is in contrast with early urban studies (of labor migration, changing forms of marriage, the meaning of "tribalism," legal change and informal social networks, changing forms of rural-urban connections) and established approaches to urbanization. The latter, according to James Ferguson (1999: 20), "have all depended, in different ways, on an underlying meta-narrative of modernization." Anthropology, history, and literature have long seen Africans as fundamentally and even essentially rural creatures, while the African city itself has been perceived as an emblem of irresolvable crisis. For a long time, the task of scholarship has been to measure the process of assimilation to the urban environment and to assess the various ways in which the relationship between the individual and the tribal community is corrupted, reinvented, or maintained. In spite of the existence of old commercial and urban precolonial cultures in the continent, the transition from a rural to an urban life has sometimes been studied as if urban ways of life were virtually unknown to those societies before European settlement.

Ways of seeing and reading contemporary African cities are still dominated by the metanarrative of urbanization, modernization, and crisis. Indeed, for many analysts, the defining feature of contemporary African cities is the slum. What is underestimated is the extent to which major African cities have been able to attract and seduce, in their own ways, certain forms of colonial and now global capital. That such forms of capital are, for the most part, predatory is without doubt. But it can be argued that this, at least partly, is what globalization is about: a set of processes that are refracted, splintered, and cracked—"a matter of highly selective and spatially encapsulated forms of connection combined with widespread disconnection and exclusion." These cities are therefore not simply made of social black holes. As Ferguson (2006: 24) explains, their geography reveals that indeed they are "globally connected," but in "a selective, discontinuous and point to point fashion." They are also cities of cash—if not quartz. The analysis Appadurai develops about Mumbai could clearly be extended to encompass Lagos, Nairobi, Abidjan, Dakar, or Kinshasa, where large pockets of privilege coexist with misery. These are "cities where the circulation of wealth in the form of cash is ostentatious and immense, but the sources of cash are always restricted, mysterious, or unpredictable . . . and the search for cash in order to make ends meet is endless" (Appadurai 2000: 628). Indeed, such fractured, colliding, and splintered orders of urban life can be seen to characterize, increasingly, many cities around the world today. Urban poverty itself is many things, some of which have to do with material deprivation; others with lack of security and dignity; others with what Appadurai calls the "exposure to risk and high costs for thin comforts"; and others still with the "terms of recognition"—the ability and capacity of the poor to exercise voice, to debate, contest, and oppose vital directions for collective social life.

Over the last decade, there have been four major attempts at reading African cities into contemporary theory. These attempts are represented by the work of Jane Guyer, AbdouMaliq Simone, Filip de Boeck, and Rem Koolhaas. Underlying their respective projects have been a series of questions related to the place of cultural imagination in the making of cities, the role of calculation and rationality in the everyday tactics of those who inhabit them, and in the way they are made to work. These works have based their readings of the African city on the assumption that in the wake of the new circulations of the global economy, African urban social life is being reshaped in the midst of uncertainty. They have also sought to rehabilitate the informal and what they see as the spectral quality of African city life—that is, its constant interplay between what is "visible" and what is "invisible," between appearance and disappearance.

For Jane Guyer it is not simply that African cities are growing demographically without necessarily developing economically or politically. It is that they are growing along unknown pathways. For instance, they are generating quite new institutions and forms of social organization, practices of everyday life that encompass systems of employment, housing and urban transport, income earning opportunities, and meaning making—a creativity of practice of at times impressive magnitude and relentless resilience. These new pathways are routed via the organizations of what she calls "the popular economy"—a system with comprehensive reach into people's lives, but without coherent properties and recognizable boundaries (Guyer 2004; Guyer, Denzer, and Agbaje 2002).

In the midst of growing gradations of stratification, instability takes various forms. Chief among these is monetary instability. Less and less money is circulating. Formal sector employees are made redundant. There are acute shortages of goods that were once considered basic. It is not clear how countries manage world markets under conditions in which state capacity hardly exists, or is being eroded. Yet, in the midst of a greater social competition and velocity, new institutions and organizations are emerging, along with new templates for trust and transactions. Cities are still more or less fed. Cross-border trade is still going on. Locally made beer is always available. New possibilities emerge, at times in surprising places.

For AbdouMaliq Simone, forms of social collaboration and people's repertoires of action are constantly shifting. Civil life appears as an inchoate mix of ruthlessness and kindness, cruelty and tenderness, indifference and generosity. Faint signals, flashes of creativity in otherwise desperate maneuvers, and small eruptions in the social fabric all provide texture to city life and are increasingly the norm. This is what Simone calls a micropolitics of alignment, interdependency, and exuberance. For him, a wide range of provisional, highly fluid, yet coordinated and collective actions are generated by African city residents that run parallel to, yet intersect with, a growing proliferation of decentralized local authorities, small-scale enterprises, community associations and civil society organizations. These practices make African cities "work" to a certain extent. The framing notions of his analysis are informality, invisibility, spectrality, and movement (Simone 2004a).

On the other hand, Filip de Boeck contends that, in ways that often leave the observer perplexed, the African city constantly undergoes the effervescent push and pull of destruction and regeneration. Focusing on Kinshasa, he argues that this is a city in which the spoken form seems to dominate the built form and in which the invisible constantly reconfigures the city's public and private spaces. In Kinshasa, it is not, or not primarily, the material infrastructure or the built form that make the city a city. The city, in a way, exists beyond its architecture. The built form is not, or is no longer, the product of a careful planning or engineering of the urban space. It is, rather, produced randomly as a living space more and more reduced to its most basic functions, that of a shelter, the heterogeneous conglomeration of truncated urban forms, fragments and reminders of material and mental urban elsewheres (de Boeck and Plissart 2006).

De Boeck describes a stunning material geography of failing infrastructure, a spectacular architecture of decay that constitutes the physical life of crisis. Simple material infrastructures and technologies, as well as their dysfunctioning and breakdown, thus create, define, and transform new sites of transportation, new configurations of entangled spatialities, new public spaces of work and relaxation, new itineraries and clusters of relations. The main infrastructural unit or building block is the human body. For de Boeck, too, Kinshasa is characterized by the first world of the day and the second world of the night—a second city, an occult city of the shadow, bathed in a constant overproduction of signs, an "overheating" or excess of the signifier that literally leads to a crisis of meaning. The struggle, therefore, is about how to reestablish control over an increasingly overflowing imaginary (ibid.).

In "Lagos: How It Works," Koolhaas takes the Nigerian economic capital to be an icon of "West African urbanity." The main assumption of this work is that African cities represent a crystallized, extreme, paradigmatic set of case studies of cities at the forefront of "globalizing modernity." This project argues that "many of the much-touted values of contemporary global capital and its prophetic organizational models of dispersal and discontinuity, federalism and flexibility, have been realized and perfected in West Africa" (2007: 138). In this context, the city in West Africa is an inversion of every essential characteristic of the so-called modern city. It forces the reconceptualization of the city itself. Koolhaas's project is "to do away with the inherited notion of the 'city' once for all." In order to do so, he interrogates the binary around which Western discourses on the city have been built. Crucial to these discourses has been the opposition between the "formal" and the "unformed." His way of transcending these binaries is to "embellish a third term—the informal," as a way of accessing the specificity of African cities' operations. The "informal" he defines as that which "is neither formed nor unformed; alternately, it looks like both." He adds: "It is not identifiable as a pattern or morphology, but nonetheless manufactures the material reality of urban form. It is an alliance of transformative ingenuity and the tactical mobilization of resources, produced from conditions of need and in the almost complete absence of centralization" (139). Koolhaas shows how the mobilization of specific kinds of everyday human labor and infrastructures end up building specific city-forms and structures. The informal, here, is the ensemble of those categories that make up the inner structure of the African city and on which the other fundamentals rest and from which urbanism unfolds.

Lines of Flight

In our rendering of Johannesburg, we depart from the global city paradigm without necessarily espousing all aspects of the alternative analytical models highlighted above. A city (whether global or not) is not simply a string of infrastructures, technologies, and legal entities, however networked these are. It also comprises actual bodies, images, forms, footprints, and memories. The everyday human labor mobilized in building specific city forms is not only material. It is also artistic and aesthetic. Furthermore, rather than opposing the "formal" and the "informal," or the "visible" and the "invisible," we need a more complex anthropology of things, forms, and signs in order to account for the life of the city in Africa. Analytically as well as in people's daily experience, simplistic oppositions between the formal and the informal are unhelpful. As Jane Guyer argues in her work on Nigerian cities, there is an entire "popular economy" comprising livelihood, employment, and capital asset creation. But to a large extent, this "popular economy" invests in, takes resources from, and generally runs up against regulated institutions. Indeed, the informal is not outside of the formal. It is related to formal regulatory institutions. The two processes of formalization and informalization work together. How they work together and how this working together ends up producing city forms and urban economies seems to be the question that we need to pursue.[3] Clearly, the "informal" itself expresses a "form." It simultaneously hides and reveals other rationalities. In African cities, forms can be thought of as conjoined with signs, and as a series of *operations* (ways of doing, of making). This book intends to capture these rhythms and operations via a rehabilitation of the concept of the "metropolis."

In addition, our aim in this book is neither to rely on a notion of Africa's difference from elsewhere, nor to assert its sameness. Africa, and by implication African cities, has so often been caught and imagined with a web of difference and otherness. The continent and its forms still frequently end up epitomizing the intractable, the mute, the abject, or the otherworldly. Africa is still seen as an object apart from the world, or as a failed or incomplete example of something else. So much so that it is tempting to revisit the frontiers of commonalities, of connectivity, with multiple elsewheres, of which the continent also speaks. Our aim is not so much to replace difference with sameness but to undercut a rigid distinction between these two terms—to allow space for the articulation of the originality of the African modern, its capacity to produce something new and singular, as yet unthought, and to find ways of accommodating this within our conceptual languages.

Finally, we have tried in what follows to identify sites within the continent, entry and exit points not usually dwelt upon in research and public discourse, that defamiliarize commonsense readings of Africa. Identifying such sites entails working with new archives—or even with old archives in new ways. One such archive is the metropolis itself. Moreover, identifying many such sites at times implies drawing on particular critical pedagogies—pedagogies of writing, talking, seeing, walking, telling, hearing, drawing, making—each of which pairs the subject and the object in novel ways to enliven the relationship between them and to better express life in motion. The above considerations explain the general economy of this book, which includes conventional academic articles, short and fragmentary essays and commentaries, interviews and images, paths into the fabric of city life—all aiming to

2 View of Mary Fitzgerald Square, central Johannesburg, 2007.
Courtesy of Constitution Hill

provide the reader with a sense of the worldliness of African life in general, and of the African metropolis as a compositional process requiring particular acts of deciphering.

The City of Gold

Although Johannesburg has historically been one of the most privileged sites of the emergence of the question of the subject in the modern African sense of the word, most studies of Johannesburg have interpreted the city as nothing but the spatial embodiment of unequal economic relations and coercive and segregationist policies. A survey of the literature on Johannesburg reveals a preoccupation with one thing: the rise, fall, and reconstruction of the segregated city. To be sure, it provides important details concerning the periodization of developments in urban policy, urbanization, and urban growth since the colonial era. It offers a range of explanations for the rise and consolidation of the segregated urban form. It documents the state's enforcement of racial privileges under the guise of public health and town planning legislation as well as public housing policies. It analyzes the political consequences of black urbanization and comments on the desegregation process and its ambiguities since the end of apartheid. Finally, it provides important clues when it comes to reading the urban landscape and identifying the historical dimensions of contemporary "urban problems." In the process, it brilliantly illuminates the dialectics between dispossession, exploitation, and struggle so characteristic of South African history, while closely tying them to the race, labor, and capital triptych. In literary studies, the central figure has been the newly urban black man—his alienation, the transformation of his identity, the commodification of his past in the conflicting spaces of the city.

That the legibility of this extraordinary place has been reduced in much recent, and less recent, literature to an experience of the abnormal is not without parallels elsewhere.[4] After all, as Stella Dong points out, the swamp-ridden metropolis of Shanghai in China was, for a long time, "ranked as the most pleasure-mad, rapacious, corrupt, strife-ridden, licentious, squalid, and decadent city in the world."[5] The loathing of Johannesburg in the social sciences should be seen as part of an antiurban ideology that has consistently perceived the industrial city, in particular, as a cesspool of vice. Writing about the industrial revolution and the process of class struggle that engulfed the Witwatersrand at the turn of the twentieth century, the historian Charles van Onselen (2001: ix) describes Johannesburg as a "concrete encrustation on a set of rocky ridges," without "fertile soil, striking natural vegetation, a lake, a mountain, a valley, a river or even an attractive perennial stream." "It lacks," he says, "the landscape of affection or mystery easily appropriated by myth-makers and nation-builders."[6]

Van Onselen's views are widely shared. Unlike bodies of literature on other cities, few commentaries on Johannesburg have been preoccupied with city form and city life as keys to understanding its metropolitan modernity. Modernity has been perceived as nothing more than the development of the capitalist mode of production and the processes by which capitalism as a socioeconomic formation in turn transformed social relations and the consciousness of black urban dwellers. As a consequence, the city that emerges from these commentaries has until recently been populated by "proletarians": a generic term that encompasses slum dwellers, migrant workers, strikers, hawkers, prostitutes, domestic servants, squatters, criminal classes, and so on (Yudelman 1984; Bozzoli 1983, esp. 151–239). Its "real story," says van Onselen (2001: ix–x), revolves around "the contest between the narrowly-based economic self-interest of the mine owners" and a "seething mass of struggling humanity" made up of a "relatively cosmopolitan labour" force that serves the industry. It is this "immediate clash of class interests around the principal industry" that does more "to excite the passions of the citizenry than any supposedly primordial yearning for cultural expression or strivings for a more encompassing identity." In fact, van Onselen concludes, Johannesburg's "shallowly-rooted, first-generation bourgeoisie and the crass *nouveau riche* of subsequent generations have always felt more comfortable in the bank, the stock exchange and the sports stadium than they have in attending a church, sitting in a concert hall, walking through an art gallery, reading in a library or even serving in the ranks of their city council."

This moral critique of early and late modern Johannesburg life as a nursery of cynicism (the pursuit of money) and a site of lack (in this case, lack of cultural compass) is widely shared across disciplines. Recognizing that Johannesburg is a product of the last quarter of the nineteenth century and as such filled with the contradictions of the laissez-faire age, the architect Clive Chipkin (1993: 10) nevertheless argues that the city's "sophistication and modernity" demonstrate "different qualities of creativity, cheek by jowl with slavish mimicry of overseas taste." Underestimating the degree to which the city always operates as a site of fantasy, desire, and imagination, recent South African historiography tends to privilege a reading of the urban as a theater of capitalist accumulation and exploitation. This scholarship constitutes an impressive body of work—albeit one that is sutured to a political agenda (the critique of the apartheid state), theoretically narrow (though empirically very strong), and almost entirely undeveloped in terms of comparative foci. These historiographical studies can be separated into three categories.

First is a long tradition of urban inquiry that focuses on the spatial dislocation, the class differentiation, and the racial polarization imprinted on the urban landscape by apartheid state-sanctioned segregation and planning.[7] Within these confines, much attention is given to the geographies of poverty, forced removals, and racially based slums and far less to the cartographies of affluence (Kallaway and Pearson 1986; Koch 1983; Hart and Pirie 1984; van Tonder 1993; Parnell 1988 and 1992). Such studies highlight the various forms of dispossession and spatial exclusion of the black population from the apartheid city. Seeing Johannesburg only in these terms also points to an important failure in most studies of the city—the failure to speak of the city on terms that warrant comparison with other cities in the world.[8] In their attempt to sort out the link between industrialization and urbanization, these accounts envision the city not as an aesthetic project but as a space of division. Planning, in particular, is perceived as that which not only recasts notions of citizenship in the terrain of racial difference but also serves to delineate different city spaces separated by boundaries of class (Mabin and Smit 1997; Turok 1994). One such space is the township.[9] As the title of Nigel Mandy's book *A City Divided: Johannesburg and Soweto* (1984) suggests, the township is both of the city and not of the city (see also Beall et al. 2002). In such studies, the emphasis has been on marginality, and the township is privileged as a site of social struggles or of contestation over the allocation of public goods.[10] Far less attention has been paid to the imbrication of city and township and, in spite of unequal social relations, to township dwellers' practices and imaginations of city-ness or the place of the township in the making of the city's many identities.

This is despite the fact that people then and now perpetually moved between the city and the township either to make a living or to access forms of urban life that the township did not provide (see the article by Mbembe, Dlamini, and Khunou in this book; see also Wilson 1996; Marcuse 1998; O'Loughlin and Friedrichs 1996). In fact, life in contemporary middle-class Soweto more and more tends to be very similar to suburban life in other parts of Johannesburg, with almost identical practices of gentrification, respectability, and patterns of consumption being played out. In middle-class Soweto and Diepkloof, an urban and cosmopolitan world thrives on sociability, hybridity, and everyday informality.[11] Furthermore, the literature fails to situate the township in relation to other kinds of urban agglomerations elsewhere (the urban ghetto, the favela) or in South Africa itself (the inner city, the squatter camp, the homeland, recent government housing schemes for poor black South Africans) and to track the traffic between these places. Such is the case in relation to informal settlements on the urban fringes whose inhabitants commute to city work zones; concentrated settlements within cities; backyard dwellings in middle-class suburbs; disused buildings in inner-city areas (parts of Johannesburg's eastern downtown section) or hostels; or similar institutions whose inhabitants live very close to their places of work ("South Africa's 'Discarded People'" 1998).

Second are post-apartheid studies, most of which fall within the urban development paradigm so prevalent in the rest of Africa and the developing world (Mabogunje 2000). Many of these studies are more concerned with whether the city is changing along vectors of institutional governance, the deracialization of service provision, and local politics than about city-ness as such (Seekings 2003). Because they approach the city as a problem to be solved, they are clearly prescriptive. They seek to contribute to policy formulation in fields as varied as community participation, housing, land tenure, service delivery (water, sanitation, roads, electricity, waste removal), local government, municipal finance and governance capacities, urban poverty, and decentralization. In most cases, these instrumentalist and functionalist accounts of the city are preoccupied with larger issues of social justice and social cohesion, equity and efficiency. Their aim is to redress the effects of inequality and past injustices through a better redistribution of public goods and the reversal of the system of spatial, economic, and social segregation inherited from apartheid (Mabin 1995). They end up mapping an urban social geography of needs, the crucial indexes of which are levels of deprivation. In the process, they underplay many other aspects of city life and city forms (e.g., see Bremner 2000; Crankshaw and Parnell 2000; Parnell et al. 2002; Cameron 1999).

Third are studies preoccupied with the spatial restructuring of the city per se. They note the sprawling, polycentric character of Johannesburg and lament the intensely privatized and quasi-anarchic vision of urban growth underlying this process. In this regard, they focus, primarily, on what the authors perceive as the "citadelization" of Johannesburg; that is, the increased barricading within the city through the constructions of office complexes and upper-class residences; the polarization of the city by income, occupation, and race; the limited public subsidies and the abdication of independent planning and regulatory action by government; the hyperconcentration of jobs in service center–oriented office buildings in the northern suburbs; and the increasing power of property developers to structure the evolution of the city (see Tomlinson et al. 2003; Judin and Vladislavić 1998). In many instances, the trope of a "city under siege" proves to be simply a juxtaposition of exclusive suburban enclaves, closed spaces, and simulated histories undergirded by a "fantasy urbanism" and odd lifestyles (see Bremner 2002; Beall 2002: 175–95; Tomlinson et al. 2003: 56–70).

Recent work on the edge city and the suburbs may signal new readings of the city. Lindsay Bremner (2004: 120), for example, describes the edge city of Midrand as a "contradictory space" inhabited by many of South Africa's new black elite, where "the color of one's money rapidly replaces skin color as the currency of showy success" and where "acquisitiveness goes hand in hand with that other must-have suburban attitude: lack of curiosity about everyone else." She argues that for these new monied classes, "middle class values and preoccupations—individual achievement, status, nuclear family life, space, security and sport—are best satisfied within the infrastructure of the security suburb," yet a "relationship with the culture of township life is maintained."[12] Developments in the inner city show that "far from being the ultimate zoned, controlled and compartmentalized city," Johannesburg is now characterized by "messy intersections and overlapping realities. Ordinary, everyday lives, which were excluded from the city by western urban management practices, town planning codes or by the legal and administrative apparatus of apartheid, have brought distant geographical, social and cultural worlds into contact."

In general, though, while recognizing the density of the empirical work referred to above, it is necessary to highlight this literature's relative lack of comparative depth, the paucity of its theoretical reach, and its overall dependence on political economy. Such a critique has two dimensions. First is that we now need a more complex theorization of race, labor, and capital to properly account for the relation between injury and personhood or the extreme acts of violation perpetrated in the name of race in the history of South Africa's city forms. A second dimension of our critique has to do with the failure of this literature to explicitly deal with the city-ness of Johannesburg and to open itself up to a global literature on metropolitan experience. The historian Jon Hyslop observes that, by and large, interpretations of early Johannesburg have suffered from being confined within two related teleologies: that of the rise of the nation-state and that of the rise of apartheid. South African urban critics have tended to focus on explaining the tragic course of twentieth-century South African history in terms of factors internal to the country and to treat it as in some sense predestined. He then goes on to suggest that much of what was happening in early Johannesburg "can only be understood by placing it within a global flow of persons, ideas, and commodities." There were "possibilities and processes contained in the early city's existence which we miss out when we simply read apartheid back into it," he concludes (2003: 7).

The Underground, the Surface, and the Edges

In Africa, analyses of capitalist modernity have not fully apprehended the fact that it is not simply in the North that, as David Frisby (2001: 161) writes, "the culture of modernity became synonymous with the culture of the metropolis." Recently, the new urbanism of the end of the nineteenth and the beginning of the twentieth century has been the main framework for explorations of modernity in places as varied as China or Brazil (Yeh 2000, esp. 31–230; Tang 2000, esp. chaps. 8 and 9; Schelling 2000: 75–126). Using the trope of "multiple modernities" or the "diversity of universals," this is indeed what a number of Asian scholars of the city have been attempting to do. Recent studies of two different yet equally cosmopolitan formations, Shanghai and Hong Kong, have helped a lot to redraw the map of the metropolis outside the box of European intellectual history. Shanghai in particular was long vilified in ways similar to Johannesburg but, as Leo Ou-fan Lee, Ackbar Abbas, and others have recently shown, it has been a "cosmopolitan metropolis" all along. A receptor of modern technological development, Shanghai was also known early on for its cultural sophistication, its prosperity in literature and the fine arts; modern media and the press; its movie studios and theaters, which earned the city the appellation "Hollywood of the East"; and its leading role in design and fashion innovation (Lu 1999). Lee (1999) has also shown how the foreign presence in Shanghai produced new kinds of public and social spaces such as cinemas, department stores, coffeehouses, dance halls, parks, and racecourses. He has argued that these spaces were appropriated by the Chinese themselves and used to construct a Chinese version of modern cosmopolitan culture. Ackbar Abbas (2000: 775) compares Shanghai and Hong Kong, two cities where splendor and squalor existed side by side. He argues that in the 1920s and 1930s, Shanghai developed a "cosmopolitanism of extraterritoriality" while, from the 1980s onward, Hong Kong developed a "cosmopolitanism of dependency."

Our rendition of Johannesburg proceeds from a different analytical vantage point. Without the gold-bearing beds of the Witwatersrand, Johannesburg would not have existed. That the city started in 1886 as a series of uncontrolled mining camps is due precisely to the presence and discovery of gold near the surface of the reef. But, as the geographer Keith Beavon indicates (2004: 5), "because of the steep dip to the strata it soon became necessary to sink shafts from positions well south of the original outcrop mines and to reach the ore-bearing seams by complex systems of tunnels and passageways, drives and stopes." It is at these deeper levels and in the way the world below interacted with the surface and the edges that the origins of the city as a metropolis are to be located. Beneath the central business district and the environs of Johannesburg lie thousands of boreholes and drilling footages of varying depths—a testimony to the way in which, in the production of this Southern Hemispheric modernity, the world of race and systematized human degradation became part of the calculus of capital and dispossession, technology, labor, and the unequal distribution of wealth (Haughton 1964: 3). In our view, this dialectic between the underground, the surface and the edges is, more than any other feature, the main characteristic of the African modern of which Johannesburg is the epitome, and perhaps even of the late modern metropolis itself.

Such a characterization relies upon, while attempting to go beyond, canonical definitions of the metropolitan form. Indeed, since Werner Sombart, the concept of the metropolis functions as a key device to problematize the relation between urban existence and crucial features of modernity, chief among which are the quantitative expansion of urban population, the corresponding increase in the quantity of commodities in circulation and their consumption, and the attendant transformations in all spheres of social and mental life. For Georg Simmel, Siegfried Kracauer, Walter Benjamin, or Max Weber, processes of abstraction, circulation, movement, representation, and the responses of the emotions and the mind to these processes, constitute the main features of metropolitan life. To a large extent, metropolitan existence is less about the city as such or how the latter is made and by whom than how it is exhibited, displayed, and represented, its colorfulness, its aura, and its aesthetics. But what is being displayed is first and foremost a "culture of things" (*Sachkultur*) in a money economy, the world of commodities and the built structures (architecture) that metaphorize them—in short, the "mental life" of the city. That the essence of the things exhibited, their quantities, weight, scale, and size lies in the fortuitous, the superficial, and the transitory does not preclude their becoming objects of artistic representation. Nor does it dedramatize the rush experienced by the city dweller to compress together the largest possible sum of acquisitions, interests, and enjoyments. There isn't, therefore, a metropolis without this aesthetic dimension. Linked to this is the ceaseless birth, destruction, and reconstruction of forms, the aim of which is, on the one hand, to distinguish nature and landscape, and on the other hand to testify to the presentness of the past while making way for the "new."

Most of these features can be found, to varying degrees, in Johannesburg, at different phases of its history. They are all the more significant because Johannesburg emerged as an instant city of strangers, aliens, and foreigners (*uitlanders*)—a city with no former history. Its urban infrastructure (its parks, its streets, the engineering of its water supply, storm-water drainage, and sewers, its monuments, its electric tramway and electric lighting, its structures of consumption and spectacle), its cultural life, and economy had to be built from scratch, without any of the constraints that usually bind other cities so tightly to their ancient past (see Spit 1976; Grant and Flinn 1992). The sole reason for its creation was the pursuit of material wealth. On the Parktown ridge, and following the high rococo style of Europe's belle époque, Randlords built huge mansions and expensive properties on the model of English country architecture and landscaping (Barry and Law 1985). The city's ascent to industrial capitalism was accompanied by human misery, degradation, disease, crime, and prostitution. But perhaps one of the most striking dimensions of the metropolitan nature of Johannesburg has been its ceaseless metamorphosis. A trajectory that in the West took ages to unfold and to mature was here compressed into under a century. The speed and velocity with which the city has experienced modernity has been in itself dizzying. Less than fifteen years after its creation, all its functional zones and residential patterns had been firmly established. It was already struggling to experience time not as fundamentally transitory, and space not as eminently fleeting. Compensating for the lack of advantages of a striking natural setting, the city planted the biggest manmade forest in the world and, through its built environment, labored to create a sense of splendor and sensory stimuli.

In fact, the entire history of Johannesburg's built structures testifies not only to its inscription into the canons of modern Western urban aesthetics, but also to the originary tension virtually built into its morphology and geological structure between the life below the surface, what is above, and the edges. After all, until very recently, Johannesburg described itself as the largest and most modern European city in Africa. As amply demonstrated by Clive Chipkin, this meant that Johannesburg was the progeny of nineteenth-century European industrial society. This inland city developed as an industrial metropolis supported by gold mining. A breeding ground for modernism, it grew as a frontier city closely tied to the global market economy and the world of consumption and at the same time was mired in bigotry and prejudice, constantly caught between what it could be (potentiality) and what it ended up being (actuality). The city's fabric and cultural styles borrowed from the major trends of the time and from an assortment of sometimes disconnected sources—from Victorian and Edwardian architecture; from the provincial versions of the French Second Empire to modernized (or neo-) classicism and futurism to Manhattan-style stunted skyscrapers; and from art nouveau to the rigid symmetry of the beaux arts, art deco, modernism, and Le Corbusier's *esprit nouveau*. Chipkin (1993: 22) explains that most technological innovations were experimented with at one point or the other in Johannesburg: "Prefabricated iron-fronted shop buildings, barrel-vaulted arcades with prismatic glass skylights, cast-iron gas lamps, electric lighting, telephone wires linking the finance houses and emporia to the central telephone exchange, horse-drawn trams with their destination signs to distant suburbs, and after 1892 the presence of the railroad linking the interior with the maritime systems of the seaboard."

But official or commercial architecture did not take its lead simply from overseas paradigms and precedents. If Johannesburg's ideas of the metropolis did filter in from overseas, cultural traffic with New Delhi, with the sister dominions (Canada, New Zealand, Australia), the East African triangle (Kenya, Tanganyika, Uganda, and Zanzibar), and Brazil also shaped them. A substantial city of the empire in the African Southern Hemisphere during the first half of the twentieth century, Johannesburg also created a metropolitan style of its own. The shifts from one style to another were themselves a testimony to its history of opulence. Right from the beginning, one of the defining features of the city was its trading square and its commercial streets. Banks, finance houses, offices, clubs, and mining company headquarters dominated the streetscapes. Everywhere in the commercial streets, Chipkin argues, "a new consumer world and new building technology had sprung up side by side virtually ready-made on this remote piece of the veld." There was evidence of contact with high fashion in London, Paris, and New York (main shopping streets, latest American automobiles, fancy lingerie, department stores, jewelry designs, polished gems, and so on), "together with the latest imported *fin de siècle* decoration from the Continent, up-to-date fabrics and wallpapers from London's West End emporia, latest lines in Manchester cotton goods and a flood of commercial products ready to clutter up colonial interiors with exotic bric-à-brac from the world market" (18).

Another crucial dimension of the history of Southern Hemispheric metropolitanism is the way in which the city was planned, governed, and in the process, came to be imagined as a body politic. This entailed specific techniques of managing difference and heterogeneity. In the modern West, urban difference was fundamentally read either in terms of class (the war between rich and poor) or in terms of the autonomy of individual existence. As David Harvey (2003: 75) shows in the case of Paris, differentiated interests, particularly those resulting from the social division of labor or from the hierarchies within the body politic, came to be organized as associations expressive of those interests. The formation of the metropolis was all along determined by the question of how much heterogeneity a city could accommodate without ceasing to imagine itself as a moral community. In Johannesburg, the question of work and labor was fundamental both to the critique of existing social arrangements and to dreams of the city that might be. Not only class, but also race (two mutually constitutive categories) was brought to bear on the ways difference and heterogeneity were negotiated. The complex social structures of the city as well as its spatial economy are, to a large extent, the result of the conflict between, on the one hand, the unconditional demand for racial justice and equality, and on the other, the imperative of white self-preservation.

In Southern Hemispheric conditions, the metropolis is formed through a process of segregation and elimination. Although swift and brutal, this process took almost a century in Johannesburg and underwent many phases. Created in 1886, the city already exhibited, by 1900, almost all the aspects that until the 1990s were to characterize the apartheid city. Beavon (2004: 67–68) explains:

> Africans had to carry passes, they were prohibited from walking on the pavements, they were excluded from public places, they rode in cattle trucks behind the Rand tram and its main line replacement, they were nòt permitted to use the regular intra-urban public transport, and they were largely confined to the single-sex "barracks" of the mines, the "Kaffir Location," and the servants' quarters of the opulent whites. Their access to liquor had been constrained, they laboured long and hard for very low wages, and they had no political rights.

Moreover, until 1927, the administration of Africans fell under the same municipal committee that dealt with the zoological gardens (Maud 1938).

The spatial framing of race and the fixing of social forms in space aimed at creating an essentially white suburban city. In this process, the discourse of race transmutated into a discourse of health and urban sanitation (1900–1940). To address the perceived blights of deviance and perversion and to clean the city of its poor and undesirable while subjecting them to the raw reality of exploitation first required that the city's inner area be rid of its slums, with their concentration of poor white Afrikaners and its multiracial underclass. Poor whites, working-class and lower-middle-class white families (as well as waves of impoverished Afrikaners) were forced toward peripheral townships in the western corridors of Vrededorp and Burgersdorp or in Brickfields. An improvement scheme known as the Insanitary Area Improvement Scheme and a Slums Clearance Act were adopted (Parnell 1988, 1991, 1992; Trump 1979; van Tonder 1993). In the context of the panic caused by the outbreak of plague in 1903, the "Coolie Location" was "surrounded by a detachment of troops, evacuated in its entirety, and immediately burnt to the ground. Two weeks later, in a follow-up operation . . . , the fire brigade was assigned to incinerate the remainder of the insanitary area. The whole zone was surrounded with a corrugated-iron fence, six street blocks were saturated with paraffin then set alight, and [1,600] 'buildings,' including a temple, were destroyed" (Beavon 2004: 77).

The city that emerged at the beginning of the twentieth century was made up of functional zones. It was articulated around an east-west axis separating lower-middle-class English and Afrikaans-speaking white residents. A distinct arc of mining land divided the southern suburbs from the lower-density and upper-income northern ones. African people and other dark-skinned minorities were confined in racial ghettoes or locked up in mine compounds, hostels, barracks, or in the servants' quarters of white householders. It was a city with various boundaries—less spatial facts with sociological consequences than racial enclaves that were formed spatially. It was also a city regulated according to the principle of proximity and social distance. This principle, in turn, governed the logic of movement through urban space. The idea was that every space possessed an exclusiveness or uniqueness, and that interactions between races should be closely identified with specifically demarcated territories. Between different racial enclaves, pieces of vacant ground and empty wastelands were used for various purposes, including the building of the slops pump station where the night soil collected in buckets, and other liquid sewage would be dumped. Another configuration was the system of squatting rights with limited tenure, or the compounds, barracks, domestic servant's quarters, and camps in which the African labor employed by the mines was housed.

In many senses, there is no metropolis without a necropolis. Just as the metropolis is closely linked to monuments, artifacts, technological novelty, an architecture of light and advertising, the phantasmagoria of selling, and a cornucopia of commodities, so is it produced by what lies below the surface. In the case of Johannesburg, the underground is not simply a technological space emptied of social relations. It does not exist only in an abstract realm of instrumentality and efficiency. In fact, it always was a space of suffering and alienation as well as of rebellion and insurrection. As evidenced by the lives and times of Nelson Mandela and Walter Sisulu, the underground of the metropolis is the repository of possibilities for invention and utopian dreams. In Johannesburg, the underground was the symbol of the powerful forces contained in the depths of the city. The French equation between underground space and revolution or insurrection (the dream of radical equality evidenced in the signifier of the Catacombs) holds in the case of Johannesburg (Mandela 1995; Sisulu 2002). David Pike writes, "The Catacombs gave material form to the principle of fundamental equality, although they did so in the brutal manner of millions of bones stacked upon and interlaced with one another" (2005: 110). The work of apartheid was to make sure that these lower depths of the city, without which its modernity was unreadable, were made to appear as strangers to the city, apart from the city.

The figure of the black migrant worker, a temporary sojourner in the city, also marks one of the limits of classical theories of the metropolis, which hold that the most revelatory facets of modern metropolitan life lie on the *surface*, in the ephemeral and the visible (shop fronts, shop windows, café terraces, street cars, automobiles), in the display of the commodity with or without its aesthetic veil (Kracauer 1995; Ward 2001; Hanak 1999; Bucks-Morss 1989). The privileging of surfaces and visuality can conceal the ubiquity of the metropolitan form. Johannesburg clearly shows that one of the characteristic features of a metropolis is an *underneath*. As the name Igoli (City of Gold) indicates, this is a city born out of a ruthless, extractive, mining economy. As such, it is one incarnation of "the actual world of human labor, of grubby production, of toil, exploitation, and minimum wage work" that Andy Merrifield so eloquently spoke about in his description of Marx's ideology (Merrifield 2002: 63). In other words, beneath the visible landscape and the surface of the metropolis, its objects and social relations, are concealed or embedded other orders of visibility, other scripts that are not reducible to the built form, the house facade, or simply the street experience of the metaphorical figure of the flâneur.

Recent work suggests that there is no surface without an underground (Pike 2005: 7). The underground is not to be understood simply in terms of an infrastructure and various subterranean spaces (sewers and drainage systems, underground railways, utility tunnels, storage vaults and so on). The world below (the underworld) is also made up of lower classes, the trash heap of the world above, and subterranean utopias. Like the nineteenth-century European city, the vertical and racial segmentation of the Johannesburg urban world was given structure and order by what it relegated beneath. As far as Johannesburg is concerned, more than the surfaces of the vertical city with its skyscrapers, the underground seems to hold the keys to unlocking the secrets of its modernity.

Living in places and circumstances not of his or her choosing, the black migrant worker is constrained to experience the metropolis as a site of radical uncertainty, unpredictability, and insecurity. Under those conditions, culture and aesthetics become an open-ended construction structurally built in existing and often misused infrastructures. Made up of stranded affiliations, the metropolis in the southern part of the African continent emerged out of complex structures—including psychic ones—that far exceed the possibilities of the apartheid grid. In fact, seen from beneath, the migrant worker more than the flâneur is the paradoxical cultural figure of African modernity—the one who is both beneath the city and outside of its orders of visibility.

Post-apartheid South Africa has given a new centrality to the figure of the migrant in general and that of the stranger in particular. Indeed, over the last quarter of the twentieth century, substantial shifts have taken place in the urban social division of labor and in the corporate organization of industrial production in the city. The process of globalization and its associated consequences—the casualization of labor, the privatization of most basic services—have fostered the emergence of multiple economies not limited to the corporate form. The inequality in the concentration of strategic resources and activities between the different segments of the city has sharpened since the 1990s. A parallel economy—informal and transnational—has emerged. As we have seen above, a socioeconomic fragmentation is also visible in the built environment of the city: a geography of fortifications and enclosures; increasing demand for spatial and social insulation; and reliance on technologies of security, control, and surveillance.[13] In this context, the *stranger* and the *criminal* now assume, more than ever, greater prominence in most cities' imaginations (see Mpe 2001; Nuttall ch. 7 of this volume). The criminal, we could say, moves between the surface and the underneath. Striking at the everyday—the woman leaving her garage, the man asleep in his bed, the young girl on her way to the shop—he navigates the ordinary surfaces of life by attacking from a darker, more underneath place. He partakes of the vocabulary of the stranger but also of the familiar: many crimes occur between people who are known to each other. Thus the man who performs this inhuman and therefore strange act is also an uncle, a father, a neighbor, a workman most of the time.

Although no single chapter in the book deals with crime, its specter hovers over the text like a shadow, raising its head in essays by Nuttall, Odhiambo and Muponde, Hornberger, de Vries and Prabhala. It is this shadowy aspect that works the way that crime itself does, along an axis that is visible sometimes and at other times invisible. As a result, the experience of fear and at times panic lies at the deepest roots of life in the metropolis. The history of Johannesburg's experience with violence is also central to Mbembe's chapter. Whether during the early period of industrialization or in the post-apartheid context, crime is more than just an index of itself. Today, homocides, rapes, robberies, and aggravated assaults are indicative of the extent to which the apartheid state and its successor, the democratic state, have failed to exercise a monopoly over the means of violence. If under apartheid the distinction between private violence, state violence, and the violence of unrest was thin, today it is the equation of democracy with the urge for armed protection that is one of the main features of metropolitan mental life. This might have something to do with the fact that the racial state in South Africa was built on the fear of the black man with a gun. But it might also have something to do with the fact that political struggles aimed at copossessing the monopoly of force instead of destroying it. Democratization, that is, has not coincided with the disarmament of the urban citizenry, and crime today has become the other side, the underneath, perhaps, of the rise of a culture of consumption.

These forms of fortification and criminality need to be counterbalanced by attention to other, varied responses to the city's transformations, but all of them together reflect the complexities of class, race, generation, and culture.

Afropolitanism

Johannesburg is a metropolis in every sense of the word. It is a thoroughly African capitalist formation closely tied to the world economy. Metropolitan existence here is "displayed" not necessarily through exhibitions or parks, but via an enticing array of consumer labels and products, highways and luminous flows, store windows and huge advertising billboards, new architecture and, more generally, technophilia. To a large extent, this is what Simmel (1950a: 45) meant by a "culture of things." For him, the representation of the metropolis occurred through the lavish display of a plethora of objects "crowded together in close proximity," which paralyzed the senses and hypnotized the spectator. From this perspective, what passes in the eyes of Johannesburg's fiercest critics as crass material trappings could very well be understood as an aesthetic of plenty.

Contemporary Johannesburg is the premier metropolis in Africa in terms of technology, wealth, and racial complexity, as well as cultural practices and formal institutions—apparent through the sheer quantification of the world of goods, of production and consumption. It is a thoroughly polyglot urban formation whose influence, connections, and identifications extend beyond its locality and well beyond South Africa (see Nixon 1994). It is also an engine of art, architecture, music, fashion, theater, literature, and religious life. Johannesburg is peopled not just by workers, the poor, criminals, and illegal immigrants, but also by artists, playwrights, craftspeople, investigative journalists, poets, writers, musicians, and civic-minded public intellectuals of all races, as well as highly skilled migrants and jet setters. It is a home to corporate headquarters, finance houses, legal services, accounting firms, media outlets, entertainment industries, and information technology ventures.

The city has become the great shopping mall for most of sub-Saharan Africa. New geographies of retailing and consumption are redefining the economic and cultural horizons of contemporary Johannesburg (Beavon 2000). Its consumer spaces (the department store, the mall, and the casino) can be read, as elsewhere, as "symbolic and metaphoric territories," in the words of Louise Crewe (2000: 275). Finally, it is a city where historical structures of racial inequity are simultaneously being sedimented and unbundled; in which conceptions of race are being reinterrogated and remade; and in which cosmopolitanism resides, flourishes, or lies dormant—an "unfinished city" thrust by the force of circumstances into a conversation between the past and the future, between Africa and the world (Bender 2002). There is no question that Johannesburg is a city that, from its origins, has symbolized novelty, exuberance, adventurism, and, to a large extent, the possibility of a kind of freedom.[14]

We have called this book "Johannesburg—the Elusive Metropolis." To assert the elusiveness of Johannesburg is to unfix rather than to fix the meanings of the African modern. We have wished to point to the gap between the way things actually are and the way they appear in theory and discourse. Cities are subjects *en fuite*. They always outpace the capacity of analysts to name them. This gap constitutes the elusiveness referred to in our title. Johannesburg is an elusive metropolis because of the multiplicity of registers in which it is African (or perhaps not at all, or not enough); European (or perhaps not, or no longer), or even American (by virtue of its embeddedness in commodity exchange and its culture of consumption). Its very elusiveness makes it especially compelling as an object of study, and the theoretical work of this introduction has been to draw its metropolitan charge into being. While the project of this book has been to work with this elusiveness (as seen in the individual chapters and the shape the book has taken), there are further questions that this book opens onto. The way in which Johannesburg relates to, and helps us to, understand other African cities requires further studies. The degree to which it invokes a Southern Hemispheric modernity more widely is still to be properly probed in comparative work. To capture the elusiveness of this city would not be to simply invoke the anthropological and developmental narratives that have dominated its representation in favor of the magic and shine of capital. Nor is it our intention to take European modernity in its literary and cultural forms as the vector of Johannesburg's contemporary life. Neither of these propositions is enacted in the essays that follow. Rather, the complexity of their imbrication is articulated by the contributors, and this is what speaks most forcefully to the elusiveness we have sought to capture.

The Structure of the Book

To a large extent, this book is a gesture of defamiliarization. In part, this implies that when it comes to things "African," it is possible to move away from the fascination with the horrors of a seemingly static world and to rehabilitate our curiosity while also insisting on this virtue as a necessary hallmark of a truly global academic project. The book is composed of two parts. The first section comprises essays written largely in an academic mode. Taken together, they generate a set of concepts for reading the contemporary metropolis, including notions of superfluity, self-stylization, and the African modern. Many work with the notions of surface and depth discussed above, adding new theoretical rigor to this set of imaginaries so redolent of the Johannesburg metropolis. Each concentrates on life worlds that signal what is emerging across the interfaces of the city, revealing its heterogeneous archive.

Working with and against Georg Simmel, Achille Mbembe uses the two notions of superfluity and surface/depth to reorder both well-known and new material into a complex theoretical argument. For him, *superfluity* refers not only to the aesthetics of surfaces and quantities but also to the dialectics of indispensability and expendability of both people and things.

More specifically, he describes two examples of the new public theaters of consumption in which space and images are both figural forms and aestheticized commodities: Melrose Arch and Montecasino. In the process, he revisits the biopolitics of Johannesburg as a "racial city" and its transition to a metropolitan form. He also explores what he calls the "city unconscious." He shows that the new political economy of this metropolis develops in and through cultural and aesthetic tastes, the main feature of which is to create surfaces and images. The creative éclat of these images and surfaces, in turn, functions to override historical memory and to replace it with the common sense of consumption and fantasy. This he interprets as foundational to "the psychic life of the city" after the dark period of apartheid. As elsewhere in the world, cultural sensitivities, aesthetics, and urban subjectivities in contemporary Johannesburg metropolitan life draw their energy from thoroughly commodified and marketed cityscapes (Vincenzo 2000). To a large extent, the commodity form becomes *the* form of existence, Mbembe argues.

AbdouMaliq Simone argues that the boundaries of Johannesburg are constantly mediated through an infrastructure. For Simone, urban infrastructure in the friction zones of the metropolis is made up of not only wires, ducts, tunnels, highways, electricity, and automobiles. It is in the first instance made up of what he calls "people," "bodies," "intersections," and "networks." These entities form the topological connections that give meaning to practices of social reproduction across city time and space. These very practices, almost of necessity, are contingent, uncertain, and unpredictable. At the same time, these people, bodies, intersections, and networks structure and delineate the material culture of the city. They constitute the fabric—or infrastructure—of contemporary African metropolises.

Sarah Nuttall focuses on the negotiation of the surface in contemporary cultural forms in Johannesburg. The city, she argues, is studied with texts—billboards, newsprints, magazine covers, road signs, and even entire surfaces of buildings constitute a stream of signs of Johannesburg representation. As surfaces, they are sometimes just that, but they also at times suggest a deeper diagnostic, a layering in which the apparent fixity of race so often privileged in accounts of Johannesburg is underwritten by the potential unfixing of the commodity-form, or in which the past resurfaces in the present. The chapter discusses two phenomena of the now. The first is the emergence in the city of a youth culture widely known as Y culture. Y culture is a "compositional remixing" that signals the supercession of an earlier era's resistance politics by an alternative politics of style and accessorization while simultaneously gesturing in various ways toward the past. Nuttall describes it as a culture of the hip bucolic that works across a series of surfaces, requiring what Gilroy calls "technological analogies" in order to produce enigmatic and divergent styles of self-making. In the second part of her essay, she discusses a series of recent advertisements that have appeared in the wake of Y culture. The ads can simultaneously be seen to work beyond, while still unwittingly reconfirming, the power of race in the contemporary public sphere of the city. She shows, too, how the market becomes an important place for projecting forms of racial conviviality and therefore a space in which the idea of living together across race is experimented with.

Jonathan Hyslop inserts Johannesburg into the narrative of modernity and modernist culture. He shows how, in the fiercely segregated years of the early twentieth century, the city became a haven of nonracial creative energies and the gathering point for activists, artists, intellectuals, writers, musicians, bohemians, and various kinds of strangers. As a modernist city, he writes, Johannesburg was a place of uncertainty and disintegration, but also "a place that stimulated the search for the possibilities of freedom. It was a city of ideas." Focusing particularly on the figures of Gandhi and Mandela, he shows that a particular role was played in the intellectual ferment of the city by the stranger. Moreover, it was the very extremity of Johannesburg's history that made its experience of modernity productive of political creativity. Hyslop takes Gandhi and Mandela as the two most globally significant and famous individuals to move on the Johannesburg stage in the twentieth century. He looks at how they were, in an important sense, the product of the peculiarly modern milieu that Johannesburg created. Both can be understood, he argues, to present us with the problem of the relation between the metropolis and nationalism, since both owed their fame to their success as leaders of nationalist movements, yet their global appeal is rooted in their transcendence of narrow nationalism. Hyslop attributes this transcendence to their markedly metropolitan and cosmopolitan experiences in Johannesburg.

David Bunn, in his chapter on the "visual city," also works with the problematic of the surface. While metropolitan modernism everywhere, from Baudelaire to Robert Frank, built an aesthetics around the idea of surfaces and reflection, Johannesburg's surfaces, he shows, and as we argue above, are based around a particular act of historical repression: the buried life of the black body, "instrumentalized and bent into contact with the coal face, or ore seam, at the stopes far below." The inability to come to terms with the actually existing life of the metropolis emerges as a particular problem in theory, Bunn argues: the problem of the incoherence of surface signs—of mediation between levels. This incoherence was long blamed on capitalist brashness, but Marxist accounts revealed little about the desires of those who inhabited the city, thus pushing the articulation of metropolitan aesthetic experience "over the horizon," after the crisis of apartheid had been "cured." It is in this context that Bunn discusses the work of contemporary Johannesburg artists, paying close attention to the texture and status of the surface explored in their work. The surface tracery of an emerging urban aesthetic, flexible affiliations which result in representational acts constitutive of a migrant modernism, collaborations between urban renewal and public art, an aesthetic of frottage and of flatness, and painted surfaces of skin indicating epitomes of both trauma and loveliness emerge from Bunn's chapter to constitute a specific and striking city aesthetic.

Writing on AIDS in Johannesburg, Frédéric Le Marcis begins on the margins of the city (in the outskirts of the township of Alexandra, next to Sandton) and follows the movement of AIDS sufferers from there to the various locations in the city where they might find relief. His is not a reading of the storefronts and windows, café terraces, streetcars, and automobiles that form the letters of Benjamin or de Certeau's alphabet of the city. The essay reveals a network and nodes of circulation, tracing a geography of the city that is very different from the visible forms of circulation we see on its highways. In the process, he shows that the city is not simply a place of mobility. It can be read from different vantage points: from above, from below, or from in between its very surfaces. It can remain largely hidden, opaque, and invisible, especially when seen from the point of view of the itinerant body of the sufferer. Its boundaries are permeable and stretched. They can be mapped only if we take seriously nonconventional urban itineraries.

Sarah Nuttall studies the emergence of Johannesburg as an idea and a form in contemporary literatures of the city, drawing out the literary infrastructures giving the city a shape. The infrastructures (or nodes of metropolitan life) she examines are the street, the café, the suburb, and the campus. From these infrastructures or nodes of city-ness, certain figures emerge, among them the stranger, walking Hillbrow's streets, recasting its conventional pathways, and negotiating its hyperreality; the aging white man and his "ecologies of ignorance"—gaps, blind spots, mistakes, paradoxes—which lead at various points to closure and to the tenuous beginnings of racial friendship; and the hustler, operating with energetic and often underhand activity, turning the codes and conventions of a newly forming human-rights culture to his own advantage. In her chapter, Nuttall explores vocabularies of separation and connectedness that surface only to recede again, and ways in which fictional characters move through and across long-established representational forms. City-ness in Johannesburg, its fiction reveals, is an intricate entanglement of éclat and somberness, lightness and darkness, comprehension and bewilderment, polis and necropolis, desegregation and resegregation.

These chapters show that Johannesburg has all along been a polycentric and international city that has developed its own brand of cosmopolitan culture. As in many metropoli of the Southern Hemisphere, it is a city where splendor and squalor exist side by side, and in which technologies of speed are dramatically changing people's experience of time, of space, and of self (Appadurai 2002; Sansone 2003). Just as in Mumbai or Rio de Janeiro, each cultural stratum has brought an intricate system of interconnections to bear upon a hybrid history that continually permeates the present. Over the last quarter of a century, its boundaries have become so geographically and socially permeable and stretched that the city seems to have no fixed parts, no completeness, and almost no unique center. Like the continent itself, it is an amalgam of often disjointed circulatory processes. Turning its back on the rigid rationalities of planning and racial separation, it has become, in spite of itself, a place of intermingling and improvisation. Its very porosity means that, released from the iron cage of apartheid, it can now continually fashion and refashion itself.

Voice Lines

The second section we have called "Voice Lines." It consists of shorter pieces and interviews. Indeed, one way of invoking the city, of bringing Johannesburg into being as a metropolis, is to make it talk. To generate the voices of the city itself is to venture into the realm of sensory intimation (Amin and Thrift 2003: 9). It is—as we have found in the process of putting together this book—not only to interpret monuments, images, built forms, and self-histories. It is also to draw on wider styles of writing, vocabularies that are not always academic, and nonconventional itineraries and mappings, such as those of journalists, artists, architects, and young people.

These voice lines point to themes and realities that have very often outpaced academic research. Mindful of what we wanted to do in this book, and of the relative poverty of the available literature on the city-ness of Johannesburg and the modernity of African life forms, we revisited the essay form and the interview form—both critical pedagogies with a long history, though often discarded in mainstream academic practice. The interventions in this section are united not only by form and style but also by theme: each concerns the remapping of physical and imaginary public spaces of the city of Johannesburg.

John Matshikiza writes about Johannesburg as the "unfinished city" of his birth and now return after many years in exile, of the "humming terminus" between South Africa and cities on the rest of the continent—Lagos, Dar es Salaam, Nairobi, Lusaka, Luanda. Two young South Africans, Grace Khunou and Nsizwa Dlamini, create personal maps of the postapartheid township in "Soweto Now." The "Arrivants" is an e-mail exchange between Tom Odhiambo, from Nairobi (Kenya), and Robert Muponde, from Harare (Zimbabwe), about living in Braamfontein, Johannesburg. They talk in ironic ways about intra-African cell phone cultures and modes of self-making in the city. Stefan Helgesson reflects on Johannesburg as seen from Maputo, via a lens of what some see as integration and others as hegemony and domination.

Music has been central to Johannesburg's metropolitan formation. Through a series of *situations* written in the first person, Xavier Livermon explores the city through its cultures of sound, and the ways in which bodies literally move through the city, in pursuit of music. Julia Hornberger reflects on the electric illumination of the night—its reenchantment—by situating contemporary nocturnal Johannesburg within its history of electric lighting. Fred de Vries writes about Sandton City, Johannesburg's largest shopping mall, and a prominent part of its dual city center, exploring it as an intriguing barometer of contemporary South Africa. Achal Prabhala writes an account of living in Yeoville, Johannesburg, once known as a bohemian, cross-racial home to the antiapartheid left, now an "Afropolitan," vibrant, and dangerous neighborhood.

The final two interventions engage with the built spaces of the city. Mark Gevisser examines how four city prisons are forming the site of South Africa's new Constitutional Court in Hillbrow. The struggle to find a form to express the new city is one that Lindsay Bremner vividly engages with in her short essay. Bremner discusses the final designs in an architectural competition for the remaking of a historical public space in Kliptown, Soweto. In an afterword to the book, Arjun Appadurai and Carol Breckenridge write of the risk of Johannesburg and of the writing of it.

Conclusion

In what follows, then, we present a city in formation, a metropolis in the making, a moment, captured in print, in the life of a city overwritten with possibility, underwritten by anxiety. As we write, a crime wave crests across the city. We have sought here to disentangle the contemporary fact of crime from a tendency to read this city in that manner—the manner of the criminological. As we write, too, citizens protest to government about crime, out of concern for the hard-won democracy from which the city is being wrought. We end this introduction, then, on a note of fragility, suffusing the achieved force, life, and political freedom of which this city undoubtedly speaks. Johannesburg, elusive as ever, in thrall to its future, speaks of a quite unprecedented African cosmopolitanism: the Afropolitan, as we have invoked it here. It is an original city, speaking in an original voice. Even in its most self-destructive moments, it is a place where a new and singular metropolitan vocabulary is being born.

Notes

1 Such characterizations are typical of the secondary literature on global cities rather than of Saskia Sassen's original formulations. For an exception, see Appadurai 1996, esp. chap. 2. Otherwise, the same assumption underlies many approaches to global cultural formations. Read Fredric Jameson's theory of the global postmodern in *Postmodernism* (1991), David Harvey's considerations of flexible accumulation in *The Condition of Postmodernity* (1989), or Manuel Castell's study of the ways in which information technology structures a space of flows of information, technology, and finance.

2 The results of the research gathered in this unpublished report were later published in a book by Koolhaus and Edgar Cleijne under the same title (Baden: Lars Müller Publishers, 2007).

3 Jane Guyer (2004) shows that in many countries, formalization has not produced predictable systemic conditions at any level: "The policy monitoring, institutional reworking, and ever more detailed synchronization in economic life that are the hallmarks of modern rationalization have been extremely partial and changeable" (98). For urban citizens who make their livelihood in the so-called informal sector, formal policies and institutions have often lacked coherence and have hardly been empowering. "What has occurred in many places is that one formal policy has undone the conditions on which another depended, producing complex 'Catch-22' circumstances that people have had to navigate as best as they could" (98). African

city forms and urban life are therefore the product of these navigations. This requires us to properly understand the uncertainty and incoherence of the formal economy. To understand what these cities are, we need to pay a very close attention to the institutional and cultural forms of economic life under uncertainty.

4 On the city of Johannesburg as a space of anxiety, fear, and terror, read Beall 2002. See also Kruger 2001 and Bremner 1998. By contrast, it is striking the extent to which both cultural theorists and practitioners articulate a different view of the city, one both less hostile and more engaged with new ways of being in the city. See Nuttall and Michael 2000, or, to take one of many examples, a recent statement by *kwaito* artist Mzekezeke—"Let me tell you . . . Jo'burg is now a place of pride, a place of history, a place of liberation. It is a place of African wealth, technology, education and culture"—in the British magazine *Face*, October 2003.

5 So much was Shanghai loathed that a missionary could proclaim: "If God lets Shanghai endure, he owes an apology to Sodom and Gomorrah" (Dong 2001: 1).

6 Van Onselen draws on a long tradition of loathing the city. Recalling the terms on which Shanghai was invoked, Winston Churchill famously described Johannesburg in similarly puritanic terms as "Monte-Carlo on top of Sodom and Gomorrah" (qtd. in Kruger 2001, 223).

7 Jennifer Robinson (1998) is one of the few urbanists who approaches city space differently. Calling for a reexamination of the apartheid spaces, she writes: "Were those spaces so fixed, so divisive, so certain in their form? Our imaginations have lived for so long with the lines of apartheid space, with the blank spaces in between, the deadening images of power drawn on the ground. We have uncovered many reasons for the emergence of these dividing lines: sanitation, health, planning, government, administration, policing, racism, disgust, employment, class, development strategies, industrialization, political order . . . Can we begin to shift our experiences and our visions to capture and understand the world of always-moving spaces? . . . In what sense was even the apartheid city—a city of division—a place of movement, of change, of crossings?"

8 For an extension of this argument in the countryside, see Beinart et al. 1986. Read the critiques by Peris Sean Jones (2000). For a critique of the thesis of "exceptionalism" in relation to cultural issues, see the introduction to Nuttall and Michael 2000.

9 See Kinda 2001: 137–52. For a summary of the literature on the township in South Africa, see Bozzoli 2000: 78–110.

10 See Bond 2000 and Mayekiso 1996. For a similar view elsewhere, see Scott 1988.

11 Detlev Krige is currently conducting Ph.D. research on this subject in Soweto.

12 For a novelistic rendition of these movements and their paradoxical nature, read Gordimer 1999.

13 Compare with the description of São Paulo in Caldeira 2001.

14 See, for example, Nelson Mandela's description of Johannesburg in *Long Walk to Freedom* (1995).

It is altogether impossible to live at all without forgetting.

FRIEDRICH NIETZSCHE, *Untimely Meditations*

1 ✛ Aesthetics of Superfluity

ACHILLE MBEMBE

If there is ever an African form of metropolitan modernity, then Johannesburg will have been its classical location. The idea of the metropolis in European thought has always been linked to that of "civilization" (a form of existence as well as a structure of time) and capitalist rationalization. Indeed, the Western imagination defines the metropolis as the general form assumed by the rationalization of relations of production (the increasing prevalence of the commodity system) and the rationalization of the social sphere (human relations) that follows it. A defining moment of metropolitan modernity is realized when the two spheres rely on purely functional relations among people and things and subjectivity takes the form of calculation and abstraction.

One such moment is epitomized by the instrumentality that labor acquires in the production, circulation, and reproduction of capital. Another moment is to be found in the way that the circulation of goods and commodities, as well as the constant process of buying and selling, results in the liquidation of tradition and its substitution by a culture of indifference and restlessness that nourishes self-stylization. Yet another is to be found in the ways that luxury, pleasure, consumption, and other stimuli are said to affect the sensory foundations of mental life and the central role they play in the process of subject formation in general.[1]

This study is highly speculative. It uses the notion of superfluity to revisit the biopolitics of Johannesburg as a "racial city" and its transition to a metropolitan form. In the wake of the collapse of apartheid (an insidious form of state racism), the collage of various fragments of the former city is open-ing up a space for experiences of displacement, substitution, and condensa-tion, none of which is purely and simply a repetition of a repressed past but rather a manifestation of traumatic amnesia and, in some cases, nostalgia or even mourning.[2] In the process, an original form, if not of African cosmo-politanism then of the performance of worldliness, emerges. It is structur-ally shaped by the intertwined realities of bare life (mass poverty), the global logic of commodities, and the formation of a consumer public. Today, the nervous rhythm of the city and its cultural pulse are made up of an unrepen-tant commercialism that combines technology, capital, and speculation.

As I use the term here, *superfluity* does not refer only to the aesthetics of sur-faces and quantities, and to how such an aesthetics is premised on the capacity of things to hypnotize, overexcite, or paralyze the senses. To my mind, super-fluity refers also to the dialectics of indispensability and expendability of both labor and life, people and things. It refers to the obfuscation of any exchange or use value that labor might have, and to the emptying of any meaning that might be attached to the act of measurement or quantification itself, insofar as numerical representation is as much a fact as it is a form of fantasy.[3]

But the abolition of the very meaning of quantification, or the general conversion of number into fiction, is also a way of writing time, of forgetting and remembering. Moreover, I argue that the post-apartheid metropolis in general, and Johannesburg in particular, is being rewritten in ways that are not unlike the operations of the unconscious. The topography of the un-conscious is paradoxical and elusive because it is bound to several distinct modes of temporality. So is the psychic life of the metropolis. This psychic life is inseparable from the metropolitan form: its design, its architectural topographies, its public graphics and surfaces. Metropolitan built forms are themselves a projective extension of the society's archaic or primal fantasies, the ghost dances and the slave spectacles at its foundation.

Superfluity

Johannesburg began as a mining camp of tents and corrugated iron buildings during the Witwatersrand gold rush of the late nineteenth century. As South Africa was consolidated as a white supremacist state, Johannesburg devel-oped into a colonial town. Like every colonial town, it found it hard to resist the temptation of mimicry, that is, of imagining itself as an English town and becoming a pale reflection of forms born elsewhere. Johannesburg's earliest settlers did not experience a sense of having genuine ties with the world surrounding them. To a large extent, this tradition of mimicry continues to determine if not the language of the city today, then at least part of its unconscious. This might explain the level of "falsehood" many analysts identified in Johannesburg's cultural life: what appears alternatively as a mélange of and a deep antagonism between provincial and cosmopolitan ways.[4]

That the city started as a tabula rasa did not mean that the new could be inscribed upon it without reference to a past. As in every settler colony, the past was to be found elsewhere, in the myth that Johannesburg was a European city in a European country in Africa.[5] It was a tabula rasa, too, in the sense that, with the displacement of earlier frontiers of accumulation (land and cattle), Johannesburg became the first site on the continent where capital, labor, and industry came together. In contrast to what happened in other regions of Africa, here the extraction of primary resources did not necessarily lead to marginalization within the global economy. People's experience of the market was constantly disciplined and brought into line with formal and, most often, coercive institutions. Money was one such institution, but so were numerical and legal frameworks for the valuation of people, property, contracts, and credit (see Posel 2000). Early on, the city was inscribed within increasingly wide networks and complex, long-distance interchanges and transactions. In the process, a distinctive commercial civilization emerged that was based partly on race, in particular through the sale of people as property. In this way, Johannesburg became a central site not only for the birth of the modern in Africa, but for the entanglement of the modern and the African—the African modern.[6]

But even cities born out of mimicry are capable of mimesis. By *mimesis*, we should understand a capacity to identify oneself or establish similarities with something else while at the same time inventing something original (see Halliwell 2002). More than any other African city, Johannesburg has evidenced this capacity to mime. In the process, the city has developed an aura of its own, its uniqueness. The mimetic structure of Johannesburg is still evident in the city's contemporary architectural forms or, more simply, in its mania for wealth, for the sensational and the ephemeral, for appearances.

From its beginning in the late nineteenth century, Johannesburg has always imagined itself to be a modern city.[7] Early on, it developed along utilitarian and functional lines, with a clear delineation between the zones of work, living, recreation, and transportation. It had its own newspapers, its horse-drawn trams, its solid stone buildings, its stock exchange, its banks, post offices, telephone exchange, railway stations, and various social clubs. Later on, it built its galleries, parks, and museums.

The modern city has a number of characteristics. It is, above all, the product of capitalism. In the South African case, industrial capitalism grew out of diamond mining in Kimberley and gold mining in the Main Reef of the Witwatersrand. This is why Johannesburg is also known as "gold-reef city" or Egoli (City of Gold). One can still see traces and markers of this early history in contemporary Johannesburg's landscape, scenery, and folklore. It is not uncommon to drive down a Gold Street, a Quartz Street, or a Nugget Street, just as it is easy to see remnants, here and there, of the machinery that lowered miners below the surface and hauled up ore. From the airport highway, one can still see the slagheaps not far from the very center of the city, those manmade hills in ochre colors, "the mine-dumps, the refuse of stamp-mill and cyanide-tank, the ghosts of the mines' earth gazing down on the world they left behind."[8]

As Marx showed long ago, capitalism is not simply a mode of production and accumulation; it also involves flow and motion (Marx 1073: 186). Capital depends on the circulation of commodities, understood here as both labor power and the means of production and exchange (see Braudel 1982). The material life of cities is made up of people and things, of images and signs. After 1873, when silver was demonetized in Europe, gold became the foundation of the global economic system or, in any case, its primary means of exchange. The discovery of gold in the Witwatersrand in 1886 immediately triggered a gold rush, not unlike the ones in California in 1848 or Australia in 1851. Within a few years, what had been until then a small mining camp experienced a population explosion.

Migrants to Johannesburg came from all corners of the earth. They included Cornish "hard-rock men" and Australian miners, Scottish and American engineers, bankers, lawyers, adventurers, gamblers, schemers, criminals, and fortune hunters, journalists, sex workers, refugees, thousands of impoverished Eastern Europeans (including Polish and Russian Jews fleeing persecution), Frenchmen, Italians, and Greeks.[9] Many dreamed of fast and easy riches. Others simply wanted to escape lives made wretched by misery and debasement. They were joined by criminals, vagabonds, hustlers, musicians, and other marginal figures (van Onselen 1982). Whether rich or poor, many had bought into an idealized lifestyle that surrendered unreservedly to the world of things—wealth, luxury, and display (Wheatcroft 1985).

Like other modern cities, Johannesburg was founded within the sphere of superfluity. Marx refers to superfluity in the context of a broader discussion on money and commodity value. For him, it is the particular usefulness of the commodity, whether as a particular object of consumption or as a direct instrument of production, that stamps it as money. But the opposite can also occur: a commodity "which has the least utility as an object of consumption or instrument of production" happens "to best serve the needs of *exchange as such.*" Such is the case with precious metals. From the outset, says Marx, "they represent superfluity, the form in which wealth originates" (1973: 168–69).[10] But for Marx, superfluity also pertains to "the sphere of satisfactions and enjoyments," to the "world of gratifications" and "fleeting pleasures." As for money and wealth, they not only have sensuous qualities, they can also be seized and lost in the same manner. Wealth, in particular, does not appear only in material and tangible forms. For wealth to be realized, it has to be constantly thrown back into circulation. More important, it has to exist in the subject's head as "a pure fantasy" (Marx 1973: 204, 232–33).

In his study of capitalism and the structures of everyday life from the fifteenth to the eighteenth centuries, the French historian Fernand Braudel defines the sphere of superfluity as a complex area of daily life located beyond the sphere of poverty and necessity. He associates superfluity with luxury, rarity and vanity, futility and caprice, conspicuous spectacle, and even phantasm (Braudel 1981: chaps. 3 and 4). A mode of relation to objects, superfluity is manifested in domains as varied as the consumption of food and drink, houses and their interiors (types of furniture, floors, walls, ceilings, doors and windows, chimneys and fireplaces, furnaces and stoves), and costume and fashion.

In contrast to Braudel, Hannah Arendt (1966) invokes the notion of the superfluous to refer to situations of misery and destitution. She argues that many European immigrants who settled in South Africa were unemployed in the societies they came from. As such, they belonged not to an actual active army of labor but to a class of superfluous men. Once in Johannesburg, they formed a mass of human material ready for exploitation. Indeed, it was believed in the nineteenth century that only the conquest, settlement, and exploitation of overseas territories could permanently solve the problem of superfluity.

For Arendt, it is a remarkable paradox that, in South Africa, the purported solution to superfluity was initially a rush for the most superfluous raw material on earth: gold (King 1867). Gold, Arendt wrote (1966: 188), hardly had "a place in human production" and was "of no importance compared with iron, coal, oil, and rubber"; instead, it was "the most ancient symbol of mere wealth." In its uselessness in industrial production, she concluded, "it bears an ironical resemblance to the superfluous money that financed the digging of gold and to the superfluous men who did the digging."

If the capital, technology, and expertise for mining came mostly from Riga, San Francisco, Hamburg, Kiev, or London, most of the "superfluous men who did the digging" were "migrant black workers without rights and with little choice but to sell their labor cheaply," Hermann Giliomee writes (2003, 323). They flocked to the Rand from as far away as Basutoland, Mozambique, and later on from Rhodesia, Nyasaland, and Zambia. Here, superfluity was not a matter simply of numbers or of surplus populations. In fact, if anything, there was never enough labor power at the beginning of the industrial revolution in South Africa. This is why, from the start, a dense nexus of overlapping and interweaving threads connected migrancy and modernity in South Africa (see Moodie 1994; Comaroff 1992: 155–80). Through the movement of bodies, superfluity came to be based on not only the prominence of money, credit, and speculation but also the obfuscation of any use value black labor might have had. Such obfuscation was itself a mode of rationality closely related to the circulation of capital. But contrary to most Marxist analyses (see Harvey 2001: 314), the circulation of capital is predicated not just on class relations but also on human investment in certain forms of racial delirium.

Delirium and the Racial City

It is by now a commonplace to assert that the city of Johannesburg grew in connection with both the forces and relations of production. Less well understood is how relations of race and class determined each other in the production of the city. It can be argued that race here became, in and of itself, both a force of production and a relation of production. As such, race directly gave rise to the space Johannesburg would become, its peculiarities, contours, and form. Space became both a social and a racial relationship, one that was additionally inherent to the notion of property.

Race in South Africa first manifested itself as a peculiar investment in the cognitive framing of people, things, and relationships (their respective qualities and the scales by which equivalences, differences, and incommensurability between them could be formally established). In the money economy of early Johannesburg, this peculiar investment took the form of a social utilitarianism applied to practical and mental forms. As a potential commodity form, black life was not only needed but also valued for its industrial utility. It could be sold and acquired through a multileveled market. But the specifics of the commodity form and the particulars of the market in which blacks circulated were predetermined by a logic of productive sacrifice that was the key underpinning of a racialized institution of private property. In the calculus of superfluity, racism was not only a way of maintaining biological differences among people, even as mining capitalism, migrant labor, and black urbanization established new connections between people and things. More fundamentally, racism's function was to institute a contradictory relation between the instrumentality of black life in the market sphere, on the one hand, and the constant depreciation of its value and its quality by the forces of commercialism and bigotry, on the other.[11] Here, superfluity was akin to the dissipation of value and its reorganization in the realm of the biopolitical. In a context in which native life had become the new frontier for capital accumulation, superfluity consisted in the vulnerability, debasement, and waste that the black body was subjected to and in the racist assumption that wasting black life was a necessary sacrifice—a sacrifice that could be redeemed because it served as the foundation of civilization. In this sense, racism was a transactional practice with radical implications for the distribution of death—as raw black labor was acquired and intensively consumed.

The pattern of labor organization in the mines of the Witwatersrand had been experimented with, and it met with relative success in the diamond mines of Kimberley. Foundational to the capitalism that built Johannesburg was the belief that black labor pertained to the domains of both need and use. Native life, in turn, was both indispensable and expendable. Because native life was seen as excessive and naturally doomed to self-destruction, it constituted wealth that could be lavishly spent. Although many whites in South Africa were disinclined to undertake manual labor,[12] they were convinced that the natives were "indolent individuals whose habitual shyness of work made them a sort of naked leisure class," the historian C. W. De Kiewiet writes (1957: 83–85). As a consequence, "confiscation of land, discriminatory taxation, and all the means used to drive [them] into the labour market" were justified on moral grounds "because they struck at superstition and sloth."[13]

The search for profit required that the same population that labored be doomed to continual depredation, if not slow death. Many studies have established the high death rates from pneumonia, tuberculosis, and silicosis in the gold mines (Crush, Jeeves, and Yudelman 1991: 41–45; Packard 1989; Johnstone 1976). Beneath the surface of the city, a labor system based on a rigidly hierarchical racial division of labor had become entrenched. Sarah Gertrude Millin (1926: 80) describes hundreds of thousands of blacks who hammered "holes into the rock for dynamite charges, their black, naked torsos . . . glistering with sweat along corridors a mile, two miles long." Vertical shafts "had to be driven into the ground to tap the reefs several hundreds of feet below the surface. That was but the beginning of shafts that would finally reach depths of a mile and more, and of underground workings with a combined length of thousands of miles." As black miners reemerged from the "sarcophagus" with the whitish-gray mine dust (the silica) upon their clothes and faces, one could hear the damage of silicosis in their coughing and see its effects in frequent funerals (De Kiewiet 1957: 157). This is why, as artist Minnette Vári argues, Johannesburg is a metropolis "that pokes and thunders at the sky while its reason for being there is thoroughly subterranean." The mine shaft evokes a sepulchral crevice, as "gleaning ore is taken from inside the earth and brought out, like a reverse internment" (Peffer 2003: 26). Built underneath the city is thus an original violence that was explicitly directed at what servile use had degraded and rendered profane (Bataille 1988: 55).

In this economy, race also manifested itself in the indeterminacy of the value and ontological status of both native life and black labor. Such indeterminacy resided in a kind of doubleness. Through the commodification of labor, the superfluity of black life could be manifested. But the same process also transformed the native into something more than the object he or she was, a thing that always seemed slightly human and a human being that always seemed slightly thinglike. The spectral power of racism in South Africa resided in the constant activation of this doubleness. For racism to acquire such power, profit and delirium had to be so closely connected as to constantly trigger the vertiginous capacity of the native to be both a thing and a metonym of something else.

This is why, far from being an accident, racism became a constitutive dimension of the city's modernity. Race thinking became a weapon in a long civil war of which the Anglo-Boer moment was but an episode. It became a device whose aim was to create walls between people. As such, Johannesburg was until very recently the physical embodiment of an apparently impossible nation. The geography of the city; its cardinal orientation; its planning, zoning, and codes; its infrastructure, streets, and utilities; and its residential patterns and distribution of wealth and income all told a larger story of conquest and the divisive power of race and capital. The settlers' denial of a common origin or destiny between them and the natives resulted in the emergence of a dual nation and a dual city.

But race in South Africa should also be understood as a mirror, a constellation of imaginary identifications, emotions, feelings, and affects. Indeed, the existence of a void in the symbolic structure is the precondition for the racist drive to emerge—for any form of racism to operate at all.[14] It can be argued that the racial city was always a psychotic city or space of delirium. This delirium was of both a political and a psychic nature. And in both cases, it had a paranoiac and schizophrenic dimension.[15] Because of this dual structure, delirium at times manifested itself through the production and overcoding of fears and fantasies, faked objects and images.

Thus, between 1890 and 1914, "periodic waves of collective sexual hysteria" swept Johannesburg, in which "white women, on an unprecedented scale, alleged that they had been sexually molested or assaulted by black men" (van Onselen 2001: 257). At other times, delirium was expressed in the form of a primal repression at once political and psychic.[16] According to Deborah Posel, the policing of sexuality manifested itself, among other ways, in the state's prohibition of cross-racial sex, the stigmatization of miscegenation, the criminalization of homosexuality, and the banning of pornography (2005; see also Elder 2003). Indeed, in order to form docile white subjects and to ensure the reproduction of the racist social formation, political coercion demanded psychic and sexual repression.[17] The Prohibition of Mixed Marriages Act (1949) and the Immorality Act Amendment Act (1950) "were two of the earliest apartheid measures designed to preserve the imagined racial purity of the White group," A. J. Christopher writes (1994: 141). For this reason, the apartheid polity produced so many slumbering and schizophrenic subjects. Deeply marked by a tremendous fear of life and used to resorting to shortcuts, white South Africans developed an extraordinary capacity to live in a world of prearranged impasses and untenable lies.[18]

From a spatial point of view, the apartheid city—its ordering and its geographical layout—has often been defined in the same terms as any other colonial city, as a rigid, segregated place divided between a center (the white city) and peripheries and outskirts (the native locations) (see Fanon 1963:

37–40). Indeed, during the years of racial segregation, architecture and city planning were both the transcription of larger mechanisms of social and urban warfare. The apartheid transcription of race took various discursive forms, most insidiously the medicobiological. It borrowed its discourse from a materialist anatomophysiology and argued that blacks had a racial predisposition to disease. Concerns about the health of whites led to the passage of a series of health acts and the forced removal of thousands of blacks from the city (Packard 1989). Although race as such could not be pinned to a stable biological meaning, it was used as a weapon in the production of a city of barriers and asymmetric privileges.

Indeed, since the early history of South Africa, state racism's function had been the biological protection of the so-called white race. This protection translated into the physical form of the city and the management of "urban problems" as well as the various bioregulatory policies designed to manage white life and black life; that is, to optimize it or, conversely, expose it to risk, random events, and accidents (see Foucault 2003: 239–53). The racial state attempted to erase class conflict among whites by conflating white poverty with white purity. For the class struggle, it substituted a race struggle. In recasting the theme of racial confrontation as a struggle for existence and survival, the state entrenched racial privileges as customary rights for whites and as the foundation for the unequal distribution of wealth and the exercise of power (Giliomee 2003: 315–54, 447–86).

Johannesburg's architecture and city planning manifested an instrumental rationality that combined a pastoral urban imaginary for white citizens with a militarization of space for blacks. Early on, this pastoral imaginary took shape in the layout of the suburbs and in domestic architectural forms. Hundreds of cottages spread for miles across the empty veld; gardens were created, and trees were planted along avenues. The first of Johannesburg's millionaires built mansions, spacious single-story bungalows with wide Victorian verandas, plenty of decorative wood- and ironwork, turrets, and other embellishments. The experience of home was determined by the sensuous impact of the building materials and investment in visual surfaces. Among the most important signs of distinction and status were marble columns, mosaics, plate-glass windows, alabaster mantelpieces, painted ceilings, and other extravagances (Rosenthal 1970: 235–26). The use of faked material was widespread among the less wealthy and was aided by an emerging culture of masquerade and artifice, superficiality and hollowness. Plastering could be disguised as marble, brickwork as stone. More important, a separation between the indoor world and the world outside, or between members of the family and domestic servants, became a defining aspect of white subjectivity in a racially divided city. In contemporary Johannesburg, this duality of inside and outside is visibly achieved by the walls that encircle and shield nearly every house or building.

As long as Johannesburg remained a racial city, this pastoral idea of the urban ensured that claims for a harmonious relation between the indoor world and the world outside formed the basis of white subjectivity. In the most extreme cases, a telluric bond and a sense of unity with the soil and the spirit of the people, fueled by a nostalgic pathos, were called upon to manifest the tragic character of the utopia of racial purity and segregation. Because it constructed dwelling as both seclusion and security, the pastoral imaginary of the racial city functioned as a way of assuaging white citizens' fears and instilling in them a morality of social conformity in exchange for racial privileges. But the dualism between inside and outside also served as a basis to reject the racial other, and indeed to legitimize a separation from the world. Urban rationality and planning sought to avoid, as much as possible, overlays or collisions. Thus, to a large extent, the apartheid city was a city of boundaries and contrasts. The role of architecture and planning was to trace partitions within well-defined spaces with clear protective boundaries so as to avoid the disruptive effects—real or potential—of race mixing.

In particular, the apartheid state attempted to establish a relationship between spatial patterns and the moral order. The physical distances that separated the races were largely understood to consecrate moral ones. Much like class relations in Paris, as David Harvey (2003: 40) has argued, race came to be inscribed in the space of the South African city (or, for that matter, on the farm) "in such a way as to make the spatial pattern both a reflection of and an active moment in the reproduction of the moral order." In the process, the arts of city building and of inhabiting the city became synonymous with the creation of an illusory harmony and purity based on the fiction of racial distance. This led to the emergence of diverse urban worlds within the same territory—strange mappings and blank figures, discontinuous fixtures and flows, and odd juxtapositions that one can still observe in the present-day South African urban landscape.

Nevertheless, the apartheid city—and Johannesburg in particular—was tubular in the sense developed by Gilles Deleuze and Félix Guattari (1987: 93–94): a space made up of leakages, of several lines of flight that not only coexisted but intermingled, that transformed and crossed over into one

another. To be sure, this was not akin to endless multiplication or proliferation: each fragment of the city interlocked with others in a space that was always undermined by fissures and cracks (see Rogerson 1989). The apartheid
state constantly tried to plug these lines of flight by fomenting a micropolitics of insecurity while inflating the discourse of separateness.[19]

Disjunctive Inclusions

In spite of its appearance of fixity, Johannesburg was never a totally foreclosed city even at the height of apartheid. The city was constantly marked
by a dialectics of distance, proximity, and reciprocal dependencies among the
different races. But each element of this dialectic contributed in its own way
toward shaping a structured racial inequality. The most obvious figure of
this is the domestic worker and, in particular, the "black nannies" of the suburbs, whom Rory Bester (2001: 222) describes as "toiling alone inside white
homes, and occasionally meeting on the pavements outside." Commenting on Ernest Cole's book of photographs of life under apartheid, *House of
Bondage* (1967), Bester points to this enigmatic figure of South African urban
modernity on the back of whom so many white children grew up and whose
"routine duties involved a daily round of cleaning, sweeping, polishing, ti-
dying and dusting," making beds, and "serving the family at meal times."[20]
The Group Areas Act of 1950 had made it illegal for black workers to live
under the same roof as their white employers. "Hence the development of
outbuildings—or 'maid's rooms'—for black domestic workers, rooms often
just big enough for a bed and a toilet," Bester writes. In this, one can see how
a logic of servility or reciprocal dependency interrupts the coded intervals
of the apartheid city while opening up a space for combined processes of re-
stratification and involution, proximity and distance.

But the black nanny was not the only living metaphor of the inextricable
relationships between blacks and whites. So was the migrant worker. As De
Kiewiet has noted (1957: 179), segregation never entailed a real separation
between two distinct communities. The prejudices that race and color engendered always hid a close weaving between black and white. Having been
deprived of free access to water and land, the natives were left with one thing
to sell: their labor. Indeed, since the earliest phase of white settlement in
South Africa, the confiscation of land had gone hand in hand with the an-
nexation of labor, discriminatory taxation, and the quasi-extinction of native

property. "Driven by destitution from their own land to seek a livelihood, the natives entered a European society that was itself economically backward and too poor and unproductive to turn their labour to profitable account." But "by the time diamonds were picked up and the first gold was discovered, black and white were far on the way to a new society in which both elements were joined indissolubly to one another in the closest economic relationships" (84–87).

In the apartheid city, racial segments interacted with one another in a number of different ways. Moreover, there was always a social shadow that escaped the apartheid binary imaginary and its attempts at totalization. Writing about black urbanization and the squatter communities in the mid-1980s, Lawrence Schlemmer (1985: 168) observed that "the well-ordered pattern [of apartheid planning] has more and more been broken, openly and manifestly, by a very visible informal phenomenon—the growth of massive squatter and shack settlements on the edge of some industrial complexes. The formal system of planned residence and controlled movement has been breached for all to see. . . . There are people building homes and developing communities outside the 'compound' gates, as it were." Illegal residence and work in the city were only part of an array of tactics that included pass law evasions, squatter struggles, various forms of boycott, and campaigns of defiance and civil disobedience (see Boraine 1989).

This pattern of disjunctive inclusion can be explained by three factors. First, the apartheid state apparatus operated as a machine that was both territorial and deterritorializing. A network of exclusive connections and disjunctive inclusions, it superposed and juxtaposed a geographic organization and the organization of *gens* inherited from the frontier wars period (Elphick and Giliomee 1979). By the end of the nineteenth century, "some territories had been entirely annexed; some were partly dependent, and others were entirely independent"; "tribal tenure and private ownership existed side by side with squatting and utter landlessness," while the dispersive forces of local conflicts and settlers' pressure caused ethnic groups to splinter or become embedded in larger ones (De Kiewiet 1965: 149). In continuity with earlier colonial policies, the apartheid state established—both among people and between territories and people—relations that were at once conjunctive and segregative. Although firmly welded to the law, segregation was only one of the apartheid state's many modes of deployment. In the cities (especially in the case of domestic servants), in the mines, and in the rural towns and farms, other interracial modalities bordered on intimacy and paternalism—which is not to imply that they were less extractive or coercive. Despite or due to the conscious desire and labor of separating, prescribing, and prohibiting, the daily microphysics of racism came to be made up of multiple forms of transgression and codependency, especially in areas where black or servile labor was needed. Because of the logic of segmentarity and overlapping divisions, *crossing* boundaries, transgressing them, or eluding them became the main modality of action for blacks in the city.

Second is the fact, mentioned above, that the apartheid state apparatus also operated as a deterritorializing machine. Cities came to play a critical role in this process as theaters of cruelty and desire. Deterritorialization involved the appropriation of land, the disassembling of older territorial lineages, the formation of neoterritories and artificial enclaves ("reserves," "homelands," and Bantustans), and their overcoding and progressive transformation into fragments and scattered partial forms hanging on to the state's body (see Horrell 1973). To a great extent, the formation of the racial city of apartheid was inseparable from the institutionalization and demise of the "reserves," those semiautonomous territories that, beginning in the early twentieth century, served to regulate the flow of migrant labor and to minimize urban welfare spending (Legassick 1974; Wolpe 1972). According to Giliomee (1985: 39–42), the reserves retained their role in the reproduction of labor even after their political functions changed. Indeed, the reserves not only served as an exclusive home base for migrant laborers, they also justified the exclusion of blacks from holding or leasing farmland in the white rural areas. Even more important, they underpinned the "policy of possessory segregation" and therefore embodied black disenfranchisement and the denial of black claims to citizenship in South Africa (Bester 2001: 219).

In many ways, the development of the reserves was akin to a reshaping of the very nature of sovereignty. The latter was partitioned according to supposed differences among black ethnic groups despite their interconnections. Under the apartheid calculus, territorial fragmentation meant to determine separate freedoms and separate citizenships depending on whether one was black or white and, above all, to express ethnoracial forms of sovereignty.

Third, as both a territorial and a deterritorializing machine, the apartheid system privileged graphism as a mode of operation. Graphism consisted foremost in tracing marks on the body and on the territory. It also entailed various acts of coding and inscription and, above all, legislative efforts to define the various races and enforce the separate use, occupation, and ownership of critical resources (Posel 1991, 1992). It was enacted through small gestures of everyday life, such as the public contexts of walking or, more generally, pass laws (Pirie 1992; van Niekerk 1989). As we have seen, territorial segmentation was a key form of the state's inscription of power onto the landscape. But the main site of this inscription was the black body itself. It could be searched every day at the end of the shift in the mines. It could be stripped naked, required to jump over bars. Hair, nose, mouth, ears, or rectum could be scrutinized with meticulous care. Floggings with a *sjambok* (leather whip) or tent rope, or striking with fists, were the rule (Simons and Simons 1983: 42; Worger 1987: 112). In order to memorialize themselves, public and private powers traced their signs on the naked flesh of the black body. They belabored it and laid it bare through various techniques: tattooing, excising, incising, carving, scarifying, mutilating, or encircling (see Deleuze and Guattari 1987: 144). This is how labor capacity was distributed; different moments of the social reproduction process isolated and singularized; torture, punishment, and death inscribed; and debts created through harm, injury, and pain.

Despite all this, one must not lose sight of the incompleteness of apartheid rule and its attempts at colonizing the city. Johannesburg, for many blacks who migrated there, offered a sense of cultural release, a partial state of freedom, inebriation, and ease. The potential for freedom rested as much on the sensory flow of urban experience as on the contingency and unpredictability of everyday life.[21] Order and disruption went on at the same time. Political resistance in response to regimentation and coercion paved the way for a powerful narrative of freedom (see Mandela 1995; Sisulu 2002). Black people reframed, juxtaposed, misled, and worked against concretions of power. Confronted with the cruelties of a bare world, they also colluded with these cruelties in myriad ways. In the process, they exposed the contingency of apartheid and the structural instability of its narrative authority. This is how Johannesburg became a heteroglot city. The making and remaking of its forms gave the city a fugitive quality. More than any other figure, the black migrant worker epitomized this experience of transience and juxtaposition, displacement and precariousness. The flux of urban circumstances and an experience of time as provisional became the hallmarks of the migrant worker's urban sensibility; nervous discomfort and improvisation became essential elements of a tactical repertoire.

The biopolitics of the mine compound and township life was in direct continuity with the earlier politics of land dispossession codified in the 1913 and the 1936 land acts. These and other laws were aimed at driving noncitizens (i.e., blacks) out of sight, relegating them to the forgotten subterrains of the outer city—the townships. They were enforced through a combination of brute force, dispossession, and expropriation, and the imposition of negative laws and sanctions. The rights of blacks to live in the city were constantly under threat, if not denied in full, which is why most social struggles of the post-apartheid era can be read as attempts to reconquer the right to be urban (Posel 1991: 61–180, 203–26). These new struggles have taken several forms, ranging from squatting to dreams of upward mobility via the new black middle class.

The racial state in South Africa combined two technologies of power. In relation to blacks, both the techniques of power and profit were, ever since the founding of Johannesburg, centered on the body: the individual body of the migrant worker and the racial body of the populace. These bodies were serialized and subjected to various forms of spatial distribution and apparatuses of capture. The township, the hostels, the mine compound, and the jail were prominent regulatory institutions that shaped the lives of black workers in the city. They were part of the urban form yet separate from it. Parallel formations, they constantly intertwined with the city, embedding themselves in the heterogeneous regime of signs that the apartheid city was. They were sites, floating spots where "inhumanity" could be immediately experienced in the body as such. Around them was instituted a field of visibility and surveillance, hierarchies and inspections.

The site par excellence of this anatomopolitics of the black body was the mine compound. Jack Simons and Ray Simons (1983: 42) describe this debasing form of working-class housing.

> The compound was an enclosure surrounded by a high corrugated iron fence and covered by wire-netting. The men lived, twenty to a room, in huts or iron cabins built against the fence. They went to work along a tunnel, bought food and clothing from the company's stores, and received free medical treatment but no wages during sickness, all within the compound. Men due for discharge were confined in detention rooms for several days, during which they wore only blankets and fingerless leather gloves padlocked to their wrists, swallowed purgatives, and were examined for stones concealed in cuts, wounds, swellings and orifices.

To a large extent, this constituted a space of exception in which a supposed labor contract was converted into a period of imprisonment with hard labor (see Gordon 1977).

One of the main characteristics of township life under racial dominion was its close articulations with biopower. Michel Foucault (2003: 256) has argued that biopower is, to a large extent, power's hold over the right to preserve life and administer death. He also showed how modern societies that function through biopower can justify the killing of populations only through appeals to race or racism, that very "precondition that makes killing acceptable." By "killing," Foucault meant not simply "murder as such, but also every form of indirect murder: the fact of exposing someone to death, increasing the risk of death for some people, or, quite simply, political death, expulsion, rejection, and so on."

In South Africa, the rights to kill, to let survive, and to let die were exercised in a paradoxical context. On the one hand, South Africa differed from the United States and Australia in that the dance of race and death did not lead to the native population's decimation. Indeed, this could not be allowed to happen since native labor was needed as raw material to keep whites alive. According to Arendt (1966: 193–94), citing De Kiewiet, it was "this absolute dependence on the work of others and complete contempt for labor and productivity in any form that transformed the Dutchman into the Boer and gave his concept of race a distinctly economic meaning." The Boers, she adds, "were the first European group to become completely alienated from the pride which Western man felt in living in a world created and fabricated by himself. They treated the natives as raw material and lived on them as one might live on the fruits of wild trees."

On the other hand, in order to kill or to let live, the apartheid state used different devices and technologies at different times. To use Foucault's terms, the apartheid city became one of the sites through which the state ensured the spatial distribution of black bodies and the organization, around those bodies, of a regime of visibility. The techniques used to control these bodies were precisely those that Foucault identified in seventeenth- and eighteenth-century Europe. Their aim was to increase the productive force of black labor in the least costly way possible; a "whole system of surveillance, hierarchies, inspections, bookkeeping" was established, at the center of which were the pass laws (Foucault 2003: 117). Other techniques were directly related to those aspects of social engineering that dealt with epidemics (like tuberculosis) and the possibility of frequent death (see Packard 1989). The end of apartheid raises anew the question of how to inhabit the city. For blacks, especially, making oneself at home in the city takes on a peculiar urgency, if only because it has been the dominant site of their exclusion from modernity.

The Waste of Affluence

Contemporary Johannesburg is undergoing a massive spatial restructuring not unlike the one that occurred under apartheid. In the central business district, blocks of dilapidated and worn-out structures are competing with government-sponsored building projects. Elsewhere, growth is fueled by private capital for middle- and upper-income residents, insurance companies, banks, and corporations. The new urban spatial restructuring is driven as much by city planning authorities as by private developers, real estate capital, architects, and designers. More than ever before in its history, Johannesburg's city space is a product that is marked, measured, marketed, and transacted. It is a commodity. As such, its representational form has become ever more stylized.

This process is not unique to South Africa. During the last half of the twentieth century, there was a global homogenization of urban space. Nowadays, Christine Boyer writes (2001: 408), "every traveler knows that airports, highway systems, downtown skyscraper centers, and suburban sprawl look the same the world around. At the local level, however, space is fragmented into separate districts of work, leisure, and living; hierarchicalized with respect to property values, revitalized and restructured with the movements of capital." Post-apartheid Johannesburg has become the regional headquarters of international banks and transnational corporations and a major site of concentration for accounting, legal, and information services. The cityscape is dominated by office developments and shopping emporiums, convention and entertainment centers, and hotels. White-collar and service employment are expanding, as are residential areas for the middle class and the wealthy elite. These developments are concomitant with the emergence of media and high-technology centers and new theaters of consumption in which space and images are both figural forms and aestheticized commodities. In what follows, I briefly describe two examples of these new public theaters of late capitalism: Melrose Arch and Montecasino.

Set in the leafy suburbs of northern Johannesburg, Melrose Arch is a private development by the Sentinel Mining Industry Retirement Fund (formerly known as the Mineworkers' Pension Fund). It is an eighteen-hectare office, retail, residential, and recreational complex located just off the M1 highway, near the megamalls of Sandton and Rosebank. The precinct resembles a miniature European city, with buildings arranged around paved piazzas. Motor traffic runs along an interconnected system of one street (High Street), one drive (Crescent Drive), and one boulevard (Melrose Boulevard), while pedestrian walkways connect its shops, restaurants, apartments, a gym and hotel, open streets, benches, and safe, covered parking. The complex is an incorporated municipality. It has its own utilities, its own police system, refuse removal, and security. It also has its own postal code and telephone exchange.

Melrose Arch is sold to residents and visitors not as a theater of consumption but as a social environment, a "community," and a place where people come together to eat, dance, listen to music, enjoy a good conversation, drink coffee, interact, and be entertained. The Melrose Arch Hotel describes itself as a destination for those who take pleasure in modern elegance and sophistication.[22] The complex aims at pleasing the senses, especially the eye and the tongue. But it is also a place for shopping. Its retail offerings include a pharmacy, an optician, a dry cleaner, a supermarket, postal services, a stationer, medical services, banks, office supply stores, gift shops, fashion boutiques, a music store, an art gallery, and a nightclub.

Much has been invested in the surfaces of Melrose Arch, including the streets and sidewalks. Tuscan paving stones were chosen for the road surfacing, and Port Shepstone stones were used to accentuate the design and colors of the buildings while maintaining an old-world, handcrafted feel. The detail and combination of colors and textures is visually impressive. Commercial and community pavings are combined. The paving links and complements the design of the buildings as well as the villagelike atmosphere of the precinct as a whole.

Another kind of surface can be found in the names of restaurants and cafés: Europa, FooMoon, Giovannis, Moyo, Latchi Fisherman's Village, the Meat Co. These and other restaurants are clustered together and spill out onto Melrose Square and along the high street pavements. The configuration was designed to create social density and interaction. The restaurants themselves offer varied menus drawn from what are described as cosmopolitan and exotic cuisines: Californian, Cape, French, Mediterranean, African, Asian, and European.[23] In spite of their diversity, all these cuisines are said to produce a titillating taste that is uniquely from Johannesburg.

Take, then, the design of the nightclub, Kilimanjaro. One enters the nightclub on a red carpet that sweeps up to an enormous, hand-carved wooden door. Visitors must be suitably dressed to gain admittance. From the entrance, one can glimpse a double-level, wire-mesh "hut" and the circular, wooden staircase around it that leads to the restaurant, bars, and lounge upstairs. The interior of the nightclub is made of carved wood, glass, and rough plaster. According to the club's promotional materials, its interior texture aims to excite a wide range of tactile sensations. Pulses of multihued light are an integral part of the decor. Off to one side of the dance floor, a huge sheet of frosted glass functions as a video projection screen or a translucent wall.

In the Melrose Arch Hotel, lighting is also used to dramatic effect. Underlit floors, oversized lampshades with cable chandeliers, a wide variety of wall and ceiling fixtures, and natural light flooding through skylights are the norm. One enters the hotel through Zanzibar doors. Steel buckets were built on the pool deck. Planted with ficus trees, they frame a pool with a shallow area in which tables and chairs have been placed. Underwater music and water that changes from yellow to red to purple complete the decor.

Another such urban development is Montecasino, a monumental (thirty-eight hectares) upmarket complex combining a casino, a hotel, and a shopping mall. The venture is owned by Tsogo Sun in partnership with the U.S. gaming giant MGM Grand.[24] The Montecasino complex has been designed to look like a Tuscan village and was named after Monte Cassino, the famous Benedictine monastery destroyed by Allied bombs in World War II. The complex is located in Fourways, between shopping malls to the south and a squatter camp to the north. It has an expanse of 8,500 square meters, 2,300 square meters of which are given to "shoppertainment." The vast gambling floor is studded with forty artificial trees (some of them eight meters high) and boasts 2,300 slot machines and table games (J. Thomas 2000b). Its exterior resembles a large, tumbledown slum. *Business Day* reports, "To replicate the effects of weathering on a real Tuscan village, designers . . . did intensive colour studies and tested various methods of layering the building materials for floors and walls. Each stone was hand-carved to match the scale of the façade. The painting and plastering techniques were perfected in a large mock-up building on site before contractors began work in the casino" (J. Thomas 2000a).

"Entering the casino complex is rather like visiting a European necropolis during the height of the tourist season," writes David Le Page in the *Economist*. "Washing hangs from lines between the buildings, paralyzed cocks leer from the roofs, ducks are poised in the middle of a stream, the old bicycle, motorcycle and battered Fiat are all there. But you know they will never again be used. The village appears lifelike, but the proper inhabitants are not there. . . . The village streets are lined with authentic metal and plastic bushes and trees, which also serve as convenient concealment for surveillance equipment. . . . Then, in an effort to renew the illusion of an Italian village, the ceilings have been painted to resemble sky by day, by dusk and by night" (Le Page 2001).

Like other casinos in South Africa, the mark of the entire complex is fakery: fake pigeons perch on fake parapets; phony ducks frolic in pseudostreams. Security guards are dressed in wine-colored Italian police uniforms. Beneath the faked Tuscan sky, slot machines flash, honk, and chatter.[25] Inside the development, an enclosed village has been created comprising various neighborhoods. These range from an elite uptown to a fishing village with fountains, piazzas, and cobbled streets. Pavement eateries and buildings apparently aged and weathered complete the panorama. Although one has the impression of being in a village exposed to the elements, the entire complex—including two-and-a-half kilometers of cobbled or paved walkways—is covered by a massive roof.

What is particularly striking about Melrose Arch and Montecasino is their incorporation of technology. Melrose Arch is surrounded by a fiber-optic ring that offers high-speed access to the Internet. Buildings, basements, and public spaces have been specially designed for high-quality cellular reception. This technological sophistication extends to security. When its three-part security system rollout is completed, Melrose Arch will be protected by a total of 1,000 cameras, of which there will be 29 Digital Sprite multiplexers, 240 cameras, and 15 high-speed domes, two 224 input matrixes, five workstations, and a supervisor station. Cameras are installed in the superbasement that spans the entire site as well as along the streets, intersections, and walkways. Digital multiplex recorders ensure that remote viewing is possible, with simultaneous hard-disk recording and playback.[26] Montecasino has a security force of over three hundred personnel. Two reaction vehicles monitor the complex and its surroundings, and regular police vehicles patrol the area. A site is allocated to the police within the premises, and the complex subsidizes a wide range of police equipment. Access to the casino is controlled and guarded twenty-four hours a day.

The increased visibility characteristic of places such as Melrose Arch and Montecasino describes at least two parallel and competing trajectories that have been inscribed in Johannesburg since its origins. One was the development of the city as a spatially bounded entity with a recognizable center and public and shared spaces (streets, squares, parks, cafés, libraries, galleries, leisure and recreational facilities), its boundaries demarcated through planning, architectural rules, transport and communication networks, and specific art forms. This vision of the urban presupposed a political city (polis) with a distinct spatial and social division of labor and the constitution of a civic sphere through cultural institutions and societies (including literary, art and music societies, libraries, theaters, newsrooms, social clubs, learned societies and other charitable and philanthropic bodies). Yet because of formal segregation, the political city in Johannesburg became the racial city. To a large extent, race defeated the triumph of the idea of the city as a site of free movement and free association. It affected everything, including the domains of taste, language, sensibility, and image. By hindering the cultivation of learning, racism precluded the development of a civilized urban society and the emergence of a polished urban culture and sociability (cf. Stobart 2002). Instead of growing hand in hand, commerce and culture (the creative and refined activities of the mind) grew apart.

This second trajectory was a metropolitanism always embedded in and enframing the "racial city" of the apartheid era. The end of legalized segregation has made it possible for Johannesburg to reconnect with this part of its historical identity as an urban form that served the needs of capital and, in the process, became the synthesis of individuality and freedom. There was always a tension between the apparent fixity of race and the potential unfixing of the commodity form, even after race itself became a commodity. Georg Simmel characterized the metropolis as the seat of money economy, as well as a site of concentration of purchasable things. This concentration is said to stimulate the individual to the highest degree of nervous energy. Because a money economy is concerned only with the exchange value that reduces "all quality and individuals to a purely quantitative level," life in the metropolis is necessarily dominated by "rationally calculated economic egoism." It is characterized by a "purely matter-of-fact attitude" in the treatment of people and things—an attitude in which "formal justice is often combined with an unrelenting hardness." This matter-of-factness goes hand in hand with what Simmel (1971: 326–27) calls the blasé attitude: an indifference toward the distinctions between things that results from overstimulation and enervation.

But above the calculating exactness of practical life and the quantification of the world, one of the distinctive features of late modern metropolitan life forms is superfluity. Here, superfluity is not merely extravagance, caprice, and eccentricity, the collapse of the distinction between meaning and form. It is the superfluity of weighing, calculating, and enumerating, of converting quantities into qualities and vice versa. Superfluity is also a mode of psychic experience in which the distinctions between things, and thus things themselves, become meaningless. Since things have neither singularity nor originality except through their quantification and their equation with money, their core can be hollowed out, their peculiarities erased, and their uniqueness decolored. As a result, the ultimate form of superfluity is the one that derives from the transitoriness of things, their floating "with the same specific gravity in the constantly moving stream of money" (Simmel 1971: 330).

In this sense, places such as Montecasino or Melrose Arch are doubly significant. First, they act as witnesses to the fractured urban space inherited from the apartheid era. With the end of legally sanctioned segregation, Johannesburg is nowadays a metropolis increasingly forced to construct itself out of heterogeneous fragments and fortuitous juxtapositions of images, memories, citations, and allusions drawn from its splintered histories. Some of its fragments seem to recall the postcolonial city form in Africa. The latter is characterized not so much by decay as by the coexistence of divergent elements of different origins brought together in a space whose limits are constantly made and remade. Life, here, is lived under volatile conditions. Small shifts, recombinations of elements from different registers, coalesce to produce a skill of improvisation and qualities of flexibility and resilience (Guyer 2004: 114).

It is possible to observe such developments in present-day central Johannesburg or in Hillbrow. For the most part, the white population has abandoned these areas, leaving behind an infrastructure now occupied, inhabited, or used by blacks in ways sometimes radically different from its original purposes.[27] New forms of spatial imagination are emerging behind the mask of modern architectural forms and apartheid urban planning. Either the space inherited from the apartheid city is drawn out and stretched, or the links of each part of the city with what used to be the whole are interrupted or saturated (see Morris 1999). In the process, Johannesburg loses its original contours; it is reduced to an empty set, or, paradoxically, gains depth. By forcing the city to open up, this process of deframing and enframing has set different repertoires of spatial imaginations and practices into collision.

It is not simply the meaning of buildings or streets that is changing. Contemporary downtown Johannesburg visually resembles other African cities in the aftermath of decolonization: a matrix of plural styles, a striated, striped city that concatenates the most formal and modern with the most informal. In some instances, these breaks signal the force of an obstacle. In other instances, they prefigure the power of a new impulse—a new intensity. In still others, inherited elements of the city are destroyed to make way for the creation of the new. All these instances belie any notion of the city as a symbolic totality. The appropriation of its different styles is not necessarily optical—as shown, for example, by the ease with which old buildings may be left to ruin as silent witnesses to the past. Mostly, the appropriation of the city space is tactile, allegorical, and onomatopoeic. Behind its disorderly convulsions and apparent formlessness, there is a recognition that the metropolis is fundamentally fragmented and kaleidoscopic—not as an art form but as a compositional process that is theatrical and marked by polyphonic dissonances.

On the other hand, Melrose Arch or Montecasino can be defined as synthetic spacetimes, constructed tableaux on which disparate images are grafted. As such, they are an integral part of the process through which late modernity and the globalization of capitalism have transformed human perception. The modes by which these spacetimes or tableaux are seen and inhabited cannot easily be subsumed under the commonplace triptych of manipulation-alienation–mass deception. It is now generally recognized that goods offer themselves as artworks not just for sale but also for use in people's fantasies and in the production of lifestyles. So, too, is the fact that late modern capitalism has effectively brought about a proletarization of commodity desire as well as a stylization of consumption (Ward 2001: 193–98). Commodity aesthetics might still be construed as a fake system of representation. And to a large extent, South African casinos epitomize precisely the "calico world" Siegfried Kracauer (1995) spoke about: copies and distortions ripped out of time and jumbled together in a dramatic geographical and temporal arbitrariness. But this still does not "address the mystery of consumer desire" Bill Brown describes (2003: 29), "without which capitalism (in any of its stages) cannot be sustained," nor does it tell us how commodity relations have come to saturate everyday life even for the poorest of the poor (see Farrell 2003). It is not simply that things are objects of consumption. It is also that they organize desires and provoke fantasies. Their spectral power (the capacity to be owned and to possess) derives from more than their evanescence and lubricity.

These spacetimes exist first and foremost as interfaces of other local and faraway places. Their architectural styles are based on the recombination of borrowed imagery and, in the worst cases, of outright "urban junk." They are marketed by private developers and property owners in contrast to an unraveling, chaotic city center besieged by swarming and inchoate crowds, incessant shouting and peddling, and a failure to contain disease, crime, and pestilence. Allusion plays a critical role in this architecture. "Exotic" local and faraway styles are theatrically restaged in simulated environments, where they contribute to the paradoxical reconciliation of place and ephemerality. I have shown how Montecasino tries to recapture the quiet life of a rustic Tuscan village, creating scenographic visions that rely on an art of verisimilitude. Take, elsewhere in South Africa, the ethnokitsch of Sun City and Lost City in the North West province. Sun City is publicized as an excursion into a "lost African empire," complete with lush jungles, a volcano, and a majestic palace. The gaming areas are filled with large leaves adorning the roof and weathered stone walls. A similar theme runs through the Morula Sun outside Pretoria, where, as *IOL* describes it, "the architecture lends itself to the style of a traditional Tswana village with conically-topped roofs, reed ceilings and colours reminiscent of those found in African beadwork" (Eksteen 2000).

These places also act as visual displays of the logic of the commodity. As scenographic segments of Johannesburg, Melrose Arch and Montecasino manifest the spectacle of capital in the same way the gold mine did in the early twentieth century: in its purest form. In each of these two instances, in the words of Boyer (2001: 63), "a whole complex of looking is held in place by the force of pure entertainment, by the very act of showing, which keeps the gaze focused on surface appearances and constructed sets of images." Thus the importance accorded to sensuous colors and tactile building materials. For instance, the façade of Melrose Arch is a planar wall assembly of glass plates twenty meters high by ten meters wide. It is supported with pretensioned stainless steel trusses and wind girders. The complex is designed to turn the urban street inward and so internalize its own set of public spaces and services within privatized layers of shops, restaurants, offices, and condominiums. By saturating its public, social, and cultural spheres with the commodity and by asserting its identity as a city of consumption mindful of the status of the ornament, the arts of commercial entertainment, and imaginary travel, Johannesburg has become a metropolis.

What does this apparently endless play of citations and allusions have to say about the memory of the racial city? It can be argued that these new spaces are setting up new boundaries and distances increasingly based on class rather than race. A political-economic reading of such spaces would suggest that private and commercial interests are reducing the nascent democratic public sphere to an arena "where private interests compete and consumer choices are displayed" but where neither critical debate nor critical reasoning takes place (Boyer 2001: 417). It could further be argued that post-apartheid commercial architecture constitutes a mode of erasure all the more dramatic because it is accomplished with painstaking care against the duties to memory ritualized by the Truth and Reconciliation Commission. But what mode of effacement is this? What is the mark of the past in these architectural forms?

In the South African context, surfaces such as Montecasino and, to a lesser extent, Melrose Arch represent new genres of writing time. But this new inscription of time is paradoxical. For it to be possible at all, the built form has to be construed as an empty placeholder for meanings that have been eroded by time rather than remembered by it. That is why they are largely the manifestation of the failure of the racial city to assimilate the passage of time. While bearing witness to a demand that the past be forgotten, this architecture asks the spectator to forget that it is itself a sign of forgetting. But in so doing, it reiterates the pathological structure and hysteria inherited from the racial city. This is an architecture of hysteria.

Hysteria, as we know, is a form of suffering. As Elissa Marder (2001: 117–22) argues, hysterics suffer mainly from "reminiscences," repressed memories that fail to be integrated into the psyche. In the process, they develop a form of *regressive forgetting,* itself an attempt to ward off the movement of time. In this sense, hysteria partakes of a backward movement through time. The architecture of hysteria in contemporary South Africa is the result of a painful, shocking encounter with a radical alterity set loose by the collapse of the racial city. Faced with the sudden estrangement from the familiar resulting from the collapse of the racial city, this architecture aims to return to the "archaic" as a way of freezing rapid changes in the temporal and political structures of the surrounding world. It is an architecture characterized by the attachment to a lost object that used to provide comfort. A magic mirror and a specular moment, it allows the white subject to hallucinate the presence of what has been irretrievably lost. This is why it is also an architecture of conjuration. In the new metropolitan psychic and aesthetic economy, the attempt to maintain oneself in "the cocoon of familiar comforts" goes hand in hand with new and reckless models of pleasure: the ultimate intoxication the bacchanal dance of consumption has become (Von Mucke 2003: 91).

But if the hallucination has its origins in a form of white nostalgia, this is not without its own ironies. Many of those who frequent Montecasino or inhabit it as consumers are white people who have never been to Europe or members of a large black middle and lower-middle class. Spaces such as these are without doubt interracial spaces.

From this perspective, the architecture of hysteria is a constitutive but unconscious aspect of the psychic life of the racial city that resists change and challenges time itself by producing a set of fantasies. As Hubert Damisch notes (2001: 18), "The unconscious can easily accommodate the survival of archaic formations beside others that have supplanted them, even on the same site."[28] It bears witness to an irretrievable loss—the loss of the racial city. This is a case of traumatic amnesia and not of forgetting, of the disavowal of time as opposed to memorialization: an active screen between the subject and the external world that filters out unwanted realities. This is not to imply that there is no mark of the past in these stories masquerading as objects. But the mark of the past here is only a trace, not a literal recollection. At times, it takes the form of borrowed elements graphed onto another context. At other times, it is but a condensation point where various "incompatible images collide and coalesce." Indeed, for Christine Boyer (2001: 373–74), this can be explained by the fact that the present is indeterminate and undecidable: "No metaphors of origins or belief in past covenants guide the present and no subject controls the future or determines the meaning of the past" in an uncontested way. Displacement is the norm. We "pass from one image to another, shifting focus and meaning, for the very definition of place is composed of fragmented strata and moving layers."

Despite all appearances to the contrary, the fabric of the racial city is in the process of being destroyed. Only its vestiges and debris remain. Blacks and whites have become wanderers among its ruins. But the play of intervals enables everyone to construct his or her own story of Johannesburg and form memories of place. This is an experience of fragmentation and of permutations that may never achieve coherence. The rupture between the racist past and the metropolitan present, between here and there and between memories of things and events, renders possible the production of new figural forms and calls into play a chain of substitutions. Johannesburg becomes the city of deconstructed images. "We are no longer offered a synthetic order that we can readily grasp, nor a reconstruction of a history we can collectively assume. Our sense of an urban totality has been fractured"—hence the juxtaposition of different images, memories of a past rejected or fantasized

(Boyer 2001: 374). Specific historical objects are ripped out of their contexts even as the state busily tries to memorialize and museumize, to build new monuments and historic landscapes that are supposed to bring together the different fragments of the nation.

Conclusion

If there is anything the history of the metropolitan form in Africa brings to the critique of modern urbanism, it is that the metropolis is neither a finite nor a static form. In fact, it is almost always a site of excess, of hysteria and exclusions. The metropolis, just like the modern city, reveals itself first and foremost through its discontinuities, its provisionality and fugitiveness, its superfluousness. Particularly in Africa, the blurring of the distinctions between what is public and what is private, the transformation and deformation of inherited urban shapes, is one of the ways by which urban citizens generate meaning and memory. To reveal the unconscious of a city, we need to track the visible marks of the passage of time and the various lines of flight that symbolize the culture of a place.

But as Johannesburg demonstrates, the unconscious of a city is made up of different layers of historical time superimposed on one another, different architectural strata or residues from earlier times. In times of transition, these layers and strata become elusive and precarious. Architecture and urban design then tend to become acts of repression, separation, and fantasy. Frequently these fantasies concern the mesmeric power of race and its relation to the surreal supplement represented by the world of things. This study has argued that the aesthetic phenomenality of things resides not so much in their surfaces but in their substitutability and in the various ways they come to life. In an age when desire is inculcated even in those who have nothing to buy, the metropolis becomes the place where the superfluity of objects is converted into a value in and of itself.

Notes

This study is part of WISER's Meanings of Money and Cultures of Economic Rationality flagship program. The research is partly funded by AIRE-Développement, a program of the French Institute for Development Research in Paris. I owe a great intellectual debt to my colleagues at the University of the Witwatersrand Institute for Social and Economic Research. I especially drew a lot from exchanges with Deborah Posel and Jon Hyslop. For extremely helpful comments on this study, I am indebted to Matthew Barac, Stefania Pandolfo, Ato Quayson, Lindsay Bremner, Lars Buur, and David Theo Goldberg. Some of my conversations with Jane Nuttall have found their way into the text. Without them knowing, I also owe a great deal to conversations with Paul Gilroy, Arjun Appadurai, Carol Breckenridge, Judit Carrera, AbdouMaliq Simone, and Bogumil Jewsiewicki. As always, Sarah Nuttall has been a generous, encouraging, and vigilant critic.

1 See Simmel 1971. For a critique, read Cacciari 1993.

2 This is not a peculiarly South African condition. Commenting on the connections between recollection and loss and what she calls the "archeology of metropolis" and "local cosmopolitanism" in Prague, St. Petersburg, and Moscow, Svetlana Boym writes (2001: 75–77), "The urban renewal taking place in the present is no longer futuristic but nostalgic; the city imagines its future by improvising on its past. . . . In some cases, such as Prague or St. Petersburg, urban cosmopolitanism is not a feature of the present but rather an element of nostalgia. . . . Places in the city are not merely architectural metaphors; they are also screen memories for urban dwellers, projections of contested remembrances." On nostalgia, mourning, melancholia, and disavowal in the aftermath of the collapse of state socialism in the former Eastern Germany, see Scribner 2003.

3 For a further discussion, see Poovey 1998.

4 According to Jon Hyslop (e-mail communication, May 12, 2004), some periods in the life of Johannesburg were more metropolitan than others. The more metropolitan periods tended to coincide with periods of opening to the world (1886–1914 and 1990 to the present). The external linkages of the city from 1914 to the 1950s tended to be more narrowly with the British Empire. A strong element of autarky and isolation characterized the apartheid years.

5 Thus, while recognizing that in Johannesburg, "there is the controlled civilization of Europe on the surface [and] the primitive unrestraint of Africa beneath," Sarah Gertrude Millin could nevertheless declare that "for all its individuality, Johannesburg is English" (1926: 95).

6 We should understand the modern not so much as a rejection of tradition or uprootedness but as both *techne* and sensibility. See, along similar lines, Harvey 2003: 18.

7 This despite the fact that the pre-1900 Transvaal state took a hands-off approach to the city. The dominant financial interests had too much of a short-term and self-interested orientation to initiate any coordinated modernist organization. Between 1886 and 1900, other than the rectangular street grid, there was little sign of modernist planning in Johannesburg. The first attempts at modernist planning were in relation to issues of race and labor under the period of direct British rule.

8 The mine dumps, Millin adds (1926: 81), "are a monument of servitude, power, the vanity of vanities and death."

9 On the Jews, in particular, see Kaplan and Robertson 1986, esp. 45–92.

10 Emphasis original. Their consumption grows, he adds, "in proportion with the growth of general wealth, since their use specifically represents wealth, excess, luxury, because they themselves *represent* wealth in general."

11 See, in another context, Anagnost 2004 and Best 2004.

12 Writing, for instance, about the white diamond digger in Kimberley, Millin (1926: 63) noted: "He sits, most of the day, on his heap of ground, watching his Kaffirs work. He does here and there a little odd job. Once or twice a week he spends an hour or so sorting gravel for diamonds. When he feels bored, he walks over to the bar and has a drink."

13 But labor itself was just as wastefully and inefficiently used: "The large turnover of workers involved high recruiting and supervisory costs. Every new batch of peasants had to learn mining techniques and undergo the painful process of adapting themselves to a strange environment," Simons and Simons write (1983: 52).

14 On this and on what follows, see Deleuze and Guattari 1987: 90–130.

15 See testimonies of terror and cruelty in *Truth and Reconciliation Commission in South Africa Report* 2003. Also see de Kock and Gordin 1998.

16 On the political side of the repression, see Webster and Friedman 1989.

17 See MacCrone 1937 and Barnes 1930: 232, 302. On sexual resentment and the old practice of white men having black mistresses, see Plaatje 1921 and Nicholls 1923.

18 As evidenced in John Coetzee's fiction and William Kentridge's art. "What I am interested in is a kind of multilayered highway of consciousness, where one lane has one thought but driving up behind and overtaking it is a completely different thought," writes Kentridge. "It's a particularly South African phenomenon of the late 1980s and 1990s to have contradictory thoughts running in tandem. You had people rebuilding their homes while simultaneously planning to emigrate. These contradictions work at an internal level in terms of the different views one has of oneself from one moment to the next. . . . I question the cost and pain engendered by self-multiplicity. . . . There is a kind of madness that arises from living in two worlds. Life becomes a collection of contradictory elements" (Cameron, Kentridge, and Christov-Bakargiev 1999: 30–31).

19 See Cock and Nathan 1989. See, in particular, the studies on troops in the townships (67–78), on the militarization of urban controls, and on the Bantustans (159–201).

20 See van Onselen 2001: 232; an extensive sociology of the figure of the nanny can be found in this book. Also see Cock 1980.

21 See Koch 1983, especially the considerations on Marabi, pp. 158–66.

22 See the description of the Melrose Arch Hotel at www.africanpridehotels.com.

23 See www.melrosearch.co.za/public/restaurants.html.

24 Over the past decade, South Africa has embraced legal gambling. Montecasino is one of five licenses held by Tsogo Sun. The other licenses include Emnotweni Casino (in Nelspruit), the Ridge Casino and Entertainment Resort (in Witbank), Hemingway's Casino (in East London), and the Suncoast Casino and Entertainment

World (in Durban). Casinos are opening in every large South African city. In 2003, South Africa's casino and gambling industry supplied 14 percent of provincial government revenues. In order to win licenses, casino operators "are obliged to create jobs in poor areas, to hire black subcontractors, and to offer shares in the business to . . . trade unions or black-owned firms." See "A Tuscan Village in South Africa."

25 "A Tuscan Village in South Africa" explains: "Most casinos in South Africa aim for Las Vegas–style razzle-dazzle. Caesar's, also in Johannesburg, boasts faux-classical statues and a restaurant on an ancient Egyptian barge. Hemingway's, now being built in East London, promises an experience that will bring back the great man's novels."

26 See www.dedicatedmicros.com.

27 "Everywhere you look," writes Bongani Madondo, "there are badly parked cars, and the remaining spaces are occupied by hawkers. It's raining hawkers in Jozi. They bring a dash of exotic; the legendary African marketplace attitude that in Jozi has turned into pavement capitalism." Entire neighborhoods have been renamed. "Turning off Bree Street into Von Brandis, I enter an area not named Addis Ababa for nothing. Here, Ethiopian hawkers sell anything from bandanas adorned with Stars and Stripes (made in Bombay) to toothbrushes and pesticides. The inner city is divided into United Nation–esque chunks—little Lagos, Beijing, Karachi, Kinshasa, Dakar, Mogadishu—and pockets of hip-hop loving township hawkers with their stew of Soweto-meets-the-Bronx-slang" (Madondo 2004).

28 Damisch shows that the city is no stranger to the operations of the unconscious. The latter retains traces of all the successive stages of psychic life. But it can only be known through scraps and figures. Its "emergence into light eludes all conscious control" (2001: 17–18).

2 ⊹ People as Infrastructure:

Intersecting Fragments in Johannesburg

ABDOUMALIQ SIMONE

The inner city of Johannesburg is about as far away as one can get from the popular image of the African village. Though it is one of Africa's most urbanized settings, it is also seen as a place of ruins—of ruined urbanization, the ruining of Africa by urbanization. But in these ruins, something else besides decay might be happening. This essay explores the possibility that these ruins not only mask but also constitute a highly urbanized social infrastructure. This infrastructure is capable of facilitating the intersection of socialities so that expanded spaces of economic and cultural operation become available to residents of limited means.

This essay is framed around the notion of people as infrastructure, which emphasizes economic collaboration among residents seemingly marginalized from and made miserable by urban life. Infrastructure is commonly understood in physical terms, as reticulated systems of highways, pipes, wires, or cables. These modes of provisioning and articulation are viewed as making the city productive, reproducing it, and positioning its residents, territories, and resources in specific ensembles where the energies of individuals can be most efficiently deployed and accounted for.

By contrast, I wish to extend the notion of infrastructure directly to people's activities in the city. African cities are characterized by incessantly flexible, mobile, and provisional intersections of residents that operate without clearly delineated notions of how the city is to be inhabited and used. These intersections, particularly in the last two decades, have depended on the ability of residents to engage complex combinations of objects, spaces, people, and practices. These conjunctions become an infrastructure—a platform providing for and reproducing life in the city. Indeed, as I illustrate through a range of ethnographic materials on inner-city Johannesburg, an experience of regularity capable of anchoring the livelihoods of residents and their transactions with one another is consolidated precisely because the outcomes of residents' reciprocal efforts are radically open, flexible, and provisional. In other words, a specific economy of perception and collaborative practice is constituted through the capacity of individual actors to circulate across and become familiar with a broad range of spatial, residential, economic, and transactional positions. Even when actors do different things with one another in different places, each carries traces of past collaboration and an implicit willingness to interact with one another in ways that draw on multiple social positions. The critical question thus raised in this ethnography of inner-city Johannesburg is how researchers, policymakers, and urban activists can practice ways of seeing and engaging urban spaces that are characterized simultaneously by regularity and provisionality.

Urbanization conventionally denotes a thickening of fields, an assemblage of increasingly heterogeneous elements into more complicated collectives. The accelerated, extended, and intensified intersections of bodies, landscapes, objects, and technologies defer calcification of institutional ensembles or fixed territories of belonging. But does this mean that an experience of regularity and of sustained collaboration among heterogeneous actors is foreclosed? We have largely been led to believe that this is the case. Thus, various instantiations of governmentality have attempted to emplace urbanizing processes through the administration of choices and the codification of multiplicity. The potential thickness of social fields becomes the thickness of definitions and classifications engineered by various administrations of legibility and centers of decision making (see Lefebvre 1991). Once visible, the differentiated elements of society are to assume their own places and trajectories and become the vectors through which social power is enunciated.

In this view, urban spaces are imagined to be functional destinations. There are to be few surprises, few chances for unregulated encounters, as the city is turned into an object like a language (see Lefebvre 1996). Here, relations of correspondence are set up between instances of two distinct and nonparallel modes of formalization—of expression and content (Wolfe 1998). Particular spaces are linked to specific identities, functions, lifestyles, and properties so that the spaces of the city become legible for specific people at given places and times. These diagrams—what Henri Lefebvre calls "representations of space"—act to "pin down" inseparable connections between places, people, actions, and things (Lefebvre 1976: 33). At the same time, these diagrams make possible a "relation of non-relation" that opens each constituent element onto a multiplicity of relations between forces (ibid.; Olsson 2000: 1242). In this multiplicity of connotations, it is always possible to do something different in and with the city than is specified by these domains of power while, at the same time, acting as if one remains operative inevitably only within them (see Rajchman 1998). This notion of tactics operating at the interstices of strategic constraints is a recurring theme in the work of Michel de Certeau (e.g., de Certeau 1984).

In other words, the disposition of regularities and the outcomes of collaborative work in the city can be open ended, unpredictable, and made singular. The truncated process of economic modernization at work in African cities has never fully consolidated apparatuses of definition capable of enforcing specific and consistent territorial organizations of the city. State administrations and civil institutions have lacked the political and economic power to assign the diversity of activities taking place within the city (buying, selling, residing, etc.) to bounded spaces of deployment, codes of articulation, or the purview of designated actors. According to conventional imaginaries of urbanization, which locate urban productivity in the social division of labor and the consolidation of individuation, African cities are incomplete.[1] In contrast to these imaginaries, African cities survive largely through a conjunction of heterogeneous activities brought to bear on and elaborated through flexibly configured landscapes. But it is important to emphasize that these flexible configurations are pursued not in some essential contrast to non-African urban priorities or values but as specific routes to a kind of stability and regularity that non-African cities have historically attempted to realize. Consider the incomplete, truncated, or deteriorated forms and temporalities of various, seemingly incompatible institutional rationalities and modes of production—from the bureaucracies of civil administration to the workshop, the industrial unit, subsistence agriculture, private enterprise, and customary usufruct arrangements governing land use. All are deployed as a means of stabilizing a social field of interaction. In part, this is a way to continuously readapt residents' actions to engage the open-ended destinations that their very collaborations have produced.

For example, the transport depot in Abidjan is full of hundreds of young men who function as steerers, baggage loaders, ticket salespeople, hawkers, drivers, gas pumpers, and mechanics. There are constantly shifting connections among them. Each boy who steers passengers to a particular company makes a rapid assessment of their wealth, personal characteristics, and the reason for their journey. This reading determines where the steerer will guide prospective passengers, who will sell their tickets, who will load their baggage, who will seat them, and so forth. It is as if this collaboration were assembled to maximize the efficiency of each passage, even though there are no explicit rules or formal means of payment to the steerers. Although each boy gives up control of the passenger to the next player down the line, their collaboration is based not on the boys adhering to specific rules but on their capacity to improvise.

Such a conjunction of heterogeneous activities, modes of production, and institutional forms constitutes highly mobile and provisional possibilities for how people live and make things, how they use the urban environment and collaborate with one another. The specific operations and scopes of these conjunctions are constantly negotiated and depend on the particular histories, understandings, networks, styles, and inclinations of the actors involved. Highly specialized needs arise, requiring the application of specialized skills and sensitivities that can adapt to the unpredictable range of scenarios these needs bring to life. Regularities thus ensue from a process of incessant convertibility—turning commodities, found objects, resources, and bodies into uses previously unimaginable or constrained. Producer-residents become more adept at operating within these conjunctions as they deploy a greater diversity of abilities and efforts. Again, it is important to emphasize that these conjunctions become a coherent platform for social transaction and livelihood. This process of conjunction, which is capable of generating social compositions across a range of singular capacities and needs (both enacted and virtual) and which attempts to derive maximal outcomes from a minimal set of elements, is what I call people as infrastructure.[2]

This concept is not meant to account for inner-city Johannesburg in its entirety. Many residents, battered by the demands of maintaining the semblance of a safe domestic environment, find few incentives to exceed the bounds of personal survival. But "people as infrastructure" describes a tentative and often precarious process of remaking the inner city, especially now that the policies and economies that once moored it to the surrounding city have mostly worn away. In many respects, the inner city has been "let go" and forced to reweave its connections with the larger world by making the most of its limited means. Still, the inner city is embedded in a larger urban region characterized by relative economic strength, an emerging pan-African service economy, political transformations that have sought to attenuate the more stringent trappings of population control, and a highly fragmented urban system whose regulatory regime was never geared toward high-density residential areas. This ensemble, in turn, has given rise to a markedly heterogeneous domain of people.

Spaces of the Inner City

Under apartheid, Johannesburg was designed as a cosmopolitan, European city in Africa, but only for a small segment of its population. When this truncated cosmopolitanism could no longer be enforced by a white minority regime, whites fled to distant northern suburbs and gated communities where cosmopolitanism was precluded, thus leaving the inner city open to habitation of all kinds. Roughly 90 percent of Johannesburg's inner-city residents were not living there ten years ago.

A drive around the circumference of the inner-city neighborhoods of Hillbrow, Berea, Joubert Park, Yeoville, and Bertrams takes less than twenty minutes. Yet navigation of their interior requires familiarity with many different and, on the surface, conflicting temporal trajectories through which Johannesburg has changed, with its sudden switches across ruin, repair, and redevelopment. For example, a five-minute walk along Quartz Street starting at Smit Street takes you from Death Valley, a strip of seedy prostitution hotels and clubs, to a concerted effort to resecure the tenancy of working families in a series of tightly controlled renovated buildings. In part, this minor effort at gentrification was motivated by a sense that the block north of Smit Street had become way too dangerous. From the late 1980s through the late 1990s, Death Valley functioned as "sex central"—with scores of bored prostitutes waiting at all times of day in the alcoves of its hotels.

There was little safety in numbers for participants in this sex market; the concentrated availability of bodies served only to increase the exploitation of prostitutes. As a result, whatever and whoever passed through this particular area of Smit Street acquired a large measure of expendability. The immediate area emptied out yet remains a kind of no-go zone, with the traces of the wild recent past still keeping other prospects at bay. Still, just one block away is the New Yorker, a relatively well-appointed block of studio apartments recently fixed up and with a long waiting list restricted to South Africans who can show five pay stubs.

Further north there is a single block along Quartz Street where hundreds of Ibo Nigerians gather on the street, usually between 2 and 7 p.m. They are here not so much to deal narcotics, for which they are renowned, but to display impunity and solidarity while buying daily meals from the curbside street vendors. It is, of course, always possible to buy a packet of drugs or arrange a larger quantity. The King's Den, a bar whose second-story veranda overlooks the street, usually hosts the more prominent middlemen, whose drivers pull up in red and black Jettas. Many of these men, now in their mid-fifties, retain the Ibo dress of *boubous* (robes) and felt skullcaps, as well as a sense of determination honed in the labor movements of Port Harcourt and Calabar, Nigeria. The block used to serve as a taxi stand for Lingala-speaking drivers waiting for calls from the airport, and a few still remain to ferry the occasional Greek, Zambian, or Congolese desperate to unload marginal contraband from Lubumbashi, Democratic Republic of Congo, so they can shop in the wealthy suburb of Sandton.

Several young Ibo men have told me that part of the reason for this public display is to reaffirm the fact that they are in Johannesburg in large numbers. But this affirmation of common nationality does not translate into ready collaboration. They cannot forget that despite whatever skills they may have—whether formal postgraduate education, vast knowledge about trade, or street smarts—there are likely to be scores of their compatriots who are more proficient in these areas. Thus, there is an incessant need to do something bold yet not rash. The older men, the ones with the real money or connections, watch to see what various individuals are capable of doing, so the younger ones submit to being watched. A few bide their time selling cigarettes and candy; almost all engage in shifting conversations. Many wait to take their turn at the Internet café just around the corner (where one can buy five hours of computer time and get the sixth free) to engage in credit card fraud, check shipping orders, or write e-mails to mom or 419 letters.[3]

Crossing Kotze Street, Quartz Street is interrupted by the somewhat frayed Highpoint Centre—a large apartment block anchored by a supermarket and other commercial properties, many of them now abandoned. Because it is watched by security guards, the mezzanine is a popular place to withdraw money from ATMS. There is also a beauty parlor and another Internet café, but the porterhouse steak restaurant, the recreational center, the American

Express travel agency, and the health food store have long been closed. A Zambian company now manages the complex and is fairly well regarded by local residents and customers because it maintains an office on the premises and has kept the local stationery and magazine store open (where the strong educational desires of children and youths translate into purchases of vast quantities of pens and notebooks). Five years ago, the residential part of this complex—some three hundred flats—used to be the turf of Coloured people, now all gone. Underneath Highpoint Center is a cavernous parking garage. The last time I ventured there, by mistake at two in the morning some two years ago, I found hundreds of women, adherents of the Zionist Christian Church, kneeling in unison.

On the other side of Pretoria Street is a block representing an early effort by the Metropolitan Council to draw street traders into an organized market with rented stalls and shedding. A variety of fruits and vegetables are sold here, as well as clothing, shoes, and kitchen goods. But the traders must pay rent for their stalls. Although the money is used to provide a clean and safe environment, its goods are consequently more expensive than those of the hawkers who still line much of Pretoria Street and whose trade this formal market was supposed to dispel. As we continue north along Quartz Street, the formal market dissipates in a contiguous block of unregulated street hawkers and alleys where stolen goods are sold. But in the surrounding arteries there are large apartment blocks, and it is clearly an area where the South African township has moved in. The pool halls and game rooms are crowded, and the block pulses with hip-hop and *kwaito* music. Corner walls are lined with hundreds of makeshift notices offering rooms for rent. Every ten yards, it seems, there is a shop or improvised street stand with a telephone—an important service for the majority of residents, who cannot afford their own phones. Ten years ago there were German pastry shops, health clubs, and tie shops on this block. On the many occasions when I have crossed this stretch between Goldreich and Caroline streets, I have always seen violent incidents: a single shot to the head, or even an *assegai*, a short spear, quickly thrust and removed. Crowds gather, mostly in silence, as calls are made to police officers who are in sight just a few blocks away, stopping cars in the cocaine zone.

The next block is inhabited by homeless squatters, whose cardboard edifices and stolen shopping carts line mounds of burnt ash from fires they use to cook and keep warm. There is an acrid smell and the incessant sounds of whistles and catcalls. Young street toughs, Congolese mechanics who use a nearby petrol station to repair and store cars, and Malawians who have long dominated the residential buildings all engage in a territorial dance for control of the block.

Finally the street ends at a major lateral artery, Louis Botha Avenue, and the Mimosa Hotel. The Mimosa is one of about ten hotels operated, if not owned, by Nigerian syndicates, where rooms are shared to keep accommodations for an army of "foot soldiers" under R10 (roughly $1.50) per night. Here, recent doctorates in designer frames mingle across street-side card tables with ex–Area boys from Lagos on the run from being framed. Some keep an eye out for everything. Others wait to unload the small quota of narcotics that will allow them to eat that night. There are those who direct old and new clients to choice rooms in the hotel in order to meet their needs; and still others are there to tell stories, often about deals both real and made up. These are imported tricksters, whose job is to celebrate the ruthless economy that most of these young Ibo guys pursue, provide occasional cautionary tales, but in the end get others to reveal what they are after, what their capacities are, where they have been, and how well they might fit certain jobs. The police and the city council have declared victory over Nigerians several times by shutting down the hotel. On the ground level, a passing observer might be fooled into thinking that the place is finished, but if you look up you might notice that the windows are full of freshly laundered clothes.

Reworked Intersections

This is an inner city whose density and highly circumscribed spatial parameters compel uncertain interactions and cooperation among both long-term Johannesburg residents and new arrivals, South Africans and Africans from elsewhere. There are interactions among various national and ethnic groups, between aspiring professionals and seasoned criminals, and between AIDS orphans living on the streets and wealthy Senegalese merchants living in luxurious penthouses. At the same time, life in the inner city fosters intense cooperation among fellow nationals and ethnics. The coupling of these trajectories produces an intricate territorialization and a patchwork of zones of relative security. Some blocks and many buildings clearly "belong" to particular national groups, in part due to the disparate practices employed by building owners and their managing agents. These actors have their own interpretations of the relative benefits and costs of renting to South Africans or foreigners.

To what extent does this narrowing of space along ethnic or national lines enforce a ghettoization of economy or mentality? For those who are rigidly ensconced in a limited territory of relative safety and predictability, everyday familial and public relations can be quite strained, even suffocating (Morris 1999b). However, such circumscribed spatial arenas are only one domain within a networked milieu of diverse locations through which residents pass, and which are actively or symbolically linked to the seemingly highly bounded inner-city territories. For many South Africans, these inner-city neighborhoods are linked to long-standing townships or periurban settlements. Hillbrow, for example, has often served as a place of both temporary and long-term escape from problematic kinship and neighborhood relations in Soweto. For those living in the vast squatter areas of Orange Farm, south of the city, Joubert Park serves as an anchor for small-scale trading across Johannesburg. Zimbabweans and Malawian sojourners and petty traders, often coming back and forth on two-week visas, use several large inner-city hotels as temporary bases of operation and storage. For many Africans across the region, Johannesburg is a site for the bulk purchase of various commodities. It is a locus of complex barter arrangements and transshipment, a site for laundering money, sending remittance, and for upscaling a variety of entrepreneurial activities through the dense intersections of actors from different countries and situations.

But a "cat and mouse" game largely prevails. Many foreign Africans cite the need for maintaining hyperawareness of their surroundings. They are constantly on the lookout for police officers, many of whom seem focused on entrapping foreigners in various shakedowns, luring them into what appear to be highly favorable apartment rentals only to then raid them and expropriate money and goods. When interviewing migrants, one notices their constant wariness about whom they can safely talk to and in what contexts. There are multiple levels of intrigue and conflict among migrants from the same region, regardless of whether they share common ancestry, politics, or commercial experience. Such infighting is typical among South African institutional personnel as well. For example, a well-known story concerns a police raid on a Senegalese mosque in Bez Valley during Ramadan, when the large Murid Senegalese community in Johannesburg was gathering contributions to be sent to the religious center of Touba, Senegal. Apparently, a Gambian immigrant dealing in false papers had targeted a Senegalese rival, whom the police threatened to toss from the window of his nineteenth-story apartment in Hillbrow unless he was able to "do something for himself" (i.e., come up with a large payoff) within twenty-four hours.

Despite this incident, the Senegalese community is much admired in Johannesburg for its ability to work together in highly complementary ways across geographical distance and commercial sectors. The political vicissitudes of almost all other African "feeder" nations generate a great deal of suspicion and internal conflict within national communities residing in Johannesburg, especially as political events constantly send new groups of varying political complexions into exile. With a few exceptions, common national identity provides only a limited platform for economic and social collaboration. The fact that the Senegalese are able to draw on such collaboration provides an important point of reference. Efforts are made to reconstitute such an experience across national identities, particularly where subgroupings of individuals sharing a common national identity are framed within a larger rubric of regional, religious, or professional commonality.

For example, common national identity can provide a concrete framework for support among individuals who may have very different kinds of jobs, ranging from repairing automobiles to teaching French at the Alliance Française. These articulations are used by larger corporate groupings—cutting across several national identities—that facilitate various business efforts through subcontracting arrangements. One such enterprise might draw on the professional legitimacy of teachers, use their students as potential customers or corporate informants, and incorporate the trading circuits developed by petty traders and the repair skills of mechanics.

The game can take on a simultaneously sinister and comical quality. Bakassi Boys chase after former Revolutionary United Front *sobels* to settle ECOWAS scores; they are aided by Gambian ex-soldiers who refused to support the Casamance rebel–backed marijuana trade that sustained Yaya Jammeh's government. Zanu-PF veterans of the liberation war rob the suburban houses of Rally for Congolese Democracy–aligned businessmen, who in turn use money earned by Lissouba-backed Zulu militias from Brazzaville to make another run at Sassou Nguesso's Cobras.[4] The inner city boasts an array of ex-combatants, intelligence operatives, and exiled politicians, all chasing one another and all running from one another, and in the process many strange bedfellows and business ventures emerge. At one time, most of these actors may have represented a cause, an ethnic group, or a nation. But these identities get lost in Johannesburg, and their new affiliations can be traced only by following how they move from one opaque deal to the next.

The relative absence of a systematic and formal framework for investment in the inner city means that the ideas, entrepreneurial experience, and networks that the bulk of foreign Africans bring to Johannesburg are largely underutilized. A prevailing xenophobia among many South Africans forces Africans from other countries to regulate their visibility—their dress, residential location, and the kinds of economic activities they pursue. As a result, many foreign actors have focused on taking quick profits and marshalling critical sections of the built environment to support the trade in narcotics, stolen goods, and various Internet-based fraud schemes like the infamous 419s and credit card scams. According to my interviews with various foot soldiers and middlemen in these loosely organized, largely Ibo-based syndicates, the profits from this trade are used to import a broad range of commodities, such as industrial parts, consumer goods, electronics, and machinery, from Southeast Asia to West and Central Africa.

Inattention to the realities of the inner city by key municipal and corporate institutions has led to an intensification of the xenophobic attitudes that force foreign Africans deeper underground. Residents' efforts to secure the range of illicit and informal trades available to them by consolidating control over specific spaces, clients, and domains of inner-city life increasingly clash with the limited upgrading and redevelopment initiatives pursued by the key municipal institutions, such as the Johannesburg Development Agency, the Better Buildings Program, and the Central Johannesburg Partnership. Normative interventions center on major building projects, such as the new Constitutional Court building just west of Hillbrow, with its anticipated multiplier effects of increased property values and the restoration of commercial zones. They also entail the demolition of residential buildings with substantial arrears and code violations, the use of existing bylaws to clear out buildings and hotels used for illicit activities, and the seizure of illegally acquired assets.[5] The complicity of some police officers and customs and immigration officials, as well as the enormous costs of continuous and targeted regulation, limit the efficacy of these interventions.

While residents of different backgrounds try to keep out of one another's way, they do form emergent interdependencies ranging from crude patron-client relations to formally constituted pan-African entrepreneurial collaborations. The sheer proximity of Africans from diverse ethnic and national backgrounds leads many residents to explore tentative cooperation based on trust. Such relationships are risky in a climate of insecurity and incessant trickery but also enable participants to exploit, in highly profitable ways, the common assumption that trust is not really possible. Given the various skills and networks that different immigrant groups bring to the table, the potential profits in combining trades, markets, and networks far exceed those from commercial activities compartmentalized within narrow ethnic and national groupings. Examples include the buying, selling, and repairing of cars or the domestic or international consigning of goods by individual traders using informal credit systems and flexible collateral. Other activities, usually managed by women, include the cultivation of informal restaurants and bars as safehouses for potentially volatile negotiations among those conducting illegal business. Young women of various nationalities are increasingly enrolled and partnered as foot soldiers in barter schemes—for example, gems for luxury accessories—that may take place in Brazil or Venezuela.

It is difficult to infer the existence of a collective system from even scores of individual interviews or multisite field observations. Yet it may be possible that this texture of highly fragmented social space and these emerging interdependencies complement each other in forming an infrastructure for innovative economic transactions in the inner city.

Operating Infrastructures

Such infrastructure remains largely invisible unless we reconceive the notion of belonging in terms other than those of a logic of group or territorial representation. The idea of people as infrastructure indicates residents' needs to generate concrete acts and contexts of social collaboration inscribed with multiple identities rather than in overseeing and enforcing modulated transactions among discrete population groups. For example, no matter how much Nigerians and South Africans express their mutual hatred, this does not really stop them from doing business with each other, sharing residences, or engaging in other interpersonal relations. The dissipation of once-relied-upon modes of solidarity, the uprooting of individuals from familiar domains, and the ghettoization of individuals within highly circumscribed identity-enclaves constitute an explosive mix of amorphous urban conflict. Residents can orient themselves in this conflict and discover profitable opportunities only through constant interactions with real and potential antagonists.

Efforts on the part of both the urban government and civil society to re-constitute viable territories of belonging and accountability through an array of decentralization and popular participation measures may have the converse effect of highlighting the failures of groups and individuals to secure themselves within any durable context. A coalition of churches, community arts programs, environmentalist NGOS, and community policy projects has attempted to transform small inner-city blocks in Joubert Park into outdoor public gathering places where local artists and theater groups can perform or display their work. Local craft markets, beautification projects, youth workshops, peace festivals, "take back the street" campaigns, and citizen ward committees have all been initiated to facilitate a sense of community and local solidarity. But this is a "community" where the negotiations, ownership, and financial responsibilities involved in maintaining a stake in an apartment are complexly layered. This is a community where the insecurity of residence and the dangers of movement generate a homegrown industry in various forms of protection and payoffs and where a certain stability to public spaces and streets is fostered by the sense that anything could happen to anyone, that no one has an advantage over everyone else. As such, community building is often perceived by residents as a peripheral disciplinary exercise that distracts residents from developing the real skills that they need to survive. Community building projects tend to micromanage a wide range of day-to-day political and economic relationships in order to promote public safety and enterprise. But this approach is ineffective, for the inner city requires not only opportunism but precisely the ability to hide one's intentions and abilities within complex relationships of mutual dependence.

The Metropolitan Council of Johannesburg has established ward committees to try to make politics responsive to local needs and styles. But as governance is relocated to the particularities of discrete places, the responsibility of citizens to embody and display normative attitudes toward managing their individual performances as entrepreneurial agents is also entrenched. Urban politics then operates not as a locus of mediation and dialogue among differing experiences, claims, and perspectives but as a proliferation of technical standards by which every citizen's capacities are to be compared and judged. In such a politics, everyone is found wanting, and group identity is reaffirmed as both compensation for and insulation from expanding fields of interaction whose implicit objective is to reproduce the compartmentalization of individuals.

The narcotics enterprises that constitute an important component of the inner-city economy are commonly seen as the purview of Ibo-dominated Nigerian networks. While this may generally be true, narcotics enterprises are by no means ethnically or nationally homogeneous. Rather, in a business that has little recourse to legal or official commercial standards, the *appearance* of ethnic or national homogeneity is used to convey a certain impenetrability. It deflects external scrutiny, infiltration, and competition and thus allows the enterprise to covertly incorporate the diversity of actors it often requires in order to constantly change supply routes, markets, and so forth. In other words, such enterprises parody a national or ethnic notion of belonging.

In the commercial culture of the inner-city narcotics economy, the discrete tasks of importation, circumvention of customs regulations, repackaging, local distribution, money laundering, dealing with legal authorities, territorial control, market expansion, and plotting traffic routes are complementary yet highly territorialized. Usually, discrete units administer each domain so that disruptions in one do not jeopardize the trade. Nigerian syndicates have instituted an interesting governance structure, which uses the hotels in Hillbrow to accommodate a large transient population that camouflages their development of a steady clientele of drug users, including sex workers. The hotels, now largely managed by Nigerian syndicates, become discrete localities housing not only workers in the drug trade but also Nigerians working in a wide range of activities. These syndicates are largely hybrid organizations incorporating elements of preexisting Nigerian organizations into evolving organizations specific to the Nigerian experience in Johannesburg. They dominate the governing committees that establish rules for each hotel. For example, there are often no-go areas for Nigerians; and fines, used for legal fees incurred by residents in criminal cases, are levied for various infractions, such as storing stolen goods in the building. Nigerians not directly involved in the drug economy are also counted on to provide a semblance of internal diversity, even if they are often used and manipulated for their access to cars, office machinery, or social connections. The individual operations of the drug trade must be integrated in such a way that complicity and cooperation become the prevailing practices. Within each domain, each operator has a specific place and is expected to demonstrate unquestioning loyalty. This is the case even though the illicit nature and practical realities of the trade constantly generate opportunities for participants to seek greater profits and authority outside the syndicate hierarchies.

Thus, it is apparent to most inner-city residents which hotels, residential buildings, and commercial enterprises belong to which syndicates and what their national affiliations are. Since any given narcotics enterprise handles only certain facets of the overall drug trade—and renders itself vulnerable if it attempts to dominate more functions or territory—neutral spaces must also be defined and maintained. But it is precisely within these spaces, where anything might happen, that the most vociferous claims of belonging emerge. These are often articulated through "contests" over women motivated by the impression (common among South African men) that economically better-off migrants are stealing local women.

Thus, the inner city has a complex geography that residents must navigate according to a finely tuned series of movements and assumptions. There are places where they know they must not go or be seen—but this knowledge often depends on highly variable notions about which places are safe and which are not. A South African municipal worker living in the well-run Metropolitan apartment blocks in Berea is unlikely to sit and read the newspaper in the lobbies of the Mark or Sands hotels, domains of Nigerian drug dealers. But even though this municipal worker would have to make his or her way along a street packed with thousands of drug dealers from noon until midnight, this would actually be safer than making a telephone call from the public stand at the nearby petrol station.

The drug economy, with its hyperactive sensibilities and codes of belonging, has been able to entrench itself in Hillbrow and Berea precisely because these dense, highly urbanized areas were being vacated both by their former residents and by financial and governmental resources. The drug operations tend to provincialize certain parts of the inner city in relation to clearly marked territories and fiefdoms. But the boundedness of organizations and territories is more a necessary performance than a description of actual operations. The more entrenched and expansive the drug economy becomes, the more it is compelled to generate ambiguous interfaces. These include interfaces between supposedly discrete groups, between illicit activity and legitimate investment, and between inner-city Johannesburg as an increasingly well-known site of the drug economy and other less visible, and often more advantageous, sites of operation.

Here the salience of belonging specifies the need for its own demise. A frequently heard rallying cry in the inner city is for blocks and neighborhoods to be restored to their "real" owners—but who are these citizens and what would they do with these neighborhoods? To what extent is the drug economy the most visible component of an otherwise invisible unfolding of the inner city onto the uncertainties of the metropolitan region? In a city preoccupied with questions of belonging, where movements and operations are insecure, there is a heightened need to identify spaces of safe residence. Yet the drug operations do not need the inner city either as market or base of operation. Already there is some indication that several syndicates are moving on, seeking other locales, and that associations over the past decade between specific agents and specific territories have become more arbitrary. One can even hear local nostalgia for this territorialization in claims that drug dealers stalled the demise of certain blocks, which are now vulnerable to an influx of petty criminals.

While immigrant networks depend on the constant activation of a sense of mutual cooperation and interdependency, these ties are often more apparent than real—especially as a complex mixture of dependence and autonomy is at work in relations among compatriots. For many foreign Africans in the inner city, Johannesburg is neither the preferred nor the final destination, especially at present. Because the South African economy is increasingly intertwined with other African national and regional economies, Johannesburg is more accessible to foreign migration than are European or North American destinations. The city's geographic location facilitates the petty-to medium-scale (whether conventional or unconventional) trade that characterizes a significant percentage of immigrant economies. In the official commercial and informal markets of Congo-Brazzaville, Congo-Kinshasa, Zambia, Angola, or Mozambique, a substantial percentage of commodities originates in or is imported through South Africa, often by South African–based immigrants.

Although most immigrants dream of a quick score that would enable them to return home with significantly enhanced prestige and purchasing power, this rarely happens. Instead, the norm is many years of toil in a series of low-wage jobs, with the bulk of one's savings remitted back home to support an array of family members. Additionally, there are often bribes to pay to policemen and unofficial surcharges owed to landlords. All traders run the risk of goods being seized, lost, or stolen. The perseverance of immigrants—especially in South Africa—only highlights the enormousness of the difficulties they would face at home. While fellow nationals or immigrants of various nationalities may band together to share living expenses, information, and risk, the possibilities for corporate action are limited. Individuals try their best to make ends meet and to deal with specific family, community, or political situations back home. Each is in some way a competitor, and cooperation is based on self-interest, self-protection, and camaraderie, not on a long-term investment in the cultivation of a place of operation in Johannesburg.

These dynamics take place in an urban environment that, however fleetingly, once hinted at the possibility of a more cosmopolitan urban South Africa. But the country has long repressed what the image of that cosmopolitanism might look like. Instead, it is reimagined primarily in politically vacuous, "rainbow nation" terms. The inner city has existed for what feels like a lifetime without any significant development of urban policy or programming—especially during the period between 1988 and 1994, when the residential controls of apartheid were suspended and a rapid demographic shift took place.

The inner city largely represents a process of running away, where the inside and the outside render ambiguous any definite sense of where residents are located and what their identities and interests really are. Black South Africans are fleeing the restrictive sociality of township life, a life too long situated in arbitrary, isolated places designed to prevent cultural reproduction. Foreign Africans, fleeing sometimes deadly conflicts in their native countries, are seeking whatever is possible to maintain a sense (and often just the illusion) of home. Still, an extensive transactional economy has developed from the range of tactics that residents use to deflect constraint, surveillance, and competition and from the varied forms of sociality that emerge to increase access to information, destinations, and support. It is to these transnational economies that the inner city increasingly belongs.

Infracity: Johannesburg and Urban Africa

On the surface, inner-city Johannesburg has many features in common with inner cities in the United States. Many of the economic and political mechanisms that produced American inner-city ghettos have been at work in Johannesburg, and these are only reinforced by the strong influence of U.S. urban policy on South Africa. But large swathes of Johannesburg reflect the failures of strong regulatory systems and the economic and social informalities commonly associated with urban Africa. To this extent, inner-city Johannesburg is a kind of hybrid: part American, part African. Indeed, it is mainly Johannesburg's American features—its developed physical infrastructure, social anonymity, and extensive range of material and service consumption—that have attracted large numbers of urban Africans. It is easy to show that changes in the global economy have substantially restructured and respatialized cities everywhere, often around residual pockets of ruin. The potential significance of reflections on Johannesburg, in contrast to other global cities, rests in how the city embodies, speeds up, and sometimes brutalizes aspects of urban life common to many African cities.

One such aspect is its urban residents' constant state of preparedness. Driven by discourses of war, contestation, and experimentation, many African cities seem to force their inhabitants to constantly change gears, focus, and location. Of course, there are some quarters whose residents have grown up, raised families, and devoted themselves to the same occupation or way of life without moving. Yet even this stability is situated within a larger, more fluid arena where people must be prepared to exert themselves. There is the need to ensure oneself against a lifetime without work or the means to establish a family or household of one's own. There is the need to prepare for the possibility that even hard work will produce nothing.

There is the need to prepare for an endless process of trickery. Government officials trick citizens with countless pronouncements of progress while finding new and improved ways of shaking them down. Parents trick their children with promises of constant nurturing—if only they would sell themselves here or there, as maids, touts, whores, or guardians. Children trick their parents with promises of support into old age—if only they would sell the land, the house in exchange for fake papers, airline tickets, or a consignment of goods that just fell off the truck.

This sense of preparedness, a readiness to switch gears, has significant implications for what residents think it is possible to do in the city. Households do display considerable determination and discipline, saving money over the course of several years to send children to school, build a house, or help family members migrate. They are in a place, and they demonstrate commitment to it. At the same time, African cities are a platform for people to engage with processes and territories that bear a marked sense of exteriority. The reference of this "exterior" has commonly been other cities, both within and outside the continent. Increasingly, it includes various interiors: rural areas, borders, and frontiers. These interiors may also be symbolic or spiritual and involve geographies that are off the map, as demonstrated in popular descriptions of subterranean cities, spirit worlds, or lucrative but remote frontiers. Cities straddle not only internal and external divides and national and regional boundaries but also a wide range of terrain and geography, both real and imaginary.

In many respects, then, Johannesburg not only displays and accelerates these tendencies by providing a rich urban infrastructure on which they operate, but it also stands as a receptacle, witness, and culmination of this preparedness. The inner city is a domain that few want to belong to or establish roots in. But it keeps alive residents' hopes for stability somewhere else, even as it cultivates within them a seemingly permanent restlessness and capacity to make something out of the city. One has to canvass only a small sample of the stories of foreign migrants to see how many different places they have been within the recent past. One informant from Cameroon showed me a passport with stamps from Congo, Angola, Namibia, Zimbabwe, South Africa, Dubai, India, Malaysia, Thailand, Singapore, China, Brazil, Uruguay, Paraguay, Chile, Peru, Venezuela, Guyana, Trinidad, and Argentina—all acquired over a seven-year period. The same holds true even for residents of South Africa, Lesotho, or Swaziland who may never have left the region but whose trajectories through diverse rural towns and urban townships encompass a very wide world.

Increasing numbers of Africans are situated in what could be called half-built environments: underdeveloped, overused, fragmented, and often makeshift urban infrastructures where essential services are erratic or costly and whose inefficiencies spread and urbanize disease. Most Africans still do not have access to clean water and sanitation. They are malnourished and, on average, live no longer than they did twenty years ago, even though the raison d'être of built environments would suggest a continuous trajectory toward the improved welfare of their inhabitants.

The international community has made a substantial effort over the last decade to help African municipalities direct urban growth and restructuring. Here, capacity building centers on developing proficient forms of codification. Not only does the city become the objective of a plurality of coding systems, it is meant to manifest itself more clearly as a system of codes. In other words, it is to be an arena where spaces, activities, populations, flows, and structures are made visible, or more precisely, recognizable and familiar.

Once this enhanced visibility is accomplished, urban spaces and activities are more capable of being retrieved and compared for analysis and planning. The emphasis is on the ability to locate and to define the built environment, specific populations, and activities so that they can be registered. The prevailing wisdom is that, once registered, these phenomena can be better administered and their specific energies, disciplines, and resources extracted.

But it is clear that much of what takes place in African cities is fairly invisible: the number of people who reside in a given compound; how household incomes that can support only one week's survival out of every month are supplemented; or how electricity is provided for ten times as many households as there are official connections.

In Johannesburg's inner city, the heightened emphasis on visible identities and the converse need of actors to hide what they are actually doing generates a highly volatile mix. But it is in this play of the visible and invisible that limited resources can be put to work in many possible ways. Throughout urban Africa, residents experience new forms of solidarity through their participation in makeshift, ephemeral ways of being social. At the same time, these makeshift formations amplify the complexity of local terrain and social relationships by engaging the dynamics of a larger world within a coherent, if temporary, sense of place. Sometimes this sense of place coincides with a specific locality; other times, and with increasing frequency, it is dispersed across or in between discernible territories. In this economy of interpenetration, notions about what is possible and impossible are upended, and urban residents are ready to take up a variety of attitudes and positions.

Take, for example, African urban markets. They are renowned for being well run and for their multitude of goods and services overflowing whatever order is imposed upon them. In these markets, cooking, reciting, selling, loading and unloading, fighting, praying, relaxing, pounding, and buying happen side by side, on stages too cramped, too deteriorated, too clogged with waste, history, energy, and sweat to sustain all of them. Entering the market, what do potential customers make of all that is going on? Whom do they deal with and buy from? People have their networks, their channels, and their rules. But there are also wide spaces for most people to insert themselves as middlemen who might provide a fortuitous, even magical, reading of the market "between the lines," between stall after stall of onions or used clothes, between the fifty-cent profit of the woman selling Marlboros and 5,000 freshly minted twenty-dollar bills stuffed into sisal bags with cassava and hair grease, tossed on top of a converted school bus heading somewhere into the interior. For it is these possibilities of interpretation, fixing, and navigation that enable customers to take away the most while appearing to deliver the minimum.

Throughout much of urban Africa, accidents, coercion, distinctly identified spaces, clandestine acts, and publicity are brought together in ways that trip up each of these categories. The clandestine becomes highly visible, while that which is seemingly so public disappears from view. More important, the apparently fragmented and disarticulated collection of quarters and spaces that make up the city are opened up to new reciprocal linkages.

These linkages are sometimes the constructions of individuals who desire to master self-limitations as opposed to merely straddling divides. At other times, urban residents invent a range of practices—religious, sexual, institutional—capable of relocating individual actors within different frames of identity or recognition. This relocation enables them to understand their relationships with other actors and events in new, broader ways. Actors speak and deal with one another in ways that would otherwise be impossible. Such unanticipated interactions can be used to rehearse new ways of navigating complex urban relationships and to construct a sense of commonality that goes beyond parochial identities. Still, residents invest heavily in opportunities to become socially visible in ways that are not necessarily tied to formal associations. For example, throughout urban Africa, the proliferating neighborhood night markets do not simply provide an opportunity for localized trade or for extending trading hours, but serve primarily as occasions to be public, to watch others and whom they deal with, and to listen to their conversations. The task is to find ways to situate oneself so one can assess what is happening—who talks to whom, who is visiting whose house, who is riding in the same car, who is trading or doing business together—without drawing attention to oneself, without constituting a threat (Bayat).

Inner-city Johannesburg raises the stakes on these realities and capacities. It does not use the residual features of its "American side" to either resolve or make them more manageable, palatable, or visible. With its well-developed communications systems, efficient yet pliable banks, and relatively easy access to daily comforts, Johannesburg would appear to have more sophisticated parallel (though often illegal) economies than other African cities. The inner city provides an intersection where different styles, schemes, sectors, and practices can make something out of and from one another. In these respects, inner-city Johannesburg is the quintessential African city. Johannesburg becomes a launching pad not only for better livelihoods within the inner city but also for excursions into a broader world, whether Dubai and Mumbai or the pool halls of Hillbrow and the white suburb of Cresta only a few kilometers away. On the other hand, the density of skills, needs, aspirations, and willingness brought to work in the inner city makes it a sometimes brutal place, where everything seems to be on the line.

Concluding Note

The intensifying immiseration of African urban populations is real and alarming. For increasing numbers of urban Africans, their cities no longer offer them the prospect of improving their livelihoods or modern ways of life. Yet the theoretical reflections that underpin an ethnographic observation of inner-city Johannesburg point to how the growing distance between how urban Africans actually live and normative trajectories of urbanization and public life can constitute new fields of economic action. In striking ways, the translocal scope and multilateral transactions displayed by these more ephemeral economic machines are similar to the operations pursued by the dominant transnational economic networks of scale. But they are just similar, not the same—for their similarity is generated precisely through the disarticulation of coherent urban space. In significant ways, both the global/regional command centers and the dispersed, provisional, quotidian economies of the popular urban quarters do not intersect.

With limited institutional anchorage and financial capital, most African urban residents have to make what they can out of their bare lives. Although they bring little to the table of prospective collaboration and participate in few of the mediating structures that deter or determine how individuals interact with others, this seemingly minimalist offering—bare life—is somehow redeemed. It is allowed innumerable possibilities of combination and interchange that preclude any definitive judgment of efficacy or impossibility. By throwing their intensifying particularisms—of identity, location, destination, and livelihood—into the fray, urban residents generate a sense of unaccountable movement that might remain geographically circumscribed or travel great distances.

Notes

1 This is a common assumption about the nature of urban Africa, but one with its own histories and disputes. See Anderson and Rathbone 2000.

2 This notion attempts to extend what Lefebvre meant by social space as a practice of works—modes of organization at various and interlocking scales that link expressions, attraction and repulsion, sympathies and antipathies, changes and amalgamations that affect urban residents and their social interactions. Ways of doing and representing things become increasingly "conversant" with one another. They

participate in a diversifying series of reciprocal exchanges, so that positions and identities are not fixed or even, at most times, determinable. These "urbanized" relations reflect neither the dominance of a narrative or linguistic structure nor a chaotic, primordial mix.

3 The 419 letter is a scheme in which mass mailings are sent out, seemingly from a prominent, usually Nigerian, figure or company that needs to get large amounts of money out of the country. In return for temporary use of the recipient's bank account or other financial instruments, a significant share of these funds is promised. The letter usually requests a faxed authorization to deposit these funds, which in turn enables the 419 fraudster to withdraw money from the account. Often, 419 victims are enticed to come to Nigeria, where they are robbed or extorted.

4 Bakassi Boys is a network of well-organized youth gangs that controls many neighborhoods in southern Nigerian cities and increasingly has operated as a paramilitary force for various politicians. *Sobels* were military personnel in the Sierra Leone Army who, in the late 1990s, joined with the opposition rebel movement, the Revolutionary United Front, to try to control the diamond trade. Yaya Jammeh is the president of Gambia; originating from a town reputed to be at the center of the regional marijuana trade, Jammeh assumed power as a young soldier in his late twenties. Zanu-PF is the ruling party of Zimbabwe, whose military assumed control of many mineral concessions in the Democratic Republic of Congo when Laurent Kabila, the former head of state, requested Zimbabwe's assistance in the long civil war (in which the Rally for Congolese Democracy is one of the primary antagonists). South Africa has hosted a protracted series of negotiations among the main armed groups to try to bring an end to the conflict. Pascal Lissouba is the former head of state of the Republic of Congo; he was replaced by Daniel Sassou-Ngueso. Both men organized private militias during their struggle for power, which largely decimated the capital city of Brazzaville during the mid-1990s.

5 Based on a series of interviews conducted by Bascom Guffin with staff of the Johannesburg Development Agency and the Central Johannesburg Partnership, July 8–10, 2002.

3 ✦ Stylizing the Self

SARAH NUTTALL

Johannesburg is a city wrought from its surfaces and depths, from that which is apparent, on display, there to be seen, ambitious, brash, innovative—and that which lies underneath, hidden in part, heaving at times to the surface, whether as earth once bearing gold, ready for extraction and manned by a labor system long based on a racial division of labor, or as a memory of the past which persists beneath, erupts, and works to shape the surfaces of the present. Several authors in this book explore the idea of Johannesburg as a city of surfaces and depths. In the introduction, Achille Mbembe and I argue that the entanglement between surface and underneath constitutes one of the defining metaphors by which to understand this city, both historically and in its contemporary forms.

One of the ways in which Johannesburg projects its surface is through its representations: in many ways, it is a city studded with texts. Billboards, newsprint, magazine covers, road signs, even the entire surfaces of buildings constitute a stream of local and global city signs, of Johannesburg representation. These texts are really a part of visual culture, and most of the time, they have sartorial and aural accompaniments. As surfaces, they are sometimes just that, but they also on occasion suggest a deeper diagnostic, a layering in which, for example, the apparent fixity of race so often privileged in accounts of the city is underwritten by the potential unfixing of the commodity form, or in which the past resurfaces in the present. Taken together, these city texts reveal something of the force and power of attempts by young black people in particular to conquer the right to be urban in the present: to occupy the center of the city, its subjective core, to produce forms of city style at tremendous velocity—in direct response, perhaps, to an apartheid past in which black people were required to work in the city but not live in it, to perform its labor, and then retreat from its center.

In this essay I want to discuss several forms of Johannesburg representation, of self-making in the city, forms that are quite different from before, even as they cite or acknowledge a past, a deeper history, which is, they assert, gone but not entirely to be discarded. Indeed, what makes these representations and forms of self-stylization they produce local in their resonances and their reach while undoubtedly spliced with the global is their remixing of a past that is South African and specific: the past of apartheid. The forms I discuss are moments in Johannesburg's history, ones that will metamorphose before long, but which nevertheless operate as important signals, even in their transience, of the remaking of the racial city toward its metropolitan form. They reveal versatile approaches to the media and information technology and produce imaginaries that are flexible, at times contradictory and eminently contingent.[1] They constitute one part of Johannesburg's distinctively modern aura, an aura, as Michael Watts (2005) has written, which derives as much from its zine culture and its metropolitan imaginings as from its memorializations, its psychic wounds, and its fugitive underground worlds.

The essay stays in part with the surface as an analytic location. It tries to capture something of the immense coincidence, so tangible in Johannesburg at present, between the end of apartheid and the rise of new media culture and cultures of consumption. It aims to show how we might take the surface more seriously in our analyses of contemporary cultural form but equally how contemporary youth media cultural forms in Johannesburg still signal to and cite the underneath of an apartheid past. As such they are firmly focused on the making of the future, while retaining a memory of the past, increasingly remade in the present. They act as screens across which emergent selves flicker, revealing traces of certain kinds of urban, bodily lives and certain sorts of investments in being in the city.

In the first part of the essay below, I explore the rise of a youth cultural form widely known as Y Culture. Y Culture, also known as *loxion kulcha* for reasons I explain below, is an emergent youth culture in Johannesburg that moves across various media forms and which generates a "compositional remixing" that signals the supercession of an earlier era's resistance politics by an alternative politics of style and accessorization, while simultaneously gesturing, in various ways, toward the past. It is a culture of the hip bucolic that works across a series of surfaces, requiring what Paul Gilroy (2000) calls "technological analogies," in order to produce enigmatic and divergent styles of self-making. While drawing on black American style formations, it is an explicitly local reworking of the American sign—a reworking that simultaneously results in and underscores significant fractures in Gilroy's paradigm of the Black Atlantic.[2]

In my analysis, I find it useful to draw on Foucault's concept of "stylizing the self." Foucault (2003: 225) invokes practices of self-stylization or self-fashioning through which individuals create "a certain number of operations on their own bodies and souls, thoughts, conduct and ways of being so as to transform themselves." Such processes of self-stylization draw on technologies of the self to ensure that what emerges from the moment of political liberation are indeed practices of freedom.

I find, too, that in attempting to understand Y Culture forms, cultural analysis that relies on ideas of translation or translatability, embedded in a model of reading, is useful only up to a point, and that what is required instead—or at least equally—is an understanding of how cultural forms move. While translation relies on an idea of a gap—a gap between one meaning or text and another—I find that what is needed in order to properly understand this cultural form is something closer to an interface in which meaning morphs continuously into something else, rather than losing its initial sense. While the idea of the gap in meaning inhabits our theorizing about culture generally, it deserves elaboration and adjustment when it comes to reading the innovations of contemporary urban cultural forms. In the second part of the essay, I consider a recent set of advertisements that have appeared on billboards and in magazines in the wake of Y Culture. I show how they simultaneously engage with and push in unexpected directions one of the most striking aspects of Y/loxion culture, an attempt at rereading race in the city. In analyzing the ads, I consider ways in which commodity images, and the market itself, come to produce some of the most powerful reimaginings of race South Africa has known in some time. At the same time, the idea of the gap (here between what you have and what you want) is continually reconstituted at the heart of the commodity in order to propel new desires.

Y Culture, Johannesburg circa 2006

Y Culture was first launched by a radio station called YFM, today South Africa's largest regional station, beamed over the airwaves from Johannesburg to nearly 2 million listeners. The station was set up in 1996. Its primary audience was young, mostly black people, who tuned in to hear a mix of popular, mostly local music. When democracy came to South Africa in 1994, there was no airspace, on the AM or FM dials, dedicated to the country's young black people. The South African Broadcasting Corporation (SABC) had a spare frequency, which it handed over to the team that would eventually found YFM. Stringent conditions were attached: the station would be granted a license only if 80 percent of its capital was black-owned, 50 percent of its staff was female and, within three years, at least half its playlist was made up of South African music. The station was to be a multilingual urban entity that informed, educated, and entertained a young audience. All of this was well in line with the founding team's goals. YFM, says general manager Greg Maloka, was to be a "phenomenon . . . for us and by us. We saw [its creation] as another June 16, 1976," he adds, alluding to the spontaneous uprising of tens of thousands of children and adolescents in Soweto, a massive call-to-action against the apartheid state that marked the beginning of the end of the white regime. Twenty-two years had passed. Apartheid was officially dead. Suddenly, the youth market was what everyone was talking about (McGregor 2005).

YFM launched *kwaito,* South Africa's first globally recognized local music form, a potent blend of city and township sound that emerged after the democratic transition in 1994, mixing the protest dancing and chanting known as *toyi-toyi* with slow-motion house, local pop (known as "bubblegum"), and a dash of hip-hop. In 1998, the station spawned a print spin-off, *Y Magazine* (or *YMag*). Making use of state-of-the-art branding techniques, the magazine associated itself closely with both YFM and *kwaito.* Its tagline, prominently displayed on the spine of each issue, is an anthem to the art of being in the know—hip, cool, plugged in: "Y—Because You Want to Know." The same is true of the name chosen by the company that owns the publication, YIRED, a play on notions of being young and "wired"—up to date and connected in all the right places. In 2002, the YFM stable launched a fashion label called Loxion Kulcha (LK).[3] "Loxion" is a text-message contraction of the word "location," a synonym of "township"; "Kulcha" is an ironic deformation of the word "culture." The brand name invokes a remixing: an infusion of black township culture, long kept at a violent remove from the urban center, into the heart of the (once white) city itself. In *YMag*, Loxion Kulcha is described as a "pride-driven line," a "brand born of the YFM era," one that remixes African American styles to its own purposes and in ways that speak to its own, particular cultural precursors (Mstali 2000: 61). Its designers, Wandi Nzimande and Sechaba "Chabi" Mogale, are "typical generation Yers, children of the 1980s who are old enough to understand what the political fuss [of the apartheid era] was about, yet young enough to keep an open mind [to the present and future]" (62).

Y Culture is located most visibly in an area called the Zone, in Rosebank, a residential neighborhood-cum-business district that has been attracting a young, hip workforce since the 1980s, thanks to a concentration of information technology, travel and tourism enterprises, retail and fashion outlets, cinemas, and restaurants. Increasingly, to serve this young workforce, a process of infill has occurred, in which shopping complexes expand by incorporating spaces and structures that predate them. The Zone—home to the YFM studios and to shops showcasing Loxion Kultcha and related fashion labels such as the popular Stoned Cherrie brand—is one of these infills.[4] Here, enclosed shopping venues and open areas are linked by indoor and outdoor "roads," in an approach to architecture that, as one critic observes, turns the notion of public space inside out (Farber 2002: 73).

In the Zone, yellow and blue neon tubes, glitter tiles, columns clad in reflective aluminum, and exposed steel trusses give it an industrial look that combines elements of the factory and the club. As one makes one's way through its spaces, one is struck by their fluidity. Distinctions—thresholds—between public and private, pavement and mall, inside and out, seem to fall away. The Zone's indoor roads sometimes feel like catwalks—and at others like a state-of-the-art gym (television screens hang over the walkways). Throughout, surfaces (shiny, mirrorlike) and colors (an energetic metallic gray flecked with primary colors) differentiate the space from the neutral beige found in the city's other shopping centers.[5] Wherever possible, the Zone's architecture maximizes the intersection of gazes: people on the escalators produce a spectacle for diners seated at strategically located restaurants; the main indoor roads function simultaneously as means of access and vantage points; signifiers one would usually rely on to orient oneself outside (street signs, for instance) are reappropriated to define interior spaces (Farber 2002: 87).

As a locus of social interaction, the Zone is complex. On the one hand, as a privatized public space, it speaks of exclusion: though it is possible for poorer citizens to come to the Zone, they are not welcome there.[6] At the same time, it is one of Johannesburg's relatively few upmarket open spaces where some manner of the unexpected is possible: theater, mime, and dance groups perform here, parades are organized, and people come from all over the continent to trade in a large African craft market located near its entrance. The Zone is by no means a place of extensive social mixing. Heavily regulated and subjected to close scrutiny by expedient mall governors, the craft market at its door underscores this. Still, as a result of its presence, there is a sense here of broader horizons: a young person (or anyone else) walking around the Zone circulates within an imagined Africa much larger than Johannesburg alone.

Thus, despite the influence on it of American models of mall design and commerce, the Zone does not yet display the nihilism that characterizes consumer culture in the United States—an approach to selling style and individuality in which each customer is pegged to a specifically managed and increasingly reified identity. This in part is due to the still-recent emergence of the black body from its history of invisibility under apartheid—an erasure from the city which Y Culture, in certain respects, seeks to recall, but that it is largely bent on transforming—and to the relative fluidity with which black middle-class culture locates itself in the urban matrix after a long period of exclusion. Elaborating on this point, we could perhaps also argue that under apartheid, black people faced the oppressive binaries of either being made entirely invisible—or being made hypervisible. It is this hypervisibility that Y Culture, but especially the advertisements I discuss in the second part of this essay, works with and parodies.[7]

The Zone, as well as housing smaller fashion outlets like the Stoned Cherrie brand store and Young Designers Emporium, is home to the ubiquitous mall chain stores. Among these are Exclusive Books and CD Warehouse. Both are found at shopping arcades throughout the city and in urban centers across the country. At this particular branch of Exclusive Books, the bestsellers are not what they are elsewhere. The books that sell the best in most Exclusive Books locations are by U.S. pulp authors like John Grisham and Dan Brown. In the Zone, they take second billing. The top sellers are Niq Mhlongo's *Dog Eat Dog* (2004) and Phaswane's Mpe's *Welcome to our Hillbrow* (2000). The first is the story of a young Sowetan trying to hustle his way through Wits University, long a bastion of white education; the second is a tale of xenophobia and AIDS in inner-city Johannesburg. The Zone branch of CD Warehouse also differs from its sister stores elsewhere in the city. It carries a prominent and exhaustive range of kwaito CDs as well as some of the best sounds from the continent and black America. Next to CD Warehouse is the YFM Internet café and the Y-Shoppe, where local designers showcase their work and whose designs generally invoke the city by name or image, draw on puns or pastiches of the past and play with the "Y" logo.[8] The shop leads to the heart of the radio station, the Y Studios, a slick, black-lined maze of soundproof booths. Through large windows, one can see DJs at work creating the Y sound at banks of sophisticated equipment. The DJs themselves are young, glamorous, mostly black-skinned and black-clad (McGregor 2005).

Remix

Y is a hybrid phenomenon that appeals to young people across borders of class, education, and taste. Key to its success in this regard is a dual remixing it effects—of the township and the city and the township *in* the city. The young designers who launched the Loxion Kulcha label are incarnations of this intraculture. Wandi styles himself a *kasi,* or "township boy," Chabi a *Bana ba di Model C* (a "Model C kid"). As such, they represent the remix at work in the making of Y. A kasi is typically someone who grew up in a black township, a world often associated with poverty, crime, overcrowding, and lack of resources. At the same time, while this is indeed the environment in which Wandi was raised and which he references in speaking of himself as a kasi, the word today has acquired so many connotations that it can now stand alone, quite apart from location, to imply a certain way of life (see Mbembe's interview of Dlamini and Khunou in this volume). Chabi's take on himself tells of a different world. When the South African education system was first integrated after 1994, privileged schools in formerly white, bourgeois neighborhoods opened their doors to black students. These schools were classified as "Model C" establishments. Though the term is no longer used as a formal education category, over time it has acquired a meaning of its own. It refers to black high-school students who have taken on a cross-racial style and social set.

Loxion Kulcha's intracultural success is less a matter of appearance than a matter of branding. The point may be to bring the township into the city, and cultural knowledge of where "township culture" is heading is certainly at the heart of what makes Wandi and Chabi hip, but Loxion Kulcha is not about spreading a "township look." The label—the brand, explicitly set forth and marketed with brio—is the thing here, as Mpolokeng Bogatsu (2003) quite accurately points out. This privileging of brand over look simultaneously reflects and shapes structures of class and race within the city's emergent youth culture.

Although Loxion Kulcha's market is intraclass (to the extent that it encompasses both city youth and those living in generally lower-middle-class township homes), sartorial markings are often seen to reveal sharp distinctions between Zone kids (well-to-do young people who make a habit of coming to Rosebank) and township kids, who do frequent the Zone but to a lesser extent and are not particularly welcome there. Rocking the brand is good, essential even, but it doesn't occult where you come from. Young people interviewed in the Zone make this quite clear: "Township girls," says one, "wear Rocabarroco [brand] shoes that are square-shaped with laces. . . . They will wear bright[-colored] jeans with a collar-type shirt. A Zone kid will wear [blue] jeans and a nice [read hip, collarless] top." Another glosses this as: "They dress similarly, but you can tell them apart. Model C girls have an air of sophistication, whereas township girls could snap anytime." Some interviewees focus less on sartorial differences than on skin color. This they do, however, in ways that stand at a distinct remove from earlier, pre-1994 discourses of race and, by extension, class. Notes one young Zoner: "In our generation, we all kind of dress the same. Some blacks dress outrageously wrong and some whites do too, but we all wear the same things. If you check around, you can't notice a difference between whites and blacks here, apart from the colour of their skin" (Farber 2002: 11–16). Difference is still located on the skin, as color, even as skin color becomes less determined within this sartorially inflected set of practices and signs.

The foregoing underscores the fact that racial identities emerging from Y/loxion culture are new in relation to the apartheid era legal classification of people as "White," "Black," "Indian," or "Coloured." These categories operated on an everyday basis through processes of urbanization, policing, and the manipulation of cultural difference to political ends. Since 1994, when this system was officially abolished, young people have occupied these categories in changing ways, using them to elaborate shifting identities for themselves in the new, "postracist" dispensation. Nadine Dolby (2000) argues that "taste" at times comes to displace orthodox constructs of race and culture as the carrier of social distinctions among urban students—this as popular culture comes to increasingly contest the church, family, and neighborhood as the primary site where racial identities are forged. The criteria that define bodies, clothing, and culture as "White," "Coloured," or "Black" are not stable, as fashion and music tastes undergo one metamorphosis after another. Class dynamics work into the constitution of racialized taste patterns, at times taking on charged connotations despite constant style fluctuations. What is clear is that new youth cultures are superseding the resistance politics of an earlier generation, while still jamming, remixing, and remaking cultural codes and signifiers from the apartheid past.

How these codes are reappropriated and transformed makes for fascinating cultural (and business) practice. Stoned Cherrie, one of the most popular fashion labels at the Zone, puts signs of the past to striking use. Notably, it recycles images of boxing champions, beauty queens, and musicians from *Drum*, a politically engaged magazine for black readers popular during the 1950s, integrating them into contemporary fashion styles. *Drum* was associated with places like Sophiatown, the heart of Johannesburg's counterculture in the 1950s. It courted and actively constructed an expressly cosmopolitan target audience, "the new African cut adrift from the tribal reserve—urbanized, eager, fast-talking and brash" (Nkosi 1983: 34). Stoned Cherrie's designs speak in several registers. In part they play on the taste for "retro" (a current global trend in styling), by drawing on 1950s imagery—imagery for which *Drum*, a showcase for some of the best urban photography in South Africa, is a particularly fruitful source. At the same time, they make extensive use of parody, as they brand unquestionably dated *vieux jeu* images onto mass-produced T-shirts. Retro and parody, in turn, combine to invoke nostalgia for "the location." Emblematic figures of Johannesburg's mid-twentieth-century past—*pantsulas*, the "bad boys" of the 1950s; migrant and blue-collar workers; black cover girls whose very existence and whose sophistication stood on its head white culture's claim to superiority—are recreated, brought to life anew and remixed, in Loxion Kulcha.[9] This past, recalled and reworked, is in turn cross-pollinated with references to African American culture(s) and styles. In an analysis of how Loxion Kulcha remakes township culture and, more specifically, blends pantsula and African American street culture styles, Nthabiseng Motsemme (2002) shows how *isishoeshoe* and *iduku* (shoes and headcloths worn by black married township and rural migrant women employed as domestic workers in the city during the apartheid era) have been recaptured, reinterpreted, and transformed into iconic fashion items on display in Rosebank. The point, here, is not a political one—not, in any event, in the sense that resistance movements to apartheid understood the term.

There is no real (or intended) engagement here with the horrors of the pre-1994 past. This is underscored by another Loxion Kulcha product: a recent line of low-cut, tight-fitting T-shirts on which liberation theorist and apartheid martyr Steve Biko's image and name appear in a brilliant, stylized red.[10] It is not so much the Black Consciousness message spread by Biko that is being commemorated here, although "BC" still has a broad resonance for young people only vaguely aware of its message. Rather, something different is being introduced: a sartorial style is being marked as an in-your-face contemporary phenomenon through the remixing and recoding of an icon.

While township culture and identity have existed as long as the townships themselves, it is the *performance* of township culture that has emerged with new vigor in the contemporary context. "Like kwaito music," writes Bogatsu, "Loxion Kulcha claims the streets of South Africa's townships as its cultural womb but occupies the centre of the city with its new forms" (2003: 14). Township culture is translated from a socioeconomically stagnant into a high-urban experience. The latter gives rise to what is increasingly known as "Afro-chic." A case in point: in the 2000–2002 Loxion Kulcha collections, overalls were big. Mostly, they were single-color outfits, inspired by the work clothes of migrant laborers and miners. Their design was similar to that of *mdantsane,* two-piece coveralls consisting of pants and a zip-up jacket generally worn by workers on a factory assembly line or by miners in a shaft. Unlike the protective garments on which they were modeled, however, the LK pieces emphasized bright, eye-catching primary colors. The utility-oriented, mass-produced overall was made chic, appropriated with great success to new cultural ends.

Here too, class and race, rethought Y-style, emerge as key concerns. In LK's designs, the township is referenced—gestured to explicitly—yet, in the same breath, cast aside. To sport LK gear is to say one wants out of (or to brag that one has definitely left behind) the location. An insistence on staying in the township, Bogatsu notes (2003: 21), is increasingly marked within Y Culture as a self-defeating show of "negritude" wearing LK's flash-in-your-face overalls makes it clear: this is emphatically not how you plan to live your life. You have no intention of toiling the way your parents did. The economic violence done them is not forgotten, but neither is it openly critiqued. Instead a largely uncritical celebratory focus is placed on the city's burgeoning service economy. LK's overall becomes the signifier, worn with pleasure and pride, of a young workforce whose members labor as waiters and shop attendants in the Zone, becoming both providers for wide family networks and, when off duty, consumers who buy clothes and music in the area and hang out in Rosebank's many clubs.

A Stylistics of Sensation

Turning to a series of images from *YMag*, we can see how Y Culture signals to, but increasingly breaks with, the past in its adoption of an elaborated stylistics of sensation and singularization. A cover image from August 2002 reveals a striking example of the foregrounding of the capacity for sensation, of the new investment in the body's special presence and powers, and of the ascendancy of the sign of blackness. Here, selfhood and subjectivity can no longer be interpreted as merely inscriptions of broader institutional and political forces; instead, the images project an increased self-consciousness of the fashioning of human identity as a manipulable, artful process (see figure 1).

Representations of the self as an expressive subject have for some time been seen by scholars to signal a subject that is fractured, multiple, shifting, and produced through performativity (Butler 1993 and 1999). What loxion kulcha's image-texts emphasize, by contrast, are practices based on specific aesthetic values and stylistic criteria and enabled by various emerging techniques of the self (Foucault 2001). The *YMag* "Kwaito-Nation" cover image (April-May 1998) bears this out, as do others published of late by the magazine. It shows sixteen *kwaito* artists. All are black men, and all are dressed in black, with one or two white shirts showing underneath. The emphasis is on the glamour and style of blackness, reflected metonymically in the color of the clothes themselves. In a fashion sequence six months later called "Angel Delight" (October–November 2002), the theme is the color white, and the shoot is dominated this time by women but also by a cross-racial group: white and Coloured women are foregrounded, and cross-racial and cross-gendered sexual desire is clearly being played with in the images. Here, then, is a quite different version of *Y Magazine*'s projected reader, and this difference is part of a broader remixing of identity, including racial identity, in a shifting signifying chain.

The identities and forms of selfhood projected here are compositional. The self in this instance is above all a work of art. So too are the stylizations of the self projected in the magazine's images based on a delicate balance between

1 *YMag,*
August 2002.
Courtesy of *Y Magazine*

actual emerging lifestyles of middle-class black youth and the politics of aspiration. An exchange in the letters-to-the-editor column in the June–July 2002 issue underscores this: "After reading Y-mag for a while now I've concluded that it would appeal more to the 'miss-thangs' and 'brother mans' living or trying to live the so-called hip life in Jozi. Some of us live in different areas in the country and you only portray a certain kind of youth. The rest of us then feel like the odd ones out, making us feel like aliens or something. Please broaden your scope so that most people can find it appealing, not just those who live in Jozi."[11] The editors' reply follows: "We are all aliens if you think about it, depending where you come from. But seriously, though, Y-mag is for you. *Y-mag doesn't necessarily portray reality as each of us would see it, that is, we're aspiring as well.* We obviously can't reflect every kind of person under the good sun but every young person can and will find at least one thing they like inside Y-mag" (my emphasis; June–July 2002, 12).

In acknowledging that their product is made for those who aspire to (but cannot necessarily claim) hip, cutting-edge, largely middle-class lifestyles in the city, the editors signal a potential gap—a gap of potential—between what is and what could be. The present and the possible interlace to form a stylistics of the future. We could also draw out this idea of a gap from the words of one young South African whom Tanya Farber interviewed in the Zone: "We understand where we come from, but I am not interested in politics and about what happened in the '80s because I wasn't there. And even if I was, I live for the future" (2003: 28). Since this interviewee is in his early twenties, he was in fact "there" in the 1980s, during the worst of the apartheid struggle and the height of the resistance to it. Indirectly acknowledging this by his phrase "and even if I was," he nevertheless insists on the fact that his project and investment lie in a search for the future. His words, we could say, mark him as a public representative of "the now" in South Africa, as he signals the remainders of the past but also speaks the future-oriented language of Y-Gen aspiration.

Y Magazine, in naming a subject who aspires, also draws consumers into a competitive system in which not everyone can have what he or she aspires to. In *Lifebuoy Men, Lux Women* (1996), Tim Burke, one of the few theorists of African consumer culture, points to pitfalls inherent in such processes. As the pleasures of consumption in the twentieth (and twenty-first) century have become increasingly and explicitly tied to satisfaction of the flesh and its needs, he asks, have we not perhaps made too much of the body as a unique site for the elaboration of forms of self-stylization? In so doing, do we not "risk separating individuals from their bodies, seeing, for example, the bodies of women as separate from the selves of women"? This, of course, is not a specifically African phenomenon. Dipesh Chakrabarty is similarly concerned with the gap between body and self that a culture of commodification would seem to imply: the commodification of culture as lifestyle, he argues, can never completely encompass the life-worlds upon which it draws.[12] On the one hand, it requires a suppression of embodied idiosyncrasies and local conjunctures, but on the other it needs the tangibility of objects and people, a "corporeal index," as Beth Povinelli (2001) puts it, to lend credibility and desirability to its abstract claims. Thus Chakrabarty draws attention to the gap at the heart of the commodity form, caught as it is between embodiment and abstraction.

Yet the making of the contemporary self is not so easily readable in the self-representations and subjective practices, the powerful parodic languages, the processes of self-styling in which the body plays such an important part—in the seductive "surface forms" of youth culture. Critics generally disavow the "surfaces" of youth culture as an insufficient analytic space (Comaroff and Comaroff 2001). Yet, arguably it is here, on the surfaces of youth culture, that we come most powerfully to encounter the enigmatic and divergent ways of knowing and self-making that mark its forms. Pursuing the surfaces of cultural form implies a reading, however, that positions itself at the limit of the by now ubiquitous cultural analytic notion of translatability:[13] it demands that we push beyond the dual notions of reading and translating to understand.

Mind the Gap

A conventional reading of Y Culture would rely on tropes of translatability—and indeed the latter can take us quite far into the analysis of this cultural form. The cover stories of *YMag* signal a transnational, multilingual hybridity that a focus on translation goes a long way toward explicating. The title "Skwatta Kamp: Hard to the Core Hip-Hop" (August–September 2002), for example, suggests the influence of American hip-hop on the local scene (Skwatta Kamp is a local rap group), even as it invokes the local topography of the squatter camp—the ubiquitous sign of homelessness and poverty in urban South Africa. "Vat en Sit: Shacking Up in Y2K" (June–July 2002) explores how young black South African couples flout older orthodoxies of sex and marriage; it draws simultaneously on the Afrikaans expression *vat en sit* ("take and live with," a colloquialism used by black migrant workers who would meet and live with women in the city despite having a wife in the rural area or town they came from—a practice of which both women were often aware) and on the English word *shack* (used to denote the makeshift quarters of the poorest in South Africa's townships and squatter camps). "The Colour of Music: Whiteys and Kwaito" (February 2000) signals an interest in and a projection of crossover cultural and racial cultural codes in post-apartheid South Africa, as does "Darkies and Ecstasy: Is It the New Zol?"[14]

Translatability and multilingualism are built into the text of *Y Magazine*. This is less visible in the body of the text, as the main articles are written in English, than in the interstices. It is in the in-between spaces—the sound bites, the gossip pages, the reviews—that language emerges most forcefully as a locus for practices of translation. Acronyms, wordplay, colloquialisms, and "deep" meanings are some of the devices drawn on within the culture of translatability at work here. A review of a new CD release by local kwaito act Bongo Maffin reads, in Zulu, "Aahyh, Ngi yai bon'indlela en'ibalwe BM" ("Ah, I see the road and it says BM [Bongo Maffin]"; Nappy Head 1998). The phrasing plays on the widely admired style and road performance of BMWS, and also recalls a classic of South African music, Dorothy Masuka's classic "Imphi indlela" ("Where's the road/the way").[15] The same review then shifts from Zulu to Tswana: "Kego tsaela 99, Bongo Maffin ifhlile" ("I'm telling you straight up, Bongo Maffin has arrived").

These shifts in language and frame of reference question standard notions of location and publics. They show us that the "world" appears increasingly as a set of fragments, bits and pieces with which young people grapple. Sutured onto these bits and pieces are the histories of isolation from, and connection to, the world that South Africans carry.[16] These fragments come to be refracted in ways that produce resemblances across different signs and languages between signs—what Mbembe (2002: 14) has referred to as "the powers of the false"—revealing the ability of Africans to inhabit several worlds simultaneously. As these fragments and their multiple meanings travel, they also encounter resistant edges, and in Y Culture one of these edges is the sign of black America. As Y youth come to inhabit a culture of selfhood shaped in part by African American hip-hop culture, they also rebel against it, resulting in a form of pastiche. A cut-and-paste appropriation of American music, language, and cultural practices is simultaneously deployed and refuted. An example of this can be found in the self-styling of Trompies, a kwaito group that epitomizes the contemporary version of *mapantsula*. The group is now sponsored by FUBU (For Us by Us), an African American clothing label often worn by U.S. rap artists. In the June–July 2000 issue of *YMag,* Trompies is accused of making a "fashion faux pas," since they call themselves pantsulas yet adopt a hip-hop style (Mstali, Masemola, and Gule 2000: 19). At the same time, it is also acknowledged that the 1950s pantsula culture emanated from America. Although the black American is embraced as a "brother," the Y reader does not want to be assimilated into his culture (Masemola 2000: 47).[17]

Tropes of translatabilty can reveal much, then, about the workings of Y Culture—but they can take us only so far. The idea of (cultural) translation relies, like the theorizations of Burke and Chakrabarty discussed above, on an idea of "the gap." Increasingly, however, scholarly work on the technologies of public forms, including popular cultural forms, has tended to move toward a focus on circulation and transfiguration, replacing or at least complicating earlier preoccupations with meaning and translation. As analytic vectors of the social, the latter rely on methods of reading derived from the tradition of the book, a tradition that stipulates that a cultural text be meaningful—in the words of Dilip Gaonkar and Beth Povinelli (2003: 388), "that it be a text and confront us as a text whose primary function is to produce meaning and difference and to captivate us in the dialectic play between these two poles." Such a tradition, moreover, implies a theory of translation grounded in the question of how to translate *well* from one language to another, as meaning is borne across the chasm of two language codes. Once we set foot in a "terrain of chasms and gaps," as Gaonkar and Povinelli note, "we are swept up in the maelstrom of debates about incommensurability, indeterminacy, and undecidability in translation": translation is seen as a productive failure (388). Rather than, or in addition to, asking what happens to meaning as it is borne across languages, genres, or semiotic modes (to "read for meaning"), we might ask what movements of cultural form and techniques for mapping them appear in worlds structured increasingly by cultures of circulation. In other words, as Gaonkar and Povinelli so usefully put it, we need "to foreground the social life *of* the form in question rather than reading social life *off* it" (394).

Such an approach proves particularly productive in understanding Y/loxion culture. It is a cultural form that cuts across sound, sartorial, visual, and textual cultures to reveal a process of "compositional remixing." In this setting, processes of circulation, parallels and slippages between genres, play a fundamental role. In the reviews pages of *YMag,* crossover styles are elaborated so that a sound might be used to describe an image, or an image a word, or a clothing line a taste. "His writing is reminiscent of Tracy Chapman's singing," writes one book reviewer (Davis 2000: 130). Another describes a book by way of allusion to a television chat show (Gule 2000: 89). A review of a CD by Thievery Corporation in *Y*'s sister magazine, *SL,* references fashion to describe sound: "Picture some cool geezer in a black Armani shirt, grey slacks, and DKNY sandals, smoking a doobie like a zeppelin. That pretty accurately describes the sound of Thievery Corporation" (Campbell 1999: 105).[18] Thus the processes of self-stylization that emerge from *YMag* further accessorize a range of cultural texts that, reframed within crossover media forms, become elements in the aestheticization of the self.[19] Race, especially blackness, as it plays out across these surfaces of form, itself becomes more of a mutating formation than before, less a finished and stable identity than something open to transformation, even proliferation—a phenomenon that actively resists attempts at reading or translation.

Revisiting the Analytics of the Gap

I turn, now, to a second set of cultural texts, a series of advertisements which have appeared since 2005 both in *YMag* and on billboards around Johannesburg. The ads elaborate on the cultural opening that Y Culture has provided, particularly in relation to the prominence given to "style" in the making of contemporary identity in the city. They take up notions of self-making and stylization in order to deconstruct South Africa's racial past—and they do so through an attempt at beginning to define notions of the "post-racial."[20] Drawing on the enormous popularity of Y Culture itself among young South Africans, they use irony and parody to work even more specifically and provocatively than *YMag* and its related brands have in the past with questions of race. A mix of image and text (a point I will return to), the ads emerge as important sites for reading the South African "now," for they just begin to make explicit ideas and passions that are "out there" in society, and therefore have an articulatory function—a function that palpably affects life worlds. Each of the advertisements can be thought of in terms of the commodity image. The latter, as William Mazarella (2003) reminds us, can be theorized as a compelling point of mediation between culture and capital and as an index of wider transformations within the field of public culture. The commodity image is at once a flashpoint for the key ideological issues of the day, a rendering of national community as aesthetic community, and, conventionally at least, a vector of cultural difference offered up for consumption.

The first two advertisements are for a brand of sports shoes called K-Swiss, an American make recently introduced in the South African market. The first is filmed against the backdrop of what was formerly a lower-middle-class section of Johannesburg and is now a mixed-income neighborhood (see figure 2). Though the neighborhood is not identified, it is in all likelihood Brixton, a part of the city popular among a certain set for its "retro" look. The ad shows a person in the process of being arrested by the police while others look on. The people on the street stand beneath a sign that says WHITES ONLY. The scene is an explicit allusion to a widely known genre of image: an urban scene typical of 1970s South Africa, depicting a black man being arrested on grounds that he is not carrying a pass to legitimize his presence in the city.

2 and 3 Advertisements for K-Swiss sports shoes. Courtesy of K-Swiss

The image relies on both irony and parody to achieve its effect: it is not quite what it seems. The crime that the man being arrested has committed, it turns out, is not a pass but a style crime: he is not dressed properly. Specifically, he is not dressed in the color white; most egregiously, he is not wearing the white sports shoes that are being advertised. The image works on many levels: it suggests that the greatest crime is now a style crime; that whiteness (and therefore blackness) is a matter less of race than of style; and that style is itself a cross-over phenomenon, working across race. It also comments on the style pecking order in contemporary urban South Africa: in the style stakes marked out on the street, the average white guy languishes at the back; next comes the black woman; coolest of all is the black man, shown here sporting a 1970s (now retro-cool) Afro hairdo and a body language that suggests cultural confidence and hipness as well as street credibility. In general, the ad plays with the notion that the way you look—the way you dress—defines you as in or out, legal or illegal, official or unofficial: it insists on self-styling as a critical mode of self-making.

The second ad in this series (see figure 3) works on the same principle: the past is acknowledged but ironically recast in the post-apartheid present. Here, the scene is a men's urinal. One man is cleaning the floor while others make use of the urinal. We might recall that under apartheid the spaces of segregation included macrospaces such as schools, churches and cemeteries, but also, importantly, microspaces, which functioned as key loci for the staging of humiliation. One such locus was the "whites only" urinal, which a black man could enter under one condition only: to clean it. The image with which we are concerned gestures to that past and its legacy in South Africa's collective memory, but with a twist. The men using the urinal are both black and white. What differentiates the users from the man cleaning the floor is not skin color but the color of their respective clothes. The users are dressed in the sign of whiteness, white clothes, and more specifically white shoes; the man cleaning the floor is *not* wearing the right shoes—he is badly dressed, the ad suggests, out of style, unwilling or incapable of playing the market to project a particular (life)style.[21]

The adverts were launched in 2004. South Africa was celebrating its first ten years of democracy, and the company wanted to run a campaign that spoke to this particular context. The target market K-Swiss was aiming at was fourteen- to twenty-six-year-olds: young people whom market research showed were increasingly thinking and acting in a cross-racial manner. The ads had been a success with this group; surveys showed that young people found the ads clever and "funny" (the only group who were not amused, he added, were fifty- to sixty-five-year-old white Afrikaans men).[22] They were based on market research showing that whereas South Africa was once the ultimate signifier of race difference, the situation is now much more striated and complex. A recent survey released by the Human Sciences Research Council shows that, in 1997, 47 percent of respondents described themselves in terms of racial categories. By 2000, the figure had fallen to only 12 percent (in the same period, references to gender- and class-related identities declined, while allusions to religious identity increased). What had been a fairly limited and predictable set of self-descriptions had given way to what the authors of the survey termed "a whole range of individual, personalized descriptions" (Klandermans, Roefs, and Olivier 2001). Another survey, "TrendYouth" (2005), which focused on black and white youth from emerging and affluent households in major metropolitan areas (and which included 2,400 face-to-face interviews and 30 focus groups), shows clothing brands to be the main ingredients in the development of a "new and clearer South African identity" and notes that the country's seven- to twenty-four-year-olds "are the most racially integrated [group] in the country, with friendships now based more on shared interests like music and fashion than on skin colour."

The K-Swiss ads underscore, on the one hand, that the cross-racial lifestyles of urban youth today, while strikingly different from those one might have encountered twenty years ago, still cite (or quote) a racially segregated past that remains in the collective memory; on the other hand, they reveal that, increasingly, "desegregation" takes place under the sign of a reinscribed "whiteness," this time elaborated around social class rather than race. Formerly, the ads state in no uncertain terms, you had to be white to adopt a particular lifestyle; now you have to know how to be stylish—stylish, that is, by K-Swiss's standards. What they don't say but of course imply is that you no longer have to be white, but you do have to be middle class, or at least you must find the money to buy products such as those celebrated in the ads. Increasingly, in fact, young people who are not middle class are buying *fong kong:* fake products available especially in the inner city that are cheaper versions of Y or loxion cultural style, thus enabling them to circumvent some of the restrictions of class and economic status.

Two further images, forming a paired advertisement, play on similar notions. Both are close-ups of men's faces, one black and one white. Together, they suggest a message that is at once subjective and "in your face." The visuals in the ads depend for their effect on the verbal text that accompanies each image, making the meaning of the paired images explicit and, again, distinctly in your face. The text in the first ad reads: "I HATE BEING BLACK. If it means some people think that they know my criminal record. My rhythm. My level of education. Or the role affirmative action has played in my career. I'm not someone else's black. I'm my own. And I LOVE BEING BLACK" (see figure 4). The second text reads: "I HATE BEING WHITE. If it means some people think that I'm not a real South African. That I'm racist. Privileged. Paranoid. Or Baas. I'm not someone else's white. I'm my own. And I LOVE BEING WHITE" (see figure 5). Taken together, these ads suggest an imperative that is both antiracist ("I hate being black"; "I hate being white") and prorace ("I love being black"; "I love being white"). The message they project is that the fact of being white or black becomes banal, that older meanings can be erased or evacuated in order to be able to inscribe onto the words *black* and *white* whatever meanings one wishes. Yet in the ads themselves, the racial habitus remains—at the same time as, socially, culturally and politically speaking, there are more possibilities for entering new racial spaces. While these ads appear to rely on the texts for their impact (as I first suggested above)—to domesticate the visual, as it were—one could also note that a visual medium itself is being used here to critique conventional notions of the image, to show the extent to which we rely on the verbal to narrate and explicate the visual.[23] Thus the ads stage a fascinating engagement with the nature of contemporary visuality.

As I remarked above, all of the ads aim to work toward what one could tentatively term "postracial" configurations, while also revealing the complexity of this task. The difficulty of it all is underscored by a striking feature of the adverts: they can simultaneously be seen to move beyond and to reconfirm the power of race in the contemporary public sphere of the city. A fine line is involved. The ads attempt to "soften" race and class difference by invoking the powerful notion of style, and in particular self-stylization. Working with the idea that "everyone" wants to be stylish—to wear good shoes, for example—the ads undercut a more "antagonistic" reading of race and class difference. As we have seen, they rely for their effect on citation or quotation of historical, political context. Simultaneously, they tap into deeper issues at stake relating to the psychic life of things. That is, they tap into the place things occupy in a given historical moment, what desires they organize, what fantasies they provoke, via what epistemologies they are assigned meaning—or, as Bill Brown (2003: 12) puts it, how they represent

4 and 5 Advertisements for Hansa beer. Courtesy of Hansa

us, comfort us, help us, change us. The psychic life of things activates deep impulses of desire that are commonly shared beyond race: it is these that the ads seek to draw out, rather than relying on less sophisticated technologies of race and class. The shift is made from a form of crude governmentality so characteristic of the apartheid period to a different sort of social potency, which displaces the terms of recognition. Earlier in this essay I considered some of the limits of a theory of "the gap." These ads return us not only to the gap of the social, which middle-class commodity cultures rely on in the very moment of aiming to bridge the gap of race, but also to how the gap (of desire) is continuously reconstituted at the heart of the commodity. For while the commodity seems to eliminate the gap, it must constantly reopen it in order to propel new desires—to sell itself.

Finally, it is worth considering the ads I have discussed above in relation to the history of consumerism and the production of the modern subject. In relation to the first, we might reflect on a long history of denial of Africans as consumers—either through their portrayal as eternally rural or as being objects of charity—that is, as receiving commodities rather than by purchasing them as modern subjects. Nick Green and Reg Lascaris (1988) show that early advertising in South Africa was aimed at the white settler. In the interwar years, there was a growing American presence in the South African economy rather than growing black participation in the market. In the 1930s, ads were aimed not at the black consumer but at the "black specifier" (the person who decides what is to be bought for his white employer). Also in the 1930s, black job seekers began to advertise themselves ("capable, clean houseboy, very quick and obliging, honest," read one ad in 1937). The latter implied an acceptance of race classification but also revealed new references to education. By 1957, a personal ad in the *Star* read: "Situation wanted: African undergraduate seeks position as clerk, general office work." By the late 1950s, the affordable transistor radio came to South Africa—and more and more black people made it a priority purchase. At this time, too, print media emerged aimed specifically at black readers (*Drum* magazine in 1951, *Bona* in 1956). Until the 1970s, Green and Lascaris observe (41), a "schizophrenic" marketing scene was in place in relation to black viewers, based on uncertainty whether (a) the black consumer would respond best to ads in black media, featuring black faces and black situations, with a message that had particular relevance for a black consumer (the assumption until then), or (b) would an ad aimed at an ostensibly white audience have such "aspirational pull" that black consumers would be irresistibly drawn into the target market? It was only in the late 1970s and early 1980s that marketers started to look at similarities between race groups rather than concentrating on the characteristics that divided them—with Brazil rather than the United States and Europe as their case study and reference point. It was then that the crossover market emerged with a vengeance, creating a system for marketing brands no longer based on race (though still revealing, in Green and Lascaris's terms, the realities of being black, white, and brown in South Africa today).

Consumerism is frequently equated with the production of the modern subject—an equal and modular citizen brought into being through the possession of mass-produced goods. What seems distinctive about post-apartheid South African consumerism (though its current crossover appeal could be seen to have taken root by the late 1980s) is that it seeks to recoup the modernist moment described above but to do so through prevailing postmodern technologies—and within an active cultural project of desegregation. Advertising, such as examples I have looked at above, emerges, then, as an attempt to give content to modernist subjectivity and to engage with ideas about citizenship—and South Africa's future.[24]

Conclusion

In the first part of this chapter, I showed that a study of Y Culture reveals the preoccupations of increasingly middle-class young black people in Johannesburg and the intricacy of their modes of self-making. The city itself becomes the engine for this self-stylizing. I have argued that the emergence of new stylizations of the self, embedded in cultures of the body, represents one of the most decisive shifts of the post-apartheid era. Integral to this shift, I have sought to show as well, is the use of a range of cultural texts, which, reframed within crossover media forms, become elements—accessories— in an aestheticization of the self. Foucault took self-stylization to be a process through which the "subject constitutes himself in an active fashion, by the practices of the self." For Foucault, self-styling implies an increased sense of singularity, performing a certain practice of freedom. I have used the notion in a similar fashion in this essay, in an effort to take youth cultures, and Y Culture in particular, beyond the problematic unidimensional types of readings to which they are typically subjected.

I argued that a notion of the gap remains central in cultural theory, while also testing its limits and the notion of translatability on which it relies, and vice versa. Increasingly, I suggested, what is needed is a theory of the circulation of forms, one that necessarily draws on technological analogies. I observed how consumer cultures (which draw on youth cultures such as Y/loxion kulcha) work to reopen the gap of desire. Thus we need a cultural theory of contemporary forms that takes the surfaces of form more seriously as an analytic construct, registers the limits of the gap, but that is simultaneously alert to the continual reopening of the gap as cultural forms and consumerism draw closer and closer together.

In the second half of the chapter, I considered ways in which a series of advertisements take up aspects of Y Culture's increasing remixing of race and attempt more explicitly to reconfigure race along the lines of the market. The market, here, comes to the fore as a powerful vector for calming racial passions in a setting characterized by the emergence of a politically empowered black middle class and the presence of a substantial white minority that holds considerable economic power and cultural clout. The market becomes an important place for projecting racial conviviality and therefore a sphere in which the idea of living together is experimented with. As an earlier discourse of nonracialism has increasingly shown its limits, the market begins to project ideas of race that rework that earlier discourse.[25]

The market and cultures addressed in this essay, I have made clear, are largely middle-class entities. Although it has not been my subject here, new work now needs to be done on the intersection of cultures of consumption and poverty in South Africa. There, no doubt, the question of the gap and its limits will prove more complex, more treacherous and, potentially, more productive still.

Notes

1 I draw here on the work of Dominique Malaquais, especially her introductory remarks to a special issue of *Politique Africaine* (2005), which she guest edited.

2 In his book *The Black Atlantic: Modernity and Double Consciousness* (1993), Gilroy introduces the idea of a transatlantic black culture—which he terms the "black Atlantic"—whose practices and ideas transcend both ethnicity and nationality. Black people, he argues, shaped a shared, transnational, diasporic culture, that in turn shaped the history of modernity. He explores this transatlanticism in black music and writing and reveals the shared contours of black and Jewish concepts of diaspora. Although he does not write about them in his book, both Brazil and South Africa partook of, and in turn helped to shape, this "black Atlantic culture."

3 Loxion Kulcha began with a collection of hand-knitted beanies (hats) that then grew into urban streetwear, mainly denims, printed T-shirts, and sports shoes. Recent designs include branded overalls and men's suits.

4 The name "Stoned Cherrie" plays on a series of puns and local references. "Stoned" refers in part to the violence of the 1980s in the townships but also to being high on marijuana. It may also refer to the pit (stone) of the cherry. "Cherrie" recalls the fruit of the same name but this particular spelling also refers to a slang term, originally from Afrikaans, meaning girl or woman or girlfriend. In 1965, for example, Casey Motsisi, writing in *Drum* magazine, wrote: "I had to invite that most fascinating cherie in this man's town, Sis Sharon with goo goo eyes." Thus the term Stoned Cherrie contains many resonances, including the retro term for young township girls of the 1950s and 1960s. It places the girl or woman at the center of its frame of reference but also stands for a general sense of having a good time.

5 I am grateful to Lindsay Bremner for her discussions with me on these points.

6 Private security at the Zone is less apparent than in regular malls around the city. CCTV cameras can sometimes be seen, but in general there are few security guards and the outdoor precincts are not secured as such.

7 I am grateful to Isabel Hofmeyr for our discussions on this point.

8 For example, one set of T-shirts is emblazoned with the word SHARPEVILLE! This is a reference to the notorious events of March 21, 1960, when thousands of Africans demonstrated against the pass-laws instituted by apartheid. It was a nonviolent demonstration but police killed sixty-nine people and wounded hundreds of others. Many view it as a turning point in the mounting struggle for liberation. The phrase also plays on the colloquialism *sharp*, which means "cool." It suggests that Jozi is a city with a past (a political struggle) but is also a cool place to be.

9 A pantsula is a young urban person (usually a black man) whose attitudes and behavior, especially his speech and dress, are of the most popular current fashion. The term is sometimes applied retrospectively to *tsotsis* (gangsters) of the 1950s who dressed in expensive clothing, particularly cuffed trousers, fine shoes, and a felt hat. More recently, a diversity of urban slang and sartorial styles has emerged.

10 Steve Biko was born in 1946 in King Williamstown, went to medical school in Natal, and was cofounder and first president of the all-black South African Students Organisation (SASO). Until then, the struggle against apartheid had been nonracial, but Biko asserted that black people had been psychologically affected by white racism and had internalized a sense of racial inferiority, and therefore that they needed to organize politically as a separate black group. Biko's aim was to raise "black consciousness" in South Africa. He was banned in 1973 and assassinated in detention by apartheid police in 1977. His political and personal legacy lives on, despite South Africa's negotiated transition to democracy in 1994.

11 The Web site www.urbandictionary.com defines *miss thang* as "a person who thinks they are, are, like so totally, like better than, like, you know everyone else,

like." In other words, a woman who thinks she's way too cool. *Brother man* would seem to speak for itself. *Jozi* is an increasingly popular term used by young residents of Johannesburg, referring not only to the city itself but to its surrounding townships, including Soweto and Alexandra.

12 Chakrabarty, n.d. "Historical Difference and the Logic of Capital: Towards a Different Marxism," manuscript. Quoted in Mazzarella 2003, 20.

13 Translatability emerges from the rise in the last decade or so of translation studies. The latter focuses on such issues as how the translation is connected to the "foreign text"; the relative autonomy of the translated text—and thus the impossibility of translation, since it is really a new text which is created; how the effects of translation are social, and have been harnessed to cultural, economic, and political agendas including colonial projects and the production of national literatures. Translation studies is beset by arguments between those who see language as hermeneutic and interpretative, opening up the gaps of meaning, and those who see it as communicative and instrumental, which seek equivalence with the original text. In sum, an analytics of the gap is at the heart of this work. See Venuti 2000.

14 *Zol* refers to a hand-rolled marijuana cigarette.

15 Dorothy Masuka (1935–) is a famous singer in Southern Africa who sang with the African Ink Spots and later with Miriam Makeba. She sang songs of political resistance that were banned in apartheid South Africa. She still sometimes performs in different parts of the world.

16 The way post-apartheid youth engage with the world has been shaped by often violent histories of international connection (through migration from elsewhere in Africa and the diffusion of British and American culture) and by the fact of apartheid South Africa's international isolation (as the figure of the grotesque in the colonial historical narrative and the international sanctions and boycotts that cut it off from the rest of the African continent).

17 In the April–May issue, the editors write: "Our relationship with black Americans is only by virtue of us all being African descendants. The reality is that their true ancestors, the slaves that crossed the ocean in the dungeons of those ships, were taken from the West Coast of the continent. We aren't preaching any anti-African-American theories. As much as we appreciate the music, there really is no need to patronize us" (April–May 2000, 52). Other instances in the magazine reveal that black South Africans turn to the apartheid struggle and explicitly not to slavery in the making of black identity. For a longer discussion of this, see Nuttall 2004b.

18 *YMag* was conceived by the YIRED publishers as a counterpart to *SL* magazine (*SL* stands for *Student Life*), which targets largely white but also crossover youth audiences. The intention was to overcome the dominant industry model, in which youth magazines targeted limited "readership ghettoes" in order to attract specialized advertising. The relationship between the two titles was initially conceived as a move toward establishing the first multiracial youth-oriented product to succeed in South Africa. *Y* and *SL* share irony and parody as dominant rhetorical modes as

well as crossover reviewing styles and the accessorization of media forms within a broader process of self-stylization. For a discussion of this, see Nuttall 2004b.

19 Cultural texts—books, for example—become forms of quotation: book reviews attest to the constant dismembering of the book, harnessed to specific textual genres as readers, reviewers, and magazine publics exercise the capacity to choose and discard: the book loses its supposed autonomy, its power as a self-contained artifact: there is no book in and of itself but only a textual fragment in the technological constitution of the self. For a more detailed analysis, see Nuttall 2004b.

20 This is a term one has to use with caution. I do so here to signal that while South Africa in general is not a postracial society, aspects of its culture are experimenting with spaces one could tentatively refer to in this way, in that the imperative, driven increasingly by what is patently a cross-racial market for goods, is that race no longer signifies as it did before, and that class, based on money, increasingly structures certain kinds of social relations. This is not to say that race doesn't—and won't in future—reassert itself in unexpected ways.

21 It is fascinating to compare these ads with those discussed by Eve Bertelsen (1998), which appeared in the years of the mid-1990s, immediately after political transition, as a measure of how much has changed in the public discourse of nation-building and identity. An ad for shoes is accompanied by the text: "When a new nation stands on its feet . . . ," while an ad for milk contains the text, "Why cry over spilt milk, when we can build a healthy nation." For a detailed analysis, see Bertelsen 1998.

22 Telephone interview with K-Swiss manager, Jeremy Nel, April 2005.

23 I am grateful to Dilip Gaonkar and Ackbar Abbas for their comments along these lines at a summer institute, Media Cultures, Everyday Life and Cultures of Consumption, held at Hong Kong University in June 2005.

24 I am very grateful to Isabel Hofmeyr for her discussion of these ideas with me.

25 *Nonracialism,* a term used widely during the antiapartheid struggle and intended to signify the idea of a society freed from the credo of race, has faded from public political discourse in the 1990s and after, as the politics of black empowerment have moved center stage and have played an important role in shifting inherited institutional power structures. This has occurred at the same time as many more choices have become available to people in terms of racial identification, especially in metropolitan centers and in the sphere of culture.

> If you know Joh'burg, the sound of a half-brick
> rattling against a policeman's helmet tells you everything.
>
> HERMAN CHARLES BOSMAN (1994: 568)

4 ⊹ Gandhi, Mandela, and the African Modern

JONATHAN HYSLOP

Sometime in the early 1930s, a Johannesburg shop owner called Fanny Klennerman imported the first copies of James Joyce's *Ulysses* ever brought to South Africa for sale at her Vanguard Booksellers. The book, originally published in 1922, had been suppressed in every major English-speaking country, and Klennerman seems to have imported the edition produced in Paris by Odyssey Press in 1932. Klennerman positioned herself at the cutting edge of metropolitan modernity. Born in Russia, she had come to South Africa as a child, attended university in Cape Town, moved to Joburg, organized white and black workers in trade unions during the mid-1920s, and been expelled from the Communist Party for Trotskyist "deviations" (Klennerman n.d.; Drew 2002). The name of her bookshop announced her purposes in life; she saw herself both as a revolutionary, as part of a political vanguard; and as a member of a cultural avant-garde, as part of the modernist movement of which Joyce's book was the English language's ultimate literary product. Klennerman had remarkably close links to New York publishing, which with her modernist eye, she recognized as the cutting edge of English language literary culture, while her fellow Joburg booksellers were still London-focused. She was proud of importing Random House's beautifully produced Modern Library series and the leading journals of the New York intelligentsia such as *New Masses* and *Partisan Review*. In the 1930s she took guidance on what to stock from *New Masses,* which, although edited by the grimly Stalinist Mike Gold, managed to attract contributions by many of America's most innovative writers. *Partisan Review,* which Klennerman stocked in the 1940s, was a hugely influential journal, but had a print run of only 6,000 copies per edition, so it is extraordinary that it should have had a following as far afield as Johannesburg. *Partisan Review* published original work by writers of the caliber of W. H. Auden, T. S. Eliot, George Orwell, John Dewey, Hannah Arendt, Edmund Wilson, Saul Bellow, and Mary McCarthy, as well as some of the first English translations of the French existentialists (Phillips and Rahv 1946; Buhle 1987). (Its leftish but anti-Stalinist politics was presumably congenial to Fanny.) To an astonishing extent, Klennerman succeeded in her project, through the 1930s and 1940s. Though she had little direct political influence, her immense bibliographic knowledge made her indispensable to the political activists, artists, and intellectuals of the city. And on Saturday afternoons, the shop became a haven of nonracial creative energies in a fiercely segregated city. In the upstairs rooms, poems were written and clandestine love affairs were conducted. Downstairs, self-appointed critics gave their opinions on their friends' new literary productions. Among the shop assistants at Vanguard was Willie "Bloke" Modisane, who was to become one of the finest of the *Drum* writers of the 1950s, and regular visitors included young Nadine Gordimer (Stein and Jacobson 1986).

I begin my account of Johannesburg history with Klennerman's bookshop partly because I want to draw on Joyce's book for the guiding theme of my discussion of the city's politics. More substantially, though, Klennerman exemplifies the way in which the story of Johannesburg is also part of the story of modernity and modernist culture. When I use the terms *modern* and *modernist,* I follow Marshall Berman (1982: 345):

> To be modern . . . is to experience personal and social life as a maelstrom, to find one's world and oneself in perpetual disintegration and renewal, trouble and anguish, ambiguity and contradiction: to be part of a universe in which all that is solid melts into air. To be a modern*ist* is to make oneself somehow at home in the maelstrom, to make its rhythms one's own, to move within its currents in search of reality, of beauty, of freedom, of justice, that its fervid and perilous flow allows.

As a modernist city, Johannesburg was a place of uncertainty and disintegration, but also a place that stimulated the search for the possibilities of freedom. It was a city of ideas: a place where notions of "reality, beauty, freedom, and justice" were explored: and nowhere was this done more energetically than among the shelves of Klennerman's bookshop.

In Georg Simmel's work, which forms a useful point of departure for my thoughts about the city in this chapter, the metropolis is characterized by, among other things, its extension in time and space, the experience of hyperstimulation, reshapings of the self which produce new forms of intellectuality, and by the presence of the "stranger." In Simmel's (1950a: 419) words, "The most significant characteristic of the metropolis is the functional extension beyond its physical boundaries . . . a city consists of its total effects which extend beyond its immediate confines. Only this range is the city's actual effect in which its existence is expressed." The metropolis, through its connections with other metropolises, provides a space in which not only the confines of rural life, but also the limits of national political frameworks can be ruptured. Simmel argues that the emotional hyperstimulation of the metropolis acts as a prompting to self-definition, both from the desire to escape from anonymity and from the need to cope with the demands of city life. This leads the dweller in the metropolis to react through an intensification of intellectuality that protects him against the "threatening currents and discrepancies of the external environment which would uproot him" (Simmel 1950a: 410). This defense of a self is productive of new forms of creativity: intellectuality "preserve[s] subjective life against the overwhelming power of metropolitan life, and . . . branches out in many directions" (411). A particular role in the intellectual ferment of the city is played by the stranger. Simmel (1950b: 405) points out that there is something in the much-decried notion of the "outside agitator"; "it is an exaggeration of the role of the stranger: he is freer, politically and theoretically; he surveys conditions with less prejudice; his criteria for them are more general and more objective ideals; he is not tied down in his actions by habit, piety and precedent."

Johannesburg was modern and metropolitan from the first. It burst into existence in 1886 as a mining camp, with no other purpose than the production of gold. This initial focus on a single commodity gave it an extraordinarily turbulent character. Four years later the town nearly collapsed because of difficulties in extracting gold from the ore. But technological innovations made it bounce back to become a city of 100,000 people within ten years of its foundation. The struggle between Boers and British over control of the gold fields produced a major international incident—the Jameson Raid—in 1896 and a major war between 1899 and 1902. The city's initial population came from the ends of the earth: miners from Mozambique, Nyasaland, Cornwall, and Australia; artisans and engineers from Scotland; storekeepers from Lithuania and Gujarat; financiers from England and Germany.

Between 1904 and 1907, Chinese workers were brought to the mines on a huge scale. In the subsequent decades came black mineworkers from Basutoland, Zululand, and Pondoland; impoverished rural Afrikaners; refugees from Eastern Europe and migrants from Greece and Portugal. These populations were not initially clearly segregated, and the process of creation of a city spatially divided by race took many years of labor by racist bureaucrats, and contained within it many ebbs and flows. By the end of the 1930s, the metropolis had a population of half a million. It was not only these flows of people that connected this city to the outside world. From the second year of its existence, the telegraph connected Johannesburg to the outside; the economic upheavals of the Rand impacted instantaneously on the London stock exchange, and investment decisions in London reverberated in Johannesburg just as fast. And the city was marked physically by international cultural trends. The city center's buildings were a mixture of styles ranging from the Victorian to the Edwardian to Chicago steel frame construction. In the 1930s the city acquired one of the world's major concentrations of art deco buildings, and a few notable examples of Modern Movement architecture (van Onselen 1982; Mandy 1984; Chipkin 1993). Johannesburg was always, then, in Simmel's sense a metropolis: its "functional extension," the range of its "actual effects" traversed the world.

Of course this city was characterized by extreme social inequalities, turmoil and conflict. Grotesque juxtapositions of affluence and penury, horrific living conditions in slum yards and mine compounds, the prevalence of industrial and epidemic disease, and violent repression of political and social protest, were all constant themes in the first six decades of Johannesburg's history. But it was this very extremity that made its experience of modernity productive of modernist cultural and political creativity. In a city where everybody came from somewhere else, social arrangements had to be constructed from scratch and everything was up for grabs. There was no sense of stability; life really was experienced as a maelstrom. As in Berman's appropriation of Marx, all that was solid in the previous experience of the migrants and immigrants did indeed melt into air. Yet it was exactly out of the destructiveness of this environment that its potential for renewal came. People did find ways of making themselves at home in the maelstrom, and of finding new pathways to freedom within it. In few other places did the environment uproot the individual as comprehensively as in Joburg, and consequently the need for new forms of intellectuality was particularly acute. And, in a city initially composed entirely of "strangers," there was an extraordinary range of outsiders able to generate new ideas. Klennerman was just one of them; her work shows the way in which the Joburg model linked to other metropolitan experiences, and how this opened new possibilities of freedom.

Fanny Klennerman, then, was a devoted but largely unknown pursuer of a modernist project. But in this chapter I will suggest that the two most globally significant and famous individuals to move on the Johannesburg stage in the twentieth century were also in important senses products of the peculiarly modern milieu which this particular metropolis created: namely Mohandas Karamchand Gandhi and Nelson Rolihlahla Mandela. They can both be understood, I will suggest, as practitioners of forms of modernist politics that Johannesburg made possible.

To think about Gandhi and Mandela in their Johannesburg setting, though, is immediately to pose the problem of the relation between the metropolis and nationalism. Gandhi and Mandela both owe their fame to their success as leaders of nationalist movements. Yet their global appeal is rooted in their transcendence of narrow nationalism. They are admired internationally for the way that they created national visions that were inclusive, rising above the cleavages of race, religion, and status, and for the way in which their moral stances appealed to humanistic values that had international relevance beyond the immediate concerns of their own political constituencies. Historically, nationalist movements have typically been the project of urban intellectuals and have been made possible by experiences rooted in urban life and by knowledge of international developments. Yet the need for nationalists to represent the movements they initiate as popular have constantly led them to invocations of the spirit of the rural; the village is inevitably invoked as embodying the nation, and this leads to a denigration of the very urban conditions that have produced the new political form. Nationalism is pulled between the discursive triangle of racial and ethnic particularisms, unitary nationalism, and universalism. The very idea of the right to "national self-determination" is grounded on an appeal to universal rights and foreign examples. But the self-regard that nationalism involves necessarily leads to an emphasis on the supposed unique national virtues of "our" nation. While nations are supposed to confer citizenship on all within their boundaries if they are to meet universal standards of human rights, in reality the call of racial or ethnic particularism frequently constitutes an effective mobilizing tool for political leaders, making for a politics where some of those within the boundaries of the state are "true" citizens and others are not.

Gandhi and Mandela both contended heroically to create inclusive nationalisms founded on universalist values. But they did not, as we shall see, fully evade these contradictions. And the representation of their lives has, through the same logic, not escaped a significant distortion of the role of the Johannesburg metropolis. Gandhi's emphasis on rural virtues and Mandela's invocation of his chiefly heritage among the Thembu have crucially shaped how they are understood. In accounts of Gandhi's life, his time in South Africa is commonly de-emphasized and his connection to Indian religious tradition foregrounded. In accounts of Mandela, his awareness of resistance to colonial conquest is often stressed, as is the oppressiveness of the Johannesburg he lived in. In this essay, I will argue that their remarkable politics were products not so much of their connections to the rural hinterlands of their respective countries, but rather of markedly metropolitan and cosmopolitan experiences.

Resistance to viewing Johannesburg as metropolitan and modern is likely to be based on a certain kind of reading of nationalist politics and liberation movements. Here I want to turn back to Joyce's *Ulysses*. For the treatment of nationalism in his book is of significance for understanding that phenomenon in South Africa and elsewhere. *Ulysses* follows the movement of Joyce's protagonists, Bloom and Stephen Daedalus, through Dublin on a single day, June 16, 1904, its structure paralleling the mythic journey across the world of Odysseus. Joyce strives for the complexity of language adequate to grasping the experience of a great metropolis.

Joyce mounts a critical, modernist attack on simplistic nationalisms. In the Odysseus myth, the Cyclops, a giant with a single eye in the center of his forehead, holds Odysseus and his crew prisoner in his cave and begins to devour them two by two. Odysseus and his surviving crew escape after driving a stake into the giant's eye. In Joyce's novel, the cave is replaced with the gloom of Barney Kiernan's pub and the giant by one of the customers, a nationalist bigot called the Citizen. For Joyce, the extreme nationalist is metaphorically one-eyed; he can see only from the single viewpoint of his fanaticism. The clichéd language of the nationalist hack is brilliantly exposed by Joyce in this passage. The Citizen is implicitly contrasted with the two-eyed cosmopolitan empathy exemplified in the novel by Bloom. This is not to say that Joyce dismisses nationalism. The nationalist sees an aspect of reality, but he is not able to relativize it or balance it with other dimensions of reality. The uncritical nationalist sees only with one eye and thus must understand the world without perspective. Bloom, by contrast, sees the ambiguity and complexity of the world.

This conflict has a tragic character. Modern nationalism emerges from the metropolis and its cosmopolitanism. But the tendency of the logic of national identity is to deny these origins. The urban comes to be represented as less truly national than the rural. The metropolitan nature of the making of modernist politics is denied. Ultimately the Cyclops wins out.

What, then, does Joyce offer against the clichés of nation? In the most quoted passage of the book, Stephen Daedalus is talking to the headmaster, Mr. Deasey, an upholder of the official history propagated by state and church:

> —History, Stephen said, is a nightmare from which I am trying to awake.
> From the playfield the boys raised a shout. A whirring whistle: goal. What if the nightmare gave you a back kick.
> —The ways of the Creator are not our ways, Mr Deasey said. All history moves toward one great goal, the manifestation of God.
> Stephen jerked his thumb towards the window, saying
> —That is God.
> Hooray! Ay! Whree!
> —What? Mr Deasey asked.
> A shout in the street, Stephen answered, and shrugged his shoulders.

As Marshall Berman (1982: 316–17) argues, what Stephen is saying is that if God is anywhere, it is not in the repressive myths of nation and religion but in the "life and energy and affirmation" that is modern and yet "radically opposed to the forms and motions of the modern world" and which expresses itself in the everyday life of the streets. In Berman's words, the street is experienced as "the medium in which the totality of modern material and spiritual forces could meet, clash, interfuse and work out their fates."

What I want to suggest then, is that when the metropolis generates new political forms, it is pulled between the one-eyed nationalism of the Cyclops and the modernist relativism of Bloom; between the nightmare history of ambitious nation-states in the making, and the creative rebellious energies of the street.

Although some time was to elapse between the publication of *Ulysses* and Eamon de Valera's creation in the south of Ireland of a sectarian Catholic state, facing off against the oppressive Protestant enclave in the north, Joyce could see that Ireland was already well along that road. Intellectuals of Protestant background had played a prominent role in turn-of-the-century Irish nationalism. But the clash of civil war led to an increasingly

Catholic-sectarian construction of the nation. Joyce knew that it was not the humane, cosmopolitan Bloom but the monstrous Citizen/Cyclops who had won their clash.

M. K. Gandhi at the Hamidia Mosque

Let us then turn to our main protagonists and explore their battles with the nationalist Cyclops. On January 10, 1908, Mohandas Gandhi addressed a crowd of supporters at Johannesburg's Hamidia Mosque. The mass meeting took place during a recess in Gandhi's trial. He had been brought to court for his role in leading the Indian migrants of the city in a campaign of refusal to register with the government in terms of legislation they saw as the harbinger of new forms of racial discrimination. Later that day, Gandhi would go to jail for the first time. Gandhi was not yet the world-famous, dhoti-clad Mahatma. He was a starch-collared, besuited figure, and one of the higher-earning lawyers in the city. Although he was a Hindu, his meeting was taking place in a mosque. His leading supporters were Muslim, but they also included Parsis, Christians, and Chinese. Gandhi was a man of high caste from Gujarat, but a substantial number of those present at the meeting were low-caste Tamil- and Telegu-speaking southerners. Gandhi was at that very moment beginning to generate a notion of Indian identity that cut through the barriers of religion, class, caste, and language (Swan 1985; Itzkin 2001). Although he was creating a nationalism, it was one linked to a humanistic universalism and one that recognized its debt to diverse sources. As Gandhi was himself to acknowledge, in the development of his philosophy, the key role was being played by a small group of Jewish intellectuals steeped in a syncretic mystical cult.

Gandhi, in my view, was able to create his politics, later to be put into world-transforming effect, uniquely in the context of Johannesburg. Given his later exaltation of village life and peasant craftsmanship, this may seem a bizarre claim. Yet I will show that the metropolitan context of Johannesburg enabled Gandhi to generate both nationalism and a universalism, and an effective approach to political mobilization, in a way that contemporary political leaders in India itself failed to do.

In an incisive study of biographical writing on Gandhi, Claude Markovits (2003) has pointed out that most Gandhi scholarship gives little attention to his two decades (1893–1914) in South Africa. Markovits (2003: 79) rightly notes that, strangely, it was in the apparently oppressive context of South Africa that "Gandhi blossomed in a way he would probably not have, had he stayed in Rajkot." But Markovits's point requires refinement. For although Gandhi did indeed gain in professional skill and confidence in his Durban years, before the Boer War, all the decisive developments in Gandhi's thought and politics took place in the metropolitan context of Johannesburg, between the end of that war and the beginning of the First World War.

When Gandhi published his autobiography, he famously titled it *The Story of My Experiments with Truth.* The most important of those experiments took place in a mining town not obviously associated with that virtue. How did this come about?

The sociopolitical context of Indians in Johannesburg was strikingly different than anywhere else. In India itself, the creation of a unified political identity faced seemingly insuperable social cleavages. The Indian National Congress had been an elite and gradualist movement. Though the crisis over Lord Curzon's partition of Bengal had recently and for the first time produced both modern mass mobilization and terrorist resistance against the British, this was largely confined to Hindus within the boundaries of Bengal. In Natal, the Indian political activity of the 1890s had been among Gujarati Muslim merchants, an elite stratum of society in relation to the predominantly Hindu southerners who constituted the "coolie" labor force on the plantations. When Gandhi came to Natal in 1893, it was as the legal representative of these merchants, who had hired him precisely to defend their social privileges. For example, one of Gandhi's early legal fights involved an unsuccessful attempt to save Indian property-qualified access to the franchise—something that would benefit only the very wealthiest merchants (Swan 1985: 83; Markovits 2003: 3–4, 80–84). Gandhi was at this time strongly loyal to Britain, mobilizing an Indian ambulance corps in the Boer War. His Natal years made him into an effective lawyer, but not into the political leader he wanted to become.

In the postwar years, when he moved his base of operations to Johannesburg, Gandhi found himself in a very different situation. Whereas the Indians of Natal were widely dispersed across the colony, the large majority of those of the Transvaal were concentrated around Johannesburg. Where Natal was an administratively and economically weak structure run by a bumbling plantocracy, in the Transvaal Lord Milner had created a brutally contemporary bureaucracy that was busy using the wealth generated by the greatest mining center on earth to remold the city of Johannesburg through authoritarian planning. Milner's bureaucrats treated the Indians with an indifference to people that contrasted with the equally racist but more paternalistic style of Natal. The nature of the Indian experience in Johannesburg is suggested by the events of 1904. Bubonic plague broke out in the "Coolie Location," the predominantly Indian slum area west of the city center. Gandhi and a group of volunteers heroically tended the victims. The administration's response was to permanently evacuate the entire population of the area to a bleak and isolated site south of the city, burn the location to the ground, and rebuild the area as an industrial site. When settler authorities began to take over the Transvaal administration from the imperial power, the rigor of the administrative process simply continued and intensified. The obnoxious legislation on Indians introduced in 1906 did not differentiate between strata within the Indian community. Concentrated in the city, the Indians found themselves in a common situation, faced by draconian measures that cut across their various ethnic, religious, and social divisions. Migration had ripped up people from their context and juxtaposed them in a dramatic way. Muslim merchants with origins in almost every part of India (although predominantly Gujarat), Tamil and Telegu small traders, and low-caste laborers lived in close proximity, and all faced common problems.

Gandhi's political genius was to find a language that would speak to this common situation. But it was a genius that seized on the discursive materials that presented themselves in the metropolitan context. His campaign was initially built through the organizational work of the Hamidia Islamic Society, an organization centered on the Mosque, led by H. O. Ally and Haji Habib. Ironically, the society was named after the then-sultan of Turkey, Abdul Hamid II, who was notorious for his persecutions of his non-Muslim subjects. But Ally and Habib proved willing and able to reach out to Hindus, Parsis, and Christians. This collaboration was in fact central to the evolution of the concept of *satyagraha* (soul force, sometimes misleadingly rendered as "passive resistance") by Gandhi. At the very first public meeting of the antiregistration campaign in 1906, it was not Gandhi but Habib who called on the audience to take a sacred oath to go to jail rather than to accept the oppressive law. Gandhi, initially surprised, accepted the idea, which provided the germ of his lifetime political strategy (Swan 1985: 119–22). It could almost then be said that Islamic conceptions of sanctified struggle were a source of Gandhianism—not a connection that chimes in with the stereotypes of the present. Through his experience in Johannesburg, Gandhi, the high-caste Hindu, embraced Muslims, low-caste Hindus, and others as fellow Indians in a way that social boundaries would have made it much harder to do at home. India was most decisively imagined in Johannesburg.

Meanwhile, Gandhi's philosophical and religious formation took place in Johannesburg in a notably cosmopolitan way, through his association with a group of mainly Jewish intellectuals who were fascinated by both Eastern religion and Western critiques of contemporary society. They became Gandhi's followers, but their ideas powerfully affected his thinking. The most important of these individuals were H. S. L. Polak from England, Hermann Kallenbach from Germany, and Gandhi's young secretary, Sonia Schlesin (Chaterjee 1992). It was Polak who gave Gandhi John Ruskin's *Unto This Last* to read on a train trip in 1904. Ruskin's condemnation of Victorian industrial civilization became central to Gandhi's critique of industrialism. It directly inspired his lifelong experiments with communal living, beginning with the Phoenix settlement in Natal and Tolstoy Farm near Johannesburg (Chaterjee 1992: 42).

Even more striking, however, is that it was through his discussions with these "Western" mystics that Gandhi fully engaged with Indian religious thought. Before coming to Johannesburg, Gandhi had had only a passing interest in Hinduism and had not seriously studied its sacred language, Sanskrit. But Kallenbach, Polak, and their associates were intrigued by Asian religion. This interest had developed through their involvement with Theosophy, a now largely forgotten religious trend, but one that attained great international influence at the turn of the century. Theosophy was constructed in the 1870s and 1880s by the Russian Helena Blavatsky and her American disciple Colonel Henry Steele Olcott. Although Blavatsky's writings are so turgid as to be reader-proof, she made two simple moves that had huge appeal for late-nineteenth-century Western intellectuals. She endorsed spiritualism (communication with the dead) and linked it with spirituality—a mysticism that invoked the East as an antithesis to the supposedly materialist West. Buddhism and Hinduism were celebrated by Blavatsky and Olcott as the most evolved religious forms. To those discontented with the hubristic pretensions of science and the bureaucratic sociopolitical order emerging in Europe and North America, this advocacy of the non-Western and the mystical was compelling (Van der Veer 2001: 55–58). Theosophists were also in the market for the ideas of another sage. The Bengali Swami Vivekananda played a major part in popularizing Eastern religion in the West. Vivekananda elaborated a doctrine that portrayed Christianity and Judaism as lesser versions of the same theology found in Vedantic Hinduism, thus providing those raised in the Western faiths with a conceptual bridge to Hinduism. In 1893, Vivekananda traveled from India to Chicago, where a World's Fair was in progress, and represented Hinduism there at a "World Parliament of Religions." His speeches there evoked tremendous interest in America and internationally. Vivekananda also, during this trip, initiated the teaching of yoga in the West, by codifying particular practices and doctrines for classes he gave to Americans in Brooklyn (Van der Veer 2001: 68–69). Thus Blavatsky, Olcott, and Vivekananda successfully packaged Hindu and Buddhist ideas for international consumption. But their work had more directly political implications. Theosophy, although overtly apolitical, by viewing the East as spiritually more developed than the West, implicitly relativized occidental achievements and was therefore proved especially congenial to western critics of their own societies. And Vivekananda was overtly anticolonial (Van der Veer 2001: 74–77).

It was in the course of his Johannesburg discussions with the Theosophists that Gandhi for the first time was inspired to study the *Bhagavad Gita* seriously. Initially he read it in English translation, before going on to teach himself Sanskrit (Gandhi 1957: 263–64). Gandhi became so devoted to the *Bhagavad Gita* that his advocacy of it played a major role in it becoming the fundamental text of twentieth-century Hinduism, a status it had not previously enjoyed (Van der Veer 1994: 113). It was also in talking with the Theosophists that Gandhi became interested in Vivekananda's work. During Gandhi's 1908 imprisonment in the Johannesburg Fort, he was able to synthesize his recent experiences and his reading of the *Bhagavad Gita,* Vivekananda, Ruskin and other religious and literary texts to formulate the notion of satyagraha (Swan 1985: 167–68). The ideology that steered the Indian nationalist movement was a product of the unique circumstances of Johannesburg.

Tragically, Gandhi, despite his extraordinary commitment to a unified India embracing all its peoples, did not succeed. The unity that was created around the Hamidia Mosque by a smart city lawyer was not maintained on the larger stage of the Indian nation by a saintly Mahatma, as M. A. Jinnah led South Asia's Muslims in a separatist direction. And Gandhi's role here was particularly tragic. He was powerfully committed to Hindu-Muslim unity, but in seeking to mobilize the Indian people, he adopted a cultural style of religious asceticism and village life that was distinctively Hindu. This made it all too easy for Muslim sectarians to portray his movement as Hindu and for Hindu fundamentalists to equate Indian-ness with Hinduism (Van der Veer 1994: 94–95). Absolutely against Gandhi's will, and despite great heroism on his part on behalf of persecuted Muslims, his movement divided along sectarian lines. In the end he was dragged into the Cyclops's cave.

Nelson Mandela at the Bantu Men's Social Centre

At Easter 1944, a group of young men (and one woman, Albertina Sisulu) met at Johannesburg's Bantu Men's Social Centre (BMSC). Among them were an estate agent, Walter Sisulu; a teacher, Oliver Tambo; and an aspirant lawyer, Nelson Mandela. They proceeded to form the African National Congress Youth League, aimed at injecting militancy and radicalism into the three-decades-old, but decrepit and cautious ANC. This was of course a crucial moment in South Africa's revolutionary history; by 1949 these young Turks would capture control of the ANC and lead it into its campaigns of peaceful resistance in the 1950s and armed struggle from the 1960s (T. Lodge 1983: 20–30).

Yet a number of paradoxes about the 1944 meeting are striking in relation to Nelson Mandela's later politics. At that meeting, Mandela was under the sway of a brilliant young ideologue of African nationalism, Anton Lembede. Though Mandela would go down in history as the great reconciler across racial boundaries, the ANCYL of 1944 declared themselves Africanists, excluding whites from a future free state. Indians were also not to be participants in the new nation, yet within a few years, the ANCYL leaders would not only work with Indian activists but also become deeply influenced by Gandhian ideas. Mandela and Tambo would, in their future struggles, develop close working relationships with Communists, yet Lembede and his disciples rejected all "foreign" ideologies.

How then did Mandela's politics take on a very different form? I want to suggest that it was through the way he worked out his metropolitan experience. Mandela's respect for tradition and his sense of authority are often, and with some justification, placed in the context of his origins as a scion of the chiefly house of the Thembu. But less recognized is that he first came to Johannesburg, at the beginning of the 1940s, as a rebel against custom and tradition, grabbing for the personal freedom of the metropolis. After growing up in the rural Eastern Cape and attending university in the small town of Alice, Mandela had faced an arranged marriage, ordered by the Regent of the Thembu. Mandela, whose education had exposed him to different conceptions of marriage, revolted in the name of a modernist individualism: "I was a romantic and I was not prepared to have anyone, even the regent, select a bride for me" (Mandela 1995: 52). With a relative who was in a similar situation, Mandela left for Johannesburg. He was not then an uncritical traditionalist, but rather a young man with distinctly metropolitan aspirations.

Despite the oppressive racial order that he was to face in the city, Mandela reveled in its modernist promise. As the car in which he was traveling approached Johannesburg through the night, he saw its lights ahead: "Electricity to me had always been a novelty and a luxury, and here was a vast landscape of electricity, a city of light. I was terribly excited to see the city I had been hearing about since I was a child. Johannesburg had always been depicted as a city of dreams, a place where one could transform oneself from a poor peasant to wealthy sophisticate, a city of danger and opportunity" (Mandela 1995: 56). Mandela never lost his taste for the cosmopolitan glamour of the city. He loved its 1940s world of swing bands and dance. When, later in the 1940s, he began to attain some success as a lawyer, he bought an Oldsmobile and ordered a suit from the city's leading tailor (Sampson 2003: 58–59). One basis then for Mandela's transcendence of the Cyclops nationalism of Lembede lies in a personal and cultural empathy with a metropolitan style that predisposed him against a continuing association with Lembede's indigenism.

The style Mandela adopted was notably Americanized. There has been a remarkable duality in black Johannesburgers' historical relationship with the United States. From the presidency of Truman to that of the elder Bush, the de facto support of successive American administrations for white minority governments in South Africa produced a visceral political anti-Americanism. Yet this was accompanied by a continuous, deep devotion to the emulation of American cultural styles, from the era of swing bands to that of hip-hop. The bands that Mandela followed modeled themselves on American stars like Duke Ellington and Glen Miller; the clothing and cars that Mandela and fashionable black youth aspired to were those they saw in Hollywood movies. At the level of self-styling, America represented personal freedom: one of the bands Mandela was associated with was the Manhattan Brothers, and a notable township gang of the era called itself the Americans.

An important conduit for American influence on black intellectuals was the BMSC. Located at the southern end of bustling Eloff Street, the city's main shopping thoroughfare, the center comprised a two-story building, in-

cluding a hall that was the venue for dances, concerts, theatricals, and meetings. It was conveniently placed for central Johannesburg office workers:
Sisulu and Mandela were among those who dropped in regularly. The center
had been founded in 1921 by the Reverend Ray Phillips, an American missionary, as a rather conscious attempt to moralize the leisure time of black
men in Johannesburg. It was well funded and in particular had a substantial
library founded by the Carnegie Corporation. But the agency of the users
of the center took them, during the 1930s and 1940s, well beyond the kind of
political quietism that Rev. Phillips envisaged (Couzens 1983). The kind of
ideological shifts that took place in the center, and the centrality of African
American influences to that process, were captured by the young black man,
Peter Abrahams, who came there in 1936. As he entered, he heard a voice
singing on the gramophone: "That was a black man, one of us! I knew it.
I needed no proof. The men about me, their faces, their bearing all carried
the proof" (Abrahams 1981: 192). The singer was Paul Robeson. Abrahams
then found a section of "American Negro Literature" on the shelves of the
center. He took down W. E. B. Du Bois's *The Souls of Black Folk,* and it proved
a life-transforming experience: "Du Bois might have been writing about
my land and my people. The mood and feeling he described was native to
me" (193). Abrahams spent all his leisure time in the next few months at the
BMSC, working through the African American writers in the center's library.
"I became a nationalist, a colour nationalist, through the writings of men
and women who lived a world away from me" (197).

For the members of the BMSC, African America provided a fiercely attractive model of selfhood, combining modernity with defiance of racial
power (Nixon 1994: 43–76). Their exemplars were black Americans whose
sporting or cultural achievements had incorporated implicit or explicit
statements of political identity. Soon after the African American intellectual Ralph J. Bunche had stayed at the BMSC during a 1938 visit to the city, he
wrote to Robeson: "Paul, you are surely an idol of the Bantu . . . when one
mentions American Negroes they all chorus 'Paul Robeson and Joe Louis'—
the more sophisticated may also add Jesse Owens and Duke [Ellington]"
(quoted in Edgar 1992: 23). African America was thus essential both to giving black Johannesburg a sense that modernity and racial liberation could
be organically linked, and in providing the city's intellectuals and politicians with discursive weapons through which inequality could be attacked.
This American modernist strand was important in Mandela's development,
for the style he adopted as a political leader in the late 1940s and 1950s was

far from the sentimentalization of tradition advocated by Lembede. This style, I would suggest, helped produce a Mandela who could look outward, beyond the verities of one-eyed nationalism.

The evolution of Mandela's political strategy was centrally connected to the cosmopolitanism of Joburg, and indeed to its Gandhian and Indian linkages. With the formation of the ANCYL, Mandela and his associates were casting around for an effective political strategy. In 1946, a Communist doctor of Gujarati descent, Yusuf Dadoo, led a campaign of resistance by the Johannesburg Indian community against racist property legislation, using volunteers who were willing to go to jail to defy the law. The campaign was explicitly based on Gandhian principles. Up to this time, Mandela had generally accepted Lembede's anti-Indian bias. But now he came to see Dadoo's campaign as exemplary and as a political model for the ANC, having "witnessed the Indian people register an extraordinary protest against colour oppression in a way that Africans and the ANC had not . . . If I had once questioned the willingness of the Indian community to protest against oppression, I no longer could" (Mandela 1995: 97). When Mandela and his cohort won the leadership of the ANC in 1949, they consciously modeled the strategy they adopted, and which was put into practice in the mass resistance movements of the early 1950s, on what they had learned from Dadoo's campaign.

Dadoo's political trajectory and his consequent ability to influence the ANC derived from the particular transnationalism of Johannesburg's history. Born in nearby Krugersdorp in 1909, Dadoo came from a family that had personal links with Gandhi. In 1920 Gandhi had, from India, intervened on behalf of Dadoo's father when the Krugersdorp municipality tried to evict him from his property. During the 1920s, Yusuf was sent to school in India. He was influenced by the nationalist agitation of the time and met Gandhi, on whom he made a favorable impression. After qualifying in medicine in the United Kingdom during the 1930s, Dadoo returned to South Africa and became active in the Communist Party of South Africa. What is striking about Dadoo's 1946 campaign is that though he was to develop a reputation as a very "orthodox" Communist, his actions in this period reflected more of the Gandhian than of the Communist influences on him. During the traumas of independence and partition in 1946–48, the Communist Party of India took an extremely hostile stance toward the nationalist movement. Turning against Gandhi and Nehru, the CPI went so far as to dismiss the attainment of political freedom as insignificant. Yet in the same period, Dadoo not only conducted his activities along Gandhian lines but was effusive in his praise of Gandhi (Raman 2004). He thus acted as a reviver of Johannesburg-invented forms of Indian nationalist practice and transmitted this tradition to the new local form of African nationalism.

In the South African democratic transition of the 1990s, Mandela famously played his role of unifier of a country on the brink of civil war. His attempts to bridge racial and class divides were then much decried by extreme leftist critics. But theirs was surely not a sober estimate. Mandela helped avoid a catastrophic war through a truly inclusive national self-definition. In his successor, Thabo Mbeki, we have seen a far narrower and more short-sighted approach. Mbeki combines ideological nationalist appeals to the "authentic" with the crassest promotion of the economic interests of a new elite. And far more dangerous to democracy is the incoherent and intoxicating brew of nativism and demagogic populism offered by Mbeki's main rival, Jacob Zuma. The one-eyed Cyclops is calling the shots.

Conclusion: Herman Charles Bosman in Rissik Street

Gandhi and Mandela were in large part products of an extraordinary metropolis—Johannesburg. In different ways, the city's cosmopolitanism provided them with contexts that were rich in new ideas. They drew on these ideas to generate thought which was nationalist, but which transcended the limits of nationalism. They became nationalist leaders who reached out beyond the narrow confines of conventional nationalist forms and who acknowledged their debts to cosmopolitanism.

James Joyce understood the urban and metropolitan origins of such political creativity. But he also saw that the logic of nationalism could undermine these potentialities. Like the intentions of the Irish radicals of Joyce's youth, Gandhi's and Mandela's heroic aims would suffer shipwreck. The humanism of Gandhi and Nehru gave way to the irresponsible populism of Indira Gandhi and the vicious sectarianism of Advani and Vajpayee. Mandela's non-racism was overtaken, much more rapidly, by the paranoid ethnicism of his successors. Too often, leaders of broad vision cannot escape the Cyclops.

But the Joycean shout in the street remains a source of hope. One who understood this was the writer Herman Charles Bosman. Bosman was, in his combination of violent destructiveness and superb creativity, a quintessentially Joburg character. He was the son of a miner who died in an underground accident. In 1926, at the age of twenty-one, Bosman killed his stepbrother with a rifle shot, over a series of apparently trivial disagreements. Sentenced to death, he was reprieved, and out of his jail experiences he created the remarkable prison memoir *Cold Stone Jug*. After serving only a few years, Bosman was released to become the *enfant terrible* of early 1930s Joburg journalism and spent the late 1930s as a poverty-stricken author in London. Returning to South Africa, he became the country's most popular short story writer during the 1940s. Bosman knew that no orthodoxy, no one-eyed nationalism, would in the end contain the energies of the metropolis (Gray 2005). On September 18, 1945, Bosman came walking down Rissik Street toward Johannesburg's Town Hall. There, the Afrikaner Nationalist politician D. F. Malan was addressing his followers. Within three years, Malan would become prime minister and initiate the policy of apartheid. Outside in the street, left-wingers and ex-servicemen, enraged by Malan's Nazi sympathies and racism, were facing off against policemen. Silence reigned. But then to Bosman's delight, it was suddenly broken:

> A shower of bottles and half-bricks and pieces of masonry hurtled out of the eerie shadows of the trees in President Street and thundered against the policeman's helmets. I breathed a sigh of relief. It was only the spirit of Johannesburg once more asserting itself. The undying spirit of the mining town, born of large freedoms and given to flamboyant forms of expression.
>
> . . . They are trying to make snobs of us, making us forget who our ancestors were. They are trying to make us lose our pride in the fact that our forebears were a lot of roughnecks who knew nothing about culture and who came here to look for gold. We who are of Johannesburg know this spirit that is inside of us, and we don't resent the efforts which are being made to put a collar and time on this city. Because we know that every so often, when things seem to be going very smoothly on the surface, something will stir in the raw depths of Johannesburg, like the awakening of an old and half-forgotten memory, and the brickbats hurtling down Market Street will be thrown with the same lack of accuracy as when the pioneers of the mining camp did the throwing. (Bosman 1994: 568–70)

We can take comfort from Bosman's understanding that the modernist energies of his metropolis would prove irrepressible. Whatever the machinations of the antiurban, anticosmopolitan Cyclops, he will always have to live in fear that the motley crew of the Joburg street will, one fine evening, drive a stake into his eye.

5 ⊹ Art Johannesburg and Its Objects

DAVID BUNN

For all intents and purposes, this is a shallow city. At least that is the way we all speak about Johannesburg: as a surface that has forgotten its depth; or as once-supple skin now hardened by violence into keloid scars; or as a free-floating signifier, detached and unanchored from a scandalous signified, now inexactly remembered.

Of course metropolitan modernism everywhere, from Baudelaire to Robert Frank, built an aesthetics around the idea of surfaces and reflection: the conspicuously superficial dawdling of the flâneur in the mirrored arcades.[1] What distinguishes Johannesburg from the metropolitan norm, however, is that this rhetoric of the surface has been implicated in an act of historical repression: in an inability to come to terms with the real origins of surplus value, in apartheid labor practices, and especially in the buried life of the black body, instrumentalized and bent into contact with the coal face, or ore seam, in the stopes far below. This chapter concerns itself with the ways in which, over the past three decades, art practice has attempted to inhabit the city of Johannesburg: first, through an active, philosophical engagement with the idea of the city as a chaotic surface, detached from reference to a buried, transcendental meaning; and second, and more recently, through attempts to create new zones of mutually habitable and aestheticized urban space, attempts that are often at odds with the logic of urban regeneration.

Separate Levels

South Africa's mineral revolution began with the discovery of diamonds in 1871. It had as its first iconic symbol the Kimberley "Big Hole," one of the largest hand-excavated, open-cast mines in the world, reaching a depth of 1,097 meters by the time it closed in 1914. Contemporary popular representations show a vast, descending pit, with precarious roadways undercut by the hungry search for diamondiferous blue ground, and a violent set of exchanges often involving black workers and white supervisors. These people are not citizens. They are already, it seems, combatants moving in distinct, racialized spheres: the one stationary, controlling the hoist, the other toiling up and down, under threat of violence.

Ten years later, in the newly discovered goldfields of the Witwatersrand, primitive accumulation began to give way to a more complex violence: the extractive migrant labor system, and the racialized and ethnicized system of labor control, in closed compounds and in the deepest mining enterprises in the world. Violence now disappears from public view. Its only remainder is earth tremors, regular news of underground accidents, and the rough, migrant men who come and go in the streets.

So the surface of the earth, on the Witwatersrand, even in its earliest representations, is frequently associated with provisionality and repressed meaning. For the historians and novelists of Johannesburg, this apparent incoherence of surface signs was exacerbated by the activities of the mine bosses themselves and their capitalist brashness. This is an argument borne out everywhere in the city, in the legacy of the overstated buildings of mining company headquarters, and crass public sculpture such as the grossly large public bronze of a white miner, pick in one hand, gleefully holding aloft a gold nugget the size of his head, which greets slowing freeway traffic on the R24 at Eastgate.

Surface and Depth—in Theory ✦ The problem of the surface began to dominate political theory in the 1970s and 1980s. As Achille Mbembe and Sarah Nuttall point out, a deep unease with the idea of the city as a livable environment haunts the South African social history of that period. In the work of the leading social historians of the day, Johannesburg is the outcome of segregationist planning, or it is imagined by left academics and activists to be a theater of class and race antagonism, the main means of transformation for proletarian consciousness. What this emphasis produces, unfortunately, is a significant aporia: the impossibility of linking an idea of being in the present, in the city, with a conception of the real source of value, the anchor of the mode of production, which for most historians was located elsewhere, in the exploitation of labor in deep-level mining. Consequently, the inability to come to terms with the actually existing life of the metropolis emerges as a particular conundrum in theory: in the problem of imagining mediation between above- and below-surface levels of being.

Art making in this city has been quite as obsessed with the same philosophical problem of schizophrenic being: in one tendency, the surface is portrayed as a kind of integument, beneath which an irreducible body of truth lies hidden; in the second, artists explore the devaluation of embodied urban meaning, which they find replaced instead by zoned and segmented neighborhoods without connection.

In the social theory of the 1970s and 1980s, residents of townships and the inner city appear to live a tenuous, shadow life, the epiphenomenal outgrowth of relations of production built on migrant labor. It is perhaps for that reason that structural Marxism exerted such a powerful influence on historical explanation in the period. The willingness with which Nicos Poulantzas was adapted into this local Witwatersrand labor history context has much to do with theorists trying to address the problem of the incoherent surface. When R. W. Johnstone, Martin Legassick, Harold Wolpe, and Stanley Trapido set about their attack on the liberal frontier thesis, they had in mind a revolutionary new understanding of surface relations of production being articulated with depth explanation in a manner that would cure the illness associated with shallow liberal explanations. The true, deep undergirdings of apartheid would be revealed. This theoretical gambit involved a reconceptualization of the state as a power bloc, or structure-in-dominance, and in a major misunderstanding of Poulantzas, as the aggregation of class fractional interests within that bloc.[2]

Fransman and Davies, for instance, attempted to show how various economic sectors such as mining and manufacturing have the capacity to arrive at joint hegemonic dominance, through the mediation of the state, with the interests of capital as a whole being served. Thus the needs of mining capital were served by a conjunctural alliance with those of surface manufacturing in a particular historical moment; this in turn leads to the development of racial capitalism and what some historians have called "colonialism of a special type."[3] Structuralist understanding was able to unite surface and depth through the conception of articulated class fractional interests; however, in the process, the texture of everyday life, for workers and producers, came to appear increasingly meaningless. Life at the surface, in other words, was reduced to shadows, and thus theory made a ghost of the city.[4]

In the heyday of South African historical revisionism, there were strident clashes between structural Marxism and the new social history. In both, however, metropolitan life is reduced to a functional effect of structure: the life of black labor in the cities is entirely provisional, in the standard interpretations, because segregation "[transfers] the responsibility for its reproduction to the 'reserve' economies" (Bozzoli and Delius 1990: 21) outside the city center. Even in the radically new urban analyses of Johannesburg by social historians like Charles van Onselen and Phil Bonner, descriptions of the making of class and community across a single rural and urban migrant labor system revealed little about the desires of those who inhabited Johannesburg. For most theorists, therefore, the key to understanding the transition to capitalism was Marx's secret of "so-called primitive accumulation" (Marx 1977, 874–75): namely, that changes in the relations of production, triggered by the expropriation of land, were at the heart of the new systems of migrant labor.[5] They were not, in the end, the result of the penetration of exchange relations from outside, not part of the flow of trade, consumption, and new desires in the street life of the city, but instead were a product of emerging class antagonism. Cities were only the terminal point of this process, which continued in the class microdynamics of the labor compound: in the evolution of racialized divisions between boss boys, *sibondas,* and workers.[6]

There is a fundamental inability in late-twentieth-century theory to accept that the stream of local city signs, of being and writing, is anything other than provisional or narcissistic. Light, reflection, flickering agency, and collective acts of representation, in this understanding, are all part of the life under erasure. Metropolitan aesthetic experience is always over the horizon, at the end of a two-stage revolution, after the present urban crisis precipitated by apartheid has been cured.

Flatness; or, an Art without Archives   ⊹   For many Johannesburg artists and writers in the penumbral decades before the first election, the question of the surface emerged with new urgency. Most obviously, the landscape presence of huge gold-mine tailings (known locally as the "mine dumps") were a constant reminder of the force needed to keep intact the cheap migrant labor system, and this notion of the surface heaving with pressure from below, as though from the mass of a buried life, is the Real that inhabits much art at the time. It is what drives the characters in Nadine Gordimer's novel *The Conservationist.* "Come to think of it," says Mehring, the main protagonist in that work, and a mining engineer, "all the earth is a graveyard, you never know when you are walking over heads—particularly this continent" (141). Gordimer's solution to the problem of the surface is to treat it as a meniscus, a tense field of pressure against which buried bodies strain. But a certain amount of generalized force—flood, or earthquake—is required to turn this into dramatic historical change. Something of that logic may be felt in William Kentridge's earlier Johannesburg films. *Mine,* the second of the Soho Eckstein films, produced in 1991, at the height of the third State of Emergency, marks a significant step forward in the technique Kentridge called "drawing for projection."

Mine opens with an underground scene, and the rattling approach of an ore truck. It quickly moves, though, to a view in section, with the shaft elevator that transports shift workers between levels. At the surface, dominating what is, alternately, a quilted bed and an anonymous industrial landscape, is the mine magnate Soho Eckstein, looming like a Goya colossus. In an argument worthy of Poulantzas, the film offers an articulation of fractions and levels: racial capitalism forms an alliance between finance houses and a super exploitative mode of deep-shaft mining, dependent, in turn, on a system of compound-based migrant black labor. There is a hideous visible inequality between nonchalant wealth above ground and the bodies crushed in the stopes below. Soho's casual gesture with the coffee plunger initiates a violent descent, as it becomes the elevator cage, passing through an older stratigraphy. Binding different eras of merchant capitalism, colonialism, and imperialism, base to superstructure, part-object to whole machine, the cage comes to a halt in the lowest levels, at the rock face, where it begins to ascend again. In the process, it uncovers the Real of the labor process: the roar of the rock drills on the soundtrack contrasts with the delicate, swift erasures needed to change the charcoal marks delineating the progress of the pneumatic drills (see figure 1).

Mine is Kentridge's most assertively materialist film. But this is unusual, and it is also the last time that we will see such confident metaphors of descent in his work. Throughout the 1980s, most images of the violent transfer of force between levels are replaced by the idea of death that has risen to just below the surface.

In Kentridge's *Felix in Exile,* produced at the time of the first democratic election, all notions of a receptive archive, and hence of depth, have disappeared. In one famous sequence, a foregrounded body lies sprawled and alone, like a peasant newly arrived in town, clumsy-footed, apparently

1 William Kentridge, drawing from *Mine,* 1991, charcoal on paper.
Courtesy of William Kentridge

sleeping rough beneath newspaper. But the leak from the head soon tells us
that this is in fact a corpse. It is the charcoal memory, the ghosting of the
erased earlier images, that signifies his death.

Violently felled, these anonymous bodies press an unnaturally traumatic
weight upon the ground, which the ground seems to receive and record for
a passage of several moments between frames. These dying bodies leave a
momentary smear on the ground. At the same time, there is another ineluctable logic by which the conventions of landscape begin, as it were, to cover
them and naturalize them. Sheets of print that come flying in seem at first
to be a poignant wrapping of the body against the elemental cold. But as
the corpse is covered and volumetrically defined, it becomes naturalized as
a topographical feature, one of the very mountains that are the product of
deep underground labor in the gold mines below. In *Felix in Exile,* for the
first time in Kentridge's work, violence plays itself out almost exclusively as
a problem of the surface, and of skin, rather than in the threat of irruption
from below. Against our will, perhaps, we watch the evidence of the body
disappear, lost to all archiving. Yet for the viewer who has seen this, it is
as though the industrialized debris field retains the memory of the death:
just as the frame-by-frame progression of the animated drawing retains the

charcoal ghost of the previous erasure, so the work of the trace now passes to the observer. It is as though every modeled feature carries the potential of a corpse. All above-ground signs, be they billboards or signposts or drive-in cinema screens, seen from the perspective of the remembering observer, are like transcendental signifiers of death: read in this manner, they are the coded memorials to a thousand minor deaths and abuses.

Drawing on the Surface ✦ It is a winter Saturday, and there is another cleanup campaign beginning in downtown Johannesburg. Hawkers, handlers, Senegalese refugees, and *amakwerekwere* are being swept up and tidied away.[7] By nightfall, overlapping with the late shifts of workers putting up braces for the new CCTV cameras, people will be on the streets again, blown up against corners and alcoves where braziers punctuate the dark. By morning, there will be another layer of peelings, ash drifts, and exfoliations.

Fire, ash, and the graying grass that stabilizes the few remaining mine tailings dumps are part of the winter aesthetic of this city. In recent years, moreover, fire and ash on the surface of the city have come to provide an idiom for more and more Johannesburg artists. By the time of the first Johannesburg Biennale in 1995, artists in the city were working predominantly within an idiom of totalized flatness. For this first biennale, Kentridge and Doris Bloom created two extensive, site-specific interventions, using fire, chalk, and ash tracing in the reduced Highveld grassland: the one (visible only by helicopter) was of a schematic diagram of the human heart; the other, closer to the Newtown Precinct, showed a Troyeville wrought-iron gate, with a generic, heart-shaped metal outline (see figure 2).

Using the flat earth as an inscriptional field, Kentridge and Bloom explore the persistence of affect. This is not a heartless city, they seem to be saying. On the contrary, matters of the heart may be read everywhere, but especially in the sign-to-sign relationships of the urban landscape, from the muted sgraffito in the burned grass to the wrought-iron motifs of a security gate. Others, like Sandile Zulu, have made a great poem out of the quickening fires that erase detail on the freeway margins and grasslands of Gauteng.[8] But the most complex and intriguing meditation on provisional inscriptions may be found in the work of another recent migrant to the city: Zambia-born Clive van den Berg.

Van den Berg's early career was in Durban. His first Natal works—produced before he was explicit about his own queer identity—trace the lineaments of repressed desire in a language of fire, fire tracings, and globular light. Early text works like *Gabriel* (a burning field of letters ignited on a Durban beach)

2 William Kentridge and Doris Bloom, *Memory and Geography*, 1995, outdoor installation, Johannesburg. Courtesy of William Kentridge

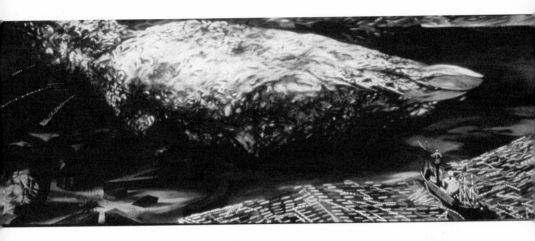

3 Clive van den Berg, *Docked in a Field of Lights*, 1987, oil on canvas. Collection South African National Gallery. Courtesy of Clive van den Berg

and *Docked in a Field of Lights* all refer to the association of light and desire. In the latter, the luminous lines, lit fishing floats, and brilliant globules trace a kind of mnemonic that is offset by the Brobdinagian, phallic protrusion of the Bluff into Durban Bay (see figure 3).

Soon after his arrival in Johannesburg, van den Berg embarked on a series of transcendent land- and site-based works that engaged with the fabric of the city. Like other immigrants and migrants, he found that the shallow metropolis had no deep archive that corresponded with his own sense of the history of queer desire. Moreover, in plumbing the late apartheid archive, he found no record—outside of court documents, the discourse of disease control, and the implementation of sodomy laws—of the love between men. Faced with this familiar erasure, van den Berg began like many others to work with the city of Johannesburg as though it were a projective surface. His *Mine Dump Project* (1997) series used the fugitive medium of light and fire to trace large-scale outline drawings on the facing slopes of mine dumps, visible only to passing freeway traffic. The images were of domestic objects, bedroom furniture, and men, the lineaments of domestic desire projected outward on a huge scale to flame out briefly then die away as burned traces, glimpsed indistinctly in the wintering grass for months to come.

These fugitive, colossal drawings are part of a larger philosophical exploration in van den Berg, of the idea of the unrealized body and of vocabularies of loving. In all of these pieces, the problem of the surface stands in ambiguous relation to the question of skin, and in his later work, to the context of a new episteme: that of the plague.

AIDS has brought a different ontology of the surface to bear on our understanding of this city and urban citizenship. Ten years ago, by his own account, Clive van den Berg lived in a state of secret terror at the idea of the hidden virus. Skin, to him, in this interregnum moment, was no longer a responsive organ but terrifyingly permeable, as though each stranger's casual touch might sink down, through hyperbolically magnified pores in the sievelike epidermis, to have the virus find a deep lodgment. Those were haunted days. In his contributions to the *Urban Futures* project, the fear of the plague was imaged in a series of billboards around the inner city, one with a doppelganger skeleton clinging like a familiar to his back. More recently, however, in his work, there has been an increasingly subtle and abstract treatment of the idea of skin surface. Two powerful new idioms have emerged: first, there is a language of fear about the progress of the disease, figured as a series of black wooden roundels applied as a surface effect to sculpted forms. These are reminiscent both of magnified pores or crater wounds and of abacus tallies, the deliberate counting of the hours. In some recent three-dimensional sculptures, exaggerated fear of the skin's porousness is dramatized in an open fretwork of pine strips, surrounding little portals that go down into another dimension. Second, van den Berg's older idiom, the globular, streaming lights that figure the tracery of desire, is turned to another purpose. Strings of lights outline and offset the disease-ravaged flesh, in a transcendental, projective aura. Against the march of the dark stains across the skin, there is the countervailing vocabulary of love. This is a great act of mediation, and of cure. The entire history of the problematic relationship between surface and depth, of an emergent subjectivity that desires containment, that is afraid of the very vulnerability of the body's outer surface to the approach of others, is here confronted. Clothed in the discourse around AIDS, this is an argument that, miraculously, denies that fear and transcends it through an act of mediation: the reassertion of the languages of intimacy.[9]

For all the artists I have discussed, the city is associated with a failure of mediation between levels, with a kind of metaphoric skin that no longer communicates properly with an interior body. The failure of this traffic between levels is variously figured: as a hardening and sloughing of the surface; as a surface that reveals only faint stencils of an older, irrelevant history; as sedimentation, rather than mining or deep penetration. Van den Berg's is certainly one of the most interesting responses to the diseased city skin and its relative autonomy. In the time of the plague, it seems, it requires a very

4 Clive van den Berg, *Love's Ballast* (detail), 2004, jeluton, life size.
Courtesy of Clive van den Berg

special aesthetic effort to find joy in the space between disease and love, between the present time of desire and the ineluctable progress of illness. In fact,
in his most recent sculptural work, the task of communicating between skin
and what is immediately beneath the surface is given over to a special new organ: the gland. For the "Personal Affects" exhibition, in the Cathedral of St.
John the Divine in New York, van den Berg produced an exquisite, three-
dimensional recumbent wooden figure, like a Renaissance tomb effigy. This
saintly victim, arms outstretched and ambiguously encompassing, turns its
face to the audience, displaying a miraculous wound: a hugely swollen neck
gland that is one of the classic symptoms of AIDS. The nodular extrusion is
polished and patinated like an ancient tree bole. Aestheticized and exaggerated, it is also the gland that communicates between the new skin surface
and the circulation of fluids and viral load beneath (see figure 4).

Écorcé: A Flayed Face   ⊕   "Mediation," says Fredrick Jameson (1981: 39), "is
the classical dialectical term for the establishment of . . . symbolic identities

5 Penny Siopis, *Pinky Pinky: Blue Eyes*, 2002, oil and found objects on canvas.
Courtesy of Penny Siopis

between the various levels, as a process whereby each level is folded into the next, thereby losing its constitutive autonomy." In the 1980s and 1990s, it seems to me the problematic of historical mediation—of making sense of a structure that consisted of contradictory elements—was explored mainly through the figure of the resistant surface. But the question of the surface is also the problem of the sign in a time of historical change: it is as though with new meanings being born, the older structures of reference are dying.

One of the most powerful, Johannesburg-based meditations on subjectivity, surfaces, and transition is Penny Siopis's *Who Is Pinky Pinky?* series. *Pinky Pinky* is a sequence of painterly essays on the philosophical condition of the face, and the city, in the present. They are all also, she says, about "the fears and phobias that have surfaced in our post-apartheid moment" (Siopis 2006: 2; see figure 5).

Despite the thickness of paint application in these works—they are all heavily impasto, and they all use palette-knife application—it is as though skin has lost its connection with underlying flesh. That is to say, skin is treated not simply as a limiting membrane, but as part of the process of the enfolding and implication that Michel Serres has described as its "milieu": "The skin," he says, "intervenes in the things of the world and brings about their mingling" (Connor 2004: 29). Normal renderings of depth are avoided entirely in these works. Broad pressure of the palette knife produces the figure, rather than tonal shifts or the punctual accretion of marks, say, from a brush.

Skin seems detached from what lies beneath: real and fake fingernails are anchored in the epidermis and pierce the surface, rather than being enfolded by it; eyes poke out from a plane below, with the dissociated stare that recalls that of the recovering burn victim, or a balaclava-clad head, or the affective paralysis of psychotic states. What is being thematized is the breakup of the portraiture sign: the face is like a loose plate moving over the subcutaneous base and without muscular anchoring; the metaphoric effect is of a referent that has become detached, that floats. Siopis's exploration of the dynamic relation of depth to surface in this work is thus very reminiscent of Levinas: "The precise point," says Levinas, "at which the mutation of the intentional into the ethical occurs, and occurs continually, at which the approach breaks through consciousness, is the human skin and face" (Connor 2004: 89).

Two other technical aspects of the method of flatness deserve special mention: first, there is an extremely narrow range of tonal value, within the spectrum of pink. The ontological strangeness of these works is due, in large measure, to the fact that Siopis uses a range of complex tints with very close color values. "So the surface," she continues, "operates to 'hold' an emerging presence rather than describe or convey completeness." Second, even though there is no conventional perspectival modeling, the ground is unusually thick, and the metonymies between paint and skin are further developed through the manipulation of relative drying times. When the paint is still tacky, in certain of the works, Siopis explains she "[hits] the surface with the flat side of the knife in regular motions and in the process [lifts] bits of paint to the point when each lifted unit forms a little peak."[10]

These performative aspects of the work, its deictic marks, are what Siopis sees as "a kind of carnal trace." "Painting," she says, "is for me a form of imagining ... and that imagining leaves physical tracks of itself" (6). Intriguingly, in the relationship between technique and philosophical method, the *Pinky Pinky* pieces approach the condition of what Gilles Deleuze has called the "haptic," in which there is a codetermination of optical and tactile experience, without the deictics of the hand being overshadowed by the lingering of the eye.[11]

Pinky Pinky is also about the long trauma of political and psychological transition, as opposed to a narrowly conceived understanding of post-apartheid citizenship beginning with the 1994 elections. There is some *thing* being born, it seems, born in a manner that mirrors our fear. In *Pinky Pinky: Teeth*, we have a good example of the philosophical discussion of the phenomenal emergence of the subject, embodied in the skin as a surface of emergence that is ill-distinguished from the world. Volume is pulled out of the sticky ground, so that the flesh apparently resolves itself into peaks and clots. This clustering of pulled shapes produces a darkening suggestive of the emergence of organs. But against this evidence of emergence, there is evidence of death; we seem also to be looking at an autopsy: the head thrown back, lips in a rictal grin, with the face falling away into the distance (see figure 6).

Another way of putting it is to say that in this work, it is as though whatever is coming into being may already be dead, autopsied, rotting internally. One might very well say about this kind of work that its subject is the "it looks" of the painting. Some *thing*, it seems, looks from just underneath a surface, a surface which is at the same time its skin, and our sense of it being like a dead thing arises from the fact that we cannot identify with its uncanny perspective. "It looks." I am not of course speaking about the glassy eyes of the ET-like creatures that inhabit this series. Rather, I am speaking about the dramatization, through a certain disconnectedness of skin and its subcutaneous attachments, of a subject position that cannot entirely be comprehended from the present time or as an integrated whole. It is like that strange grammatical tense, the "I died," that Derrida (1991: 157–58) assigns

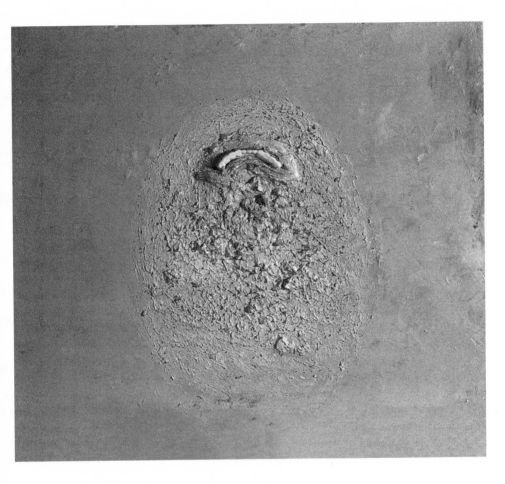

6 Penny Siopis, *Pinky Pinky: Teeth*, 2002, oil and found objects on canvas.
Courtesy of Penny Siopis

to the work of his art-historian friend Louis Marin, whose revelatory text he reads shortly after the man's funeral.

These revenant figures appear to us like this with their loose, glovelike skin because we do not yet know the position from which they speak or the new discourse that will make them whole in the future. The paintings of course also allude to a complex genealogy of occult figures that have been associated, in the public imagination of the past century, with the changing nature of value, commoditization, wage labor, and the structure of the social under apartheid. The figures I am speaking about are personifications of playful evil, of witchcraft, of modernity: they range in style and form, from the phallic, dwarf figure called *tokoloshe* feared by migrant African workers in cities, to the mythical snake *mamhlambo* which feeds on money and blood, to a huge array of zombie figures directly associated with traumatic transformations in the condition of the cash economy, and the relationship of labor and time.[12]

Such occulted, zombie figures are also frequently associated with the color white, a color of death and mediation of states for most Africans as well as for Melville's Captain Ahab. Siopis's *Pinky Pinky* is from the same ghoulish stock. This is how she describes its etiology:

> Pinky Pinky is an urban legend that seems to have emerged in 1994. A pink, hybrid creature . . . , described sometimes as a white tokoloshe, albino, bogeyman, stranger, it is an imagined character that finds shape in the various tellings of the myth. Pinky Pinky, for example, terrorizes prepubescent children, lying in wait for them at school toilets. It attacks—even rapes—girls (especially those wearing pink underwear). It is visible to girls but invisible to boys, who feel its presence through a slap or scratch on the cheek. . . . As much as Pinky Pinky is a perpetrator of violence, it also seems a victim of, and scapegoat for, violent uncivil actions. . . . The myth seems to mirror unspeakable psychic states of fear and moral panics. . . . These could translate as the fear of residual white power or the nameless dread associated with failing confidence in continuity, stability, and tradition.

These very suggestive remarks speak of the skin not only as a surface of emergence, but also of the inchoate forms of citizenship associated with white and gendered identity in the last two decades of transition. Just as the Pinky Pinky myth is most prevalent in Model C schools, where young black elites rub up against the sons and daughters of older white privilege, so Siopis's creatures are often the locus of what she calls "excited fright." Such a lovely phrase that! Yet it marks the locus of another kind of fear: the threat of sexual violence against women, totalized into a kind of background/foreground effect of the disembodied but ever-present look.[13]

Consider *Pinky Pinky: Stomach*, with its long torso and the saintly gesturing. The effect is very menacing and very bizarre, but the threat is communicated through a childlike understanding. The devouring bogeyman seems to have borrowed its form from Dr. Seuss's *Cat in the Hat* and Jason in *Friday the 13th*. Its stomach full of gobbled-up babies is a projection of preadolescent fears about incorporation, such as one might find in Freud's Wolf Man.

So in the end, the uncanniness in these pieces does not result only from the awful slippage between epidermis and underlying cartilage. It is also occasioned by conflicting references to new forms of subject and citizen in historical time. Associated with past legacies of skin inequality, and with the contradictions of neoliberalism at a time of national reconstruction, Pinky Pinky figures arise out of a milieu of fear, playground rumor, and the anticipation of the reemergence of a certain kind of past whiteness. It is, in this reading, the fundamentally urban expression of a next generation's fantasy of the past, of the whiteness of the Third Force, and of Vlakplaas, propped on a much older and occult iconography.[14] For the white viewing subject, the uncanniness resides in an inability to inhabit the position that precipitates that fear: the "it looks" cannot be recognized as a potential of our own. "Whiteness," in the eyes of the other, is given back to us as a severing of the face from its supportive musculature.

Separate Spheres

Artists under the Sun ✢ My maternal aunt lived in Finsbury Court, a red-brick apartment block overlooking Joubert Park, the largest public park in Hillbrow, the country's most densely populated urban area. My friends and I would crowd onto the first-floor balcony, drop birdseed onto passersby, and shout greetings at the "flat boys" drowsing in the sun with their girlfriends in the park across the street. For my aunt, Joubert Park was not Africa; that name was reserved for the north, not this place of servants and surfaces. Her apartment was crowded with a variety of central and east African curio art, like Kirchner's Dresden studio.

I'm sure that my aunt wanted to be a kind of Beryl Markham.[15] For her, Hillbrow was an exciting, chaotically dangerous place; but it was also a temporary staging point for the real journeys that would follow, to the places that produced the real masks and drums: Tanganyika, Kenya, the Congo. Some Sundays in spring, she would help my mother run a stall in the Artists under the Sun bazaar, which consisted of mainly middle-class white Sunday painters and potters, hemmed in by a fantastical collection of East Rand opportunists trying to hawk beaten Rhodesian copper fire guards, tea towels emblazoned with images of Bushman rock art, batik prints, and other lesser wares.

Artists under the Sun still exists. In the wake of business flight north, it packed its bags and moved to Zoo Lake, close to the road edge so as to be under the safer gaze of northbound traffic on Jan Smuts Avenue. The Joubert Park it left behind, depending on how you look at it, is either still one of the most dangerous public spaces of the city, or, alternately, the place where art is beginning to have a new kind of engagement with the flow of superfluities upon which new inner-city identities are being built. Whereas through one lens, an older problem of the surface was pursued and explored through an ontology of the surface, a new generation of Johannesburg art now concerns itself with another kind of horizontal mediation between separate spheres. To understand this logic, we have to imagine literally moving through the inner city, in a long, looping tour. What I propose now to offer is an imaginary circuit, beginning with Hillbrow, Joubert Park, and the Johannesburg Art Gallery, moving across to Newtown, the Faraday Street taxi rank, then over the Mandela Bridge, up the new "Cultural Arc" to Constitution Hill.

Joubert Park: Stranded ✥ Andrew Tshabangu's *Joubert Park* series of silver prints (1997) offers a dramatic record of how this part of the city has changed. In one image, a group of African women lean into the task of preparing food and stoking braziers.[16] The irregularly pierced metal drums glow, smoke, and fan themselves into coherent flame. All about them, the ground itself has a deep sediment of ash and maize husks, the immediate detritus of informal commerce that serves the mobile minibus taxi industry that now has Joubert Park as one of its main hubs. These may look like ephemeral lives, but they are regular and intensely lived, part of a complex remaking of locales. Glimpsed through the dematerializing haze in the photograph, parts of Hillbrow loom, a taxi skids by, and there are frayed edges of an ornamental palm from the last epoch of white civic gardening. The new rubs against the evidence of the old architectural styles without engaging it directly as a memory event. It could be Rio or Mumbai (see figure 7).

Joubert Park now is a hub that spins off centrifugal traffic and collects the centripetal journeys of migrants arriving from around the country to Park Station. As a space of flows, and temporary associations, it epitomizes what AbdouMaliq Simone (2004b: 408) has called "people as infrastructure." In the Hillbrow region generally, there is a high proportion of refugees, and while their connection to the city might in some respects seem superficial—a matter of surface exchanges and not deep roots—an extraordinarily detailed and complicated set of connections provides a grounding for their daily lives. Unlike the earlier generation of social historians, our new understanding of the city cannot be based on the stereotype of the *amagoduka,* the young crop of mine recruits arriving in Egoli to be fleeced by *tsotsis.* Instead, in and around Joubert Park, there are scores of Burundian, Ethiopian, Kenyan, Senegalese, and Congolese refugees with a deep investment in the idea of urban living. Surveys conducted in Johannesburg reveal that almost 80 percent of forced migrants "reported living in cities for most of their lives before coming to Johannesburg" (Jacobsen 2004: 58), and 21 percent of them (as opposed to 1 percent of South Africans) are engaged in inner-city, micro-enterprise trading (Landau and Jacobsen 2003). Faced with the uncertainties over housing, employment, command of South African languages, and being shaken down by the police and local kingpins, many refugee communities turn to ethnically determined forms of self-identification organized within mutual-aid societies. Congolese refugees, for instance, in many South

7 Andrew Tshabangu, *Joubert Park,* 1997, silver print on fiber paper. Courtesy of Gallery MOMO, Johannesburg

African cities, have organized themselves into tightly structured mutual-aid societies called "tribes," based on area of origin and language (Amisi and Ballard 2005: 3). For many of these groups, long-distance trade with Congo-Kinshasa has involved the export of South African manufactured goods and the importation of Congolese crafts, especially curios.

The loose citizenship that manifests itself in and around Joubert Park imparts a sharp element of danger, threatening an older order of art: visitor traffic to the Johannesburg Art Gallery—which had been minimal anyway in this brash city—began to slow to a trickle, with tourists and local gallery patrons having to run the gauntlet of the taxi crowds around its edge. With gallery funding at its lowest ebb, and no improvement in visitor traffic in sight, the City Council at one stage proposed to relocate the gallery to Turbine Hall in Newtown, at a cost of R110 million.

The relocation proposal is symptomatic of the frustration of developers and other agents of urban regeneration wishing to improve this part of the city. In fact, to some, Johannesburg's very future seems undermined by the rapid, horizontal affiliations of the majority of its citizens. To planners, the residents of the inner city who appear to live lightly on its surface are not citizens in the conventional sense of the word; their lives are not directed toward the making of phenomenologically lived spaces. From the perspective of an urban aesthetics, however, this part of the city is like a screen, across which flickering desires track. Representation itself, under these conditions, is always a kind of frottage: a rubbing of a new layer of meaning against an indirectly perceived texture below, without direct sight of it. Amnesiac in nature, the present acts of being encounter the older urban footprint very indirectly; the ash of the present is bedded down on the recent past, showing vague outlines.

It takes a special kind of representational vantage point to understand the city spaces as virtual or potential human flows, a vantage point located outside the aesthetic conventions of landscape. One such departure, located in the experience of the townships ringing Johannesburg, may be found in David Koloane's 1993 series *Made in South Africa* (graphite on paper), in which busily aggressive dogs rear up against an urban backdrop figured by a series of graphite striations. The dogs, it seems, stand in for the aggressive survival tactics needed by township residents; it is as though the crowded cross-hatching of marks against which they rear is a blurred collective record of the aura of myriad shack dwellers.

Working from his studio in Newtown, Koloane frequently uses rubbed and abraded surfaces, in layered oil pastel, charcoal, or graphite, to give a sense of existentially lived space. At the same time, this buzz of static or surface tracery reveals only indistinctly the record of urban lives. For the logic of urban planning, such representations are evidence only of the failure of the collective, instances of "weak citizenship . . . in which only the ghosts of an older, more idiosyncratic civil society live on" (Retort 2005: 21). Seen from the perspective of the surface, however, these are far more complex human infrastructures, forms of flowing and collaborative identity that may be called into being or dissipated as quickly as the whistle brigades used by young comrades in the years of 1980s urban protest.[17] But these same flexible affiliations amount to a knotting of the social, in a manner that is repeated throughout Africa: households and income-sharing units are profoundly adaptable, changing according to need and split across distinct locations. Their logics stand in sharp antithesis to the demands of planning and urban betterment. They also do not conform to the sociological imperative that defines "households" in terms of pooled resource use or consumption. For most urban sociologists of Africa, case studies founder on the same definitional problems. Fiona Ross (1996: 67), in an astute recent study of households in Cape Town's Khayalitsha, speaks of the difficulty in studying "changing conglomerates": "children lodged with relatives and friends while their parents were mobile; adults moved between domestic units; people ate in different units to those in which they slept. The residents of the settlement had extensive movement histories, not merely indicating mobility at the regional level, but also at the intra-settlement level."

Joubert Park is not only a chaotic place. It is part of the mise en scène of a larger plot involving Johannesburg and the continental imaginary: the desire of migrants and work seekers, from Kinshasa to Beira, to find jobs and enrichment in Johannesburg, and to move through the city fluently, like a native. For African working-class subjects, this drift into the city has always, since the origins of migrant modernism, been anchored with representational acts. When in 1971 Oswald Mtshali published the seminal poem "Amagoduka at Glencoe Station," his was still a portrait of Egoli mine worker migrancy in which proletarian subjectivity was presumed to be split between the lure of city cash and the nostalgic distant prospect of fat cattle and young women in the reserves. But in truth, no matter how binary the opposition, or how cruel the cyclical movement between Park Station and some distantly imagined rural homestead, workers have always been involved in the fantasy of the city, and the representation of imaginary pleasure in the city systems, whether near or far.[18]

Given this long history, it is no surprise that in the new city, sites like parks continue to be important places of self-representation. In that sense, Joubert

Park has come to be an imaginative supplement to migrant and refugee desire, and this has led to a clustering of street photographers alongside the taxis and hawkers. This idea of the park as supplement is a crucial one: if the city is a place of housing and work, crossed by instrumentalizing and disciplinary functions, then the park enables a kind of excess, a kind of writing, self-dramatization, and contact that has little to do with survival. Older, Edwardian logics of civic aesthetics—the garden with its formal Gertrude Jekyll plantings and axial paths—brought together the idea of pleasurable retirement and the arts. Just as in public gardens in cities around the world, there is an imagined garden circuit associated with decorous bourgeois wandering and which culminates in an architectural apogee, in this case the Lutyens showpiece Johannesburg Art Gallery building.[19] Now the older civic armature has been turned into a backdrop.

It was with this in mind, perhaps, that the Joubert Park Public Art Project was formed in 2001. Curated by Bie Venter, Dorothee Kreutzfeldt, and Jo Ractliffe, this was one of a series of inner-city regeneration projects, some of them corporate-funded, many of them initiated by the city and metropolitan government.[20] In the main phase of the project, Ractliffe, Kreutzfeldt, and Venter invited fifty local and international artists to interact with the Joubert Park space. Terry Kurgan was one of those invited. She wished to understand the practice of a large and eclectic group of Joubert Park photographers, and began to document their individual histories, producing extensive archives on forty of the forty-five recorded photographers in the Park. What emerged was a minutely defined sense of the collectively negotiated site and workspace, and a complex history of the participants themselves.

In 2001, Kurgan began to work more intimately with six of the photographers. Studying their methods and clientele, she then collaborated with them and a corporate sponsor around the introduction of a mobile studio, a tentlike structure that boasted changeable backdrops. As it turned out, the politics of use and locale was far more complicated than she had originally imagined; the photographers were more alert to the complexities, and they carefully democratized access to this sudden resource, so that the logic of donation did not overwhelm the fragile commercial ecology of the park.[21]

"Park Pictures," an exhibition Kurgan produced in 2004, consists of portraits of the photographers, an "aerial map marking their inviolably fixed working positions," as she puts it, and "a large collection of their photographs that have never been claimed by their clients." In Kurgan's aerial photographic map, the thick clustering of short- and long-distance taxis frames the old park. Superimposed onto the older grid, and along the axial divides, are the photographers' stands. In many cases, those customers desiring portraits also desire particular kinds of studio backdrop: especially those that speak of distant places and of transformative, alchemical luck, two ingredients captured in the one studio backdrop that far outshines all others in the popularity stakes—Sun City. In portrait after portrait, young couples newly arrived in Johannesburg dream themselves out of Joubert Park again, depicted, for those at home, against landscape backdrops of the faux architecture of Sol Kerzner's infamous casino.

Corporate sponsorship of the Joubert Park photography project was unusual in that it recognized an already existing network of street-level practices. Elsewhere in the city, however, the collaboration between urban renewal and public art has been grander in scale and defined around thematized and rejuvenated precincts.

These initiatives imagine public art in Johannesburg as the prophetic forerunner of development, capitalizing on the links between arts and gentrification that stabilized many run-down neighborhoods in European metropolises. Newtown, in the inner city, has always been imagined as the core cultural precinct. Other precincts are part of the cellular, defensive strategy that have City Improvement Districts (CIDS) at their core. These tend to be sterilized, modernist block developments, organized around corporate anchor tenants who are able to seal off the district as a defensible space with CCTV camera surveillance and privatized police and waste collection. Public art, for the most part, in the imagination of corporate clients, plays a mainly anchoring role: statuary, monumental parkland, artistic street furniture, these are all the new *points de capiton* that stabilize the contradictions of the cleaned and emptied spaces.[22] They provide visual points of reference for audiences in surrounding buildings who flow along defended tunnels of space to defended lunch rooms. Patrolled zones and monumental images such as these are of course at odds with the loosely connective alliances of street vendors, informal garbage collectors, refugee networks, and park portraitists who make up the actually existing city.

A Faraday Street Crucifixion ✦ Art in the inner city is actively engaged with urban planning. This kind of symbiosis is best exemplified by the special relationship between the Johannesburg Development Agency and the Trinity Session, a project-based, public art collective comprised of artists Stephen Hobbs, Marcus Neustetter, and until recently Kathryn Smith. Currently based at the Premises gallery at the Civic Theatre in Braamfontein, Trinity has been directly involved in some of the most ambitious attempts thus far to put art at the heart of urban regeneration. Currently, they are collaborating with the Johannesburg Development Agency, and the Wits School of Arts, in public art commissioning along the imaginary Cultural Arc, which stretches from Constitution Hill, down past the Civic Theatre to the University of the Witwatersrand, and across the new Mandela Bridge into the Newtown Cultural Precinct.

Of all the founder members of Trinity, artist Stephen Hobbs is perhaps the one who has made the most sustained attempt to come to grips with a new aesthetics of the city. Hobbs describes his own life as being isomorphic with the birth of the New South Africa: on April 21, 1994, he took over as young director of the Market Gallery; seven days later, he cast his vote for the African National Congress in the first democratic election.[23] As a brash young organic intellectual, Hobbs was interested in the intersecting vectors of his own life as a white boy in the city, and the territorial and inscriptional patterns of other residents. Some seven years ago, he announced an extraordinary new aesthetic with stills from an imaginary suicide fall, fifteen seconds recorded by a crude 8mm film camera attached to a shopping bag parachute then dropped down the central well of one of Hillbrow's most notorious skyscrapers, Ponte City. Since then, creating no grand narratives like fellow urban photographers Guy Tillim or Santu Mofokeng, he has worked obsessively to record fragmented but emerging locales, glimpses of localized placemaking in the heart of the city:

> I would document the informal settlements behind the French Institute which have now become the Brickfields developments and all those Newtown low cost housing developments. I would literally fucking watch how they rebuilt their shacks, then they were trashed, then they would rebuild them again and some learner's truck driving school would open up there and I was fascinated by their makeshift test driving signs. I was just interested in the endeavors of daily human activity and because I photographed it so much I could literally say whether a piece of pavement had changed texture because someone lit a fire on it the day before, but the day before that it had looked like something else. So there was a cyclical analysis of the daily transformation of the fabric of the city which I was obsessed with.

Collecting fragments of the city, Hobbs became very conscious of the manner in which his own public art practices crossed over the inscriptional efforts of others: the emerging publics of the inner city, new forms of neighborhood-based micro-alliances, often involving refugees or immigrants. To capture these fleeting intersections, he began to use a form of rapid notation, combining photographic record, Beuysian lectures, and mind-mapping diagrams. His work on the Daimler-Chrysler group show employed this "scriptovisual" language, combining erratic textual notation with a complex archive of representations of the city skyline.

Most recently, the Trinity Session has been invited to participate in the Dakar Biennale. Thinking about their possible contribution to the event, and at the same time doing a survey of Hillbrow neighborhoods, Hobbs and Neustetter were on one memorable occasion suddenly accosted by a French-speaking Senegalese resident. Pulling them aside to warn of the dangers of the area in which they were walking, he fluently defined for them the invisible spheres of influence, spatial alliances, and fire zones that crisscrossed the neighborhood. This description of the invisible boundaries of newly constructed immigrant locales will become their key signifier in the Dakar intervention. The installation they envisage records the remembered cognitive mapping of the city of Dakar, as told to them by Senegalese labor migrants in Johannesburg.

Hobbs's Trinity Session is one of the most intriguing of the recent instances of urban art making in collaboration with civic and municipal authority. At their most successful, they dramatize forms of existing representational practice in the city. For every attempt to create sanitized and patrolable zones, there are acts of relational aesthetics, to use Nicolas Bourriaud's term (2002: 24), that create "free areas and time spans whose rhythm contrasts with those . . . 'communication zones' that are imposed on us" (McIntyre 2007: 37).

There is a recent set of photographs recording the Trinity contribution to the regeneration of the Faraday Street market. To approach that area on foot, crossing the city from Newtown (itself a CID) through the financial and mining houses areas would be to pass through several zones patrolled by private security companies. Arriving at Faraday, say, on a Friday, when the delivery of *muti* materials from KwaZulu Natal is in full swing, one is deeply conscious of the flow of long-distance taxi trade. Hobbs's images reveal graphic evidence of the unstoppable production of conviviality, gathered around forms of illicit and brutal trade. Faraday Street represents a classical example of the attempt, on the part of municipal government, to "emplace urbanizing processes through the administration of choices and codification of multiplicity" (Simone 2004b: 408). In Johannesburg, this "emplacement" logic has been aimed at the most unstable interactive environments: *muti* markets, street hawkers' stalls, curio sellers' stands, and taxi ranks. For each of these planning interventions, however, there are "tactics operating at the interstices of strategic constraints" (409). For Faraday Street, as for Joubert Park, the attempt to flush away the dirt and detritus of informal sociality produces a swarming of resistant representational practices: from the first hours of their being moved, displaced muti sellers started to prop their own advertising onto the new signifiers associated with the hygienic space. Herbs and skins were arranged around the fire equipment brackets; and on the fringing, spiked palisade fencing—a style of boundary associated with gated bourgeois communities across the city—the pathetic corpses of monkeys are crucified to dry in the sun.

Heritage Boom, Heritage Bust ⊕ Johannesburg is a place of flows, not in the simple neo-Smithian sense of commodity exchange, but as a place of desirous greeting, where desire traces itself (to play on Derrida) and defers its valued returns.[24] Most citizens are loosely here, deferring any sense of locale. Because there is no recourse to an ontological or topographic model of encountering the city, we are forced to take seriously the aesthetics that is present everywhere in the art and popular culture of the day—the aesthetics of flatness.

There are two transitional moments in the history of the surface that exemplify the present problem of urban aesthetics. City residents will remember kwa Mai Mai, the bustling informal trading center best known for serving the needs of migrants and hostel dwellers in their endless round between rural homesteads and the city. Chief among the representational tactics of men moving through this zone was the purchase of a chest in which to carry goods; on the outside of the chest, and divided into thematic panels, were cutout images of film stars, religious icons, and lottery motifs, a representational swarming designed to magically enhance the transformative goods within. In 2006, this same woodworking collective now specializes in the manufacture of another object much in demand: paneled coffins, in which the body of the diseased is transacted home.

Some of the public art practices I have been describing thus far spring from a long history of urban activism, an activism that has at its heart the understanding of separated "communities." What is at play here once again is a desire for mediation, the underlying desire to bring into association radically distinct spaces separated by planning blockades, differential policing, racial identity, and fear. At its most successful, this practice extends the traffic of signs between previously distinct zones. That is no simple task.

Johannesburg today is a significant site of flow and counterflows, of varying "ontopologies" (to use Derrida's term for the "specific conjuncture of identity, location, and locution that most commonly defines the particularity of an ethnic culture" [Bhabha 1998: 34]), that incorporate exchanges with the whole of south central Africa. "In the narrow passage between rootedness and displacement," says Homi Bhabha, "when the archaic stability of ontology touches the memory of cultural displacement, cultural difference or ethnic location accedes to a social and psychic anxiety at the heart of identification and its locations" (35). What he is speaking about here is the distribution of a kind of anxiety between spaces that is manifold in Johannesburg. Unlike post-national European states, or older colonial urban spaces, South Africa's largest city has achieved a variety at its center that exists and yet is not recognized in terms of ontology. In each of the sites I have mentioned—Hillbrow, Joubert Park, Faraday, Newtown—the work of urban "improvement" ends up being at odds with intercontinental forms of sociality, exchange, and trade. The challenge facing organizations like Trinity is to bend public art to the service of "an idea of urbanism that is already social, already cultured . . . and already densely populated" (Place and Nuttall 2004: 543), and not to have art resolve itself down to sentinel public sculptures, or the aestheticized boundary markers that define corporate precincts. Recognition of this need would lead us to look more closely at models of desire, consumption, sociality, and space in market environments elsewhere: in south Asia, for instance (e.g., see Favero 2003).

These days, many of the artists working in and around the inner city of Johannesburg, concerned with the flow of new street-level economies, are also caught up in the vortex of a new kind of governmental intervention: that of state heritage programs. What before would have manifested itself in community arts projects, and collaborative public art, is now centripetally attracted to massive early-twenty-first-century heritage projects in the city such as Constitution Hill, and here lies our final example of attempts at mediating between distinct ontopologies of the city.

Con Hill, as it is affectionately known, is a vast construction site in which the old bastion of apartheid penal control, known as Number 4 to most black South Africans, and the Fort to others, is being redeveloped. When it is completed, it will be a moral backdrop to the ambitious new Constitutional Court. Millions of Africans passed through Number 4, often on petty pass offices, and unlike the sanitized site of Robben Island, this place still has a crude carceral brutality about it. A makeshift guard tower of corrugated iron looks down on a yard where prisoners would work and defecate in pit latrines; another thin strip of corrugated iron, two feet high and forty feet long, meant to mask the genitals of the squatting workers, ticks in the winter Highveld sun.

This intensely affective, ruined site presented a major dilemma to the artists and consultants asked to imagine temporary didactic displays. One of the most effective strategies they employed was to work very lightly on the surface of the site, with haze, gossamer, and indirection. In one very effective temporary information display, on the Fort ramparts overlooking the remains of the Awaiting Trial block and the construction site for the new court itself, Terry Kurgan, Mark Gevisser, Nina Cohen, and others installed a series of framed gauze panels, imprinted with images that recalled individual clauses of the new constitution. One of the most memorable, referring to the right to housing, was oriented so that the viewer looks through it and onto a dilapidated Hillbrow low-rise block, with the washing of residents, migrants, and refugees on the balconies. However, in an unsettling reversal, the image through which you squint depicts the view from the flat itself, the interpellating view of the refugee family itself, back toward the same spot on which the visitor now stands.

Vigils: This Body, This Precinct ✦ My argument thus far has described a circular, directed tour through some of the key sites of public art in urban Johannesburg, beginning in Hillbrow, descending to the southern outskirts of the city, and ambling back to Constitution Hill, the biggest heritage building project involving public arts in post-apartheid South Africa. To be fair, though, art has been both a direct witness to and an instigator of the violent clashes between the contradictory views of citizenship fought out in these regenerated spaces. Nowhere was this more spectacularly demonstrated than in Steven Cohen's evocative *Chandelier* performances. Cohen brings the spectacle of the perverse into spaces and situations associated with the limits of the new democracy. Among the most testing of these situations is that of the new forced removals: for the neoliberal agenda of the Mbeki government, the spectacle of urban squatters and illegal land occupation is deeply problematic. Trying to encourage investment capital back into the inner city, and a precinct-based separation of defended spheres, yet faced with problems of job creation, increasing embarrassment over corruption scandals at a time when World Bank debt write-offs are being tied to anti-corruption drives, and the problem of a recalcitrant Robert Mugabe, city authorities regard illegal land occupation as a terrible symbolic dilemma. Municipal projects to clear slum areas of illegal squatters (the Better Buildings Project would be one example), are fueled by a wider public paranoia about illegal work seekers. Quite literally, these are haunted civic programs, in that they both evoke and are fearful of the return of the ghosts of forced removals from the apartheid past.

But there is another type of spectral return that is feared by local government, and that is the apparition of apartheid era liberalism. The figure of the passive watcher and witness to events—events that are then discursively and morally constituted as equivalent to past apartheid practice—is an especially volatile trope in present conversation. What it conjures, for the state, is the ghost of "feminized" moral vigils, best represented by the silent protests of the Black Sash in the 1970s around issues like detention without trial and forced removal. Infuriating in its silence, passivity, and sculptural immobility, the Black Sash represented a position on resistance to apartheid associated with public shaming to which the apartheid government was always vulnerable.

As a queer performance artist, Steven Cohen stands in a similar "moralized" position in relation to citizenship, rights, and constitutionality. In 2001, Cohen created a performance piece called *Chandelier,* in which he strayed onto the site of a forced removal of illegal squatters by municipal workers in the characteristic red uniforms that has earned them the name "red ants." Seminude, in a revealingly corseted tutu, powdered and whitened, head shaved and inscribed, and wearing a beautifully balanced armature of lights consisting of an elaborate crystal chandelier with lit elements, Cohen tinkled around the site and interfered in the most active scenes. Over the past years, Steven Cohen has specialized in testing the limits of the new citizenship at its most sensitive points and in its most contradictory urban manifestations. Like prominent activists in the Treatment Action Campaign, he has been singularly successful at dramatizing perverse responses to AIDS and queer identity, and he has systematically tested surviving institutions of prejudice, from dog shows to mall beauty-queen ramp parades. Cohen has staged perverse claims on citizenship in a series of spectacular performances. These have usually combined the public use of sex toys, the display of anal eroticism, rhetorics of sadomasochism, and the flagrant use of abject bodily fluids like blood, urine, and excrement. *Chandelier* is an apparently less controversial piece. Its language is self-consciously that of the aesthetic, but of a second-order aesthetics borrowed from bourgeois privilege: Christmas-tree ornaments, and the language of northern suburbs privilege, are returned and recast into forms of queer white performance that are very problematic. Cohen's art constitutes the body as a site of perverse pleasure, and aesthetics, in another troubling respect: in the regenerative logics of city planning, art and its objects help to create pleasurable vistas; what Cohen underlines is the pleasure and aesthetics of other senses apart from sight, most especially the desire to be touched (see figure 8).

8 Steven Cohen, *Chandelier,* 2002, performance in Newtown, Johannesburg. Courtesy of David Krut publishing

In *Chandelier,* and other pieces, Cohen inserts himself into quite volatile situations where the violence resides in separation: the separation of gender and sex; or the physical removal of communities. Having occupied these spaces, he then appeals to the desire of bodies to mingle, calling up a phenomenology of pleasure based in bodily curiosity. This logic is entirely opposite to the law of the "precinct." This kind of witness performance approaches the city as though it is an aesthetic project in the making; that is to say, it stands in opposition to the zonal logics of urban planning and refocuses attention on the distributed, human sources of present value in the city.

A similar form of existential witnessing—reminiscent of Rilke's angel of history or Wim Wenders's *Wings of Desire*—may be found in Minette Vári's spectacular recent Lamba prints and two-channel video work (I am thinking especially of *Sentinel, The Calling,* and *Riverrun*). Vári's inner city has an achieved aesthetics, and the new subjectivities associated with this urban landscape represent it as metamorphic outgrowths of older architectures. Like Wenders's parapet angel, Vári stages herself in *The Calling* as a transforming gargoyle, brought into flesh by the city. A similar sense of identity as flow, in relation to the achieved city and a newly complex democracy, may be found in her *Riverrun* series of prints: here the phenomenological space-time experience of the city is compressed into a series of blurred sequences, reprojected onto the body and imaged as a sort of looming urban cloud.

What I have been looking at, in this synoptic essay, is the engagement of Johannesburg artists with the problem of mediation. Expressed first in the 1970s and 1980s in a concern for surfaces that fail to engage with meaningful depth, or a significant archive, these philosophical considerations are further refined in the examination of the figure of skin in contemporary Johannesburg-based artists like Siopis and van den Berg. Scars, in their work, are not simply the mark of a generalized episteme of trauma; instead, epidermal coarsening, on the one hand, or the uncanny permeability of skin on the other, points to an uncertainty about the future of the body, time, and the conditions of intimacy that have yet to be built. Imagining a strange change in the nature of the surface, they have been able to herald in their work a new kind of emergent public being. Similarly, the public arts I have surveyed attempt to mediate between the enclaved zones of the corporate precinct, and the present existence of migrant communities, sometimes coming into direct conflict with the new forces of urban planning. Only very recently, however, has art itself begun to achieve a philosophical inwardness premised on an acceptance of Johannesburg in its present state. In the end, such work anticipates a loveliness to come, flowing from this city and its aesthetics.

Notes

1 See Buck-Morss 1989; Mbembe and Nuttall 2004. My reference, naturally, is to Benjamin's *Passagen-Werk,* but the sense of flatness, of surfaces that will not yield to a penetrating gaze, is paralleled by the modernist sense of a self that is dulled and anaesthetized by the "technologically multiplied shock" it encounters in the city. See Hansen 1999: 317.

2 Poulantzas also exercised huge influence over the revisionist understanding of the transition to capitalism. In Mike Morris's structuralist understanding, a capitalist mode of production comes into being in the countryside through the transformation, from above, of semifeudal relations of peasant production. This thesis on the "Prussian path" to capitalism depended on the understanding of a brutal, class-fractional alliance between the state and farmers to produce a steady farm labor supply. See M. Morris 1976 and Bradford 1990: 65.

3 This seems like a bad dream now, but the colonialism-of-a-special-type thesis on South Africa was at one point in our political history the common hypothesis that united left historians, the South African Communist Party [SACP], and the African National Congress. The SACP advocated a "two-stage revolution," the first stage aimed at achieving national liberation, and the second at achieved forms of socialism. However, because this strategy was derived from the study of colonial situations, it required a peculiar kind of modification for the South African case: that is, that colonialism is internal to South Africa, and of a special type in which black South Africa is a colony of white. See Callinicos 1986.

4 Some of the breakthrough articles would include Johnstone 1970 and Wolpe 1972. For early social history critiques of the structuralist position, see Clarke 1978; for overviews, see Davies, Kaplan, Morris, and O'Meara 1976, and Bozzoli and Delius 1990.

5 Differences of opinion about the origins of racial capitalism in South Africa characterized both academic and activist rhetoric from the 1970s until the 1990s. This was at one and the same time a very productive debate, leading to major new theories about the development of class affiliation in the countryside, and very destructive, when it was used to distinguish one form of party political affiliation from another. A Leninist line would follow Marx's argument in *Capital,* vol. 1, about changes in the relations of production in the countryside (including the dispossession of the peasantry), and would in the same period have been antagonistic toward the Sweezy and Wallerstein "neo-Smithian" account of the growing influence of exchange relations. The latter, perhaps, was more amenable to discussion of the nature of commodity exchange and urban identity than the former.

6 The complex, masculine hierarchies used to police mine-compound life are well described by a variety of writers. "Boss boys," or *indunas,* were on the top rung of the racial hierarchy, whereas a *sibonda* was a dormitory leader appointed by fellow workers. See for instance, Moodie 1994.

7 *Amakwerekwere* is the dismissive, xenophobic term sometimes applied to foreigners seen to be competing unfairly for local jobs and services.

8 For an excellent analysis of Zulu's use of fire as a transformative medium, see Richards 2005.

9 For a nuanced account of van den Berg's recent work, see R. Morris 2004.

10 Siopis, personal communication with the author, June 2006.

11 This is reminiscent of Francis Bacon, who, Deleuze claims, attempts to give visible expression to the simultaneous experience of a variety of allied senses. See van Alphen 1998: 32.

12 For an influential analysis of the proliferation of zombie-like figures during the crisis of political transition in South Africa, see Comaroff and Comaroff 1999.

13 This element of the Siopis series has been elegantly described by Sarah Nuttall (2005).

14 Vlakplaas was the notorious death farm used by various secretive apartheid assassination squads. In the last decade before the 1994 election, a significant portion of apartheid's violence was fuelled by secret alliances between the government, the police,

the military, the Inkatha Freedom Party, and underground hit squads and assassins. Before its true nature was revealed, this shadowy evil was routinely referred to as the Third Force.

15 Beryl Markham's autobiographical epic of pioneer African flying, *West with the Night,* was an object of deep fascination for women of my aunt's generation.

16 This is one of the key images chosen by David Koloane for the entry on Tshabangu in the controversial *Ten Years/One Hundred Artists* volume.

17 The use of whistle alarm calls is a fascinating feature of public life in townships. During the 1980s state of emergency, young comrades at the center of street committees would use whistle calls to warn of the arrival of the police and to knot together informal kinds of sociality. This remains a permanent feature of street governance and vigilantism in South Africa today: criminals in the act of committing crimes may find themselves surrounded by residents blowing whistles to call up squads of helpers. As Melinda Silverman recalls (Silverman and Myeza 2005: 46), even the photographers in Joubert Park use whistles to call for help from fellow artists when they are threatened or in danger of being mugged.

18 Some of this noninstrumental, fantastical investment in the city's projective possibility has been captured in the anthropology of witchcraft. Some years ago, for instance, Mark Auslander showed how the witch-finding rituals of Ngoni diviners in eastern Zambia drew heavily on the bureaucratic strategies for inducting labor into the South African gold mines; and in a classic analysis, John and Jean Comaroff discuss the representational "madness" of a Tshidi mine migrant, who uses a proliferation of Johannesburg gold mining references to work through the crazed splitting inherent in the new cash economies and the loss of subsistence based in cattle value (Comaroff and Comaroff 1992: 174).

19 Silverman and Msizi Myeza (2005: 44) draw attention to the regular geometry of the nineteenth-century plantings, which "emphasized regularity and order in contrast to the chaotic streets of the rapidly expanding town" in the late nineteenth century.

20 The 2002 Creative Inner City Initiative, for instance, concentrated on training young artists in and around Hillbrow and Joubert Park.

21 Terry Kurgan, interview with the author, June 15, 2005, Johannesburg. For a fuller account of the entire project, see Kurgan and Ractliffe 2005.

22 The Lacanian notion of the *point de capiton* is applied by Slavoj Žižek (1989: 87–88) to those nodal quilting points that stabilize an ideological field and prevent its disseminating drift.

23 Stephen Hobbs, interview with the author, Johannesburg, July 3, 2005.

24 The charge of "neo-Smithian" Marxism, as described by Robert Brenner (1977) in "The Origins of Capitalist Development: A Critique of Neo-Smithian Marxism," was often leveled at left intellectual South African academics intent on examining questions of the subject and the commodity form, rather than (of course) the relations of production. The effect of this intellectual hostility was to delay very substantially any serious discussion of the meaning of desire as well as consumption in urban South Africa.

Translated by Judith Inggs

6 ⸭ The Suffering Body of the City

FRÉDÉRIC LE MARCIS

Since 1990, parallel to the period of transition to a democratic society, the AIDS epidemic in South Africa has increased dramatically. The level of HIV infection in the adult population (ages fifteen to forty-nine) rose from 1 percent in 1990 to more than 20 percent in 2000. However, this figure conceals a disparity in the distribution of the disease. The townships are affected far more than the largely white suburbs, while in the townships themselves the highest levels are found in the so-called squatter camps (Shisana and Simbayi 2002).[1] The combination of pandemic and democracy has wrought changes specific to sufferers living on the periphery of Johannesburg. People obtained their freedom and fell sick at the same time. The newly acquired sovereignty has enabled individuals to explore previously unavailable urban spaces, to develop innovative forms of political mobilization, and to access, in new ways, health services that had once been forbidden to them. The practices of these suffering bodies are the focus of this essay.

Generally the body that is inscribed in most scholarly work on the city is the healthy body. Theorists of modernity regard the city as the place par excellence for the realization of the individual. If the individual suffers, it is usually from isolation and anonymity (Simmel 1971). Otherwise, the individual is autonomous and free from disease. It is with reference to this presupposed healthy body that typologies (Hannerz 1980) and concepts such as mobility, trickery, and poaching (de Certeau 1990), strolling (Baudelaire 1968), and wandering (Benjamin [1982] 2002) have been developed. These concepts have also subsequently been used to give meaning to a whole set of daily urban practices (Gibbal et al. 1981; Bourgois 1995; de Villers, Jewsiewicki, and Monnier 2002). In these works, the body is considered as a medium for or object of various practices, which are in turn the subject of analysis. Even if such practices lead to a deterioration of the body (Bourgois 1995), the body sui generis is not present in their definition as such.

In what follows, I take the suffering body as the starting point for a discussion of the city. In making use of the life stories and itineraries of AIDS sufferers living on the periphery of Johannesburg, I redraw the map of the city outlined by the bodies of those who are poor, hunted, suffering, and in search of care. I show how, far from being immobile, the sick body moves and travels. In doing so, it shuttles constantly between private and public spaces, unveiling the city through its movements. I show how the body afflicted with AIDS itself constitutes an archetypal figure in the city of Johannesburg and how, in its search for care and for sanctuary, it acts as a place of mediation and meeting between the public and the private, the official and the unofficial, the here and the elsewhere.

Most of the sick have no fixed income. Some receive a disability grant of R700 a month on the basis of their HIV status,[2] but for many, mobility and trickery are the means of survival (de Certeau 1990). Underlying their struggle is a quest for social and therapeutic support and, for some, a quest for social recognition through militant involvement in HIV/AIDS associations. The Johannesburg itineraries described here do not cover the entire experience of those living with HIV/AIDS, but they do allow an understanding of certain fragments of that experience and urban reality. Johannesburg, in this reality, appears as a series of dots, with cardinal points in certain public places (health centers, administrative buildings) and other sites where sick people are hiding or where they are known only as nearly dead bodies (houses where the sick find refuge, unofficial places of care, hospices for the dying, and finally, the cemetery). There are also other destinations, places of transit and stopover that together weave an urban fabric, the fibers of which are familiar only to those who are HIV-positive.

Along these journeys, Johannesburg also appears in its ambivalence; that is, the city appears as an expression or sign of the harshness of the world but also, occasionally, as one of compassion. Just as it authorizes the exploitation of the sick, so it opens up a myriad of possibilities in terms of care and mobilization. The itineraries of these suffering bodies in the city thus draw a map of the management and the geography of AIDS in Johannesburg.[3] An exploration of these journeys is not limited to that of care. It brings to light the fact that these bodies and selves belong to the urban reality and, more broadly, to the field of national issues as well as to the globalized world. They are integrated, for instance, into the exchange of pharmaceutical products on a global scale, an integration that exposes them to the violence of the market and to exploitation. Other circuits are also explored that allow the suffering bodies tracked here to become people of the polis. In this capacity, they form part of the emergence of a civil society.

Places of Suffering and Places of Mercy

For those who do not work or whose families have no income, the capacity to travel in the city often depends on the receipt of the disability grant. This is the case for Dalene, a twenty-eight-year-old woman who lives in Alexandra. Formerly a part-time cashier in a supermarket, she was the only person providing for her mother and sisters, with whom she lives. Her father left them long ago. Now she is seriously ill, and her monthly disability grant of R700 is the sole source of household income. Receiving it at the end of each month revives Dalene's vague desires to travel within the city; it also means she can afford a taxi and hospital consultation (R15). When Dalene's health was good, she used to enjoy visiting the shopping malls in Sandton, the nearby wealthy suburb, but today such excursions are barely possible. In addition to being generally very frail, she is suffering from a suppurating abscess on her hand, which gives off a foul-smelling odor. The arrival of visitors with transport makes the family more amenable to Dalene's wishes. We agree to take her to Edenvale Hospital, a few kilometers south of Alexandra.

Logbook, Alexandra, June 5, 2002: We arrived and waited for her to get dressed. She was wearing a beige jacket that had clearly just been dry-cleaned (the label was still attached) and a pleated lilac skirt. She was also wearing very nice evening shoes. These clothes must have been one of her best outfits. She clearly wanted to make a good impression. Her sister and mother helped her to get ready. Her mother combed her hair and cleaned her hand (the reason for going to Edenvale Hospital). Her sister got her papers together and put them in a multicolored woven straw bag. Despite these devices, Dalene's generally feeble condition, the bad smell that surrounded her, and her thinning hair meant that all these efforts were rather pointless. When she went out into the street to get into the Beetle, the neighbors gathered round as if at a show, silent and curious. They were as intrigued by our presence as by Dalene's outing.

Dalene had already seen several doctors about her hand, first at the university clinic in Alexandra (First Avenue), then in Parktown, at the Johannesburg General Hospital. But the treatment she had been given (betadine and antibiotics) seemed to have had no effect. Edenvale was a last try. It was there that she had given birth and discovered her HIV-positive status, but she had never been back.

Normally, Dalene would have had to take a minibus taxi to get to Edenvale Hospital. The journey costs R9 round-trip. She would have walked up the length of Hofmeyr Road to reach the western edge of the township. A business zone called Pan Africa is situated there, the departure point for the township taxis at the north end of First Avenue. She would have waited until a minibus taxi going to Edenvale Hospital filled up with the requisite twelve people before leaving. She had made this journey several times before, but now it would have been impossible, given her ill health. We leave the congested streets of Alexandra and drive into Canning Road, after crossing London Road, which marks the southern boundary of the township and which is lined with factories. Some are disused and inhabited by squatters. One factory still in operation manufactures the condiment *achar*, filling the road with the smell of oil and spices. Furthest from Alexandra, on Vasco de Gamma Road, other factories have been turned into churches, such as the Rhema Church. The same phenomenon can be seen in the center of the township, where the Universal Church has been established for some time.

Once over the "industrial quarantine line," a vestige of apartheid politics dedicating the place of work as a privileged meeting place between blacks and whites, the road winds down through a small valley passing through the suburbs of Bramley View Extension, Lombardy West, Corlett Gardens, and Rembrandt Park. Before the demise of apartheid, these suburbs housed middle-class white families. After apartheid, some of these families sold their homes and gave way to an emerging black middle class. Canning Road eventually becomes Wordsworth Road and then joins Modderfontein Road in Edenvale.

The whole journey follows the Jukskei River. This narrow river traverses the township and links it, like Ariadne's thread, to Edenvale Hospital, whose grounds it runs through. In Alexandra, there are still shacks in some places along the banks of the Jukskei River. In Edenvale, the river is bordered by open fields, where children from the neighboring suburbs used to play before the end of apartheid (today the area seems less secure and these fields remain empty). Edenvale Hospital is situated on a leafy green hill, accessed by a road that links Modderfontein to the center of the city. At the entrance to the hospital, street traders sell sweets, cigarettes, and other goods to people waiting for minibus taxis to take them back to the township. During the apartheid period, this hospital was a public hospital reserved for whites. The inhabitants of Alexandra had to go to Baragwanath in Soweto. Today Edenvale Hospital is inundated with patients referred from various Alexandra clinics.

From clinics to hospitals, Dalene tries to hedge her options by rewriting her medical history and hiding her HIV-positive status, which she feels, often justifiably, to be an obstacle to good care from the health services. Following this logic, although she is doomed to failure because of her physical appearance, Dalene opens a new file when she arrives at the hospital rather than handing in her old one. The files of patients known to be HIV-positive are marked with signs or abbreviations recognizable to health professionals, which alert them to the patients' status.

The coding of HIV-positive patients is linked to the politics of hospital management. Faced with a major shortage of hospital beds, the doctors often choose not to admit HIV-positive patients at an advanced stage of AIDS, because their chances of recovery are limited, while they would admit someone with the same symptoms who is HIV-negative. By not admitting an HIV-positive patient, the doctor can keep the bed for an HIV-negative patient or someone at a less advanced stage of the disease. Days of hospitalization may be saved, since the results of treating HIV-positive patients are somewhat unpredictable.

By changing her file, Dalene is changing her status. After a two-hour wait for an outpatient consultation, she leaves the hospital, fed up with queuing and with little confidence in the outcome of the consultation. In any case the nurse at reception had remarked, even before greeting her, "Here, we don't deal with that"—gesturing toward Dalene's purulent hand. Later, her condition deteriorating, Dalene's family has her admitted to Mother Teresa House, a hospice in Yeoville. She stays there for a few weeks before dying.

When families can no longer take care of the sick, or when those who are ill live alone and home visits by volunteers are not effective, some make a final journey to one of the hospices near the center of town, for example Mother Teresa House or the Rhema Church Service Foundation in Hillbrow. Once again, the trip leading to death passes through the city or, more accurately, through the places of pity and mercy that reinscribe the instability of life in the city at the center of the subject's consciousness, an instability that we can see as part of the nature of modernity itself. While elsewhere the city seeks to show itself in the shape of the bar, the café, the restaurant, the shop, or the motorway, here it appears as a final attempt to render the last moments of life humane.

Protected behind high walls, Mother Teresa House is situated on a quiet street and surrounded by small houses. Apart from the name MOTHER TERESA HOUSE inscribed in blue letters on the front of the building, there is nothing to hint at the drama that takes place behind its walls. The hospice is unobtrusive; only the arrival of emaciated bodies betrays its anonymity. It is a two-story building. On the ground floor there are a chapel, a waiting room, and a men's ward. Upstairs there are two women's wards. It is a clean and tranquil place, where patients are given a courteous welcome by a sister of the order of the Missionaries of Charity, dressed in a sari and smiling reassuringly.

Patients must give the hospice advance notice of their arrival to avoid being sent away for lack of space. Once patients have been admitted, they receive care and food. This welcome contrasts sharply with the long wait required to be admitted to public hospitals and, generally, for any consultation in the public health sector. Admittedly, the health services have to deal with a large number of patients and small, overworked staffs, who are unable to attend to patients quickly. In practice, in a primary health care clinic—the first stage in the system—patients normally wait about two hours before being seen by a nurse who, in less than two minutes, sends them to a colleague dealing with the particular problem presented. The patient then finds him- or herself in another queue and is finally examined by a nurse for an average of five to ten minutes. Sometimes the patient will be redirected to a health center further up the ladder, either to be seen by a doctor or to be hospitalized. For the suffering body, the rhythm and the temporalities of the city are often characterized by waiting. There is no movement. Only knowing how to wait.

The outwardly gentle appearance of the hospice should not conceal the seriousness of admission to Mother Teresa House: one comes here to die. The patients have no misconceptions about this; nor do those who accompany patients who have no family support: they sign a discharge form authorizing the organization of a pauper's funeral. These funerals are provided by the Department of Social Services. A dismal cycle then begins in which the patients impotently witness the regular departures of their neighbors on the ward, awaiting their own turns. Here the city comes to a standstill. Here, too, the journeys of the sick come to an end. What leaves the hospice is no longer a body, but the remains, a corpse. The body as such is henceforth confined to bed, all but immobile. The city, for its part, grows dark—and then disappears. And so vanish the city's boundaries as much as the limits of the body and life of the sick person.

The Networks of the Sick

Visits to clinics, then to hospitals, thus form a first circle of exploration, before the hospice. Turning to the hospital offers an opportunity for leaving the area where care is organized around the clinic. In Alexandra, the Health Centre and University Clinic (a clinic that has the status of a nongovernmental organization [NGO] and is better known as the First Avenue Clinic) is found at the western edge of the township. In contrast to public clinics, which offer primary health care services, the First Avenue Clinic has doctors, an emergency service, and a laboratory. Recently renovated, it offers its patients a safe and peaceful haven in addition to treatment. Even the architectural structure of the clinic (several houses linked by corridors around a grassed courtyard) breaks with the unimaginative model of the public clinics (usually rectangular red-brick buildings with consulting rooms distributed along a central corridor). The patients and their families often sit in this courtyard, turning it into a convivial waiting room. During the states of emergency in the 1980s, the clinic was reputed to have protected United Democratic Front (UDF) militants from the police. It is said that nurses used to "lose" the files of patients wounded by bullets, because the police would try to identify participants in the clashes by examining the consultation records.

A symbol of Alexandra's involvement in the struggle against apartheid, the clinic maintained its involvement with the people of the township during the violence that rocked Alexandra before the 1994 elections. In order to reach patients for whom the area around the clinic had become a no-go area, mobile units were set up that traveled around the suburbs. The older employees have nostalgic memories of that period of the struggle when the clinic was united around a shared sense of service to the community of Alexandra. Today the clinic faces a huge influx of patients. From seven in the morning, the benches along the walls of the corridors are filled with people waiting for treatment. Both patients and nurses complain that medicines are often lacking. Nevertheless, for the people of Alexandra who are HIV-positive, the First Avenue Clinic remains the closest and most effective place of treatment. It is often there that they are tested for the first time and learn of their HIV-positive status.

However, it does not take long for the clinic to reach its limits, forcing patients to search elsewhere for treatment. Medicines that are normally distributed free of charge (immunity boosters, vitamins) are rarely available in the pharmacy. Other places, such as the Johannesburg General Hospital (JGH), seem to have adapted better to the demand. The JGH in particular has a dedicated clinic for AIDS sufferers. The hospital has greater technological resources and often a wider range of medical specialists. Yet it still features the same structural problems as the clinics. At Baragwanath Hospital in Soweto, the admissions procedure takes an exceptionally long time, and patients must be present for the entire process even if they are quite weak.

The admissions area at Baragwanath is filled with patients lying on stretchers, files in their hands or, if they cannot hold them, slipped under the mattress or under a leg. This admissions process—which limits the possibility of fraud by preventing the admission of virtual patients—creates, in effect, a glut of bodies, more or less living. At Edenvale Hospital the situation is somewhat different, as the hospital still benefits from its former status as a hospital for whites. It is situated on a hill, and the large windows in the reception hall provide a panoramic view of Johannesburg. The admissions procedure is no less cumbersome than at Baragwanath, but the hospital has the advantage of a more modern infrastructure and a more humane admission process. For example, the patients are invited to sit in a booth so they can complete the admitting forms in privacy.

AIDS thus quickly demands ever-increasing circles of exploration, obliging sufferers little by little to crisscross the city. The options provided for HIV-positive patients by the public services (clinics, hospitals, social assistance), the NGOs and the churches (support groups for patients), and the various therapy or education options are spread out across the metropolitan area. The patients circulate among these different places depending on their means of transport and the quality of the service offered. This applies, for example, to patients wishing to obtain a medical certificate on the grounds of physical incapacity, a prerequisite for receipt of a disability grant. The rules state that a medical certificate can be issued only if the individual concerned is physically unable to work. Some doctors consider an individual with a CD4 T-cell count of two hundred or lower to be eligible for the grant.[4] Others are willing to sign a medical certificate as soon as the individual is HIV-positive.

These movements around the city often begin with support groups for people living with HIV/AIDS. The activities of these groups, which vary according to their coordinators and institutional affiliations, include the exchange of information, advice, and experiences of patients, organizing home care, and delivering food parcels. Generally, the advice given to the members of support groups focuses on the idea of a "healthy lifestyle." The literature distributed at the clinics by the Department of Health advises patients to "take care of your health (eat properly, do physical exercise, get enough rest), have a positive outlook on life (set personal objectives, believe in yourself, see the positive side of things, be aware of your strengths and weaknesses), try to get the support of those around you (family and church), practice safer sex": all designed to ensure a "healthy lifestyle." The coordinators generally sum up the expression "healthy lifestyle" by condemning alcohol consumption and tobacco use and encouraging the use of condoms.

To address participants' nutritional problems, meals are sometimes provided at the meetings, or food parcels are delivered. The groups vary considerably according to their institutional affiliation. Some are run by local or international NGOS, others by churches. They may also be organized in the context of research programs on HIV/AIDS. The support groups' knowledge of the pandemic and related issues, as well as their financial resources, depends in some measure on their institutional support. Some groups develop income-generating projects (e.g., handicraft workshops, vegetable gardens). Memory boxes are another type of project. These allow sufferers to prepare for their demise by leaving traces of themselves for their families in the form of texts or photographs. The groups also serve as a forum for discussing common dilemmas, such as disclosing one's HIV status to family and social circles or the possibility of having a child.

HIV-positive individuals are referred to support groups most often by the clinics, but word of mouth also plays a role. A young HIV-positive woman who had recently joined such a group said, "When I was phoning, Elsy saw me. She called me. She said she was going to take me there and there, and she started telling me about the support group. If it was not because of her, I would have known nothing." The arrival of a new member begins with an interview with the group coordinator. This interview takes the form of a confession during which the newcomer relates his or her personal history. The newcomer is then introduced to the other members who in turn introduce themselves briefly by giving the date on which they discovered their HIV status: "HIV positive since 1999, for three years." The newcomer introduces him- or herself last. Each person's story is revealed little by little or not at all, in full or in part, depending on the relationships that develop within the group. The initial sharing of the date of infection gives a common base that provides a driving force for these groups. It does not, however, imply any unconditional sharing of experiences or suffering. The coordinator normally remains the primary facilitator among the members of support groups. He or she often enjoys a privileged relationship with the social or health services and as a result may be able to intervene positively if necessary—providing access to grants, assistance in cases of domestic violence, and consultation on specific health problems.

Attending a support group sometimes means journeys over long distances, not because the groups are few but because patients tend to look for confidentiality. Porshia lives in a shack in Dobsonville. She found out that she was HIV positive after she was raped during a visit to her family's home in the Transkei. She attends a support group in Diepkloof (about twelve kilometers from Dobsonville), which allows her to conceal her HIV status and her rape from her neighbors. Similarly, individuals living in Orlando East, rather than attend the support group in their neighborhood, avoid unwanted encounters by attending the Diepkloof clinic's group in the adjacent suburb. In effect, weekly visits to a neighborhood clinic (groups generally meet once a week) could lead neighbors to gossip about one's HIV status and raise suspicions within one's own family, who are often unaware of the situation. In some cases, the disclosure of HIV-positive status leads to discrimination by the family: family members may stop sharing food with the sufferer, or he or she may be asked to stay alone in a backyard shack instead of staying inside the house. The family may also fear being seen as a "host" to the illness in the neighborhood. Of course these reactions are not systematic and differ from one place to another, from one family to another. Nevertheless, they often justify people's need to hide their HIV-positive status.

Elisabeth lives in a shack in Diepkloof and does attend the support group at her local clinic. To explain her frequent visits to the health center, she says that she is being treated for tuberculosis. A young man living in Yeoville attends a clinic and support group in Alexandra. In his case, the desire for confidentiality goes together with a search for quality treatment. The clinic he attends in Alexandra seems to him to offer a better service than those that are closer to where he lives. Domestic workers in the northern suburbs of

Johannesburg, not far from Alexandra, also provide the township clinics with their quota of patients in search of free treatment. The city drawn by the support group is thus made up of juxtapositions and enclosures. It is made of fragments of anonymity. The individual wanders through it wearing, of necessity, a mask. This is a dispersed metropolis, where place has sense only in relation to a duplicate that simultaneously hides and erases it.

Epidemic, Sales, and Profits

As centers of information exchange, the support groups also act as places of recruitment for therapeutic trials or for commercial activities, introducing sufferers to more and more complex networks that effectively turn the city into a veritable labyrinth.[5] Individuals' participation in these different networks is inscribed within the framework of a search for treatment. Confronted by the absence of a definitive therapeutic response to their disease, HIV-positive individuals who cannot purchase antiretroviral drugs through private doctors seize any opportunity that presents itself and thus serve up their bodies to therapeutic trials.

Some tests are legal and are supervised by competent authorities. This is true of therapeutic trials conducted at Baragwanath Hospital in the PHRU (Perinatal HIV Research Unit). Here, all tests are subject to a validation request from the ethics committee of the University of the Witwatersrand. When tests concerning new medicines are involved, they are submitted to the MCC (Medicines Control Council) and to the Gauteng Province Protocol Review Committee. In some cases, the Faculty of Health Sciences Institutional Review Board is also consulted.

Other tests are conducted secretly and carry no guarantee for the volunteers. A young HIV-positive man belonging to an Alexandra support group was recruited in the street to take part in clandestine trials in Yeoville. On this particular day, his only mark of identification was a T-shirt on which was written HIV POSITIVE. A white man approached him and explained that he was looking for volunteers on behalf of a friend. These volunteers were needed to take part in AIDS therapeutic trials. He invited him to come along and bring with him any HIV-positive friends. Five members of the young man's support group turned up at the selected venue. There they found other patients who had been sent by a nurse at the Johannesburg General Hospital in Parktown. For three months, they received ultrasound therapy once a week in a flat in Orange Grove, an opulent northern suburb of Johannesburg. The contract the participants signed required them to keep the treatment secret because, they were told, the government refused to take care of HIV/AIDS sufferers and would probably try to eliminate anyone who was able to find medication.[6] During the trials, these guinea pigs were given nutritional supplements and sent to a private Parktown clinic to evaluate the effect of the treatment on their CD4 counts and viral loads. Their transport costs were covered. Later, they were taken to a public hospital in Pretoria for control tests because the costs were lower there. The trials ended without any results being communicated to the volunteers. The participants in these trials revealed their experience to the rest of the support group only later, when the feeling of having been exploited got the better of their hope for a cure. Moving in an economy where limited treatment is available favors the concealment and the compartmentalization of networks.

Within the framework of these secret therapeutic trials, sufferers are displaced from home to clinic and obliged to make trips out of the townships only to serve as guinea pigs. When these journeys are finished, sufferers often have nothing more to show than a worthless contract and a few laboratory bills. One of the volunteers claimed that an opposition party seeking to oppose the African National Congress (ANC) on the issue of AIDS had financed the trials in which he had participated. There was no proof of this, but it may well be that the epidemic has become a factor in the party political struggle. The more Thabo Mbeki's denial was publicized, the more the issue of AIDS became a key aspect of the opposition's criticism of the government.[7] If the debate concerned the question of the delivery of antiretroviral drugs, it was also deeply inscribed in the history of race relations in South Africa and more generally in the context of North-South relations (Posel 2003). Experiences of such therapeutic trials in the opulent northern suburbs leave a rather bitter taste in the mouth.

Similar things happen in the townships. The same impunity protects those who, on the pretext of looking for an African cure for AIDS, exploit the bodies of the sick and thereby earn money, charging patients up to R1,500 to participate in these so-called trials. In these networks, business and disease turn out to be good bedfellows. Here the logics of individual care at a local level intersect with the logics of profit, politics, and ideology at the national level. In political projects and ideological debates, those living with HIV/AIDS seem to be little more than raw material to be exploited. The intervention of President Mbeki and the then–minister of health Nkosazana Zuma in the Virodene trials of 1998 is just one example of the collusion between politics and the search for treatment.[8] These debates are also ideological, because the legitimacy of ethically dubious trials is based on the Africanness of the research carried out. In the name of a search for an African response to the pandemic, some doctors are authorizing the establishment of therapeutic trials without supervision from the MCC and without backing from an ethics committee.

In fact, alongside networks of therapeutic trials—whether official (such as those at Baragwanath Hospital) or unofficial (such as the ones in the townships)—commercial networks are being established from within support groups. One such network is the South African company Pharma Natura, which has specialized in the sale of so-called natural pharmaceutical products for the last forty years.[9] Under the name of one of its divisions, Optilife, it has established a medicosocial orientation center in Wynberg, an industrial area situated near Alexandra township.[10] This center recruits patients from the nearby Alexandra support groups and provides a holistic treatment for the sick. There they can consult a university doctor specializing in AIDS, who points them toward appropriate hospital services, while a social worker gives advice on accessing social assistance. In the waiting room, the patients find a wide range of pamphlets on AIDS, as well as brochures advertising a variety of natural products manufactured by the company.

These products range from vitamins and nutritional supplements to products for diseases of the skin. The company's leading products, inspired by anthroposophical medicine, are the Sutherlandia Formula and the VMA Formula.[11] The first is a cocktail of plants (*Sutherlandia frutescens* and olive leaves), vitamin E, and selenium, while the second is a nutritional supplement. The description of the Sutherlandia Formula draws on idioms of scientific discourse as much as of indigenous knowledge. Vitamin E and selenium are described as "antioxidants" and "immune boosters." Without ever explicitly mentioning AIDS, the vocabulary used belongs to the register of the epidemic. Along with the scientific term *Sutherlandia frutescens,* the common South African term is also given—the Afrikaans name *Kankerbos* (cancer bush). According to the Sutherlandia Formula leaflet, the plant "is regarded traditionally as a medicinal plant in Southern Africa and has enjoyed a long history of use in southern Africa." Optilife advises users to complement this cocktail of vitamins (two tablets morning and evening, at a cost of R50.50 for a box of 120) with the VMA Formula nutritional supplement (two capsules, one to three times a day, R45.60 for 60 capsules). The terms

HIV and AIDS do not appear in the leaflet that describes the supplement, but the disease appears beneath the surface. The nutritional supplement is aimed at those who suffer from "skin rashes, constipation or diarrhoea, weight loss, infections, night sweats"—and other characteristic symptoms of AIDS. Optilife's business strategy is to not mention AIDS directly so that the stigma attached to the disease does not chase away potential clients. One should be able to purchase these products without signaling one's HIV-positive status to family and friends.

The initial consultations were offered in the support groups free of charge. Optilife also invested in the refurbishment of the clinic and paid the salaries of the doctor and social worker. Because of low sales, a charge of R30 was introduced for each consultation. However, after a year, in February 2003, the clinic closed down, although there is a network of agents still operating in the city. Each agent receives, after a short period of training, a medication kit worth R150, which he or she is meant to restock as the contents are sold. The more products the agent sells, the greater the profit margin on each product. While Optilife uses a variety of ways to reach its clientele (getting patients to come to them, establishing agent networks, and contacting the medical services of large companies), others focus primarily on recruiting an army of small-scale traders who travel across the city, visiting HIV/AIDS support groups in various treatment centers. City of trade and city of disease, the informal and the formal, the visible and the hidden—all are intertwined, each embedded in the other.

The dialectic between indigenous knowledge and biomedicine is more marked and the reference to AIDS more explicit in advertisements for the following products than for Optilife. One such product is a Forever Living Products drink called Aloe Vera Gel, which is manufactured from the aloe vera plant and said to boost the immune system. Forever Living Products has had a presence in South Africa since 1995, via local distributors; in 2001, worldwide sales reached $1.3 billion.[12] On its Web site, the company states that its product has been used for centuries: "Aloe vera's skin smoothing emollients and healing capabilities have been known for centuries. The earliest reference to aloe vera was discovered with an Egyptian mummy from 1550 BC. Alexander the Great used aloe vera to restore the health of his troops. Cleopatra relied on it to help preserve her legendary beauty."

Aloe Vera Gel is recommended to support groups by retailers who report that aloe vera has been used for many years in black communities in South Africa. This discourse echoes the current South African debate around the recourse to local "traditional" knowledge in response to the AIDS epidemic. Although it has a local legitimacy, Aloe Vera Gel remains a global product. The company that manufactures it is based in Tempe, Arizona, in the United States. The one-liter bottle costs $16.95 (R125) on the U.S. Web site of Forever Living Products, while the bottle is sold in South African townships for between R250 and R300 ($36–$43). Staff in clinics who are responsible for pre- and postcounseling (individual interviews with patients before and after taking an AIDS test) are targeted by a number of retailers selling this kind of product. They are encouraged to direct those who are infected to the retailers, either by telling patients where to find them or by giving out a cell phone number. Once a specific number of patients has been referred, the counselor receives the total profit of one sale from the retailer.

This type of network marketing, a function of overlapping roles and common interests, also exists outside of places of treatment. For example, a civil servant responsible for processing applications for a disability grant (accessible to HIV-positive patients) might take advantage of this position to introduce sufferers to a trade network extending throughout the city. One such network was established by a company called Nature's Health Products based in Rietfontein, a town on the west side of Johannesburg. It extends across all the large cities of southern Africa. Nature's Health Products has a branch in Florida—a suburb southwest of the city center—and another in Soweto. It markets many products that are supposedly effective against AIDS. The heterogeneous names of these "anti-AIDS" products demonstrate the cosmopolitan nature of their market. For example there are products called Amandla (a Zulu word meaning "power"), African Potatoes/Inkomfe, Aloe Vera, Viraforce, Powerlife, and Miracle Muti (*muti* is a generic term for medication in traditional African medicine). The Nature's Health Web site indicates the multiple ways that the company ensures the value of its products:

> All of Nature's Health's products have undergone safety studies and we have scientific proof that they work. They are all manufactured according to international standards and all the regulations as laid down by the South African Medicines Control Council. Nature's Health's products are widely recommended by both medical and traditional doctors as well as hospitals and Aids clinics. Currently Miracle Muti is being given on a regular monthly basis to Aids patients at an Aids clinic. Research is being conducted on an ongoing basis to develop new products and to improve existing ones. Our range of products increases every

month. As a network marketing company we are actively recruiting new distributors all the time so that we will be able to service our clients and introduce more people to Miracle Muti.[13]

There is an underlying tension here between a Western reference ("international standards"), a scientific reference with universal value (the South African Medicines Control Council, "medical doctors"), and a secular African knowledge ("traditional doctors"). These three elements form the cornerstone of the sales techniques used by this company. They are also at the center of the debate on the methods of treating AIDS in South Africa as well as at the center of the dynamic of networks explored by those living with HIV/AIDS in the city. When the civil servant in the social services sees an HIV-positive individual, the civil servant distributes a copy of a promotional article extolling the merits of Miracle Muti. The tension manifested on the company's Web site can be found here too. In addition, this product is presented as an alternative to antiretrovirals, because it treats just about everything and is, moreover, nontoxic and has no side effects, at least according to the promoters: "MIRACLE MUTI now includes AMANDLA, a powerful combination of five of Africa's most potent herbs, which in scientific tests has proved to be very successful in the fight against HIV/AIDS because it is anti-viral, anti-fungal, anti-bacterial, antiseptic, and anti-inflammatory. Amandla is completely safe, non-toxic and without any side effects." The article encourages the reader to contact the distributor of the medication and includes the phone number.

Nature's Health locates potential customers in part through the intricate networks of HIV/AIDS patients, as in the case of Ntombi, who lives in Alexandra. She discovered her HIV-positive status a year ago, when she was pregnant. She has tried all kinds of treatments ranging from immune boosters to healing rituals in the Zionist Christian Church to muti purchased here and there. After joining a support group, she was directed to the nearest welfare office to apply for a disability grant. When she read the article referred to above, she made the telephone call. A white woman replied, which surprised Ntombi since she thought she was dealing with a black African muti. Indeed, some companies exploit the contemporary mood for an African herbal cure for AIDS, and in so doing they transgress the racialized assumptions about so-called indigenous cures. Ntombi described her symptoms (weight loss, diarrhea), and the woman assured her that if she took this Miracle Muti she would feel much better. She also explained to Ntombi that the bottle would cost R295 on the day of the conversation but the price would increase by R100 the following week. She asked her to take a minibus taxi to Florida and to phone again once she arrived so that she could be fetched from the taxi rank.[14] This city of suffering bodies is thus also a stream of stories and narratives accumulated by individuals, as well as of disappointments experienced along the myriad paths they traverse in search of treatment.

Ntombi's physical weakness and the fact that she does not have access to diverse social networks make her vulnerable to all kinds of exploitation. On one occasion, she visited her area clinic, where a nurse informed her that there was a shortage of medicine. The nurse advised Ntombi to buy some Bio Sil (an immune system booster sold both in pharmacies and door to door) and directed her to a nurse at Baragwanath Hospital in Soweto who sells herbs and medicines that counteract AIDS. There are countless such examples of people unable to receive care from public health services and referred to the private sector for muti or drugs.

The vitamin cocktail High Impact Vitamins has been on the market for several months. In the product description, it is called HI-Vite, which leaves little doubt as to the HIV status of the target market. The leaflet in circulation has three photos. The first shows "cold sores and fever blisters," the second "shingles and skin rash," and the last "thrush in the mouth and throat." The photos are preceded by a list of AIDS-related symptoms, presented as a rhetorical question: "Is someone in your family suffering from [list of symptoms]? They are! Then they need Hi-Vite to boost their chances of fighting their infections." A cell phone number and e-mail address are provided. Like the other products described above, HI-Vite claims to bring together indigenous knowledge and biomedicine. The cocktail's ingredients include, among other things, the African potato (known for its supposed effect as an immune-system booster), selenium, various minerals, and amino acids.

In the support group that Ntombi attends, not everyone has been systematically exploited in these trading networks. Some members have taken advantage of the system and have assumed more active roles as volunteers. They attend clinics outside their own areas to counsel patients. They then collect medicines for their own use or for their relatives to alleviate the chronic lack of supplies in their own area. The turn to new cures available in the city may result from a family member's initiative as well as from financial constraints. Adelina, a young HIV-positive woman, was taking AZT (Zidovudine, an antiretroviral medication) at a cost of R700 per month. This expense was covered by Adelina's aunt, a domestic worker for a white family in the north of Johannesburg. After one year of treatment, Adeline was advised to switch to a tri-therapy treatment, but this was very expensive and her aunt could no longer finance it.[15] Adeline's aunt advised her to go to the center of town to see an Indian doctor whom she knew who practiced Ayurvedic medicine. While trying not to cure her but simply to improve her general condition, this doctor prescribed a treatment based on roots and herbs that brought the monthly cost down to R125. Satisfied with this medication, Adelina is still taking it. She has also joined a support group in Alexandra where she provides home care as a volunteer.

Vast, anonymous, inscribed in the exchange of goods on an international level, and also caught up in a local epidemic and ideological context, Johannesburg allows individuals to invent their own cures. Cosmopolitan, it makes accessible all kinds of avenues, from Ayurvedic medicine and Chinese green tea, said to prolong life, to antiretrovirals sold in the offices of private doctors. While exploring these networks, or by creating them, sufferers cross the urban boundaries between rich and poor, black and white, and travel across the townships, the city center, and the northern suburbs. The area clinic and the hospital are the initial range of any exploration of the city. This circle then enlarges to include other clinics and other hospitals. Ever alert, patients take advantage of any opportunity that presents itself. These inscribe sufferers, often without their knowledge, in national or even global contests, both ideological and financial, and make them vulnerable to exploitation. The city, however, is creating the conditions for political mobilization, allowing people to exist not only as suffering bodies but also as political actors.

The Open City and the Creation of a Civil Society

For many people living with HIV/AIDS, the urban experience encountered on the edges of the townships is inscribed in wider life histories that often begin outside the city. Such is the case of Jesus and Elsy. After failing his final high school examinations in 1991, Jesus, originally from Limpopo (three hundred kilometers north of Johannesburg), decided to come to the city to try his luck. As he notes, "Egoli is still the City of Gold."[16] Jesus stayed for a while with a cousin who worked as a houseman for whites living in Rosebank, and he enrolled in a commercial college with the financial support of an older brother working in Limpopo. One year later, he found a job in Mayfair at an Indian-owned factory. There he met a young woman and moved in with her. He quickly discovered that she was a prostitute in Hillbrow, close to the city center. They stayed together for a while, and then one day she left, without a trace.

Elsy, meanwhile, left KwaZulu-Natal to escape a stepfather who was abusing both her and her sister. She joined an aunt living in Johannesburg, who found her employment as a domestic worker in Mayfair. Elsy used to go to a shebeen near the Diplomat Hotel and Tavern 702. She also used to visit the park near the police station to eat lunch or to have her hair done. Elsy and Jesus met each other in a local supermarket and started living together in a flat in Yeoville that they shared with some of Jesus's friends. In 1993, this group of friends took AIDS tests, out of bravado more than anything else. Elsy and Jesus were found to be HIV-positive. They did not really pay much attention, however. In 1997, it became difficult for them to share a flat with friends, and Elsy decided to buy a shack for R1,000 in Alexandra. She and Jesus moved in together. In the meantime, Elsy left her job as a domestic worker. She bought fabric at the Indian Oriental Plaza in Fordsburg and in President Street in Newtown and started making and selling cushions. In 1998, Elsy gave birth to a little girl who died nine months later at the Johannesburg General Hospital in Parktown. It was then that Elsy and Jesus fully recognized the significance of their HIV status and became involved in new networks—those of treatment and support.

Jesus and Elsy put together their meager funds and asked for contributions from friends and acquaintances in order to bury their daughter. The whole experience proved too much for the couple, and they separated shortly afterward. Jesus stayed with various friends until he found a place at a Protestant mission in Soweto that was about to open a hospice for HIV/AIDS patients. After staying there for several months, during which he served the mission by developing contacts with various sponsors, Jesus decided to leave Johannesburg and go back to Limpopo, where he married and put his efforts into AIDS prevention. Elsy stayed in the shack that she had bought and became a volunteer caregiver in a support group for those living with HIV/AIDS.

She subsequently attended the HIV clinic at the Johannesburg General Hospital in Parktown for treatment for herself and for the child she was expecting by another HIV-positive boyfriend. The clinic provided her with Nevirapine (a product given to pregnant women or to newborn babies that reduces the risk of mother-to-child transmission of the virus). After her baby was born, Elsy continued to attend the HIV clinic, working as a volunteer counselor. This work enables her to supplement her disability grant by an extra R800 per month.[17] In addition, her presence at the clinic allows her to take advantage, when necessary, of personalized care. In fact, volunteers and employees are often included in therapeutic trials, thus giving them free access to antiretroviral drugs that would otherwise be available only from a private doctor—and hence financially inaccessible.

Voluntary work is not restricted to searching for sponsors and funding but also implies a learning process for people who left school long ago. In order to become a volunteer, Elsy attended a training course with the Gauteng Department of Health in the city center of Johannesburg. This was the first time she had gained access to an official building. Shortly afterward she took a job with an organization for AIDS sufferers, the Treatment Action Campaign (TAC), whose offices in Johannesburg are situated in Braamfontein, which is close to the city center. Through her involvement in this association, Elsy is gradually obtaining social recognition not only as an HIV-positive individual but also as an actor in the affairs of the city. The TAC plays a militant role in the fight for a national program that would provide general access to antiretrovirals. As part of her work for the TAC, Elsy participates in public information campaigns and in other actions directed at political figures or at the public health service. She moves from meetings in Braamfontein to participation in actions in Pretoria or Johannesburg. She also takes part in various meetings and lectures, which have given her the opportunity to travel to Durban and Cape Town for the first time. These journeys are paid for by the TAC. During the campaign of civil disobedience organized by the TAC in 2003, Elsy, along with others, protested a speech given by Minister of Health Manto Tshabala-Msimang at Public Health 2003—a conference held on March 25, 2003, at the Eastern Boulevard Holiday Inn. The following day, an article titled "Activists Give Health Minister the Boot" appeared in the *Star,* a daily newspaper. The press's favorable response to these actions confirmed Elsy's feelings: because of her involvement in this movement, she is being "taken seriously."

Strengthened by this new legitimacy, Elsy is claiming her rights and carrying with her other HIV-positive individuals. If legal advice or support is needed, she accompanies them to the AIDS Law Project at the University of the Witwatersrand—a group that is seeking to establish legal precedent in the area of HIV/AIDS-based discrimination. There, they have access to pro bono legal counsel, and they are given the opportunity to expose and condemn the abuse to which they are subjected. Elsy also visits the AIDS Consortium, which is found in the same district—Braamfontein—and which is the central organ for information on AIDS.

The TAC benefits from strong international support, of which its members, such as Elsy, are well aware. The NAPWA (National Association of People Living with HIV/AIDS) does not have the international profile that TAC enjoys. However, it does offer HIV-positive people the same room for mobilization on a national level. Each uses the network of support groups and takes advantage of its accessibility across the city. This was the case in April 2002, when a group of people, all HIV-positive, visited Johannesburg support groups to collect the number of signatures required to create the HIV Support Party. The cell phone may be a fashion item and status symbol, but it is also a vital instrument of socialization for members of these networks. Individuals are able to keep in contact via SMS (Short Messaging Service). They are informed of events that they might want to participate in, from workshops to burials of AIDS victims. The purchase of a limited amount of airtime allows them to send an SMS to someone with more funds in order to be contacted. It is not unusual for the first disability grant payment to be used to buy a cell phone.

The Final Station

Increasingly, the members of support groups are openly participating in the funerals of their deceased members. It is common to see militant members of AIDS organizations at these funerals. These actions are part of a movement to eliminate the stigma around the disease, a movement that can be seen at burials in Johannesburg and surrounding areas. Instead of attending anonymously, the members of the support group display red ribbons, which they also distribute to those present. Some of them wear TAC or NAPWA T-shirts. When the funeral convoy leaves the home of the deceased to go to the church or the cemetery, the hearse is preceded by the members of the support groups.[18] Just as during the struggle against apartheid, they sometimes toyi-toyi.[19] They also sing religious songs and chant slogans promoting the use of condoms. These demonstrations are not limited to the funerals of active members of associations of AIDS sufferers but are also organized for ordinary support group members who request them before their death.

At the cemetery, the support group members generally form themselves into a separate choir, as do work colleagues if there are any present. At funerals for people whose HIV status is known, it is not unusual for an anti-AIDS sticker to be affixed to the coffin. It could just be a simple red ribbon or sometimes a red ribbon on a blue background with the question, "I care, do you?" It is at this final event that the city welcomes, in its very depths, the body that has traversed and crisscrossed it. A body or a human wreck—it no longer matters. The death of an AIDS sufferer has an ambivalent effect on the support group. It reinforces the unity of the group by mobilizing its members around the deceased and provides an example, to those who are left, of the quality of the escort provided by the support group members. Ntombi (the young, HIV-positive woman living in Alexandra discussed above) reported that she could not stop thinking about her own funeral during a huge toyi-toyi at the burial of an Alexandra woman. She imagined it would follow the same pattern. The thought of a close and unavoidable end is also expressed in the bodies of those members of the support group surviving the deceased. They often complain of falling ill and suffering from diarrhea as a result of stress at the thought of their own deaths.

Conclusion

The metropolis that emerges from the journeys of suffering HIV-positive bodies living on its periphery is both visible and invisible. Initially, it is structured by official AIDS sites at various levels. Support groups, clinics, hospitals, and social service agencies constitute the emerging part of this structure. Here the epidemic is overt and measured (the number of patients testing positive, the number of volunteers trained and supervised). However, the patients' search is not restricted to the public sector. It also extends to the unofficial paths of treatment and resources. And here the city becomes hidden. The city submerged in suffering bodies begins in the domestic sphere, where the sick retreat or hide; it then extends to the churches attended by sufferers and includes the illicit AIDS networks that lead those living with HIV/AIDS from therapeutic trials to the sale of unauthorized products—sales that exploit the lack of an official response to the treatment of AIDS. This city is drawn in dots. An exploration of the networks of people living with HIV/AIDS clearly does not exhaust the question of how the metropolis is experienced. However, it does reveal a part of the essence of urbanity. Local and global, the metropolis inscribes the sick, who maneuver within these networks through exchanges and debates that go beyond the city itself. The links between sufferers, product distributors, and organizers of therapeutic trials are made not on the basis of linear, rigid networks, but on the basis of encounters that are sometimes random, sometimes orchestrated—opportunities that by nature do not last.

The quest of the sick does not acknowledge the administrative health divisions of the city but follows the principle of a search for optimum care. This quest transcends the suburbs of the rich or poor, black or white, just as it transgresses the rules of a medical system that sends patients from one health center to another higher up the chain. It involves journeys that are as much a function of an individual's state of health (the body is finally forced into immobility) as his or her financial resources. In this context, mobility is not a temporary state but—for the poor population living on its periphery—the very condition of survival in the city. This mobility consists of coming and going, incursions into the official city and retreats into the city of the poor, frozen in its suburbs and impermeable to the daily life of the sick. Johannesburg appears simultaneously as a space whose resources may potentially be exploited but also as a dangerous place where suffering remains largely invisible, despite the Department of Health's slogan reproduced over and over again on T-shirts and stickers: "I care, do you?"

There can be no place more poignant to ask this question than the cemetery. Today, the cemetery in Alexandra is full. Families are now being advised to bury their deceased in Midrand, an hour from Alexandra. Once the ceremony is over, it is no longer the disease that hinders visits to the dead but the financial resources needed to make the journey. The frequency with which individuals attend burials of members of their networks is a reminder of the brevity of their own existence. As for the city, it is clearly in its nature to survive its dead. But the city hardly exists without this submerged component, the depths in which the scraps and the remains finally come to rest.

Notes

The facts and biographies recounted here were collected between September 2001 and September 2003 as part of a research project funded by the French National Agency of Research into AIDS (ANRS) and with the institutional support of the Department of Anthropology at the University of the Witwatersrand. The people quoted in this article were first encountered in Diepkloof and Alexandra as part of regular visits to support groups for HIV-positive individuals and later visited at their homes. The names and the details were changed to avoid identification of the people concerned. I am grateful to Todd Lethata, who accompanied me during the collection of this data, and to all of those infected who shared with us part of their experiences, joys, and pains. I thank Achille Mbembe and Sarah Nuttall, who read and commented on the first version of this essay.

1 This essay will not be dealing with the black suburban middle and upper classes, who tend to live in the affluent northern suburbs as well as in suburbs on the edge of the city (e.g., Midrand).

2 The exchange rate varies between seven and eight rands to the dollar.

3 The Department of Health in the municipality of Johannesburg provides the following statistics on its Web site (www.joburg.org.za/services/health1.stm#hiv): "At Johannesburg Hospital about 30% of pregnant mothers tested are HIV-positive. Of children tested on admission to the paediatric wards, 40% are HIV-positive, and 75% of paediatric deaths—mostly children under the age of two—are AIDS related. The overall infection rate for Johannesburg of 26% is greater than the average for Gauteng, which stands at 23.9%. The City of Johannesburg is home to a population of 2,883,226 people in some 791,367 households. The population is projected to rise to 2,986,228 in mid-2005 and 3,103,182 in mid-2010. The average rate of population growth for the City of Johannesburg between 2000 and 2010 is projected to be 0.9% per annum. The HIV/AIDS epidemic is largely responsible for this low rate of growth, along with a low fertility rate in Johannesburg."

4 CD4 T-cells are known as "helper" cells. They track down germs in the body and destroy them. The HIV invades the cells, reproduces itself within them, and eventually kills them. A CD4 count indicates the different stages of the HIV infection. A healthy body has a CD4 count of 1,000–1,500 cells per cubic millimeter of blood. A CD4 count below 200 indicates that a person has reached the fourth stage of the illness. This person would be said to have AIDS (i.e., he or she is no longer simply HIV-positive). See Evian 2000.

5 The support groups, in fact, are one of the few sites where churches, pharmaceutical companies, and social science and medical researchers come into contact with sufferers.

6 The idea of a government conspiracy against poor HIV-positive people is shared by many living on the fringe of the townships. The government's nonintervention policy is seen as an attempt to reduce the number of poor people in South Africa. This idea developed in the midst of a controversy in South Africa over President Thabo Mbeki's denial of a link between HIV and AIDS. The controversy came to an end in November 2003 when the government announced a comprehensive plan to distribute antiretrovirals. For an analysis of the controversy, see Fassin 2002, 2003; Fassin and Schneider 2003.

7 For an example of the AIDS debate, see the exchange of letters between President Mbeki and Tony Leon, the leader of the Democratic Alliance (*Sunday Times* 2000).

8 For further information on the Virodene saga in South Africa, see Smith and Nicodemus 1999.

9 See Pharma Natura's Web site, www.pharma.co.za.

10 See Optilife's Web site, www.optilife.co.za.

11 Anthroposophical medicine, which appeared in Europe at the beginning of the twentieth century, advocates a holistic approach that takes into account the body, soul, and spirit and advises the use of medicines based on natural substances.

12 See Forever Living's Web site, www.foreverliving.com.

13 See Nature's Health's Web site, www.natureshealth.co.za.

14 *Taxi rank* is the South African term for a taxi stand.

15 Tri-therapy treatment attempts to reduce the level of viral load in the body for as long as possible in order to maintain the strength of the immune system. It is a combination of three antiretroviral drugs, usually a combination of one or two transcriptase inhibitors with one or two protease inhibitors. For more information on HIV and AIDS, see Evian 2000.

16 Egoli is the Zulu name of Johannesburg and means "city of gold." This name was given to the city in the nineteenth century, when working in the Johannesburg gold fields was the only way for rural migrants to earn money. More than one hundred years later, the city still attracts rural migrants, for the same reason.

17 This work is considered volunteering, though people do receive a stipend after they have shown themselves to be committed to the work. However, the stipend still falls far short of a living wage. The volunteers often view it as a temporary income or a step toward a salaried job in the field of health care.

18 After a ceremony at home, the bereaved go directly to the cemetery or they go via a church or temple, depending on the religious affiliation.

19 *Toyi-toyi* is a demonstration in which the participants form a compact group, stamp their feet, and chant slogans—something that came to symbolize the struggle against apartheid in the townships.

7 ⊕ Literary City

SARAH NUTTALL

What might a Johannesburg text be? How does Johannesburg emerge as an idea and a form in contemporary literatures of the city? What literary "infrastructures" are giving the city imaginary shape? Which vocabularies of separation and connectedness surface—and recede? What representational forms? City-ness in Johannesburg, as it emerges in the texts below, I will argue, is an intricate entanglement of éclat and somberness, lightness and darkness, comprehension and bewilderment, polis and necropolis, desegregation and resegregation.

The most influential body of work on the literary city in South Africa is that which has focused on the emergence of Sophiatown and its writers. Sophiatown was the vibrant and racially fluid inner-city suburb of Johannesburg that flourished and then was forcibly removed in the 1950s. Its writers fired literary critical imaginations in new directions, capturing some of the multisidedness of Johannesburg's modernity, showing it to be a place occupied by the black poor, squatters, and slum dwellers, and also a center of urban black culture that, as Paul Gready (2002) has written, "offered unprecedented possibilities for blacks to choose and invent their society from the novel distractions of urban life" (145). Openly critical of liberalism, Sophiatown's writers, most of whom worked as journalists for *Drum* magazine, neither romanticized the rural nor condemned the moral degradation of the city, contributing to a new tradition of writing which focused on black experience in the South African city.[1] Much of their fiction tried to capture the racial landscape they inhabited: "The inter-racial frontier," writes Gready, "was fraught with contradictions and anguish, but while some like Themba later turned their back on it, others made their fictional and actual home in the quagmire of its tensions" (148).[2] Rob Nixon (1993) has shown how, at a time when the very idea of belonging to the city was coming under increasing legislative pressure, the Harlem Renaissance helped emergent South African writers fortify their claim (16).

Sophiatown and its writers, then, dominated the critical imagination of the literary city, drawing the city as a subject more explicitly into being. At the same time, other writing, less focused on by critics, also gave the city voice. In Peter Abrahams's *Tell Freedom* (1953), for example, the worlds of Vrededorp and Fordsburg, where he grew up, give way to an encounter with the city at large, which was also the making of "a new kind of black person" (195). Born into urban poverty, the son of a Coloured woman and an Ethiopian man, Abrahams begins to encounter himself in the city through the few books he could get his hands on: "I desired to know myself . . . I was ripe for something new, the new things my books had revealed . . . I felt lonely and longed for something without being able to give it a name . . . impelled by something I could not explain, I went, night and night, on long lonely walks into the white areas of Johannesburg" (161–65). Impelled by longing, but denied access to the city and a new kind of self at every term, Abrahams finds a job as an "office boy" at the Bantu Men's Social Centre and here begins reading "everything on the shelf marked American Negro literature" (188), a process out of which he learns to interpret his reality, and to propel himself out of "life in South Africa." Two decades later, Mongane Wally Serote would publish his famous poem "City Johannesburg":

Jo'burg City
I travel on your black and white and robotted roads,
Through your thick iron breath that you inhale,
At six in the morning and exhale from five noon
Jo'burg City
That is the time when I come to you,
When you neon flowers flaunt from your electrical wind,
That is the time when I leave you.[3]
(Serote 1982: 22)

Over two decades later, Lesego Rampolokeng deliberately echoes Serote's poem to the city:

Johannesburg my city
Paved with judas gold
Deceptions and lies
Dreams come here to die
(Rampolokeng 2004)

Both poem and lyrics draw out, with equal power, the dark eroticism, the failed promise, the intimate knowledge, like the body of a lover, the drama of entanglement, the claim to belonging ("my city"), the inability of the city to be a home. While Serote attributes this relationship to the city to apartheid, Rampolokeng suggests that such a relationship persists, like "judas," into the post-apartheid present.

In contemporary literature, particularly fiction, the city emerges in an even more self-conscious way as an aesthetic, a political and an imaginary site, a vivid and explicit template for an entire array of social fears and possibilities (Gunner 2003). The city skyline begins to appear on many book covers, signaling its status as subject at the center of these narratives. While several critics (Titlestad 2003, Hoad 2003, Mpe 2001) have begun to work on recent novels as fruitful sites for understanding city culture, the texts' insistent focus on the city as an idea has still to be properly explored. It has, in fact, been the urbanist Jennifer Robinson (1998) who has offered one of the more overt methodological challenges to reading the city from the vantage point of the now: "Our imaginations have lived for so long with the lines of apartheid city space, with the blank spaces in between, the deadening images of power drawn on the ground. . . . Can we begin to shift our experiences and our visions to capture and understand the world of always-moving spaces? What do the spaces of change and dynamism look like? In what sense was even the apartheid city—a city of division—a place of movement, of change, of crossings?" Robinson invokes the figure of Toloki in Zakes Mda's *Ways of Dying* (1995):

In the afternoon Toloki walks to the taxi rank, which is on the other side of the downtown area, or what is called the central business district. The streets are empty, as all the stores are closed. He struts like a king, for today the whole city belongs to him. He owns the wide tarmac roads, the skyscrapers, the traffic lights, and the flowers on the sidewalks. That is what he loves most about this city. It is a garden city, with flowers and well-tended shrubs and bushes growing at every conceivable place. In all seasons, blossoms fill the site. (46)

Toloki passes across the lines of the apartheid city, across its cruel divides; he generates crossings, not so much—as Robinson notes—undoing the spaces of poverty as refusing to treat those spaces as one-dimensional. We are in the realm of Lefebvre's "representational space," and each time we move, we potentially use space differently. Robinson views the apartheid city from the fresh, experimental vantage that is opened up by the political transition. The new South African city is still a space where nightmarish divisions may be witnessed and where the fear of crime delimits dreams of truly public space (see Kruger 2001). But she nevertheless suggests that we think not only in terms of fixed structures, but in terms of movement, journeys through the city.[4] Rita Barnard (2006) writes that Mda's shift away from an "earlier poetics of a grim documentation of physical surroundings to a new, more fluid sense of black urban experience" parallels shifts in South African urban studies from a "near-exclusive concern with the location of physical structures and the visible aspects of urban organization to a concern with the city as a dynamic entity." Barnard notes, too, the difference between Toloki's "proprietal strutting" and the "servile, if ironic" movements of Serote's narrator in "City Johannesburg."

In the last decade or so, an international body of scholarship on the city has turned for inspiration to, but also begun to critique, the writing of Michel de Certeau (1984) and Walter Benjamin ([1982] 2002). It has returned to these writers as a way of trying to name neglected urban spatialities and to invent new ones, to unearth emergent city figures to connect that which has been held apart, to draw out the city's theatricality, its improvisations, its ironies (see Amin and Thrift 2002). De Certeau's key insight was that people use cities by constructing who they are, producing a narrative of identity. They make a sentence or a story of particular places in the city, and the city is not available as an overview—the city is the way that it is walked. Much of an earlier terminology of location and mobility—vocabularies of the nomad, the decentered, the marginalized, the deterritorialized, border, migrant and exile—was, by contrast, seldom attached to specific places and people, representing instead ideas of rootlessness and flux that seem as much the result of ungrounded theory as its putative subject (Solnit 2000). Benjamin's figure of the flâneur (the esthetic bohemian, drifting through the city like a film director) invites us to "read the city from its street-level intimations, to encounter the city as lived complexity, to seek alternative narratives and maps based on wandering" (Amin and Thrift 2002: 11).

For Zygmunt Bauman (1996), the figures which populate the Western metropolis, in addition to the flâneur, include the tourist (for whom the city is a spectacle); the player (who knows the rules of various urban games); the vagabond or vagrant (who moves at the borders of the establishment through the practices of transgression); and the commuter (who treats the city as a place you enter, park, work and leave—an autopolis). Interestingly, he fails to include the figure of the sex worker, and like most theorists of the city, he seems uninterested in what a gender-related city consciousness—the experience of the flâneuse, among other figures—would look like. African cities suggest a number of other figures, which could be read back into European cities as well: one would be the figure of the *sâpeur*—the figure of spatial transition, operating in the interstices of large cultures, participating in a cult of appearance, especially expensive clothing; a mobile individual who, following Janet MacGaffey and Remy Bazenguissa-Ganga (2000), creates ramifying networks extending through time, space, and multiple cultures as he circulates between countries, pulling off coups in otherwise invisible spaces in and between cities. Others, as we will see below, include the figure of the migrant worker, the aging white man, the "illegal immigrant," and the hustler.

Much of the emergent work I have discussed above tends to overstate the city as a space of flow, human interaction, and proximate reflexivity. Although the figure of the flâneur draws important links between space, language, and subjectivity, it fails to consider whether the transitivity or transitioning of the contemporary city, based on an endless spread and multiple connections, is best grasped through the trope of wandering/wondering—or requires other imaginary means (Amin and Thrift 2002: 14) and underestimates the extent to which striating openness and flow are a whole series of rules, conventions, and institutions of regulation and control, a biopolitics (26).[5] In the case of Johannesburg, Michael Titlestad is right to have observed that it has been characterized less by practices of flânerie and drifting than by a set of divisions contrived by law, surveillance, and threat, hostile to errant and nomadic meaning, to improvised selves and versions of social hope (29). Yet, as Amin and Thrift warn, we need to be careful about how we analyze space: "The city allows for juxtapositions at all kinds of levels—the meeting in the street, the rich and poor areas cheek by jowl, the lack of control of public spaces and so on. All kinds of forces may conspire to nullify these juxtapositions . . . the fact remains that the city, through these juxtapositions, is also a great generator of novelty" (40–41).

Jennifer Robinson, in her more recent work (2004), foregrounds a set of tensions emerging from two competing approaches, by practitioners and academics alike, to reading the city. South African urban studies, Robinson argues, is tossed between a left Marxist critique, which caricatures the present city in the resonant binaries of the past, and a form of poststructuralism that insists on seeing spaces and identities as profoundly uncertain and always subject to dislocation (271). Yet at this moment in the remaking of the city of Johannesburg, both intellectually and in our political imaginations, Robinson argues, "something more is demanded of us." That "something more" requires, in her view, that we pay more attention to the moment when "something is made" (271). The challenge, she argues, is to find a view of the past through the lenses of the post-apartheid present rather than through a "persistent apartheid optic" (275). The city here, as elsewhere, both fragments and brings together (280).

In what follows, I work with these ideas in relation to fictional accounts of the city. AbdouMaliq Simone, in this volume, uses the term *infrastructure* to refer to people in the city, to the "ability of residents to engage complex combinations of objects, spaces, people, and practices," to form "conjunctions," which "become an infrastructure—a platform providing for and reproducing life in the city." I explore the imaginary infrastructures that surface in fiction, producing writerly, metropolitan maps. The fictional infrastructures I have chosen are the street, the café, the suburb, and the campus.

The Street

Phaswane Mpe's novel *Welcome to Our Hillbrow* (2000) explores, via a modality of pedestrian enunciation, the inner city quarter of Hillbrow, in Johannesburg.[6] Using the second person, Mpe's narrator describes how to cross this part of the city:

> Your own and cousin's soles hit the pavements of the Hillbrow streets. You cross Twist, walk past the Bible Centred Church. Caroline makes a curve just after the Church and becomes the lane of Edith Cavell Street, which takes you downtown; or, more precisely, to Wolmarans at the edge of the city. Edith Cavell runs parallel to Twist. Enclosed within the lane that runs from Wolmarans to Clarendon Place (which becomes Louis Botha a few streets on) is a small, almost negligible triangle of a park. On the other side of the park, just across

Clarendon Place, is Hillbrow Police Station, in which you take only minimal interest. Crossing the park, you walk alongside the police station, still in Clarendon Place. A very short distance later, you join Kotze Street. In Kotze you turn right to face the west. (10)

Mpe offers a revised inventory of the city, composing a path along its streets, both tracking and breaching historical constructions of city space. Built sites along the streets symbolize specific practices, demarcate racial identities in particular ways, and in turn determine how one walks.[7] Thus one might feel oneself to be at the "edge of the city," "enclosed within the lane," "walking alongside," or "facing west," depending on where one is—a complex combination of built structure and felt identity. Significantly, Refentše takes "only minimal interest" in the Hillbrow Police Station, one of the most notorious sites of apartheid police repression in the city. Street names, too, mark the trace of colonial and apartheid epistemologies and practices, but these proper names also, as de Certeau notes (1984: 104), make themselves available to the diverse meanings given to them by passersby in the know, detach themselves from the places they were supposed to define, and serve as imaginary meeting points on itineraries. These words operate in the nature of an emptying out and wearing away of their primary role, as de Certeau sees them (105), and insinuate other routes into the functionalist order of movement.

Throughout Mpe's novel, the streets are marked by "incidents," things happen with greater intensity or regularity in certain streets, and where the danger spots are is a matter of great contention ("the notorious Esselen," "the notorious Quartz" [6]). The coming of what Mpe calls "black internationals" into Hillbrow invoke the streets and their names as "receptacles for other routes." If Mpe doesn't know who Edith Cavell or Wolmarans are, he knows or chooses to remember that the Hillbrow Tower is really called the JG Strijdom Tower and recalls the civilized labor policy of the 1930s, as well as the historical irony that Hillbrow is now a largely black neighborhood.[8] Hillbrow, for Mpe, is figured as partial and now patchy inventory of the old apartheid city and as revised inventory of a largely black, highly tensile, intra-African multiculture. At the beginning of his book, Mpe makes clear that the novel's preoccupation with writing the map, navigating the streets, has much to do with the figure of the migrant itself: "Your first entry into Hillbrow was the culmination of many converging routes. You do not remember where the first route began. But you know all too well that the stories of migrants had a lot to do with its formation" (2000: 2). These migrant "routes" refer to those who gravitate to the city from South Africa's hinterland but can also be taken to refer to the cross-border migrants from elsewhere in Africa that the novel increasingly refers to and who now make up much of the demographic outline of Hillbrow. The figure of the migrant comes to overlay the earlier trope of race (whites seldom appear in the novel, though not because Mpe is making a deliberate political point, and race conflict is not a theme or major subtext of Mpe's writing) and even dominates the urban spaces that the novel explores.[9] Hillbrow is composed of a city of strangers, in which the terms of civility and incivility have to be negotiated. The novel sets up a tension between xenophobia, the hatred of the unknown, the "foreign," and "humanness," invoked throughout the book. Much of these tensions are played out on the street itself.

Neville Hoad (2004) reflects on how *Welcome to Our Hillbrow*, in its title and its content, invokes both a geographical specificity and a "form of worldliness." It invokes, that is, the geographical place to which we are being welcomed (in the oft-repeated title phrase, "welcome to our Hillbrow") and the potential expansiveness of the "our." Hillbrow has long been a place that has given its inhabitants an experience of urbanity and vivid street life, both of which offer possibilities, he shows, for different kinds of relationships to oneself and to strangers (what Lauren Berlant has called "stranger intimacy," a form of citizenship). Hoad traces Mpe's descriptions of possible connections between strangers in "our Hillbrow." Thus, for example, despite Refentše's cousin's warning that "you do not go around greeting every fool in Hillbrow" (Mpe 2000: 12), he "again responds" to an elderly, poverty-stricken man living on the street, with whom "you had become friends without ever saying anything to each other" (16).

Moreover, Hoad argues, bodily fluids like tears, sweat, semen, and blood provide transpersonal yet deeply personal metaphors between people—lovers—in the city. Some of these fluids are also the primary means of transmission of the HIV virus, just as they are "also deeply symbolic of the human capacity to feel, to create and to work" (2004: 7). This vulnerability of the body, Hoad suggests, becomes the ground for both community and intimacy, and the terms of the welcome become clear: "to be embraced by the hospitality of the cosmopolitan is to accept the invitation to share the work of mourning" (10).

Mpe is engaged in an act of renegotiating the terms of recognition set up on the street. Whereas many black South Africans in Hillbrow (themselves migrants from the villages and towns of the hinterland) see foreigners as *makwerekwere* (*kwere kwere* being a derogatory imitation of unintelligible foreign languages), Mpe's narrator describes Africans from elsewhere as "so-journers" (2000: 18) like himself, "people taking their unplanned and hap-hazard journeys through our world" (111), and xenophobia as the work of "ostracizing the innocent" (20). Moreover, the real heart of xenophobia, he suggests, is less the city than the village itself ("Tiralong danced because its xenophobia—its fear and hatred for both black non–South Africans and Johannesburgers—was vindicated" [54]).

Welcome to Our Hillbrow disavows a politics of hatred in favor of an ethics of hospitality. In the stories it tells of lovers in the city, the dramas of Refentše and his friends and their relationships with women, their duplicities, betray-als, and confusion, the narrative repeatedly performs an act of embrace: "Yes, she is. And so am I and all of us" (64); "Refilwe was only doing what we all did" (111); "You do not own life" (67); "Welcome to our All" (104). It is sig-nificant, though, that the story is written in the second person: the narrator refers throughout to a "you," most often a devise used in fiction as a way of addressing the reader directly, but here a way of talking to the dead (the "you" addressed here is Refentše, who has died). The book begins with the words "If you were still alive" (1), addresses a person who is "alive in a different realm" (67), and ends by reflecting on heaven itself: "Heaven is the world of our continuing existence" (124). Heaven becomes a place from which to reflect back on life, and the narrator makes use of addressing his dead protagonist to achieve this self-reflexive space. The book is not directly autobiographical, but Mpe would freely tell (before his own untimely death) how it was written at a time when he himself felt suicidal—the book, that is, becomes an ex-tended suicide note that also comes to save his life—by giving him a renewed desire for writing: this much at least we can extrapolate from Refentše's own recorded desire to "explore Hillbrow in writing" (30) and from the line "you wrote it in order to steady yourself against grief and prejudice, against the painful and complex realities of humanness" (59). There is much to suggest that the dead Refentše is in part Mpe himself, and that his embrace of a place in which one can be "alive in a different realm" speaks of a place of deeper humanity or healing. Heaven, in the book and within Mpe's frame of mind at the time of writing, "is not some far off place" (47) but rather a continuum between life and death, a place of insights, from which to view and review "our world." Mpe's own sudden death in 2005 in his early thirties, and his stated desire just before his death to train to become a "healer," are both prefigured in the novel's highly unusual second-person form of address, drawing the worlds of the living and the dead closer and closer together.

For Zygmunt Bauman, civility is "the activity which protects people from each other and yet allows them to enjoy each other's company. Wearing a mask is the essence of civility." Masks, he argues, permit pure sociability, detached from their circumstances of power, malaise and the private feelings of those who wear them. "Civility has as its aim the shielding of others from being burdened with oneself" (2000: 95). In order for cities to become sites of civility, Bauman argues, people need to be able to occupy public spaces as "public personae," without being "nudged, pressed or cajoled to take off their masks and "let themselves go" (96). Mpe's novel offers a different vision of stranger civility as he maps the practices of Hillbrow's streets. Civility, here, is learned from a consciousness of vulnerability and humanness, self-reflection and imperfection, the fact that you "do not own this life" (117). It is less the mask of the self than "the face of the other" (Levinas) that provokes Mpe's ethics of civility on the street. It is this Levinasian ethics of entanglement that is most striking about Mpe's book. The face of the other communicates what is human, injurable, precarious. It involves the work of finding out who else suffers. This is the book's affective structure. Told in the second person, "to you," it expands our understanding of form in the context of an ethics of entanglement. It is a process in which the narrator becomes someone else and in which, as Judith Butler says (2004: 23), we are "undone by each other," especially in a context of grief, within which Mpe writes. It is, then, a notion of civility less interested in the bounded being that the "mask" implies than in being awake to what is precarious in another life, or rather, the precariousness of life as such.

The Café

Ivan Vladislavić's novel *The Restless Supermarket* (2001) is also set in Hillbrow, this time at the Café Europa. Aubrey Tearle, its main protagonist, is an old hand at the café, their most venerable patron, an incorrigible "European," as he describes himself, playing on the name of the café, though he has never been to Europe. Tearle is a disgruntled, aging white man, a proofreader by profession, who devotes his life to the task of eradicating error. Tearle is obsessed with language, a device the author uses to place language itself at the very heart of his narrative of the post-apartheid city. He is preoccupied by the maintenance of "standards" (259), of order, and prides himself on his "sense of discrimination" (15), his "civic duty" (28), his decency, his "respect for rules and regulations" (42), and so on. His epistemological fetish soon segues into a political predisposition toward the maintenance of apartheid social engineering and censorship.

The novel is set at the time of the political transition, and Tearle is not taking it well. In the café, where he spends most of his time, he regards the tables and chairs as "travesties of their former selves" (10); the public spaces of the neighborhood he finds deficient since there "were no pavement cafés à la française" (16). On the wall of the Café Europa is a painting of the imaginary European city of Alibia, which Tearle describes as "a perfect alibi, a generous elsewhere" (19). Alibia is for Tearle, as Michael Titlestad has written, "a cityscape of displacement, a composite imaging of the *not-here* of white (European) apprehension of South Africa," his "imaginary homeland" (77–78). The fantasy of Europeanness is also the refusal of Hillbrow, and Johannesburg, at least as they are becoming after political transition. Specifically, it is the refusal of the transformation of Hillbrow from a mostly white, orderly suburb inhabited by large numbers of Eastern European immigrants who benefited from apartheid privileges into a diverse, disorderly Afropolitan inner city quarter. When Tearle hears that the Café is about to be closed, in favour of a "whorehouse or a disco or a chicken outlet" (11), he fears that with it, will be the final loss of his fantasy of "elsewhere."

At the "Goodbye Bash" for the Café Europa, the place is trashed (even though Alibia is still there, "lights twinkling gaily in the dark" and "the big wheels turning"): "We picked our way through the debris of paper cups, monkey vines of coloured streamers and tinsel and toilet paper, tattered dollars, carrot tops, bottles of every shape and size, the jewelled shards of the stained glass. And Cheese Snacks everywhere, crunched into powder, like shed gilt. The newspapers lay scattered on the carpet, with their pages curling from the wooden spines, like moths that had flown too close to the chandeliers" (299). The trashed café, the debris of paper cups, the tattered dollars and Cheese Snacks—the café in a sense becomes a figuring of the street of the new city. Tearle, in describing the "trashing" of the anachronistically named Café Europa, also unwittingly describes the brilliance and banality of the metropolitan city street, strewn with old newspapers, its beauty and violence ("moths [that fly] too close to chandeliers"). In the final scenes of the novel, he finds himself out in the streets of Hillbrow, with a young Coloured woman called Shirlaine, eating chicken at a chicken outlet. Tearle, perpetually out of touch throughout the novel with his city, even though he calls himself a "true Johannesburger" (19), finally comes to actually inhabit its streets, to fall kicking and screaming into the future.

The hermeneutics of city-ness in this novel are embedded in language itself. While Tearle bemoans the linguistic banality and vacuousness of the consumer city (women's names at the café—Raylene, Maylene—sound to him like "household cleaners"; and the commercial detritus of the city is reflected in shop names like Mr. Exhaust, Mr. Cash and Carry, and Mr. Spare Parts), Vladislavić, as Stefan Helgesson (2004: 782) points out, plays with the stylistic potential of such words by treating them as "print objects" akin to Marcel Duchamp's found objects. The words, that is, appear in the text as pieces of printed language that stand out as changeable and contingent, susceptible to the transformative power of the imagination. Thus what Tearle reads under the rubric of decay and decline, Vladislavić finds constitutive of a different form of city-ness, the language of which has been reshuffled and defamiliarized, and which requires other acts of decipherment. What Helgesson calls the "entropic blandness of consumerism" (786) is opened, by the author, to the pleasures of visual and aural playfulness. Vladislavić begins to find a language for Johannesburg's Los Angeles–type of urban sprawl, commercial strips, and industry, excavating a kind of cultural potential hardly yet drawn into the surfaces of fiction.

In Vladislavić's 2004 novel *The Exploded View*, Egan, a sanitary engineer who designs sewerage reticulation systems for the new townships arising on the outskirts of the city, finds himself one evening with his black colleagues at Bra Zama's African Eatery. The eatery is in "a peri-urban no-man's land, where a dying business district petered out in motor town" (78). Vladislavić, like one of his characters in this novel, is interested in detaching the component parts of the city, disassembling them (thus the "exploded view" of the title, which invokes while also perhaps parodying, the "service delivery" and its trope of "building" in which most of the characters are involved).

Tony Morphet (2005) refers to the events at the eatery as a "comedy of manners," one that makes for an interesting contrast with Tearle's jaded authority in the dying days of the Café Europa. Egan has been taken to dinner by the township bosses, and he's pleased to be at Bra Zama's, where he finds the Afritude sauce unexpectedly delicious. Theirs is the only mixed party in the eatery, and he is proud to be working with these black men to construct homes and services for the poor. While he has worn a "Madiba shirt," the black men are in suits, a discord he finds initially embarrassing, but as he begins to feel like one of the boys, he refers to them as "gents" (85).[10] However, as the drinks flow, his black dinner guests abandon English for Sesotho and he's left feeling an idiot outsider: "Slowly, peristaltically, Egan felt himself moving to the edge of the conversation. They were talking mainly in Sotho now, switching back into English occasionally to include him. . . . the real purpose of the exchange, in which he appeared to be an equal partner, was in the sidelong chatter, the small talk he didn't understand" (86–87). The rupture is only partly about language: as the conversation proceeds, he feels he can't read the signs, the register, nor does he know which jokes to tell because he's not sure what his colleagues would find funny. Vladislavić again uses the figure of the aging white man to register the changing city, to reveal what are in part ecologies of ignorance—gaps, blind spots, mistakes, paradoxes, ironies, anomalies, ambiguities, and invisibilities—but also in part the complex entry and exit points, fragmentary encounters that inhabit the making of racial friendship or collegiality in the city.

In contrast to earlier South African fiction, white characters in *The Exploded View* are, as Helgesson notes, just as likely to be subjected to powerlessness as black characters (2006). Racial entanglement, here, is an unfixing, a quality of identities having been exploded, and of reforming into not-yet-coherent entities. In this "exploded view," "every solid thing has exploded . . . into its component parts. . . . Each part hovered just out of range of the others it was meant to meet" (171). The form of the book itself is that of a novel "exploded" into component parts which almost, but don't quite, add up. In 2005, Vladislavić's book was excluded from the short list for the country's major fiction award on the grounds that it "was not a novel"—a view widely contested in public debate around the issue. It was, of course, a critique of the novel form, of the conventional novel structure as a way of capturing contemporary Johannesburg.

The café and the eatery operate in Vladislavić's fiction as material and allegorical infrastructures of the self in the city, here the aging white self, a self which, in the figure of Tearle, is prone to refuse the present in favor of the past, and in the figure of Egan is eager to embrace the present without properly understanding it. The post-apartheid city itself, it would seem, is being built at this very intersection, at least from the perspective of whites of an older generation. Vladislavić makes use of the semipublic space of the eating house to explore his characters' own struggles to inhabit their private and public worlds, to understand their entanglement with the old and with the new, positioned as they are on the boundary lines of the past and future.

The Suburb

Just as Hillbrow and the inner city have formed a potent urban imaginary in fiction of the city, so too has the suburb begun to surface as fictional infrastructure in current South African writing. A complex assemblage of residential areas, highways, shopping malls, and office parks, the shape of the suburb is hard to decode; it is hard to define where it begins and ends. The suburb is what used to be thought of as the noncentral city parts of the metropolis, but which is becoming an increasingly dominant urban cultural landscape in Johannesburg (see Hayden 2003). By comparison with the inner city and the trope of the street that dominates that urban imaginary, in Johannesburg's northern suburbs, the streets are often relatively empty; one could say too that on the suburban street, there have always been sharp differences between those who walk—some children, many black adults—and those who do not.[11] As these suburbs deracialize, many in the middle classes still seldom walk, at least in the suburban streets. In Muff Andersson's novel *Bite of the Banshee* (2002), urban space is negotiated through talk, as the new middle class hang out in Rosebank, Killarney, and Melville. Talking, here, is a means of doing something, not just a means of representing things. For Bakhtin, language is like the living, concrete environment—it is never unitary, it is somebody talking to somebody else, even when that somebody else is one's own inner addressee (Holquist 1981). In Andersson's conception, which replaces language in its city context, urban talk involves making speculations on states of affairs and rendering them intelligible and legitimate for those around us. The city, here, hums with talk, based on shared conversational contexts, in which categories and identities are constantly articulated (Amin and Thrift 2002: 86–87).

The novel name-drops, as does the celebrity culture of the suburbs, and it is written in the spirit of the new journalism, echoing Hunter Thompson, in which "resemblance to real life figures is 'entirely intentional' " (inside title page).[12] The story turns around a murder, but it is the way in which the murder —the ugly—surfaces in light and sharp banter among friends in a suburban bar that Andersson draws attention to. Abby Moeketsi says: "Dodie Katz is dead . . . I wonder what she would think if she could see and hear us now, so heartlessly making merry in Primi Piatti restaurant in Rosebank, talking about her murder with no more emotion than if she were an expendable movie extra" (10). And: "Again it strikes me that our conversation is far too flippant. Most of the party around our table knew Dodie Katz. I can't help thinking that it wouldn't hurt for us to be a bit more respectful in the way we talk about her death" (12). Andersson, then, reflects in her story on the nature of suburban talk, the quality of conversation, in the face of the expendable, of death itself.

On the issue of crime in the suburbs, Andersson similarly draws her characters, describing themselves as "urban youth" (10), as both flippant and callous. Making fun of those who "pack their possessions and make their plans for their new life in Toronto" (37), Abby says to her friends: "Just don't bleat, OK? Understand who is doing the crime, and why. It doesn't cancel the act, but it makes such a difference to your attitude" (38). In the suburbs, too, cocaine and psychotherapy have their place. Only in this novel, the bag of powdery white substance which changes hands at a crucial moment in the plot is not cocaine but C2Z, a new antiretroviral drug being secretly tested on Africans in Hillbrow (packaged in crystal form that looks like crack). And while Abby gives up on her psychotherapist, her "dream man," while continuing to use some of his methods to diagnose the lives of her friends, she opts instead for the force of the "banshee" in people's lives, and as a key to the unfolding mystery of the murder itself. "Banshee" is the "no-rules player, the 'live-for-today' hedonist," who "does not prepare for the future, or appease the gods, or pray." Banshee is ruled by "what feels good, by the unknown, by what should not be done" (24). The banshee, which Abby turns into a bestselling rap song, is really the force of urban youth itself, let loose in the suburbs.

Bite of the Banshee is described as "creole" in form by its author: an Anglicized and Africanized creolité (Boehmer and Gaitskell 2004) in which the white author writes in the voice of a black woman, and which draws for its narrative register, Andersson says, on a local mix of Mikhail Bakhtin's dialogic voicing, the romance and melodrama of West African fiction, and Mbembe's relations of "illicit cohabitation" and "mutual zombification" between rulers and ruled in the postcolony.[13] In this novel, Hillbrow is the place where Pindi and Cornelius go to escape their right-wing fathers (only hers is rich and his is poor and dispossessed, she black, he white) and to make love.

Andersson's novel of the suburbs, and a murder, echoes in part Nadine Gordimer's 1998 suburban novel *The House Gun*. In this novel, Claudia and Harald Lindgard live secure in their middle-class professions (she a doctor, he a business executive) and in their townhouse, until they are told the news that their son has been arrested for murder. The immediate effect, writes Stephen Clingman (2000), is one of dislocation: in particular, a loss of authority and a dependence on the help of others, especially their lawyer, Hamilton Motsamai. Increasingly, the townhouse, despite its well-maintained grounds, security-monitored entrance, and electronic gadget, "provides no refuge" (35) because "what has happened has brought into the order of the townhouse what it wasn't built to contain" (104). Suddenly, that is, they have to cross a series of social boundaries that life in the townhouse was meant to shelter them from: their life is no longer "outside but within the parameters of disaster" (128). They are "invaded by a happening that had no place in their kind of life" (69). By telling their son Duncan as he was growing up that they would be there for him whatever happens, that he could tell them anything, "they could feel Duncan was safe. They had made him so" (69). Now, the fact that he had murdered another man means that "the townhouse is a court, a place where they turn on each other, where there is only accuser and accused: 'What have I done to Duncan that you didn't do?'" (95). They feel themselves increasingly to belong to "the other side," specifically "the other side of privilege" (127), as they confront issues of violence and death from which their secure(d) lives had shielded them. Gordimer writes, "Neither whiteness . . . nor money . . . had kept them in safety" (127). Now, faced with the murder their son has committed and his possible death by hanging, the "townhouse ethics of doctor, board member, are trivial" (145).

The novel offers a brilliant diagnosis of the townhouse as a metaphor for exploring a society in transition and the challenges to whiteness as that society undergoes radical change. Despite their attempts to occupy a "safe" space on numerous material and symbolic levels, Harald and Claudia have to confront the fact that "there is a labyrinth of violence not counter to the city but a form of communication within the city itself. They no longer were unaware of it, behind security gates. It claimed them" (141). Their son, Duncan, has murdered a man he found sleeping with his girlfriend (the man himself having been formerly Duncan's lover too). He has done so by picking up a gun lying around in the suburban house he shares with friends—a gun lying around "like a house cat; on a table, like an ashtray" (271). During the course of his trial, the judge remarks that Duncan's action can be attributed in part to the "conscious availability of the gun" (263) and in part to "an unconscious sanction of violence" (227), a general resort to it in society as a whole.

As it turns out, Duncan escapes death, since his case is the first to follow the scrapping of the death penalty by the new Constitutional Court. Instead, he faces seven years' imprisonment. Whereas at the beginning of the novel Claudia's suburban life as a doctor is characterized as operating along "the divide of the ultimate, between life and death" (13), Duncan, Gordimer writes in the last sentence of the book, now has to "find a way to bring death and life together" (294).

In this novel, like Andersson's, a key structural device is that of talk. Invoking Harald and Claudia's exchanges, Gordimer refers often to "he-she," a place of narration which, as Clingman (2000) observes, is "outside both characters, yet rather than simply expressing an antithesis between Harald and Claudia, also seems to inhabit both of their minds and reverberate between them" (146). Hence the style "registers as if to suggest not only that Harald and Claudia have already entered into a life where the old syntax —rules of combination, association and sequence—might not apply, but where there is also no fixed point of observation" (146). Thus awareness is distributed, collaborative, Clingman suggests, as Gordimer explores a different version of communication, superimposing voices on one another, setting them beside each other, and having them reflect off one another (153). This profusion of voices, hearing and mishearings, movements back and forth, Clingman interprets as a profusion and cohabiting of voices necessary in post-apartheid South Africa, a version of opening to the future rather than closing into the present and its pasts. Clearly, too, though, it is indicative of the dislocation that Harald and Claudia feel as their ordered, upper-middle-class view of the world erupts through the action of their son, and more symbolically, through the confrontation with violence that comes with a city is profound transition. Thus when Gordimer writes, "It doesn't matter whose thoughts those were, Harald's or Claudia's" (78), she suggests a terrain where the writer can only etch what is a shifting form of consciousness —among whites, but also in society as a whole. Where Clingman is perhaps right is that the novel elevates talking, though the status of talk is rendered complex in the novel.

Harald and Claudia, in the wake of the murder, "shut themselves up in the townhouse and talked" (120). But when Duncan shoots his ex-lover, he does so to "put an end to all the talking" (156). That is, he shuts down all the endless talking with his girlfriend, who betrayed him, the drama and dissection of their relationship ("He could not know what it was he thought, felt under all the talk, talk, talk . . . it was that he must have put an end to when he picked up the house gun" [156]). Talk, then, characterizes suburban life, as it does in Andersson's novel. Yet talking can lead not so much out of, but into, violence. For a society being born out of negotiation(s), talk(s), the ambiguity is clear.

Like Andersson's, Gordimer's novel is founded on a murder, and in many ways, as Clingman observes, "murder underlies the foundations of Johannesburg" (156). Yet the city under which the man lies buried is also, writes Gordimer, "where this court is the seat of justice" (261). Instead of giving a life for a life, Duncan is subject to a "different form of rehabilitation" (156). Moving beyond the "fixed geometry" of the old, the book offers openness to "the possible."

Taken together, then, these two novels of the suburbs suggest a preoccupation with the modes of talk that structure people's lives. Both explore forms of dialogism, in the wake of apartheid's assertion of its monological privilege.[14] While Gordimer's novel offers an astute reading of waning forms of whiteness in the suburbs, Andersson's dialogism is embedded in a crossracial younger generation, in which the suburbs become the subjective center of the city, the place where action is generated as much through gossip, the manufacturing or rumors about crime, and namedropping as through events. Talking here becomes an alternative kind of urban practice that takes place less on the street than in the modulated spaces of the café, the townhouse, and the car.

The Campus

In Niq Mhlongo's novel *Dog Eat Dog* (2004), Dingz, the main character, is a Wits University student "monitoring the atmosphere" (27) in order to make it at Wits and to avoid sinking back into township life. Running out of money fast and having just been refused a student bursary, he hustles his way into the financial aid office on campus and cons a Dr. Winterburton into reopening his case:

> "It's really difficult. Our electricity and water have been cut off because the bills have not been paid for the past two years," I lied. I was not ashamed that I lied. Living in this South Africa of ours you have to master the art of lying in order to survive. As she looked at me I hid my hands under the edge of the table so that she couldn't see my gold-plated Pulsar watch, which I had bought the previous year at American Swiss. (20–21)

The novel is set at the time of the first democratic elections. Dingz is a sharp reader of the changing political landscape and how he can use it to his advantage. He tests "the race card" by using it against a white woman in a bank queue and later plans to use it against the university authorities over a missed exam. Confronted with an obstinate dean, he and his friend "planned to complicate everything with tradition, and if the dean refused we would accuse him of something to do with race discrimination" (197–98). Tradition becomes a particularly useful playing card when it comes to explaining why he·can't produce a death certificate for his cousin and why he didn't submit it in time to be granted permission to miss his exam: "Is it possible to extend that deadline for me? It would be very difficult at this point in time for me to ask for the death certificate at home. According to my culture, the deceased's property is regarded as sacred for about a month after the burial" (158).[15] Dingz is in the meantime trying to hustle an old township lady with the same surname as him to hand over the death certificate of her deceased family member (because of course his cousin didn't die at all). In order to persuade her of his credentials he tells her that he and his friend "both work for the new ANC government. We are registering the names of orphans . . . so they can receive monthly grants from the government" (192).

Dingz's version of the city is that of the hustler: when a policeman tries to stop him drinking in public and then requests a bribe to keep quiet about it, Dingz tapes their conversation on his Walkman. The tactics of the hustler are learned from the community at large—township residents, especially those who live in the "affirmative settlements," name their areas after famous political activists: "People use the names of famous political leaders to attract the government's attention to the urgent need for housing. It is also a clever tactic to delay any possible eviction that might follow" (81–82). Though his actions are politic to his needs, Dingz is not into politics. Assigned a set of readings for his political science course on democracy, he decides that "there was no way that I would waste my time reading about that tired, misused term" (142). In the pub, his friend parodies Mandela: "We must live together, black and white, in this land of ours. You must not fight. When conflict arises, let us go to the negotiation table. We will find solutions. Like Mr. de Klerk and myself did in CODESA. We shook hands. I thank you" (213).

Dingz, the hustler, operates with energetic and often underhand activity, turning others into suckers, luring less skillful players into competing against him in a game of chance. Hustling, in this novel, often carries a politically charged meaning, as he turns the codes, conventions, and clichés of a transitional culture of "human rights" to his own advantage, in acts of ventriloquism and parody. Parody, writes Linda Hutcheon (1985), carries with it a range of intent—from the ironic and playful to the scornful and ridiculing. It is repetition with critical distance, at play with multiple conventions, a stylistic confrontation, a modern recoding that establishes difference at the heart of similarity. It is a process of revising, replaying, inverting particular works or iconic conventions, and it relies on a sophisticated and competent reader. The pleasure of parody's irony, writes Hutcheon, comes not from humor in particular but from the degree of engagement by the reader in the intertextual "bouncing" between complicity and distance.

Being at Wits is a way of being in the city; being in the city is a way of being at Wits. Dingz's friend Theks says to him: "Once we are let loose in the real world you'll realize that life is a matter of dog eat dog" (218)—but life is already like that, permeating the university walls and halls, in order for Dingz to survive outside the township. Dingz is, throughout the story, in pursuit of a death certificate (in order to justify having missed his exams and to try for reentry). Death itself, one could say, is his means of survival in the world he seeks to belong to, the exchange currency, the city commodity, that he deals in. City life in *Dog Eat Dog* is a tactical construction: power and that which contests it become not only about domination and oppression by certain kinds of actors and institutions, but constitute a mobile, circulating force, based on momentum, a force field of affect (inciting, inducing, seducing, hustling).[16]

In each of the fictional urban infrastructures I have discussed above, the surface and depth of the city are entangled, as are the polis and necropolis. Death and dying structure Mpe's narrative of the city. Vladislavić's characters inhabit a realm where social and racial death have to be resisted or explicitly turned away from by finding new ways of being in the city. Andersson and Gordimer's books both deal with a murder, and Mhlongo's text traces a hustler who deals in death. At the same time, the novels explore among them an emergent ethic of hospitality in the city, a form of whiteness under duress and just beginning the work of its reconstruction, a newly self-conscious view of life in the suburbs, and a humorous if ironic take on emerging forms of urbanity in Johannesburg. City-ness in Johannesburg, then, is an intricate entanglement of éclat and somberness, light and darkness, and it works itself into being via the metaphors and material histories of both.

Conclusion

Early on in this chapter I considered the idea, via Lefebvre and Robinson, that each time we move in the city we potentially use space differently—an idea that also suggested the need to resist reading space and identity, including racial identity, as one-dimensional. This "always-moving space," a constant revising of the inventory of the city, is a tracking and a breaching of its historical construction, and a way of conceptualizing the contemporary city. As a means of tracking city space, I looked for fictional architectures, infrastructural figurations in the making of an urban biography—the street, the café, the suburb, and the campus. Into these infrastructures surfaced figures of the city—the *stranger;* the *aging white man,* a new minority figure, trying to remake a public self; the *suburban talker,* name dropper, insular professional; and the *hustler,* deftly rummaging among the conventional modes of institutional life with a view to rerouting them.

In each case, I sought to draw out formations of race identity embedded in these city fragments. Blackness, no longer locked into an overarching binary with whiteness as in most of earlier South African fiction, comes increasingly to be mediated by the notion of the stranger, here the African other, the demise of certain forms of whiteness and the rise of the black middle class, and the parodic rendering of the democratic new, as discursive effect and as generative of material practices of living in the city.

I considered, within these urban narratives and styles of subjectivity and language, moments when "something gets made," while also paying close attention to the effects of an apartheid past. Much of that process of making lies of course within the constructing of narrative, the making of language itself, the act of summoning the city—in this case the African city, here the city of Johannesburg—into words. Thus we might think of Mpe's second-person narrative, itself a way of summoning the dead to life and opening the living to the dead; Vladislavić's hermeneutics of city-ness, prizing open the meanings of the city through language as such; Andersson and Gordimer's dialogism, and Mlongo's art of parody. Together they could be said to constitute an "architectonics," a term used by Bakhtin to signify that which concerns questions about building, about how something is put together—in this case, the literary city itself.

What, then, is the Johannesburg text of the now? For the moment, it is still a text finding its form. Much of what is most exciting about Johannesburg fiction of the present could be said to be the new content that it is drawing into being, into writing. Yet it is a body of writing suggestive in terms of form, though it is perhaps Mpe, Vladislavić, and Gordimer who work most fully on this level. The elevation of the other through second-person narrative, the idea of language as "print object," and the location of a dispersed, narrative consciousness less binary than before all work symptomatically to give the novel and the city their contemporary form.

Vladislavić, in *The Exploded View,* dissects the proliferating, competing, and contradictory infrastructures of the city, its cars, roads, and its flickering television screens: "An endless jumble of body parts and ruins, a gyrating hip, an enigmatic navel, a fossicking hand, a pointing finger, sign language for a secret alphabet, fragments of city streets, images flaring and fading, dissolving, detaching, floating in airtime, dwindling away into nothing" (24). He invokes assemblages of city-ness, infrastructures of the urban that are continually being reassembled in both historical and psychic time.[17] The city is a vast narrative structure that constantly re-presents itself. Considering what a Johannesburg text might be, we see that critical work on the present is necessarily firmly tied to the work of writing the city.

Notes

1 These writers include Es'kia Mphalele, Arthur Maimane, Todd Matshikiza, Bloke Modisane, Can Themba, Nat Nakasa, Casey Motsisi, Bessie Head, and Lewis Nkosi.

2 Gready argues that the writers were offered what Berman calls a "shadow passport" to an unreal reality and the frustration of a world that they could taste but not make their own (2002: 149).

3 See also Sipho Sepamla's bitterly ironic poem "To Whom It May Concern": Subject only to the provisions / of the Urban Natives Act of 1925 . . . He may roam freely within a prescribe area / Free only from the anxiety of conscription" (1975: 9).

4 I am grateful to Rita Barnard for our discussion on this point.

5 Biopolitics, as Amin and Thrift show, engineers the body and its senses—and life more generally—so as to produce governable subjects: "Cities cast spells over the senses, spells which come to be engineered by the state" (2002: 28).

6 At least 90 percent of Hillbrow's population live in blocks of flats. The remainder live in hotels, on the streets, in domestic quarters on the roofs of blocks of flats, or in the negligible number of residential homes still standing. As Alan Morris (1999a) notes, Hillbrow is one of the very few neighborhoods in South Africa that, despite the Group Areas Act, moved from being an all-white neighborhood (in terms of flat dwellers) to being predominantly black.

7 I am grateful to Tom Odiambho for our discussion on this point.

8 Mpe, interview with the author, Wits Institute for Social and Economic Research, Johannesburg, April 20, 2003.

9 Of course migrants are not necessarily always-moving figures but may instead be forced to follow well-beaten tracks. In the case of Johannesburg, it may rather be

the new black middle classes who are really on the move in the city. Nevertheless, in fictional representations, migrants are shown, thus far, to be quintessentially "moving" figures. Alan Morris (1999a) has found that while race and racism in Hillbrow are still beset with contradictions and anomalies, most inhabitants say that racial barriers have broken down and that acts of overt racism are not common. On the other hand, the over 23,000 Congolese and 3,000 Nigerians living in Hillbrow faced xenophobia and "political racism" in a context in which the antiapartheid struggle did not breed a pan-Africanist consciousness, or an instant ethos of international solidarity or respect for diversity (316; see Simone 2000) but which is nevertheless leading to the unofficial forging of the highly tensile beginnings of an Afropolitanism.

10 "Madiba shirt" refers to the specific style of high collared, loose, often patterned shirt worn by Mandela in place of a more formal suit, and widely reproduced for sale in South Africa.

11 Alan Mabin (2003) writes that "suburbs have been a silent presence in the widely disseminated 'models' of the apartheid city, but meanings attached to the term, and its relationship to other quintessentially South African terms such as 'township' have been underexplored. Apartheid may have helped to shape the South African suburb, but its disappearance, if anything, accelerated the development of new forms of suburbia." Mabin remarks that increasingly technologies of race that long segregated the suburbs from the townships are being replaced by technologies of security, image, and style, as well as new forms of spatial segregation.

12 Early in the novel, Abby Moeketsi says of herself: "So I wear Stoned Cherrie gear, with pictures of early Drum magazine cover girls on my T-shirts, and get invited out a lot. . . . along with Gwen Gill, Rudeboy Paul, Tom Modise, Phat Joe, Khanyi Dhlomo-Mkhize and Darryl Bristow-Bovey, I still get invited to the opening nights of every play in town, as well as every show biz party—and, in fact, to anything that even remotely embodies the words 'art' or 'culture'" (9–10).

13 Andersson, interview with the author, University of the Witwatersrand, Johannesburg, September 14, 2003.

14 Barta et al. (2001: 4) argue that monologism is always subject to its own disintegration: "However much a given official or privileged form of speech seeks to assert its own monological privilege, it is in fact always already constituted out of the same dialogic relations as gave rise to its unofficial, centrifugal other."

15 Dingz also tries out these parodies to get what he wants, to hustle the dean of the faculty: "According to our culture I'm not supposed to touch anything connected with the deceased. And since it's taboo, I had to get permission from the elders"; "We are a very communal people and so, even though the corpse has decomposed, we still had to agree as a family about the funeral arrangements " (209).

16 See Amin and Thrift 2002: 105. Mlongo's novel recalls David Lodge's campus novels of the 1960s, 1970s, and 1980s. In his novels *Changing Places* (1969) and *Small World* (1979), Lodge treats the university as a piece of territory somewhat removed from the hurly-burly of ordinary life, a "small world" in which ambition and desire

generate comedy rather than tragedy. By the time he writes *Nice Work* (1986), the pastoral seclusion of the campus, whether literal or metaphorical, from the real world of social, political and economic forces, has gone forever. Lodge (2005: 1) remarks that this occurs roughly at the same time as the "rise of Theory, which subverted common sense and was virtually incomprehensible to the layman" (1).

17 Gilles Deleuze and Félix Guattari (1987: 3–4) suggest that an assemblage is constituted by "lines of articulation or segmentarity, strata and territories; but also lines of flight, movements of deterritorialization and destratification. Comparative rates of flow on these lines produce phenomena of relative slowness and viscosity, or, on the contrary, of acceleration and rupture." While for them assemblages constitute a regime of signs, here I have tried to draw out assemblages of contemporary city-ness and urban objects in which the material life of the emergent city intersects with the implicit immateriality of the sign as such.

Voice Lines

Instant City

JOHN MATSHIKIZA

There must have been something here, where Johannesburg stands, before the gold rush, but it was never recorded in history. So Johannesburg became and remained, by default, an instant city, periodically growing and being torn down as the gold seams shifted course in one direction or another and the needs of its fickle residents changed. Beer halls, brothels, and bioscopes rapidly outnumbered places of worship.

And speaking of places of worship—in the early days, when each cathedral was built it was granted a full block of the city's infrastructure to stand on, but Paul Kruger, president of the Transvaal Republic, permitted the Jewish synagogue only half a block, arguing that Jews read only half of the Bible.

So it has always been a politically and racially charged city. It is said that Johannesburg has been built up and torn down no fewer than five times since it first appeared on the Highveld in 1886. And each time it has reemerged even uglier than before.

It has its charms. They say that Johannesburg has the most extensive greenbelts of any city in the world—grassy parks with swimming pools and jacaranda trees. But to return to politics, we have to remind ourselves that it is only relatively recently that these beautiful amenities have been available to all its citizens, regardless of color.

Ten years after we liberated the city from its oppressive past, most of the parks have turned into brownish wilderness—particularly those around the center of the city, where the former inhabitants have abandoned their green pastures and moved on to armed townhouse complexes and shopping malls in the north. It is a wealthy city indeed that can simply abandon its tallest buildings and move onward when the imminent arrival of the barbarians is announced. It is also a mark of a culture that accepts that its very existence is purely temporary and that a day will always come when it is time for the tribe to move on.

Johannesburg is an ever-changing movie that no one has quite managed to produce. It is a screenplay in progress. Like movie directors, leaders are thrown up out of the soil of the surrounding area to try to bring a sense of order to what Johannesburg is.

Of course, there was Cecil John Rhodes, who couldn't stand the place but played his part in making it the mining town that it would later become, drawing the world to its waterless shores.

Then there was Paul Kruger, whom I have already mentioned. And in more recent times, we have had Winnie and Nelson Mandela. No one has really been able to wrestle Johannesburg into any kind of civilized order. The city remains what it is, with its own personality—here today, gone tomorrow.

For the millions who throng to it, Johannesburg is the perfect haven, all things to all people. It is a movie set with a host of superstars, starlets, heroes, villains, minor personalities, and as many extras as you could possibly want. Yet Johannesburg never quite comes together as the perfect movie, the picture you could make to turn Hollywood green. Johannesburg is an unfinished movie.

Johannesburg, the Unfinished Movie

What is tough is not to make a picture; what is tough
is to make a deal.   BILLY WILDER

If ever there was a town that was about making a deal, it is Johannesburg. Cape Town is known for scenic beauty: the sea, the mountains, the ever-changing sky hovering over its naked history. Pretoria has lyrical avenues of acacia trees framing its tidy business center and austere, gray-brown miles of government buildings that speak of a dedication to mind-control and other forms of order. Durban, on the Indian Ocean to the south, has the enticingly seedy air of a tropical seaport with the accompanying sense of easygoing disorder. Bloemfontein, the other great provincial capital, has yet to develop a describable identity.

But it is Johannesburg, ugly, hectic Johannesburg, that draws the energies that make the rest of the country tick.

Johannesburg wears its lack of style garishly on its sleeve. Johannesburg is proud that history and beauty and all that bunk aren't a significant feature of its landscape. Rome wasn't built in a day, but Johannesburg was. In Johannesburg, as soon as you've finished putting a building up, it's time to start thinking about pulling it down again and erecting something even more graceless in its place. Johannesburg can afford to be perpetually throwing things out because—well, because it can *afford* to.

Johannesburg is the African mecca of the Deal. And that started when the legend of gold—the legend that would make El Dorado sound like a hick town in comparison—stuck fast in the imaginations of the early mining magnates, from Europe, from America, from anywhere, it seems, but Africa. And so the rush began.

I regret to say that my ancestors, the lyrical peasants of the blasted hinterland, followed that rush and have stayed here ever since. Hoping, vaguely, somehow, to one day become part of the Deal.

Nothing has changed.

Pilgrims from the African Hinterland

Gold turned Johannesburg into an African mecca. The heydays were the 1930s, the 1940s, and the 1950s. People rushed in from all over the subregion—from neighboring countries like Portuguese East Africa, Angola, Namibia, the Rhodesias, and their poor baby sister, Nyasaland; but also from further afield, countries like Tanganyika and Congo and Kenya. Some came looking for El Dorado. Most came because they were coerced, with the connivance of their colonial governments, to supply the sweat of their labor in extracting the thin but lucrative seams of gold that seemed to go on forever underneath Johannesburg.

Some came to be educated. Joshua Nkomo, Robert Mugabe, Samora Machel, and Seretse Khama—men who would become the leaders of their independent countries—came and drank at the trough of learning at Fort Hare and Lovedale but would have spent most of their time hanging around the fast streets of Johannesburg, the most modern city on the African continent. The fact that it had a serious race problem only sharpened the development of their own philosophies of liberation back home.

People came to work as garden boys and kitchen maids. The suburbs of Johannesburg offered a meager living, while there was only desperation back home. Northern Rhodesians came to Johannesburg and discovered the joys of ballroom dancing, shebeens, and a racy lifestyle, which they exported when their contracts expired. The beat of Sophiatown made the stay-at-homes back in the townships of Lusaka, Kitwe, and Chililabombwe sit up and listen when the been-to's came and told them what they had seen.

Then there was Clemens Kadali, a young man who walked all the way from Nyasaland (now Malawi) to find work on the mines and ended up founding the Industrial and Commercial Workers' Union (known as the icu), the most powerful black trade union in southern Africa. He also founded a dynasty of brilliant offspring who went out into the world and multiplied— also multiplying the intellectual frameworks of the liberation struggle.

Johannesburg was the humming terminus of a two-way street between South Africa and the rest of the continent. There is a very good reason Peter Abrahams, later to become a world-famous writer, bore the huge, staring eyes and delicate features of an Abyssinian icon: his father was an Ethiopian who had come from that ancient, unconquered empire to seek out the mysteries of Johannesburg. Then there was David Kgobe, a young man from the Orange Free State who decided to take Johannesburg for a ride, hustle an easy living, and sidestep the horrors of the invidious pass system all in one stroke by claiming to be an Ethiopian prince. Everyone in Johannesburg's black society knew exactly who he was, but he insisted on going around calling himself Prince Wani Yusuf, from abroad. This did not stop him from living the high life of Johannesburg—the dream of Prester John alive and well in the South Western Townships that cling like poor relatives to the skirts of the City of Gold.

Distant Images from a Liberation Struggle: Lagos, Dar es Salaam, Nairobi, Lusaka, Luanda (*Getting Close to Home*)

The 1960s saw a hemorrhaging of Johannesburg's black talent. Virtually all of the show-business world left for London with the jazz musical *King Kong.*

From there, many of them struck out for New York, the city in whose image black Johannesburg had always fashioned itself. What had come down from the silver screen at the Odin Cinema in Sophiatown—the gangster culture, the molls, the glamour, the live-fast-die-young attitude—was now laid at the feet of the superstars who had given Johannesburg its modern identity: Miriam Makeba, Hugh Masekela, Letta Mbulu, the Manhattan Brothers, the Woody Woodpeckers, and many others.

But there was a hemorrhage of a different kind also taking place. Politics had come to a head with the Sharpeville shootings and the subsequent banning of all legitimate avenues of protest available to black people, whose leaders—figures like Walter Sisulu, Nelson Mandela, Dorothy Neymbe, Yusuf and Amina Cachalia, and many, many others—all gravitated toward Johannesburg from their respective places of birth. Johannesburg had always been hot. Now, with clampdowns by the newly empowered Afrikaner security apparatus, it became too hot to handle. Thousands of people drifted into exile.

Exile was a double-edged sword. For some it was a prelude to a slow and calculated suicide, cut off from the very lifeblood of home. For others it was the dawning of the discovery of a new world—particularly the African world that had always seemed so distant and so tantalizing.

Alf Hutchinson set out on the *Road to Ghana* (the title of his autobiography). Ezekiel Mphahlele, who had worked his way from the rough streets of the Pretoria township Marabastad to the pages of Johannesburg's racy *Drum* magazine, left for Ibadan, Nigeria, then Kenya, France, the United States, and Zambia before returning home in the mid-1970s, in defiance of the many obstacles that had been set before him. Oliver Tambo and Thabo Mbeki drifted between London, Moscow, and Lusaka, with staging points in other exotic places—particularly Dar es Salaam and later Lagos. Africa became the place to be, the vantage point from which to look back on the accursed land they had been born in. With them, and the thousands of ex-thieves, intellectuals, good-time boys and girls, nurses, teachers, jailbirds, gunslingers, and dedicated revolutionaries, they brought a new element of excitement, danger, and curiosity to Africa's cities.

Johannesburg's sophisticated black monthly, *Drum* magazine, had always been a forum for Africa to speak to and for itself. Through the pages of *Drum*, black South Africa watched the unfolding drama of Africa's surge toward independence from colonial rule. Kwame Nkrumah; Kenyatta the

Burning Spear; shock-haired Kenneth Kaunda; the rise and fall of Sir Abu-bakar Tafewa-Balewa; and the haughty dignity of Emperor Haile Selassie, Lion of Judah, King of Kings, direct descendant of King Solomon of the Jews—all were part of the day-to-day gossip of Sophiatown.

In return, *Drum*'s regional offices in Dar es Salaam, Accra, Lagos, and Salisbury (now Harare) pumped that urgent, urban image of Johannesburg and its swagger, its triumphs, its trials and tribulations into the streets and speakeasies of metropolitan Africa. The dialogue had already been firmly established by the time the exiles started swarming in, infecting the fiery continent with their own angry, anguished agenda.

We talked. We philosophized, shared meals, and swapped partners, learning how to Africanize ourselves. And Africa, simultaneously impressed and unimpressed, talked back.

People would become intimate with you as soon as you said you were from South Africa. "Ah, South Africa, Johannesburg," someone said to me one day in Nairobi. "That's a great place. How's Winnie doing?" They were referring to the embattled Winnie Mandela, icon of the struggle, public face of the jailed Nelson Mandela, flawed hero of the people, and a symbol of female pride and durability. How could I tell them how Winnie was doing? I had been in exile for twenty years by then. Yet they were talking to me as if Winnie and I chatted over the garden fence in Orlando every morning, muttering inanities about the weather.

Then there was the Yoruba fellow who invited himself into my hotel room in Lagos in 1977 and, after conversation about life in general, and Africa in particular, suddenly leaned forward with a scowl on his face and said, "What is wrong with you South Africans? A Nigerian would never allow white people to push us around in our own country. Why aren't you fighting?" My protests that there was indeed a fight going on were brushed aside with a click of the tongue: "You just give us the green light," he said, "the Nigerian army will walk into Johannesburg tomorrow and sort this thing out."

Dakar

Although most of our thoughts were about guns, we also had days of roses. Exile gave us access to parts of Africa we never even knew existed. Most of the time in exile, we felt cut off not just from the atmosphere of South Africa, and Johannesburg in particular, but also from what Africa meant in the world.

Months and years could go by in Lusaka or Luanda or Dar es Salaam, and while we knew we were living the daily life of the continent, many of us were stuck in refugee or military camps where there was no room to maneuver, where you barely felt human—let alone African. "African" became an abstract condition. What was there to identify with when your main aim was daily survival, wondering when the final battle that would take you home would actually begin?

Early in 1982, I had the privilege of being invited to teach in Dakar. Nothing could stop me from getting there. I took the cheapest ticket I could find, an Aeroflot flight via Moscow. I was stranded three long days as the airline changed its schedules, but finally landed in Senegal in the dusty early dawn of a February morning. In Dakar and the slave island of Gorée, just a couple of miles offshore, I found space to ponder my place in the world and the relationship between the African city, history, and the present we were still fighting to take possession of.

It is 1982, far from home, twenty-two years on from the defining moment that catapulted me out of my native city of Johannesburg. I am sitting at a sidewalk café, the Metropole, on the Avenue Georges Pompidou, the main drag of the endlessly energetic city of Dakar, clinging to life between two vast and threatening oceans: the Atlantic to the south and west, and the Sahara desert to the north and east.

What this extraordinary city opened up for me was a different perspective on humanity and what it means to be human. I have come here as a teacher but find myself humbled, learning from the Senegalese. I walk the streets of Dakar by day and by night. I observe these people who have such beauty, grace, and elegance in the midst of their poverty. Tall, beautiful, black—and proud. This is important. The South African struggle is about blackness, whiteness, and indignity. The hidden side of our struggle, which begins to reveal itself to me here, is about where you find your source of pride. In Senegal, this sense of an unbroken link to your own history hits you in the face. In South Africa, even as South Africans in exile, we carry ourselves with an arrogance borne of coming from the City of Gold, from the powerhouse of the African economy. Subtly, imperceptibly, we have bought into our own colonization. We have come to agree with our own oppressors that we are better than other Africans because we come, even if as servants, from the promised land: the land given to the white man through a covenant with God himself. Or so we'd been told. And sneakily, in the absence of evidence to the contrary and broken down by four centuries of debilitating war, we began to believe the propaganda in spite of ourselves.

Dakar taught me how to find pride again—not the borrowed pride of the fleeting black image that sometimes appeared out of Hollywood, or the lessons of assimilation from the truncated civil rights movement in America. Nor the pride by association that had become part of our skin through the novels and essays of James Baldwin and LeRoi Jones (whose *Blues People* accompanied me on this journey to Senegal) and Zora Neale Hurston, Richard Wright, Frantz Fanon, Toni Morrison, Gabriel García Márquez, Aimé Césaire (whose undiscovered plays littered the sidewalks of Dakar, waiting for me to stumble on their untold riches). It was about the simple things of being black, of being human, of having been round the block and coming back, and still not giving a damn—except about the things that are important.

In Dakar there are open, flowing sewers left by the French colonial administrators, the stench rising or subsiding according to the season, the time of day, or the ebb and flow of the tide from the Atlantic, into which they bring each day's waste. Cheek by jowl with this is the midday ritual of sitting round a communal dish and eating *tieb bou dienne* with your bare hands, your host or hostess separating for you the best morsels from the pile of rice, vegetables, *tiof* (known as the prince of all fishes), and red oil so that you leave satisfied, feel accepted as part of the human family.

I walked restlessly, relentlessly through the streets of Dakar, too scared, too astonished at this endless palette of life to stop, to rest, to close my eyes even for a moment, if I could. I stared at women in their elegant boubous, their turbaned heads poised on their long, sleek, black necks, their cheeks or temples slashed with scars that told whether they were Peul, Wolof, or Lebou. Men built like gladiators of the ring rasped out at one another as they hurtled through the streets in the jaunty, careless, classical language of Wolof, integrated with casual bursts of French, just to show they were all part of the same modern/ancient world.

Dakar focused the mind. How could such strong, gregarious people ever have been colonized, subdued, enslaved? And how could they have bounced back, generous, amusing, filled with all the mysterious rhythms of life, controlled and respectful in their interactions with one another and with strangers like myself?

Beggars were everywhere: women and men, girls and boys, small children, people with withered limbs and sightless eyes, hobbling round on steel crutches, dragging their stick-thin, lifeless legs behind them, determined to survive and with no sense of self-pity, calling on you to give in the name of Allah—for the grace of the God that has made us all and made all things. My atheist soul was humbled. Sometimes I gave. Most times I stood and watched, trying to find my place in the wild mosaic. An accidental awakening.

One day, in the heat of the afternoon, I was walking along a busy street off the Place de l'Independence, thinking my own thoughts, when I became aware of a man who had been persistently following me, addressing me in the nasal tone that is so much a part of the Wolof tongue, trying to persuade me to buy some of the unappealing, tinny gold jewelry he was carrying in his hand. I was almost an old *Dakarois* by then, three months into my Senegalese odyssey. I had learned to defend myself, to switch off the outer soundtrack, the constant barrage of provocation and temptation, the hard sell that swarms through the *trottoirs* day and night.

But something made me take notice of this man. He might have overstepped himself, aware that I was ignoring him, and tapped me on the arm. Whatever it was, I found myself violently awakened from my reverie. I stopped in my tracks and turned on him. I yelled something in French, telling him I was not interested in his wares, that he should go away and leave me alone. He looked at me with the pained stare of a child who has just been unjustly slapped. "Je suis nègre comme toi, hein!" he said disapprovingly, the gold trinkets still tinkling uselessly in his hand. We stared at each other, and then I burst out laughing. He did too. We had made eye contact. He knew there was no way I was going to buy any of his wares. But at least I had acknowledged him. Wars begin when people pretend that they cannot see each other. And anyway, our blackness, he was telling me indignantly, united us in the struggle against an infinitely unjust world.

Once again, I had learned my lesson.

The sensuality of that very different African experience, the people who hold themselves with such poise in the midst of a poverty I had never seen so overt anywhere in the world, wretchedness, disease, flies, malaria, but also music and movement at their highest forms of expression on every street corner, and an argumentative, aggressive type of capitalism that would have you fleeing from street traders as soon as you stepped out of your apartment—all this signaled a different kind of arrival and a different perspective on what it was to be an African. And it reinforced all the things we had been denied as black Africans in South Africa, whether at home or in exile.

And then, finally, eventually, surprisingly, it was time to go home.

Home Run (Transcribed in a Furious Scribble on
Pages of the *Weekly Mail*, Jan Smuts Airport, September 11, 1991)

*It's all started now, of course. Nerves at Heathrow, but on landing, a strange
feeling of—nothing much at all. As if some form of energy has long ago been
bled out of the atmosphere. We could be anywhere. Especially coming straight
from JFK and then Heathrow, and most fellow travelers looking the same here
as they did there.*

*Queue for passport control, a nation full of relatives waiting unseen beyond
the barriers. I'm given back my passport, then called back—for the first time
anywhere in the world my name has appeared on the computer. So . . . wait and
wait while I protest and they say they'll call Pretoria when the offices open. Sitting in the coffee bar—what's changed? Everything.*

Coming off the apron, away from the dozens of orange-tailed jumbos of SAA,
*bidden "Welkom in Suid Afrika" by the signs around the endlessly rebuilt ter-
minus, walking into it past a pathetic stuffed zebra rampant on a plinth, emas-
culated and dead, barely even black-and-white anymore, just gray-brown and
dead. Welcoming foreigners to this brave country.*

*Waiting. Cross through curmudgeonly security controls to get a coffee. Dazed
up the up escalator, the white boys with their killer evasive eyes and Nazi-
brown shorts and guns. Down the down escalator, remembering how, when the
moving stair was first introduced in* S.A., *round in 1961 in the* "OK" *Bazaars,
or somewhere, a sop after Sharpeville, terrified platte-land whites forced their
cringing laborers to get on first to make sure it worked and didn't grind you up,
this thing that was supposed to take you upstairs without walking. The tsotsis
soon slipped on their bravado, swaggering "staff" onto the rows of iron teeth,
grinning backward at the irritated Boers as they rode into the air above the
shop floor. Nowadays, with the reluctant, step-by-step retreat from the far side
of apartheid, blacks are made to go down the up-escalator, and up the down. As
a challenge. To see if they are up to being part of the twentieth century. Just to
keep things in a rumpus. Fear in the sunken eyes, the long war raging now too
long, too wearing on a diet of pap and* tausa.

*Browse through the bookshop where Nelson Mandela's books now stare out
shoulder-to-shoulder with Wilbur Smith, only Wilbur Smith's a better seller. By
far. Always will be.*

*The blacks have dead eyes, dead like the zebra, and yellowy-red. Blitzed-out
in the beer halls and the streets of horror and shame.*

The whites—a little subdued, not so horny-cocky as they were in '72, when the war was still an exciting prospect on the horizon. But what's this? I see one white woman mopping the floor along with all the blacks. She looks ashamed. So am I.

Stage Two

In and out of Josies like a bullet that changed its mind. Unimpressed, actually, by how small and small-town it feels. We hang out with Aunty (who welcomes me home profusely, though I wish I was feeling something) and Sunnyray and others around the Market Theater, taking pictures of each other by Kippie's Bar (sad memorial to a hard-drinking genius who deserved much more 'cos he was much more). Aunt V. points out John Vorster Square, still there, still huge, still evil. She closes one eye to run her finger along the row of windows that mark the infamous tenth floor, where she and Cicely and thousands of others were locked in, in raw fear, the adrenaline pungent like the slaughterhouse, and some were pushed out onto the pavement below, not floating but dropping like stones and disintegrating on the carefully laid paving stones like bags of offal.

John Kani shouts "Hey" at me from across the street and we hug, but it's not like that great homecoming we all thought it would be. Just us here on another street. . . .

Back to the primitive, shabby halls of Jan Smuts, kissing them all "Totsiens" for now. Run for the so-called Namib Air plane, which is SAA in new colors, that's all.

Out on the tarmac, now, the SAA planes are no longer the only game in town. Air Zimbabwe and Air Malawi have slipped in under cover of daylight.

Up into the ether again, looking down on the white suburbs, each and every house with its turquoise, kidney-shaped pool in the yard, some with two pools. The ones with two pools belong to the most liberal whites, I suppose, proud to tell native visitors like me that one pool is for mixed bathing ("I use that one myself") while the other is for hardliners who don't want to share their water with blacks at this stage. Democracy, your host will point out, means freedom of choice.

We are flying deeper into South Africa. I don't think this is where I'll be living for the rest of my life.

Soweto

Soweto is a symbol of revolution all up and down the continent. Soweto is also where I spent the first few years of my life—although I was no longer in Soweto when the shit hit the fan.

In Lagos, people would ask me, "How is life in Soweto?"

As if I had a clue.

Soweto Diary, Sometime 1991

One a.m. Wake up in shock, after barely an hour's sleep. Pain and itching round my neck, on my back, both arms. Blistering barnacles, bedbugs! Reality is beginning to bite, literally. This experience, this familiarity is breeding contempt among the locals. What was it that Todd wrote about bedbugs? The time when he and the Nkunzana were in jail for drinking liquor at the white man's behest. They were shouting to each other about the fresh, soft flesh of these mission boys slung in among the hardened People of the Stone, and tucking in, careless and callous as Big Fives.

I've snapped on the bedside light and slap and scratch at myself, reach myopically for my specs and search the bedclothes in terror, wondering what a bedbug will look like when I see it, will I be able to handle it. Look round the little room, Aunty's bedroom, much smaller now in sharp, unromantic focus. This is Soweto, boy, where you ran away from. The walls are yellow and sooty. Things are packed in cardboard boxes alongside and on top of the shabby old wardrobe, the tiny desk is useless as a desk, it is a bedside table and store cupboard, the government has built hovels for the people, and the people are trapped in them, shoulder to shoulder, step out of your front door and how can you avoid seeing your neighbor knifing her husband in the gloom of her stoep because she's gone crazy, or Sherry being chased down the street by must-be-a-hundred Bushies grinning and waving sticks in anticipation of a little variation in this cruel life, all wanting to take part in corrective, instant punishment of Sherry, 'cos she, this middle-aged seventeen-year-old, had the audacity to leave her two-year-old and the baby with her ninety-year-old father who's a drunk, alone and without food and milk from her horrified breasts, for three whole days, looking to fit some fun into the weekend and make it last a little longer. Here's Sherry running barefoot past my Aunty's stoep, and the "community," from four to sixty, running hopefully after her with sticks.

They corner her down in the creek, where Mr. Snit found that snake in '58 and couldn't resist bringing it all the way up the hill in a sack to terrorize us kids playing in the yard of Mama's crèche, which is still there, on the corner over Mamlankhunzi, just as I left it, with regrets. Let the snake writhe before us while Mama wasn't looking and then burned it, in its death throes, with fire. What the hell were we supposed to make of it all? Aged three?

The dust rises from around the creek as they lay into Sherry. They finally catch her and tell her what's what, no matter how bad they all are. Jesus says, Who dares to throw the first stone? Me, they all say. We go back to what we were doing, watching television, drinking beer, talking politics. Staring like into a mirror at the identical township pouring away in every direction over the rounded hills. This must have been a beautiful landscape, once, until they discovered the gold. The piles of mine dumps, left there for the township to crouch around, the white man's dirt abandoned where he decided he was finished with it, the skeletons of mine-head gear rusting over sucked-out shafts where the Coloureds can fall in if they want to, I've got work to do. . . .

The house is sleeping. This little bedroom feels like a trap. I am, after all, not used to this. The river doesn't return to its source. Two nights I've hardly slept, not out of excitement, but because the mattress is amazingly uncomfortable. This is poverty, and knowing my aunt the way I know her, I can't believe that this is really happening. I mean, this is deep *poverty. Like, why don't any of these dozens of useless sons and sons-in-law fix the lavatory? Why doesn't somebody paint the walls? Why, why, why? In fact, why should they? This has been going on for as long as any of us can remember. It's enough just to hold on under the pressure. So your granddaughter comes back from the mean night streets and gives birth to another girl-child right there before your eyes, and won't or can't tell you who's the father. So you make some more space where there's none, and life goes on. Because we're black, and nobody is ever turned away. Or so it goes. . . .*

But in the quiet house I'm alone with invisible bedbugs. I scratch and slap my skin, hoping someone will wake up and come and keep me company. Nothing. Prepare for sleep again. Just drawing the sheet up to my chin, gingerly, when, damn me, if the fattest thing, big and brown like two cents, comes marching out of the folds and straight toward my face. I haven't even switched off the light. I am shocked. It's so fucking big. Stamping across the white sheets, out of nowhere, fearing nothing.

I clap the sheet hard. Hold it, breathing heavily. How do you kill a bedbug? An ax? I open the fold a crack. There he is still, squirming. Released, he starts marching again. I squeeze the sheet tight, twist it, grind, dig my fingernails into the patch where he is, in there where I can't see his ugly, township mug and don't want to. Me and him, the same.

Fearfully, gingerly release my grip. Peer into the folds, my knuckles white. My blood seeps out of him and his mangled body, smearing the sheet. And that terrible sweet smell they always said bedbugs give off when you squash them. He's dead. I look around the room. Why? This has all already been written by guys like Casey Motsitsi. Why do we have to go through it in person?

Didn't sleep any more.

September 18, 1991: Why I Love Johannesburg (*From an Erratic Diary*)

Walking uptown at lunchtime to fetch my daughter from school.

Black people rushing to catch Russians-and-chips on the pavement in the hot, dull lull. Security men with shotguns, watchmen with knobkerries also racing to finish the greasy packet of chips before the baas opens up shop again.

A Coloured man in his kuffertjie, *sitting on the edge of a concrete rubbish bin, from which, this sacred Friday, he pulls a full gin bottle, pours into a polystyrene cup, looking quickly up and down the street, replaces the bottle in its hideout amid the rubbish, and drinks, raw and strong. Blazing midday heat, no muezzin in sight or in earshot.*

Fast, erotic town. Rape and violence. No time. All the time in the world to wait for this madness to pass. And every minute, new children being born.

Black children hurrying through town in orange gym slips, white socks, missionary sandals. Blue/black gym slips, ending halfway down their fat brown thighs. Running down Bree Street to the bus stop. Kidding hand-in-hand with black schoolboys in white shirts and grey trousers. Sex is old. Sex is fast. Sex is new, yesterday, tomorrow. To reach out and grab your arm, grip you belly-to-belly and whisper "Let's love tonight," while the white man works, builds concrete, greases his guns, and grinds groins in the Escort Agency, grows grim as he thinks of the sagging white flesh he made the mistake of marrying for good, for the sake of the race. And all this glowing black flesh to relate to.

Time flies in Joburg. Men go mad. Women know who and what they are.

"Control through submission," says Violet G. "Otherwise men, you know, men, like you, they panic and say 'no' and then they want to beat you, because they're scared. But if you say, 'OK, you're right, Papa, now straighten your jacket and don't come home late,' they'll say, 'Oh, yes my dear.' And that's how

you get things done. That's what love's about. Love in Johannesburg, anyway. That's how it's been from way, way back."

That's what the women say. . . .

You have to remember that it's very high, very dry up here. It's a high plateau, and people are only living here in these numbers because there's gold here, somewhere in the hills. Or nowadays, in the deeps. It's drawn every one of our crazy bones, pull or push or kicking and screaming. Now we scream anger if we get in each other's way, and push on, rushing down Bree Street as if time mattered.

It's high and dry in this part of the Transvaal, and in winter it's cold as all hell. Forget the oily forests of Venda and Zululand, we're here in Johannesburg, and if you don't Vaseline your limbs before you go out hunting for work, your black hide turns grey, cracks, and makes you itch. It's not where you'd naturally be, being human, unless you were on the run. But it's alive with prospects. So oil your loins and grease your arms, and move. Oil your machine.

Xenophobia

It is true that we have an uncomfortable problem of xenophobia in South Africa. It is a xenophobia that is particularly nasty because it generally seems to be an intolerance exercised by black South Africans toward black people from elsewhere on the continent.

Thousands of nonblacks also have swarmed into this country and at an increasing rate in the 1990s as all sorts of restrictions began to fall away. Tens of thousands of Russians, Bulgarians, Yugoslavs, and other eastern Europeans flocked to South Africa as the socialist regimes that controlled their countries disappeared and the haywire free-market economies that replaced them (not to mention civil wars) put intolerable strains on their lives. Not all of these immigrants are engaged in legal or responsible forms of employment. But you don't hear about xenophobic mob lynchings being carried out against them. Nor are they rounded up in random police sweeps on the streets of Hillbrow or downtown Johannesburg and threatened with deportation.

Let us be clear from the beginning, then: it is not an issue of "South Africans against foreigners" but a feeling of resentment by *some* black South

Africans against black Africans who are legal or illegal residents of South Africa. Who can tell how many black South Africans feel this way? Surely not all of us, but the numbers are enough to make life very uncomfortable for many black people from this vast and fascinating continent we are all part of.

The worst cases make the headlines, as is usual with news reporting, and disappear unresolved soon after. A case in point is the fate of three West African traders who were hounded off a moving train between Pretoria and Johannesburg—two of them electrocuted as they scrambled onto the roof for safety, the third pushed to his death on the tracks. Whatever happened to that story? The grim thing about it (since I am trying to find statistics about this kind of xenophobia) is that neither the police nor the reporters who tried to investigate the case could get any information from the many witnesses who sat passively in their seats while this outrage played out before their very eyes. Is this complicity or just fear? After all, in the past these same witnesses have probably sat transfixed in their seats on other suburban trains as politically inspired massacres were conducted at random, or even as criminal gangs carried out—as they still do—terror campaigns of robbery, rape, and murder in those sealed and speeding carriages.

Is this xenophobia simply an extension of the violent acts of self-loathing that stem from the degrading conditions of township life and the disempowerment that black people have been consigned to? I am sure this is an important part of it. But there is more.

I lived away from South Africa for thirty-two years. Exile, even when it is described as "voluntary," is always involuntary. Who likes being barred from their own place of birth? On my return, I was filled with such a flood of desire to make up for lost time, to create a space for myself in this complex and unknown country, and to get to know my own people that I must admit to moments of resentment that thousands of others who have no roots here should be competing for the same space.

But there was a parallel problem. Many of the millions who had stayed behind also expressed resentment against me and my fellow exiles for swanning in with our big heads and funny accents and seemingly trying to take over. As far as we were concerned, we were simply trying to normalize our lives as quickly and as painlessly as possible, but it didn't seem like that to many of the "inziles." They, too, were trying to reclaim a space that had been denied them for as many generations as anyone could remember. We were all rushing to make up for lost time and all getting in one another's way. There was no United Nations relief program to help us sort the whole thing out. It was a free-for-all, and the so-called makwerekweres from the north just had to take their chances like the rest of us.

We exiles spent a lot of time living in the makwerekwere (the rude term for foreign) countries. In some cases, there was resentment from citizens of those newly independent states who were also trying to find their identity after decades of colonization. Exiles from southern Africa, however, were never murdered just because they were foreigners. On the contrary, for the most part we received the kindest hospitality, and our host countries sometimes suffered terrible military reprisals for offering it.

Were we always good guests? I'm afraid not. In many cases, we brought our dangerous township energy with us.

Julius Nyerere was said to have pointed out that the difference between a Tanzanian and a South African was that if you put an untrained Tanzanian in a helicopter, the Tanzanian would take one look at the complicated mess of dials and levers and walk away, defeated. A South African, on the other hand, would tinker around for a bit and finally get the hang of the thing.

"The problem is," said Nyerere, "the South African would then fly the helicopter to the nearest shebeen and leave it there."

This comment comprises the mixture of the fear, respect, and contempt that (black) South Africans have always engendered on this continent. Those complicated emotions still inform the uncomfortable relationship that exists between ourselves and our siblings from the north.

An Epilogue—or a New Beginning

I live in Johannesburg now. I wouldn't live anywhere else. It is hard to tell if I am just another African immigrant gravitating to El Dorado, destined to be subdued, disappointed, robbed, raped, or murdered on its grisly streets. My perspective on my old hometown is that of a foreigner, but of an African foreigner—an important difference.

I stake my claim. I was born here. My forebears built this ugly city but were never allowed to make it their own. I have a duty to perform on their behalf.

And the rest of Africa is swarming in behind me. There is some comfort in this. Makwerekweres get beaten up in Hillbrow if they don't know how to answer a greeting in Zulu. But I can find many friends with whom I can converse in French or Swahili.

And I continue to move. My African exile has taught me that I am more than a South African. I strike out into my continent at regular intervals, inhaling those extraordinary perfumes; the dust; the wood smoke; the incense in the flowing robes on the plane to Bamako; the gutted fish and the raw, hacked pieces of meat lying on open slabs in the downtown markets in Sandaga or Nairobi or Dar es Salaam; the noisome, appalling sewers of Yaounde and Douala; the raw potato odor that hovers over the ground in Lusaka after the first rains have fallen; the cow dung in the village; the sweat of black bodies in perpetual motion; the sharp, sweet tang of the baobab fruit.

Somehow you find a way to stitch the textures of home and exile together. But my anchor is now at home, in Johannesburg. It's a strange place. But we certainly have come through a revolution in this Johannesburg, this place of gold, this jangling bag of nerves, even if it is an unfinished revolution.

South Africa, as they say, is finally becoming African.

Soweto Now

ACHILLE MBEMBE, NSIZWA DLAMINI, AND GRACE KHUNOU

*Over the past few decades, historians, geographers, sociologists, urban develop-
ment specialists, and political scientists have produced numerous and sophisticated studies of this specifically Southern African social and urban formation
called "the township." Most of these studies have dealt with the hypervisible
issues of poverty and dispossession, chronic hunger and malnutrition, and expropriation and disenfranchisement in the context of state-sponsored racial
violence. Other studies have examined in detail the conditions of social reproduction and political mobilization in the township.*

*Yet almost fourteen years after the end of apartheid, we have very few postlib-
eration ethnographies of everyday life in the township. We have even fewer academic or theoretical reflections on its place in the city, its rhythms and senses.
That the township both is and is not urban, that it is proximate to the city
while at its margins, and that city and township were inextricably linked under
apartheid—all these points are incontestable. So is the fact that the township
still suffers from a lack of basic amenities, even as it exhibits the extremes of
poverty and wealth characteristic of the city. Nevertheless, we are left with a
negative definition of this highly syncretic urban formation that is integral to
city life in South Africa and deeply embedded in the nation's social imaginary
and political unconscious.*

*The objective of the following conversation with two young black South Afri-
cans is to open a small window onto postliberation township life and experience.
The questions put to Grace Khunou and Nsizwa Dlamini, then both doctoral*

fellows at WISER (Wits Institute for Social and Economic Research, University of the Witwatersrand), begin a conversation about the township within analytical territories that help to defy ready-made categorizations of this site of extremely complex interconnections. As their responses make clear, Khunou and Dlamini do not hesitate to read township life and experience as a text and as an emblem of the global city. Both of them seem to suggest that in spite of the overwhelming poverty of many of the township's residents, new cultures of commodification are emerging. These cultures underlie new aesthetic forms, of which cell phones, cars, and various registers of fashion are but examples. Both also point to various ways in which the township, although invented by the apartheid state, was and continues to be produced well beyond the apartheid moment. In very subtle ways, they seize on apparently marginal details of everyday life to show how, gradually, township residents are moving beyond the spatialities and temporalities of apartheid. A. M.

ACHILLE MBEMBE: How would you define "the township"? What distinguishes it from, say, the city, the inner city, the squatter camp, or the homeland?

NSIZWA DLAMINI: Well, when I think of "the township," I think of it as a largely racialized space created by the apartheid state—and in this sense it differs from the deracialized space of the city. The homeland was the result of the state's creation and definition of ethnic identities and differences. In the township, of course, people of many ethnicities live together in the same space. Squatter camps are different from townships only in a material sense; they are more deprived and are home almost exclusively to the unemployed—those who have come to be seen by society as disposable people. To me, the township is also a space in motion. People are perpetually moving and commuting. This sense of always being in motion is captured in the language of township residents, their dress code, and their music—kwaito in particular.

GRACE KHUNOU: For me, history, politics and culture, and language are what make the city, the homeland, and the township different from each other. To this should be added the fact that in the township everybody knows everybody else, where they come from, how their parents met. The city is a no-man's-land. Everybody has a stake in the township and can call it home. The city is for passersby. In the township, there is a strong sense of a community, of continuity and certainty. The township has a little bit of the homeland in it in terms of these kinds of social relations. In the city, the individual is his or her own master.

AM: In your view, what have been the main ruptures and continuities in everyday township life since the end of apartheid?

ND: A major rupture has been the upsurge of crime. Acts which could have been classified as criminal before 1994 were justified as acts of political resistance that allegedly sought to cripple the apartheid system. These included the hijacking and looting of vehicles carrying furniture, bread, and so on.

I have also noticed that many sites of everyday life I remember have lost their symbolism. Take shops, for instance. Shops used to be sites of recreation for male youth. It was here that habits deemed negative by township moralists were first learned and performed. These habits included the smoking of cigarettes and *zol* [marijuana]. Alcohols, such as benzine, and glue were used to intoxicate the youth. Shops were also sites where the mugging of smaller kids took place. And they were sites of a special kind of sport played only by streetwise males in the township. The use of tennis balls to perform tricks associated with soccer was significant in this regard. One needed special footwear to perform them, like the Converse All-Star takkies traditionally worn by *amapantsula* for dancing, running, or chasing.

What remains are social events organized by and for adults, including jazz sessions that are held on Sundays. During these sessions, there are no live performances. Rather, CDs are played by the host, who will benefit from selling alcohol and food [*chakalaka*]. Monday evening social sessions are also still highly regarded. They are given different names in different townships. In Alexander and Kwa-Thema, they are referred to as *amaphati omgodu* [tripe parties]. Tripe is sold during the sessions. It is understood that tripe is useful for overcoming hangovers and recovering from Sunday drinking.

GK: More taverns operate today. More women go out by themselves. Women who used to have flats or claim to have friends in the city, where they could sleep over, were suspected of being involved in sex work. If they were seen getting into a taxi to "town" in the evening, they were labeled. This is no longer the case. Young people are less political and more excited about life and about the world in general. People are keen to make it for themselves. At the same time, the number of funerals has increased. "Community" is still built around such tragic events. There are very high unemployment rates; as a result, alcoholism and youth suicides are up. Amid all of this, people keep dreaming and looking for new opportunities and ways of relating to one another. Some move out of the township in order to make it in the new world. Women are under less pressure to get married and to have babies; they are expected to go to school and to make their families and communities proud. There is a decrease in teenage pregnancy in Diepkloof, for example. There are more young girls going as far as they can in their studies. Such is not the case with young men, many of whom would like to become soccer stars or to work just after they graduate.

AM: In people's everyday experience and discourse, how is Johannesburg read from the township?

ND: People have always perceived the city as a different place. It is where one goes to make money. It is also viewed as a clean space. In that sense, people will not just get up and go to town. Some of these views are changing, though. The city is more and more experienced as just another place where you walk in and out. It is no longer viewed as "white only." A lot of old people complain about how the city used to be clean but is now populated by hawkers and thugs. This means that a new imagination of the city is in the making, in which the city appears as the place where you can become a target. It is no longer the state that is targeting you, but a threat of a different order. People therefore prefer to go to malls because the latter are seen to provide security. One can talk on one's cell phone without fearing that it will be snatched. One can also sit in a restaurant and look respectable or walk around without fear of being mugged in daylight.

The city is read as a space of opportunity. Take the example of petty criminals. Usually on Fridays and Saturdays, they go to the city to mug those who earn and can spend money. It is believed that Friday and Saturday are when the economically advantaged engage in acts of consumption. The youth read the city from the perspective of specific sites or streets. For example, sites such as City Outfitters in Jeppestown, the area from Small Street to Carlton Centre, as well as various sites in Hillbrow are significant in this regard. Small Street is popular because of its affordable designer labels. City Outfitters is known for dressing up pantsulas. Hillbrow is famous for sexual experiences; the Moulin Rouge is regularly visited by pupils willing to indulge in forbidden activities. Places such as the Summit are also popular, if only because they offer strip shows, preferably by white women.

AM: Township life under apartheid was, to a large extent, a mode of inscription of people's lives in a space subject to high levels of surveillance. What, in your memory and the memory of township residents, were the principal markers of the township landscape and what has happened to those markers?

GK: Memories of those times are shaped by the form and size of the houses, road access, the everyday parading of the army with their big war cars and guns. There are also memories of almost clean and empty streets during the afternoons.

ND: To me, the sizes of the plots were the key marker. They are very small and overcrowded. The plot usually consists of the "main house" and other dwellings such as *izozo* or *amazozo* [a shack or shacks]. There are other markers, some of which are hardly noticeable or noticed. In most streets, there are Eskom electricity main switches. They used to be painted yellow until township residents added green and black to the yellow; the green and black symbolized the colors of the African National Congress. This colorful landscape has been disappearing since 1994.

Other important markers of the township landscape were the Apollos. These were very tall, steel township lights. Most were installed in the 1980s, during the heyday of the struggle. They transformed the township evening darkness into daylight and were important for state surveillance. Some of these tall structures are still present but now largely dysfunctional. Today, townships at night are darker than they used to be. Only electrified houses save some townships from complete darkness at night.

AM: In a number of studies, the architecture and overall design of the township is read horizontally and in relation to the structures of the apartheid state. It seems as if, since 1994, we should add to this horizontal reading an aerial one. What, in your view, have been the major transformations in the aerial landscape [the airscape] of the township since 1994? What does one see when one reads the township from the air?

GK: Seen from the air, the township is being sold as hip and as a place to be. Some of the adverts seem to suggest that if you can have it in Sandton, then you can have it in the township, too. The idea is that you do not have to be in Sandton. So, adverts are playing on the elements of desirability, accessibility, and opportunity. Everywhere you go in Soweto, for example, you will meet adverts for MTN and Vodacom cell phones, not to mention beauty products. They all sell a lifestyle, and in many ways, the youth are buying into it. Through acquiring these products, the youth want to be seen as connected and as beautiful. One can also see the "rainbow nation," with its celebration of blackness as talented, wealthy, making it. For example, the TV advert for Metro FM ["The African Beat"] depicts blackness as rhythmic, poetic, cultured, and possessing style.

ND: The airscape is dominated by the radio, its sounds and noises. People do not seem to be keen to listen to vernacular radio. Before 1994, you could listen to drama, and the latter had strong currency. With the prominence of YFM and Metro FM, there is a rejection of stories in favor of music shows. Kwaito and house music are dominant among the youth. Hip-hop music and, with YFM, poetry are fast gaining a following.

AM: If the aerial landscape is so dominated by advertising and other media and technologies, what type of aesthetic sensibility do you think derives from this and what types of accessories best signify this new aesthetic moment?

GK: A cell phone is the best accessory ever. Those without disposable income find ways of owning one and having airtime. A lot of the hip guys do not leave their cell phones in their cars or put them in their pockets. They hold them in their hands. Funny enough, as they walk in a crowd or in a public space, it starts ringing or they somehow have to make a call. Another thing they have to be seen as having are the smallest cell phones. You lose points if you are seen with a heavy and big cell phone. The heavy cell phones are called "heavulla." The idea is that your neck will need to be massaged if you use the heavulla. No hip guy or girl wants to be seen carrying a heavulla.

Cell phones are also very much a female accessory. For some women, having accessories such as these are a reason for having multiple boyfriends, whom they refer to as "ministers"—that is, different boyfriends to provide for their different needs.

ND: It is considered degrading to give someone a landline phone number, as it suggests that one does not have a cell phone. Even those who have one are not off the hook, as their phones have to be tiny, lighter, and look good. The stylish carry small and light cell phones. Those are the expensive ones. Bigger ones are given names such as a "brick."

AM: How do cars figure in this postliberation imaginary?

GK: A man with a car is the man. He gets all the women. But not just any car: VW Golfs and BMWs used to be linked to being fast, having money, and challenging the apartheid system. Men with Golfs and BMWs used to be associated with shady activities, dressing up in high fashion. Today, Golfs and BMWs are still the cars that every young man dreams of owning.

They represent access to women, drink, and a good life. A lot of women do drive cars, but this is a new phenomenon. Although most women from the township can be seen driving the same loxion-style cars, like Golfs, some also break away and drive different cars, like Audi A3s, BMW Kompressors, and Mercedes Benzes. Mostly they go for cars that are not high risk.

ND: A BMW, a Golf 3 VR6, and VW GTI are the major attractions. They are cars that bring women home for a guy. An Alfa Romeo 147 also brings status. These are cars that a young man is supposed to drive. Cars such as Mercedes Benz or Audi [with the exception of the A3 and S3] are considered unsuitable for the youth. An SLK and other smaller, two-door models are appropriate Mercedes Benzes, but these are usually not affordable by the youth. When it comes to stealing cars, the Mercedes Benz is considered untouchable. In fact, there are no quick buyers of such cars within the township.

AM: The end of apartheid seems to have facilitated the emergence of new sites of erotic performance. What are the most visible of these?

ND: Erotic performance increasingly happens on the dance floor itself. Men and women dance in a "circle." They dance either face-to-face or the male dances from behind. A woman is never behind. Usually, men are encouraged by the chanting and dancing of the crowd. Sexual acts are performed either outside the venue, in cars, or in other corners. Gayness and lesbianism are important dimensions of township sexual relations and are publicly discussed.

GK: Men go to the pubs to pick up women. They use their economic power and their ability to buy drinks as a way to access women. It is also said that they use all sorts of substances to get women sexually excited and to go to bed with them without the trouble of a relationship. Currently the most popular aphrodisiac is Spanish fly.

There is a lot of fear and denial about HIV/AIDS. There are endless discussions about condoms. People react to the possibility of death in different ways. Some people seem ready to use condoms, but as a license to have multiple sex partners. They are being incorporated into the discourse of machismo: "If you do not take care and do not use them, then you are not a real man." Other people still do not use any protection during sex. Many do not disclose their status because they cannot deal with the changes that come with such a disclosure.

AM: What are the new registers of black beauty and fashion?

GK: African beads, hemp, jeans, and sneakers are predominant. If you want to be harassed, wear gold jewelry. The fashion items related to mapantsula involve expensive shoes from shops such as Spitz, as well as Italian cuts.

ND: Pantsula dress codes are persistent. In addition to clothes bought from City Outfitters in Jeppestown in a shop referred to as "Mohammed," the reservoir of pantsula has been increased by Loxion Kulcha designs. The concept of these designs specifically targets township youth.

Among males, there are also the *amantariana* [youth who wear Italian clothes]. Their clothing is supposed to be expensive; designs that are believed to be made in Italy are preferred. They are obtained from malls. Important shops here include Exceptions and Oreb in Eastgate and Versace and Hugo Boss in Sandton Square. Those who cannot afford these designers but who want to belong to this group buy from shops lining Small Street to Carlton Centre in Jozi.

The other group is the one that is influenced by a hip-hop dress code. They draw their inspiration from hip-hop artists, both outside and inside the country. Their main designer label is FUBU [an African American design company whose name stands for "For Us by Us"].

AM: A word on the "traffic" between the township and the city and the various ways that people move in and out?

GK: You move out because the lifestyle you want is not catered for. You want to break the cycle of five generations living in *gogo's* [grandmother's] house. You move out because privacy at home exists only for boys, who are allowed to build *izozos* in the backyard. You move out because you found a job in Durban, Cape Town, or elsewhere. And you move out because you cannot take that way of life anymore.

However, whether you like it or not, the township remains home. You go back every weekend to attend a funeral, a *stokvel*, a graduation party, or a twenty-first-birthday party. This is where your circle of friends originates. People come back from different suburbs every weekend. You also have cases where people move out for, say, six months, and because they are not used to life in suburbia, they move back to the township. You might work in the suburb, or you might like hanging out in Melville, but at the end of the day something or someone will make you go back to the township.

ND: Most people use taxis and trains to travel to and from Jozi. The young black elite uses both taxis and private cars. Trains are a significant feature of the movement between the township and the city. It is not unusual to find preachers on the train. Although not ordained, they are respected by some commuters. Trains are also sites of trading. Different commodities are sold at cheap prices. The language used by the traders can be traced back to pantsula culture. These traders have a distinct name—*snaman* [snack man, because they used to sell snacks]. There is a kwaito song by Mashamplan that recognizes this subculture. Crime also happens in trains. This ranges from pickpocketing to the three-card game, where commuters are asked by the facilitator who has three cards to pick a selected card from the three. If they pick the right card, they win. Players must have cash in their pockets. If they do not, they cannot play.

The Arrivants

TOM ODHIAMBO AND ROBERT MUPONDE

From: "Tom Odhiambo" <odhiambot@wiser.wits.ac.za>
To: "Chikoko R. Muponde" <chikokomuponde@hotmail.com>
Subject: the arrivants
Date: Mon, 21 Feb 2005 09:42:44 +0200

Robert,
I hope that the weekend went well and you still have your cell phone. In fact
since you wrote me when I was in Nairobi about "donating" your cell phone
to Joburgers, I have been wondering why some of you fellows walk around
advertising your phones. I thought it was peculiar to Joburg that people hold
their cell phones in their hands all the time but I discovered that people in
Nairobi and Kampala do the same. Is it that we are mesmerized by technology
or are we just strongly attached to our property? Or is it different in Harare?

From: "Robert Muponde" <muponder@wiser.wits.ac.za>
To: "Tom Odhiambo" <odhiambot@wiser.wits.ac.za>
Sent: Monday, February 21, 2005 7:25 PM

Tom,
Cell talk is valued in Harare, where I am supposed to come from, and belong.
The cell phone is called "runharembozha" in the new Duramazwi (Shona dic-
tionary), meaning, the phone ("runhare") for the bourgeoisie ("mbozha").

But I don't want to tell you how embarrassing it can be to be seen carrying around "chidhinha" (a brick), by which is meant the big and heavy cell phone handset when you are supposed to be "mbozha" in Harare. I don't think it is only about showing off, but about being in the circuit, in the right orbit, knowing what's circulating, and being in circulation, with the right velocity, and the right-size baggage.

I should have told you what happened on the day I was relieved of my 3310 in a Hillbrow pub. I have since been advised by those who know better that it is hardly a story to tell anyone. It would have been something else if I had been hurt, abducted, raped, wounded, or lost a few body parts. The 3310 itself is not an item that attracts self-respecting thieves, as one Hillbrow thug said to me. He took great offense at being frisked by the security officers for a mere 3310. "I don't do 3310s!" he said, and they let him go. He went on to threaten a young Zimbabwean prostitute in the pub who had seen him "work" on me. "You are a bitch; I am a thief, so keep to your portfolio or else. . . ." I bought a new cell, with camera, all sorts of new things, but have now lost it to my spouse. You see, how else would people know what you have if you don't wear it on your body, where it can be seen? Isn't this the same problem you will have with people back home, or people from home who know you are here, and at WITS? What's your great learning for if you don't drive, you don't drink, you don't take up with those cigarette-smoking, lager- and cider-drinking South African girls? What kinda story you gonna tell them brothers back home? Books, my foot!

From: "Tom Odhiambo" <odhiambot@wiser.wits.ac.za>
To: "Robert Muponde" <muponder@wiser.wits.ac.za>
Sent: Thursday, March 03, 2005 10:18 AM

Yes Robert, what worries me most is the weight placed on the shoulders of those of us who have traveled. Indeed, I get asked about the type of car I am driving, if I am soon marrying a Xhosa girl or whether I have settled here permanently, etc. It seems that people "back in Africa" have this notion that Joburg is some kind of America, with all kinds of jobs and the rand easily available; and that travelers like us are either mean or unwilling to share information and our wealth with them. But even more worrying is to meet the latest arrivant who thinks those of us who have been here for this long are examples of unsuccessful Africans because we don't yet live in the suburbs, drive new cars, or have the latest cell phone. But

I have learned to wait patiently for their stories after a few months here when they discover that it is difficult to make an easy buck in Joburg and that the cost of living here is far higher than wherever they come from.

From: "Robert Muponde" <muponder@wiser.wits.ac.za>
To: "Tom Odhiambo" <odhiambot@wiser.wits.ac.za>
Sent: Thursday, March 17, 2005 10:52 AM

I was at the La Rumba nightspot last weekend, and it is good that I was there. It's the first time that someone from Zim (Zimbabwe), a Zimbo (as we call ourselves), drunkenly kissed everyone on the tops of their heads, and said, "Tirikugara muHarare tirimuJohannesburg," meaning "We live the life of Harare while in Johannesburg"! Yes, "your back in Africa" is here too in Johannesburg. This is home, so there is no need to carry anything that you can't carry, because my brother, never mind, this is home. For Zimbos, South Africa, especially the vibey Jozi, has become a place of work, and a place of memory, a place of self-making in many senses. All of Harare is also here: the rich and the poor, the well-meaning and the pickpockets, the pimps, the poets, the politicians, the prostitutes! You only need to go to Braamfontein Centre, to see all the eleven or so floors full of NGOs manned by Zimbos, doing talk shops on the Zimbabwean crisis. You only need to go to Hillbrow to see how Zimbos are no longer having to get into dogfights about "local" girls (meaning Zimbos from home) because there are so many of them in Johannesburg.

Then, Zim politics is everywhere in Joburg: right from Mbeki's high office, down to the street. You really have to come from an undiscovered planet not to have some knowledge of, or opinion about, Zim, if you are in South Africa. So, that makes this place familiar.

Here, I read the *Zimbabwean*, a weekly launched two months ago in London and Johannesburg, to address the news-needs of Zimbabweans in the diaspora. There is a concrete physicality to the feeling of being here, of being everywhere in the same place. And I think Johannesburg is the only place I have ever felt as evenly dispersed and multirooted as a black Zimbo.

From: "Tom Odhiambo" <odhiambot@wiser.wits.ac.za>
To: "Robert Muponde" <muponder@wiser.wits.ac.za>
Sent: Thursday, March 17, 2005 2:33 PM

I used to buy beer at a place down the street from La Rumba called Raja Raja but stopped after being caught in the midst of an argument over the likely results of a match involving Arsenal and Manchester. Since I support Arsenal and they were in ascendancy in the English Premier League at the time, I wasn't willing to lose the argument till I was told that since no Kenyan plays for any team in the premier league I had no case to make. So much for African brotherhood in the diaspora! What I discovered thereafter was that relationships in the place are made and unmade depending on what European soccer team one supports, especially if one comes from West Africa, given the large numbers of Nigerian, Ghanaian, Senegalese and Cameroonian players in those leagues. So soccer has come to mark social boundaries for these African travelers from north of the Limpopo. What a life!

I have found it interesting to observe how these itinerants have started the "small business" culture bang in Braamfontein. When I arrived here five years back, you couldn't find a shoe repairer or shoe-shine boy anywhere around here. One had to pay twenty rands for a haircut—a full 140 Kenyan shillings, at the then–exchange rates. Now, that was unacceptable for a poor Kenyan student like me who was used to paying around ten Kenyan shillings or less to have my hair clipped. What I mean is that these fellows are progressively introducing the "small man's" lifestyle into a place such as Braamfontein, which was initially meant for big business and "big men." Surprisingly, very few fellows from your place seem to be involved in such businesses, even in Hillbrow and Yeoville, where most Zimbos are to be found. What is it with you people? Is it that your small population hasn't made you guys as desperate as Nigerians, or even Kenyans who a few years back had the highest birthrate in the world? Or is it due to what I hear South Africans claiming: that you guys are actually another province of Azania (the unadopted name of South Africa). Waiting to start collecting social grants?

From: "Robert Muponde" <muponder@wiser.wits.ac.za>
To: "Tom Odhiambo" <odhiambot@wiser.wits.ac.za>
Sent: Monday, March 21, 2005 10:23 AM

I used to be sad when I heard about Zimbabwe being the ninth province of South Africa. Well, at the moment it is. You should see how our uncle Mbeki defends Zimbabwe, while South African companies loot it of all the platinum, and flood all the shops and our homes with South African gadgets.

So, Zimbos don't invest in South Africa in small ways. They go big. Because that's where the Zimbabwean money is going, so they follow it like big game. You have forgotten that the chief executive officer of the *Mail and Guardian* is a Zimbabwean, who stays in Zimbabwe! There are many more in other fields. But as far as small business is concerned, you don't beat a Zimbo at roasting chicken tripe and gizzards in Hillbrow. One stick of roasted tripe and gizzard goes for R5, and it's only enough to help you swallow a bitter lager, so you will have to go back again for some more. Better than begging at the street corners, blaming black empowerment for loss of jobs and status as the whitey (really formerly white, if you look at the grime on their skins) beggars and their Coloured scion tend to do. So, we Zimbos live here with a vengeance, we are making this place, and it is our place, so we bring our money, our music, our foods, our lingo, and our politics right into every home in South Africa.

From: "Tom Odhiambo" <odhiambot@wiser.wits.ac.za>
To: "Robert Muponde" <muponder@wiser.wits.ac.za>
Sent: Monday, March 21, 2005 1:08 PM

Well, it seems that Zimbabweans have the knack of being sensible, despite Robert Mugabe's mischief back home. But it doesn't surprise me much because things are not that different in Kenya. After Moi's years of misrule, Kenyans, for some strange reasons, are doing quite well in Kampala. As you would possibly know, Kampala compares to less than a half of Joburg. Run-down facilities all over the city. Terrible roads. Slow Internet. Poorly maintained pubs. Road killer machines akin to South African taxis. But unlike Joburg and Nairobi, one can walk the streets at night without much fear, although I guess this depends on which street or residential area one stays in.

There are thousands of Kenyan young men and women seeking an education there. Kenyans still worship the advanced high school–level certificate. So, just like they are here in numbers seeking what they believe to be an "acceptable" and universally worthy degree, they are in Uganda in droves for an "A" level education. That means that they trickle into the job market. So they literally, together with South Africans (mainly whites), run the information technology industry. As you know, South Africans own huge chunks of the Ugandan economy from chicken business (junk-food outlets) to the information and electric power companies, mining, etc. Xenophobia seems to be creeping into Ugandan society, if what I heard in Kampala reflects wider social reality. Kenyans—by which they mean mostly Nairobians working for companies listed on the Nairobi stock exchange with Ugandan subsidiaries—are taking over their jobs, South Africans are grabbing their industries and god knows who will soon be recolonizing Uganda. So do you see how these cities are interlinked? Goods, information, students, national sentiments, fear of arrivants, stock exchanges, owning cell phones, etc., are all colluding to make our world smaller every day. So, brother, fear not the day when Zim becomes the ninth province of South Africa. After all, I know you'd rather take the demotion if you can have rands rather than Zim dollars in your pocket.

From: "Robert Muponde" <muponder@wiser.wits.ac.za>
To: "Tom Odhiambo" <odhiambot@wiser.wits.ac.za>
Sent: Monday, March 21, 2005 2:28 PM

I'd of course like to have a strong currency in my bank, but a secure city is a plus. Johannesburg is not a place of safety. It's a place where babies as old as five months are raped; AIDS carts away loads of dead bodies to the cemeteries every week; hijackers and gangsters slit throats the way they do it at makeshift abattoirs; and almost every small crook has a gun or some ganja in his pocket. Harare has its own perils: the aged and violent veterans of the liberation struggle who torture members of the opposition party. They have bombed presses of newspapers that are critical of Mugabe's ruling party and have killed white farmers. Then the so-called youth militia who rape and maim the population in the name of national service. But Zimbos agree: this is sponsored state terrorism; it's not like in Johannesburg, where crime seems to just burst from the ground like it has always been in the soil of this city.

See, Botswana is about the only other African country I have visited apart from Zimbabwe and South Africa. But make no mistake: I have been to more of these African places because I cut through them in the streets here in Joburg, almost all the time. The famous Nigerians you meet in the pubs, on campus, in their cell phone accessory and Internet shops, as well as banana shops, and then on DSTV on that channel "African movie magic"; the Kenyans and their *chapati;* the Zambians (who often masquerade as Zimbabweans in order to get attention); the Mozambicans, who hang around Zimbabweans only to remind everyone that they were once domestic workers for Zimbabweans . . . it's all so mixed up in titillating ways.

A kind of xenophilia. It's not all about the stranger as unwanted, but also as a curious object of possibility, excitement, representing borders beyond one's own, and an object of all sorts of speculation. Sometimes you wonder if we strangers are that special. If you are not the much-maligned Nigerian, then they ask you about why you have such a beautiful accent, such a good education (when you come from a poor, genocide-prone, hunger-stricken, floods-harassed, AIDS-tormented country), and they buy you a beer. And hey, Zimbabweans have given Oliver Mtukudzi to the world, so every one of the locals who sees us, wants to show they know "Tuku," and love him through you.

From: "Tom Odhiambo" <odhiambot@wiser.wits.ac.za>
To: "Robert Muponde" <muponder@wiser.wits.ac.za>
Sent: Monday, March 21, 2005 3:14 PM

Travel, brother! Forget the illusions of "home" that we itinerants are fond of creating around here. Forget about sneaking into Hillbrow, sampling some yam *fufu,* and claiming that you know your fellow brothers and sisters like some armchair postmodernist American anthropologist who doesn't know the difference between Nigeria and Algeria. Travel to Lusaka and discover a one-street African city. Go to Dar es Salaam or Mombasa and you will find African cities where people hardly sleep. They drink their coffee and chew *khat* all day and find no sleep in the evening.

From: "Robert Muponde" <muponder@wiser.wits.ac.za>
To: "Tom Odhiambo" <odhiambot@wiser.wits.ac.za>
Sent: Tuesday, March 22, 2005 3:42 PM

Aren't we all in the great belly of the whale called South Africa? From Cape to Cairo? Look, besides South Africa looting the platinum in Zimbabwe, the diamonds in the DRC, and the oil in the Sudan and this other place where some seventy South African mercenaries were going to topple an obscure African tyrant to get his oil fields, just think of how Mandela and crew sold South Africa as the continent in order to host the 2010 soccer World Cup. For a very long time to come, we will see more roads being paved to Joburg.

From: "Tom Odhiambo" <odhiambot@wiser.wits.ac.za>
To: "Robert Muponde" <muponder@wiser.wits.ac.za>
Sent: Sunday, April 03, 2005 12:50 PM

Robert, one of the things that intrigues me about arrivants is the way they live here in Joburg. Take my case. I live in a block of flats of about sixty units. Yet in my two years of living here, I still hardly know my neighbors. I do not know what most of them do, although most claim to be students. We meet on a personal level only when there is a complaint to be raised such as when someone has nicked another person's clothes from the drying line (and they do this a lot, especially around wintertime, when jackets and cardigans just happen to disappear); or when there is a commotion over "boyfriends" or "girlfriends"; or some latest arrivant has decided to announce that he has a new sound system by playing it at the maximum; or the caretaker feels compelled to "warn" every other tenant about abusing some undefined communal code of conduct.

From: "Robert Muponde" <muponder@wiser.wits.ac.za>
To: "Tom Odhiambo" <odhiambot@wiser.wits.ac.za>
Sent: Wednesday, April 06, 2005 12:13 PM

For some reason I find I now like staying in this decaying apartment, on the top floor, with a leaking roof, and all sorts of ethnic cockroach armies, ones that come in different shapes and colors, the ones that take a whole atomic bomb to kill. I haven't tried killing them again, since the ninth can of pesticide in ten weeks nearly precipitated my final meeting with my Maker. On the can it promises certain doom to roaches in "superfast triple action," and I imagined myself a Clint Eastwood, eyes squinting in thick spray mist, shooting right into every nook and cranny where the damned prehistoric hide. But, God, I inhaled the spray big time, because I was screaming (I think crying) right from the depths of my navel.

So, I live and let live. And this, Tom, is a useful strategy. Because if I didn't have that sort of attitude, I could have killed my neighbor, whom I hardly know: the one to whose room I have to drag the ganja-smoking security guard to ask him to turn off his radio in the early hours of the morning and every Wednesday night when his big, hoarse-voiced woman comes to visit. I have done that five times, so far, since moving into the catacomb-like place, and that's how close I am to my neighbor. I don't care much that I have to relate to him this way, because I don't fancy his music: "Love me love me oh baby love me," "Love is a liar" . . . Why all this sickness, this whining!

Everyone in this place screams love—the corridor is full of huggy-huggy pairs, and the rooms are loud with all sorts of merrymaking. But I do like the place. I don't have to know anyone that much beyond "heyta"! You know. I don't have to say what I do, I don't have to explain anything if I'm not greeted, or I don't say hi to anyone. The place is so full of us, you would think that sort of space wouldn't exist—the space, I mean, to be someone else, and to do anything, without having to do it with anyone living there.

From: "Tom Odhiambo" <odhiambot@wiser.wits.ac.za>
To: "Robert Muponde" <muponder@wiser.wits.ac.za>
Sent: Wednesday, April 06, 2005 12:44 PM

I understand your seeming unease about "loving Joburgers." But then, the world is so "unloving," you know. How did humanity arrive at a state of affairs in which there is so much available but so little that is shared? Take the shopping malls that are all over Jozi. I must confess that the first time I walked into what we call "supermarkets" back at home, my knees almost buckled. I was used to only the kiosks around the slum I grew up in. I was mesmerized by the rows and rows of goodies. My head swirled. I was dizzy. But when I walked into one of the Game stores here in Jozi for the first time, it seemed all unreal. I can't describe what I felt then. So, here you have all this stuff, all these foods, clothes, electronic gadgets, whatever, but just outside the mall are beggars, street people, starving abandoned children. What a world of surprises, contradictions, and ironies! The sum just does not add up.

It is a world that has me totally confused. I quite like this arrangement made possible by the mall to walk into a place and have breakfast, gaze through glass windows of rows and columns of goodies, have lunch, sample free music at the store, buy a cheap (or, equally, outrageously priced) pair of jeans, take afternoon tea and come back to my flat. A day well spent, you could say—oh, yeah, because the credit card affords me all this! Yet something about the setup rumbles in my stomach, but I am afraid I don't know what it is. Do you have some answer for me, brother?

From: "Robert Muponde" <muponder@wiser.wits.ac.za>
To: "Tom Odhiambo" <odhiambot@wiser.wits.ac.za>
Sent: Friday, April 08, 2005 9:07 PM

I am no longer in the habit of looking for answers in this city, I just get on with my business, which I think is the answer to much of what is asked here. Everything seems to be so much about how you negotiate your being here.

The mall beggar and the street beggar have a plan, and some notches in the social climbing business, as well as someone to blame for everything. I have often been surprised by the inventiveness of the beggars. Just check how they splash your car's windshield with soapy water right at the traffic light, just before it turns green, and you have to quickly give them the contract to wash the windscreen, or else hell breaks loose when the light turns green. The more cyber-inclined beggars have an e-mail address and a Web site: www .trafficrobot.com. And they have a streetwise little kid weaving in and out of the stream of traffic, and you talk of upbringing! Then the urban legends doing the rounds about beggars who have three cars each and go begging to fill the tank of one of the cars, as well as to buy a McDonald's burger. You can't be too pope-like here, with these street guys, because one day they will stick something up your backside.

From: "Tom Odhiambo" <odhiambot@wiser.wits.ac.za>
To: "Robert Muponde" <muponder@wiser.wits.ac.za>
Sent: Wednesday, April 13, 2005 2:12 PM

I guess every other city, country, or continent has unresolved histories, more so these places that used to be governed by the servants of the mighty queen or king. And I doubt if these histories ever want to be resolved; really, the task is to make the present work. And I can tell you that there are many people in Jozi working quite hard at making the rainbow dream work. There is a positive vibe out there, and occasionally it restores my faith in poor old mother Africa. Look, when you go to Sandton and see these builders struggling to erect the "tallest" structure on the continent (remember, the Carlton Centre is already one); and you go to Rosebank and observe the "mixing and matching" of the Asian/European/American and African cuisines, attires, music and tongues, smells, gaits, colors; and you go to Yeoville and smack in your face are all these diehard bohemians, whose dreams apparently were never troubled by apartheid and are hardly unsettled with the current fad, "African renaissance"; and you take a taxi to Johannesburg International Airport and sense some kind of worldly connectedness; or maybe just walk around Wits and feel the airs, smells, and glares of optimism, yes, you feel that the dream is livable, attainable. I have learned that human exertion can make things work, and sometimes I marvel at the creativity of the bands of eagle-eyed capitalists, struggle-drained toyi-toyists, clueless socialists, and failed Marxists and communists who roam the streets and offices of this country. It is actually a good thing to have a country where everyone has something to tell or sell to someone else. Whether it is a fake business venture or an illegible blueprint on how to make South Africa the new communist center of the world or even a half-baked policy paper on how to make social welfare work, it just goes to show that people are concerned about their country's future, which is not something that one can say about most African countries.

From: "Robert Muponde" <muponder@wiser.wits.ac.za>
To: "Tom Odhiambo" <odhiambot@wiser.wits.ac.za>
Sent: Wednesday, April 13, 2005 6:28 PM

Tom, I agree, and I think I should sign off with your stubborn optimism, which of course is the signature of the continent. Haven't we all survived all manner of plagues and histories? Slavery, colonialism, apartheid, pestilences and other pandemics that include not only malaria, HIV/AIDS, and famine, but also man-eating dictatorships and horrendous genocides? And with all this in the background, and alive on the continent, right here is born a Nelson Mandela, rising above all this mess and misery to sow hope in crestfallen hearts and bring the best of the world closer to the fingertips of all ye that had abandoned hope. The ancient histories of Cairo have remained guarded by the sphinx and have failed to ignite hope in Africa. Apart from them becoming part of the biblical heritage, they have remained frustratingly ancient and Egyptian. So Cecil John Rhodes's Cape-to-Cairo dream will be reanimated by a new breed of dreamers in Johannesburg, and it will be a different kind of exploration, hunting, mining, farming . . . I mean, our own black imperialism headquartered in Joburg. I am glad to be living in my time, and glad too there is this sense of something palpably new, other than spectacles of death and disease, here in Joburg.

NOTE: The title of this conversation is inspired by the Barbados poet Edward Kamau Braithwaite's *The Arrivants* (1967–69).

Johannesburg, Metropolis of Mozambique

STEFAN HELGESSON

Where does Johannesburg begin? Perhaps roughly ten kilometers from the center of Maputo, Mozambique's coastal capital. This is where you hit an impressive tollgate and fork out 10 rand or 15,000 meticais to cross the boundary between the normal, dilapidated roads of Maputo and the N4 of the Maputo corridor, a smooth highway that takes you through the border post of Ressano Garcia—visaless since April 2005—and all the way to Johannesburg, 500 kilometers inland. Every day, vast numbers of trucks, cars, and minibuses pass through the tollgate, many of them on their way to and from the South African megacity.

The corridor is a lifeline. Landlocked Johannesburg relies entirely on the ports of Durban and Maputo for its import and export of food, cars, fuel, clothes and electronics. Much of Maputo's surprisingly vibrant economy is, conversely, dependent on everything from South African milk to South African chain stores with head offices in Johannesburg. Not to mention the regular remittances from hundreds of thousands of Mozambican immigrants in South Africa, both "legal" and "illegal."

As one of the largest infrastructural projects since the advent of South African democracy in 1994, the Maputo corridor has been rhetorically invoked by President Thabo Mbeki as an example of regional integration: a step toward making the African renaissance come true. This is not without its ironies. What some call integration, others call domination. Not only would the corridor have been impossible without South African capital, but it continues to generate capital on South Africa's behalf. In downtown Maputo in 2005, Standard Bank put up huge billboards in Portuguese, hoping to soften its South Africanness with a quote from Kwame Nkrumah: "We do not look to the West, nor to the East. We look ahead." Next to the quote was the bank's slogan: "Não há nenhum lugar como África," there is no place like Africa. At a minimall (the real thing still hasn't hit Maputo), South African Woolworths and Checkers have established themselves, at odds with the "tropical European" style of city planning that still makes Maputo more enjoyable to walk around in than any South African city.

These images of South African economic dominance are not without historical precedence. In fact, the desire to boost democratic and independent southern Africa's regional economy is destined to repeat old patterns. One could argue that the corridor has been in place ever since Johannesburg started to exert its magnetic pull on the region in the late 1880s. The gold mines' thirst for labor was quenched in part by southern Mozambique, the Sul do Save region. The WNLA (Witwatersrand Native Labour Association) had offices as far north as Inhambane Province. To go to Lourenço Marques and get on the train to the mines in "Jone" was to escape—if temporarily—from forced labor to paid labor. To some, it became a rite of passage that made a man eligible for marriage. It was invariably risky, but also a full introduction to the elusive pleasures of Anglo-Saxon modernity—its clothes, its films, its music.

Moving in the opposite direction in the 1950s and 1960s, white tourists from Johannesburg and Pretoria would court risk among Lourenço Marques's prostitutes and enjoy the exoticism of the Portuguese colonial order. The heirs of these tourists, post-1975 and postwar, now ride in convoys of SUVs with GP (Gauteng Province) plates, heading for the "pristine" coast of Mozambique and oblivious of the people and the country. To drive along the Estrada Nacional and meet these monstrous cars, equipped with refrigerators, tents, and anything imaginable needed to spend a few comfortable days in "the wild," is to see the aggressiveness of Johannesburg in condensed form.

In Mozambican writing, the modern tradition of which dates back to the 1940s, the longstanding link between Johannesburg and Maputo has been a continual preoccupation. One of Noémia de Sousa's best-known poems is "Magaíça" (1950). *Magaíça* or *magaiza* is a Mozambican term for migrant laborer, synonymous with the mineworkers who went to Johannesburg.

In Mozambican poetry it has been a common theme, so much so that the *magaíça* at one point became an Everyman, an allegorical figure for the Mozambican experience of modernity.

De Sousa starts at the train station in then–Lourenço Marques, the beginning of the corridor in its earlier phase (my translation):

> The blue and gold morning of the billboards
> engulfed the ingenuous migrant,
> bewildered by the incomprehensible
> bustle of whites at the station,
> and by the restless shuddering of the trains

> A manhã azul e ouro dos folhos de propaganda
> engoliu a mamparra,
> entontecido todo pela algazarra
> incompreensível dos brancos da estação
> e pelo resfolegar trepidante dos comboios (de Sousa 2001: 64)

It is a moment of apprehension for the *magaíça,* whose baggage carries "enormous anxiousness" but is also woven from "the unsatisfied dreams of the ignorant migrant." The word *mamparra,* meaning "childlike" or "ingenuous," is often used in connection with *magaíça* and has a certain associative link with cattle, which are both innocent and a source of wealth. In "Magaíça," a destructive economy of innocence and wealth prevails. As the worker returns with "suitcases full of the false brilliance / of the scraps of the false civilisation of the Rand compound," his illusions are shattered, his youth gone, yet they are transformed:

> His youth and health,
> the lost illusions
> that will shine like stars on the neck of some lady
> in the dazzling nights of some City.

> A mocidade e saúde,
> as ilusões perdidas
> que brilharão como astros no decote de qualquer lady
> nas noites deslumbrantes de qualquer City. (85)

This is one inevitable view of Johannesburg from the horizon of Maputo. The city is seen as a Moloch, devouring Mozambicans in the "mines of Jone" and transforming their labor into luxury for the few. What is striking, however, is the metonymical link that de Sousa establishes between, on the one hand, the beauty of jewelry and the allure of the generic metropolis (*City* with a capital *C*), and, on the other, the beauty of the young worker. Although bitter in its analysis of Johannesburg's exploitative economy, de Sousa's image manages to hold, at the figural level, radically disjunctive meanings of "Johannesburg" together.

Maria Tereza Santa Rita, a contemporary of Noémia de Sousa, also records a fragmented experience of Johannesburg, but from a distinctly different position. Whereas de Sousa was a *mestiça* who identified intensely with the colonized, Santa Rita belonged to the liberal, "white" circles of postwar Lourenço Marques. Just after the National Party reached power in South Africa, she wrote a brief travelogue in the avant-garde monthly *Itinerário:* "Coisas que eu vi" ("Things That I Saw," October 1948). In sharp contrast to the magaíças, she could travel to Johannesburg purely for reasons of pleasure. Anticipating Rui Knopfli, she explains how "In Lourenço Marques, Johannesburg exerts the same attraction as Paris does in Lisbon," and her article waxes lyrical on the spectacle of the city—the tall buildings, the endless amount of commodities for sale, the escalators, the restaurants, the parks (8). Yet a note of discord soon enters her article. Johannesburg is not a "happy" city, not like Lisbon, and this sense of unhappiness feeds into her description of the muddy streets and impoverished inhabitants of Alexandra township. It is a short, impressionistic example of socially indignant journalism. Santa Rita offers no analysis but chooses to moralize: "How can there possibly still be 'Alexandras' in the rich city of Johannesburg? They stain, in a big way, its bright white pages of civilisation and progress" (10). The visibility and sordidness of racialized modernity are comparable to what we find in de Sousa's poem. In contrast to de Sousa, however, Santa Rita is incapable of linking the two halves conceptually. Her notion of "civilisation and progress" in Johannesburg remains simplistic and parochial.

The key Johannesburg writer in Mozambican literature is Rui Knopfli. A resident of Mozambique until 1975, and eventually recognized as a major twentieth-century poet of the Portuguese language, he belonged just like Santa Rita to the privileged class for whom travel as enjoyment was a possibility. However, having been born in Inhambane, he also identified more strongly with Mozambique than most Portuguese colonials. This helps to explain his continuing fascination with Johannesburg, the only metropolis that was available to him.

In his first two collections, *O País dos Outros* ("The Country of the Others," 1959) and *Reino Submarino* ("Underwater Kingdom," 1962), there are a number of Johannesburg poems—some in English—that try to reconcile the detached gaze of the flâneur with an intense unease caused by the Manichean order of the apartheid city. "Kwela for Tomorrow" from the first collection is a particularly effective montage of discrete "frames" of life on the Rand (in Rui Knopfli's own translation):

A thousand and more negro children
play with mud toys
in the heart of the slum.
A thousand and more athletic boys,
blond, red-cheeked, dressed in khaki,
raise up in the air the glinting gun breeches
at the Union grounds.
Precisely two minutes ago, the Mayfair bus
knocked out a miner
and blood breaks out a net of paths
over the sooty skin face.
A million people
at the early morning rush
moving automatically
on the tarmac thread

. . .

Moenie du Preez attends a meeting
with Moenie Potgieter and the stock prices
of the Diamond Co. (Pty.) Ltd. go up.
Since dawn at the General Hospital
one hundred and two casualties
have already been cared for
(Knopfli 1968: 2)

As so often in Knopfli's poetry, redemption is to be found only in music, in the "kwela for tomorrow" of Spokes Mashiyane. Later, in *Mangas Verdes Com Sal* ("Green Mangos with Salt," 1969), the political immediacy of "Kwela for tomorrow" is replaced by a more decisive flâneur optic, but with a postmodern twist. The high point is the poem called "À Paris" ("To Paris," French title in the original). Its first half goes like this:

My Paris is Johannesburg,
a Paris certainly less bright,
cheaper and more provincial.
But Johannesburg reminds me
of the Paris I've never known:
the same mad rush, the traffic cop's white gloves
the shining show windows of shops
the fashionable colours, the same lovers
shamelessly embracing on the benches
of sunny pavements, the Seine
that isn't there and the Eiffel Tower
that isn't either. Here I buy myself
banned books and see the latest
Antonioni. Here I'm your genuine
foreign tourist, greedy for surprise.
At night I dine at the *Montparnasse*
in Hillbrow, the local Latin Quarter,
gazing at women who are strange
and very beautiful in sweaters and Helanca slacks
at bearded beatniks
who are weird and hideously ugly,
all with the sincere and unconvincing look
of "made in the USA." (Knopfli 2001: 192)

O meu Paris é Johannesburg,
Um Paris certamente menos luz,
mais barato e provinciano.
Mas Johannesburg lembra-me o Paris
que não conheço: o mesmo movimento
endemoninhado, as luvas brancas
do polícia sinaleiro, o brilho das montras,
a cor da moda, os mesmos amorosos
que se beijam sem pudor nos bancos
das áleas ensolaradas, o Sena
que não há e a torre Eiffel
que também não. Aqui compro
o meu livrinho proibido e vejo
o último Antonioni, aqui sou

bem o estrangeiro cobiçoso de espanto.
À noite janto no "Montparnasse"
de Hillbrow, que é o Quartier Latin
do sítio e olho essas mulheres
excêntricas e belíssimas
de pullover e slacks helanca
e esses beatniks barbudos
excêntricos e feíssimos,
tudo com o ar sincero
mas pouco convincente do made in U.S.A.
(Knopfli 1972: 29, trans. Suzette Macedo)

The poem reads so unobtrusively, almost like a diary entry, that it is easy to miss the subtle tension it stages between signification and experience. Steeped in an inherited metropolitan discourse, Knopfli's poetic subject invokes Paris in order to make sense of Johannesburg. Or should we say: to let the reader—*mon semblable, mon frère*—make sense of Johannesburg. Since Johannesburg itself has not been woven into the canonical texts of "world literature" to which Knopfli aspires, Paris comes in handy as the generic image of the metropolis when representing a day's experience of the South African city. The poem evacuates this generic notion, however, by emphasizing—in a twist reminiscent of Fernando Pessoa—that it is the *absence* of Paris that creates the meaning of Johannesburg ("the Seine / that is not"). And not only Paris: it is the absence of metropolitan authenticity as such that constitutes this metropolis and, by implication, the very notion of the metropolis. We end up instead with simulacra, signifiers standing in for other signifiers—"Montparnasse," "USA"—that circulate a generalized desire for contemporaneity and social weightlessness.

A similar irony can be observed at the level of the speaking subject. While any reader of Knopfli's poetry may appreciate how powerfully the comparison between Johannesburg and Paris indicates a sense of homecoming, the poem ultimately refuses any correspondence between self and place. After stating that the jazz, "at least, / is real and has a wholly local beat," the alienation of the flâneur takes over:

The neon lights and silent dawn
the glistening tarmac,
the early morning light, the glow
of advertising signs, my solitude,

would be just the same in Paris.
Here no one knows who I am,
here my importance is nil.
As it is in Paris. (Knopfli 2001: 192)

O neon e a madrugada
silenciosa, o asfalto molhado,
a luz da aurora e a luz dos reclamos
misturando-se, a minha solidão,
aconteceriam assim em Paris.
Aqui ninguém sabe quem sou,
Aqui a minha importância é zero.
Em Paris também. (Knopfli 1972: 30)

There is a hint of romanticism here, a seeking of solace in solitude. Knopfli's poetics defend the authority of the absolute outsider. "I am really the
underground," as he writes in another poem (1972: 102). His "outsiderhood"
is nonetheless a relative position, generated at times in relation to Africa but
generally in connection to western/metropolitan culture. In "À Paris," this
leads to the exceptionally ambivalent operation of both appropriating and
evacuating the name of Paris (and hence the experience of Johannesburg)
as an object of desire.

Differences remain. When I take an early morning taxi to Mavalane airport
(with the taxi driver explaining that all the really good films are about taxi
drivers) to fly from Maputo to Johannesburg, I get delayed seven hours. I am
told that I am not on the list. This is in February 2005 and the list is, atavisti-
cally, really a list: a printout on a long sheet of paper. Not a computer monitor in sight, just a throng of agitated passengers and fatigued functionaries
that grant the list absolute authority over who should be allowed into the
transit terminal. As I spend my uncertain hours of waiting pacing up and
down the airport with its signage from the 1970s, the ticket in my bag feels
like nothing more than a piece of scrap paper. Finally, with some help from
a Mozambican friend, I am assigned a seat on a later flight. Exactly what did
or did not happen will remain a mystery.

Once in Johannesburg—the flight is ridiculously short—I check in at the
domestic terminal for my connecting flight. I am confused at first: now I
have no ticket to present, only a printout of my itinerary. However, I am told
that this is as it should be. My domestic ticket in South Africa has never been

destined for paper: it is an "e-ticket," a short string of letters and digits that guarantee my right to occupy a certain seat in the skies at a certain time. It works seamlessly. The rationalization of time, space, and people has always been far advanced in Johannesburg.

Despite the close historical links between Maputo and Johannesburg, the voyage from one to the other is a voyage across discontinuous space. As a young child, traveling from Johannesburg to what was still Lourenço Marques, I marveled at the warm nights, the screeching bats, the different sense of urban space created by broad pavements, shops that were open late in the evening, and the presence of people everywhere, both black and white. This was definitely not apartheid Johannesburg in its late Calvinist phase.

Yes, there was also talk of "the guerrillas," of a vague war going on in the north, but it was subdued. Or perhaps merely hidden from my childish ears. When I traveled in the opposite direction in the early 1980s, differences were at their most extreme. In practical terms, it was a question of moving between a place with nothing (Maputo) to a place with everything (Johannesburg). Having become used to Maputo in its phase of scientific socialism and endless queues for bread or rice, I walked incredulously among the aisles of the supermarkets in Eastgate (a mall in eastern Johannesburg). The teenage consumer that I was at the time felt relieved that things and food still existed, but also nauseated by the overabundance. Where did all this stuff come from? Who bought it? How could any population need to eat so much?

Johannesburg and Maputo could be described, respectively, in terms of ordered concealment and chaotic visibility. In Johannesburg, so much of what happens in human terms occurs behind some sort of a screen: a wall, a mall, a security gate. The roads—the space of flux that is a constitutive element of Johannesburg—are inhabited by people behind the enclosure of the car window. Although immigrants and minibus taxis now encroach upon spaces formerly reserved for other purposes, the legacy of razor-sharp distinctions and orderliness lives on, down to the geographical delimitation of "ethnic" zones and the hyper-cleanliness of the malls. Much as I love Johannesburg, it frequently makes me feel that life is going on slightly outside my field of vision.

In Maputo: a truckload of people singing at the top of their voices. A patch of pavement transformed into a miniature smithy. Life is what you see, survival is what everyone is struggling to achieve. This has been constant in the socialist and capitalist phases of Mozambican history, although capitalism has intensified street life. The chaotic visibility of Maputo makes it painful but also humanly accessible. It has less of the class- and race-ridden protectiveness that alienates Mozambicans in Johannesburg. Despite the difficulty of getting by in Maputo, and despite the fact that so many Mozambicans try to make their way to Gauteng to study, to work, to do business, I never hear anyone speak kindly of South Africa.

It was 1975, the year of the Mozambican revolution, that marked a rupture in the relationship between Maputo and Johannesburg. Following the exodus of the Portuguese, the border all but closed. Very few migrant laborers continued to go to South Africa. As the conflicts between South Africa and its neighbors grew uglier in the 1980s, the South African cross-border raid came to typify transnational relationships in the region, as Lília Momplé thematizes in her novel *Neighbours* (1998). This was also a period of growing revolutionary and nationalist orthodoxy in the reception of Mozambican literature. It would seem that Johannesburg, by fiat, no longer should figure in the poetry of the new and unified nation, unless to represent the historical exploitation of Mozambicans.

Interestingly, the large generation of writers that emerged in the 1980s engaged with the nationalist project in an independent and even subversive fashion. A key figure of that generation, Nelson Saúte, is arguably the most cosmopolitan of them all. His latest collection of poems, *A Viagem Profana* (2003), makes a point of almost deliriously naming places all over the world, particularly the kind of big cities that Rui Knopfli would have longed for—Johannesburg included. This is not surprising, since Saúte explicitly names Knopfli as a poetic forefather. In South African and North American contexts, it is worth pointing out that Saúte is black and Knopfli white, if only because this distinction is of no consequence in Saúte's writing. The historical distance between the two is important, however, and one way to describe *A Viagem Profana* is as an attempt to transfer Knopfli's modernist outsider poetics to the postrevolutionary, globalized context of Mozambique.

Like previous writers, Saúte evokes Johannesburg from the perspective of a regional outsider. There is no Johannesburg as such in this poetry, only aspects of Johannesburg. "Não é preciso ir à América" ("I Don't Need to Go to America"), which is clearly a response to Knopfli's "À Paris," starts tangentially by claiming that

I don't know where America is.
I've never been to America. America

never possessed me. I'm ignorant of America.
I've heard Ginsberg shout through my window
but I confess that I don't know America.

Não sei onde fica a América.
Nunca fui a América. América
não me possui. Desconheço a América.
Ouvi gritar Ginsberg na minha janela
mas confesso que não sei América. (Saúte 2003: 86; my translation)

Saúte carries on in the same vein, compiling a long pop-cultural catalog of a notional America. Films and literature are what have represented America, an experience that seems entirely familiar to virtually any reader today until the abrupt announcement that

I now know
that I don't need to go to America. I say this
as I get lost in a street in Johannesburg.
I have my domestic America. So what?
It is my America. It doesn't matter that it is not
because after all, it is available. My America.

Sei agora que
já não é preciso ir á America. Digo isto
quando me perco numa rua de Joanesburgo.
Tenho a minha América doméstica. Que importa?
É a minha América. Dá-me jeito quanto mais não seja
porque, afinal, me fica à mão. A minha América. (86)

America as the intertext for Johannesburg would certainly have pleased the Sophiatown writers and musicians of the 1950s, who felt passionately for an imagined America as a template of modernity. In Saúte's case, the recognition of America is more blasé, even weary, in an era suffused with hyperreal images of America. It places Johannesburg in a global economy of representations, yet this familiarity is also mixed in the following poem, "Joanesburgo" ("Johannesburg"), with apprehension and fear:

In Europe I told myself I was a lover of the big cities,
I challenged them openly.
. . . .

So far from Lisbon, Madrid, or London.
Without even leaving my maternal Africa.
Fear of the city jumps at me. I who thought
I was urban since the first minute
that Maputo, under another name, took note of me

Na Europa dizia-me amante das grandes cidades,
desafiava-as de peito aberto.

. . .

Tão longe de Lisboa, Madrid ou Londres.
Sem sair desta minha materna África.
Assalta-me o medo da cidade. Eu que me
julguei urbano desde o minuto primeiro
que Maputo, com outro nome, de mim deu conta. (87)

The *Unheimlich,* the uncanny amid the familiar, springs at the subject. The alterity of Johannesburg demands recognition. This alterity also includes the regional stranger's complex sense of being at home and away in Johannesburg.

⊕   ⊕   ⊕

Sounds in the City

XAVIER LIVERMON

Ever since my first visit to Johannesburg, I have been struck by the extent to which the feel of the city is reflected in its sound. The mixture of different African and European languages, the loud clap of thunder on a summer day, the clicking of shoes on the pavement, the incessant honking of minibus taxis, the pounding beats coming out of corner stores, the noisy birds that populate the trees in one of the largest manmade forests in the world—all of these incessant sounds stimulate my senses. According to Henri Lefebvre (1996), one way to understand a city is to consider its rhythms, which compose the basic fabric of the life of the metropolis. They include the rhythms of the interior (for example, the heartbeat) and the rhythms of the exterior (the chiming of the bell in a clock tower, the laughter of children on their way to school, the sounds of a traffic jam during rush hour).[1]

In the black South African tradition, the sonic encompasses a kaleidoscope of secular and religious expressive practices involving music, oratory, poetry, drama, and dance. Music is a form of urban social memory. In Johannesburg, sounds in general and music in particular are key channels of an Afro-cosmopolitan identity (e.g., see Masekela and Cheers 2004). Music has not only been central in the city's formation. It has contributed to its high levels of social energy, which made it permeable, flexible, and defiant, especially in times of struggle and racial conflict. The social memory of the African metropolis can be located to a profound degree in its music and world of sounds.

The most popular post-apartheid musical genres are kwaito, hip-hop, and house music.[2] Emerging almost simultaneously with the new political dispensation of 1994, kwaito has been by far the most commercially successful of these genres. For many young South Africans, it represents something that is quintessentially local. One of the most unusual sonic features in kwaito is the thumping slowed-down house beat. Played at least twenty beats per minute slower than in Europe and the United States, it is combined with the urban street language of *iscamtho*.[3] Iscamtho is deftly employed by the artists to create neologisms and playful double entendres, which mark the sound that one is listening to as something that could come only from Mzansi.[4] The combination of improved production quality and the growing number of artists rapping in vernacular languages have contributed to the rise and success of kwaito. The emergence of kwaito has gone hand in hand with the explosion of the popularity of imported hip-hop, R&B, and house music. House music in particular has benefited from the rise of local DJS, who not only create their own house compilations but also produce house tracks that incorporate forms of music not often associated with youth culture, such as gospel, *maskandi*, and *mbaqanga*.[5]

If sound structures the city, so the city structures sound. Johannesburg, the unofficial financial capital of the continent, is a critical node in the circulation of global sounds that characterizes the increasingly networked age of late capitalism. Although kwaito can be said to be quintessentially local, much of its sound could not be produced without material gleaned from the city's position as a node of circulation of capital and commodities in all its forms. In the early 1990s, *kwaito*'s borrowings placed it firmly within black diasporic musical traditions. For instance, the early sartorial regime of Boom Shaka's female leads (short shorts, revealing tops, black boots, and elaborate, multicolored, long braided hair) recalled a style made popular by Jamaican dancehall queen Patra in the mid-1990s. AbbaShante's "Girls" was heavily indebted to the sonic textures of Caribbean sound. In addition, most early kwaito groups featured one male member who rapped in a ragamuffin style. American hip-hop and R&B also figured prominently in such early classics as "It's about Time" by Boom Shaka. The influence of Congolese rhythms and phrasing (prominent in Mafikizolo's massive hit "Udakwa Njalo") as well as the reinterpretation of popular Congolese dances such as *kwassa kwassa* in the latest dance crazes in urban South Africa meant that such borrowings also looked north into the African continent. Just as earlier South African genres of popular music had drawn on African diasporic and

international sounds, kwaito represents an example of contemporary inter-
diasporic musical remixing identified by scholars such as Paul Gilroy (1993),
George Lipsitz (1994), and Michael Titlestad (2003). It is the music form
through which young black South Africans refashion themselves away from
the ossified identities of apartheid.[6]

Township Metropolis

If anything characterizes kwaito, it is the velocity of its circulation throughout the city. Since the end of apartheid a generation of newly mobile young
blacks, more financially secure and confident than previous generations of
black youth, has emerged. For a great number of young blacks, the late 1990s
and early 2000 have been a period of social mobility. To be sure, the dis-
locations of apartheid, which have in various ways structured their lives,
have not totally been erased. But with the abolition of state-sanctioned racial segregation, new opportunities have arisen, of which many are taking
full advantage. As the most popular post-apartheid musical genre, kwaito
circulates through the vast metropolitan area of Johannesburg, referred
to in local cultural semantics as Jozi. The spatial circulation of the music
defies the tendency to geographically and culturally divide the city into a
white, predominantly wealthy city, and a black, predominantly poor, township space. The music in and of itself does not erase the differences in the
economic and racial composition of the city. But the manner of its circulation strongly highlights post-apartheid symbiotic (if unequal) interactions
between town, township, and suburb. To a large extent, from a kwaito perspective, it is futile to consider Soweto as a city separate from Johannesburg.
This is revealed through an examination of the way in which the new black
youth navigate the city. The music is culturally reconfiguring the relationships between township space and city space to the extent that, for many,
the township is no longer *apart,* but rather *a part* of the city. City architect
Fanuel Motsepe uses the term *township metropolis* to describe the increasing
imbrication and mutual influencing of each space, city and township, with
or on the other (Motsepe 2004).

The music also reveals a geography of the township which is somewhat
at odds with the taken-for-granted assumption that the township is almost invariably black, poor, and lacking—a space of poverty and despair.
To be sure, an important part of the music conveys the anger still felt at

the unequal allocation of resources and life chances. Some of it is mere escapism, machismo, and fantasy. However, as Murray Forman remarks in his discussion of U.S. rap music (2002: xix), "it is too frequently accepted without evaluation that rap is implicitly conjoined with spaces of urban poverty existing as both a product and a legitimate voice of a minority teen constituency that is also demographically defined as part of a social underclass." The same could be said of kwaito. Indeed, while many young, upwardly mobile people have left the townships for a variety of reasons, there are significant numbers who have not. They are responsible for the creation of bourgeois suburbs in areas such as Diepkloof Extension, where some homes have recently fetched over R1 million in the housing market. To be sure, many still go to bed hungry or live in intolerably cramped conditions. But there are also moments of joy and celebration. People love, they get married, and friends come over for dinner. These relatively mundane acts of everyday life are important facets of township music and culture, as evidenced, for example, by the proliferation of restaurants and nighttime club venues in Soweto, the increased mobility of its residents, and its inclusion in local circuits of tourism and consumption.[7]

The Car

A crucial mediation through which music circulates in the city is the car. Traditionally, much has been made of de Certeau's (1984) thoughts about walking in the city. The city has been conceptualized as a place of encounters that are structured through walking. A defining feature of Johannesburg is its identity as a city of automobility for the upwardly mobile, while the train, on the other hand, has always been one of the main means of transportation for blacks. As far as young, upwardly mobile blacks are concerned, the nature of encounters in the city is increasingly defined by the movements made possible by the car. Here, automobility is "the combination of autonomy and mobility" (Featherstone 2004: 1). Just as in other cities in the post-Fordist age, it influences individual patterns of consumption, pleasure, and ideas of achievement among the growing black middle class (Urry 2004: 26). Johannesburg can therefore be said to be a city that is first a city of mobility and second a city of mobility structured, to a certain degree, through automobility. Here, John Urry writes, trains, private cars, and taxis "extend where people can go to and hence what they are literally able to do." Indeed, among the black and white middle classes, much social life in Johannesburg "could not be undertaken without the flexibilities of the car and its 24 hour availability" (28). At the same time, the mobility rendered possible by the use of the car is paradoxical, if only because the car highlights the very segregated and divided nature of the urban metropolis. Yet it also reveals it to be a segregation or division that can be disturbed or shifted. With an automobile, a city is more easily traversed and its temporalities more easily refigured. In Johannesburg, time is extended through automobility: nightlife would be virtually impossible without this mode of mobility.

Even more characteristic of the rhythms of Johannesburg is the relationship between the auto and sound. Taxis in particular are spaces of performance, where individuals engage in dialogue with radio programs and sing at the top of their voices to their favorite music (Bull 2001). As Mike Featherstone notes, "the experience of the aural has become the definitive form of car habitation for many contemporary car drivers" (2004: 9). Yet what many theorists of the car and its aurality focus on is the privatized and solitary nature of the act. For Michael Bull (2001), much of the pleasure of aurality and car space depends on the control the driver has over musical selections and the closed-off nature of listening to music inside the car. Bull (2001) suggests that consumption patterns in the car differ from those of home, and the driver unencumbered by the need to be mindful of other household members or neighbors feels more in control of his or her musical selections.

What emerges in almost all accounts of automobility is the car as privatized space and the fundamentally antisocial nature of the car (Gilroy 2001). However, my experience of musical cultures in Johannesburg suggests something entirely different. Far from being a privatized space of antisociality and solitary encompassment, the car functions not only as the mode of travel through which individuals move from space to space, but also as an aural arbiter. As people move from one location to the next, the car itself (along with attendant technologies such as the cell phone) becomes a space of high sociality, with interactions between members of the vehicle and those who are outside the vehicle. Sound in general (a hooting horn, a human voice) and music in particular are extremely important ways through which interaction occurs with the community that surrounds the vehicle. Rather than being consumed in solitary privacy, many of the cars of young people are specifically designed to facilitate public consumption of the music. Powerful speakers ensure that the music from a car sound system can be heard at considerable distances. Impromptu parties are organized around car stereo systems. A constant verbal exchange involving passengers and drivers informs the selection of the music. Those on the street can get to know the latest and most popular sounds by the frequency with which they hear a particular tune blaring from a passing car or minibus taxi. Drivers often consider the tastes and desires of their passengers when choosing music. To blast the wrong music out of the car can completely affect the social perception or positioning of the driver within that space where the music can be heard. The music played draws attention to the car and therefore the driver. One typical aspect of street bashes held in townships is the converting of the car into a space for performance. The street itself serves as the dance floor, and dancers use the headlights of the automobile to highlight their dancing prowess. On many occasions, the dancers literally dance on the vehicles as they pass through the gauntlet, body parts writhing against the car as if the car were their actual dance partner. Their movements may be facilitated by the car stereo of the passing vehicle or the outside sound system that accompanies the street bash. The car and its mobilities are central to the musical cultures of Jozi, and the connection between automobilities and the aural is highly social and rarely private.[8]

Situation One: Soweto-in-Melville

I live near the Melville bar and restaurant area. On this particular evening, I had invited a few friends from Soweto to join me for drinks and dancing. I was tired and did not feel like going far from home. Melville is one of those areas that define the post-apartheid city of Johannesburg. It is known as one of the liberal areas of Johannesburg, with a quirky and economically well-off crowd. As a resident of the San Francisco Bay Area for most of my life, I felt right at home in this suburb, which prides itself on being a desirable place to live for its imitation of European-style café culture and nightlife. It is also one of the few places in the city where one can comfortably walk the streets of Johannesburg and browse the many shops, bookstores, and galleries centered on the perpetually busy Seventh Street drag.

As busy as the street is during the day, it becomes even busier at night. The narrow streets of the suburb are congested with cars parked on both sides, effectively turning most of the main thoroughfares into one-way streets, whose right of way is the subject of constant negotiation. Melville has always struck me in relation to its lack of integrated party scene. Given its trendy nature, one would expect to find more upwardly mobile blacks hanging out in the evenings. Indeed, during the day, one finds many blacks at bars and cafés such as Spiro. It might well be that most of the upwardly mobile black professionals want to let loose on Friday and Saturday nights on the dance floors in the township. However, on this day, my friends and I marched from bar to bar looking for a place that was unusual enough to peak our interests and inviting enough so that we wouldn't feel uncomfortable or out of place. We walked by a club that I hadn't noticed before. The doorman was a young black man. He asked us to take a look at the place. The song being played thumped with a pleasant bass that could be heard by passersby. The house anthem was among one of the many tracks that made up the heavy rotation on stations like Y and Metro, and could often be heard at street bashes and on minibus taxis in town. Some of my friends have affectionately labeled these popular tracks "ghetto house," for one is likely to hear them at most venues where a predominantly black crowd is expected, particularly in the township. Later, I noticed that the chalkboard marquee announced that Metro FM sponsored the evening, and one of their more popular DJs would be playing the gig.

We were not the only people bar hopping and bar shopping on that evening, and the pavement of Seventh Street was congested with people meandering around looking for the place that best suited them. The combination of the cars, pedestrians, and bar hoppers literally spilling out onto the street made for a festive atmosphere on what was turning out to be a warm spring evening. After much walking up and down, we chose the supposedly gay bar/coffee shop Statement. A DJ was playing what my friends described as nice house music and we could get a table. Some members of our group identified as gay. They felt they would be more comfortable at this spot. But on this particular evening, most of the couples enjoying drinks at Statement seemed to be mixed-sex partners.

After we finished a couple of rounds of drinks and drew attention to ourselves by being the only ones dancing to the music, we decided that it might be good to change venues. I was hoping that my crowd would want to go to the Metro FM party a couple of doors down. As we were enjoying our drinks, I saw a number of young black people heading there. It was a crowd that was unusual by Melville standards, and I thought it might be fun to join the party. I was wondering what more luck my friends and I could ask for: a black party in the heart of Melville that was also quite gay-friendly, judging from my casual glance at the crowd. However, my friends took one look at the crowd and refused to enter. At first I thought they might be concerned with the cover charge, which I assured them I would pay, if they wanted to go to the party. But one of my friends finally turned to me and said: "This place is just like Soweto. The music, the crowd, it's like township in town, we didn't leave Soweto to come to a place like this. Why leave Soweto to come to a place that's just like Soweto?"

I protested that there was nothing Soweto about this crowd. In fact, quite a few of my Melville friends were present at the club, enjoying themselves, and I could not possibly fathom what was "ghetto" about this party at all. "First," explained a friend of mine, "let's start with the over-commercialized common house music, that you can hear on any taxi in town, any street bash in Soweto, or any car passing by while you're doing chores on Saturday morning." "Then there's the crowd itself," explained another. "They obviously drove from Soweto to come to this party." "All you have to do is look at the way most of the girls are dressed," a female friend told me. "They are from Ekasi, the dresses, the jeans, not that there's anything wrong, I mean we're not dressed much different, but then what was the point of coming to Melville?" For my group of friends, the sartorial styles and the music combined to turn this small corner of Melville into a facsimile of Soweto. On this particular evening, my friends wanted a different experience. Interestingly, the issue was not race. One of my friends had stated that it reminded them of Ekasi because it was so black. The perception was that the bar was offering nothing particularly novel for them in the way of experience. I got the impression that had we gone to Kilimanjaro in Melrose Arch or the trendy hip-hop and house nightclubs of Rivonia or even the Rock in Soweto itself, my companions would have been satisfied. These places are the playground of the black bourgeoisie. My unwillingness to drive to these places meant that we settled on Oh! club for our evening of dancing. As I looked around the predominantly white, male, gay club throbbing to the beat of recycled techno music, I smiled to myself and thought: "This is definitely as far away from Soweto as you can get."

Situation Two: Township Festivals in the Park

Any understanding of how music travels in Johannesburg would be incomplete without an examination of the use of the city's parks and open areas as impromptu concert venues. Some events may be billed as festivals. An admission charge may be required, unless sufficient sponsorship has been obtained. The park is then reworked into a concert venue, complete with security checks and body searches before you enter. Private security firms as well as Johannesburg police officers are omnipresent, in case the crowd should get out of control. One section of the park is partitioned, and a stage is set up. Local DJS are hired. Usually, these bashes are labeled as kwaito festivals, even when a wide range of musical genres is performed. Free festivals tend to take place during the day and usually end by dusk; the crowd is expected to clear from the area by sunset. Admission fees range from R10 to R60 per person. Festivals usually draw huge crowds. This is all the more the case if they are held during the day and in township spaces. Those who do not live in the township will normally come for the day just to enjoy the crowd and the inexpensive entertainment. Partygoers are allowed to bring coolers and *braai* stands. It is not unusual for people to arrive in the early afternoon and stay until long past midnight if the festival goes into the evening.

The outside venue of the festival is a mingling of people parking their cars and hanging out while they blast their stereos and drink from their cooler boxes. Here, any keen observer can judge just what music is popular at any given time, as minibus taxis and private vehicles vie for sonic supremacy. On this particular day, it is clear that house and kwaito rule the airwaves. The music blasting the loudest from the speakers polices what other forms of music get played. Nobody wants to be perceived as being behind on the latest musical trends. Attendance at these festivals and parties often requires some form of advance planning. One of the highest priorities is transportation. The most well attended festivals are those that are taking place on the outskirts of the city. They are close enough to the townships to draw the young black crowd that is likely to be attracted to the mix of hip-hop, kwaito, and house stars. Yet they are not in the township, therefore giving the event an aura of distinction. Given that there is no adequate public transportation system in Johannesburg that operates in the evenings, those without their own vehicles must negotiate with those who have vehicles in order to participate. The other popular option is the hiring of minibus taxis to ferry groups of partygoers from spot to spot.

Two of my friends and I began to load the car in the early evening shortly after the sunset. The essentials for the evening included jerseys and a cooler filled with juice. We then headed for the first stop, which for my friends was a local hangout at a twenty-four-hour gas station next to a shebeen.

The gas station is an important stop for any festival or big party attendant. Here, information is exchanged and directions are handed out or explained. Caravans of cars streaming to the festival are formed. Additional passengers are picked up. The area between the shebeen and the gas station also serves as a spot for young people to acquire and, in some cases, to smoke *dagga*, in an effort to attain the correct buzz prior to and during the festival. After making one final stop at yet another twenty-four-hour garage, we met and exchanged information with other groups of people, buying sodas, chips, gum, and other snacks that I assumed would fuel us through what was expected to be a long evening. After picking up the last of our provisions, we headed for the park where the festival was held. While I understood the fee to be R10 per person, we managed to talk the fee collector to let us enter for only R30. Making an entrance is an important ritual of any festivalgoer. The cars with the sleekest looks and the most prominent sound system get noticed. Cars such as Citi Golf and BMW 325i are associated with the youthful kwaito vibe. They must be fitted with the latest mags on the wheels, tinted windows, and sport kit. The minibus taxis with the liveliest crowd and the loudest thundering boom also get their fare share of attention. Partygoers hang out the windows, drinks in hands, bouncing rhythmically to the beat at hand. I quickly realized that my car, a Nissan Sentra, was woefully inadequate by comparison, and our crew made a relatively meek and unostentatious entrance. At one point, one of the partygoers looked at my car and remarked: "This is a no-name car, I can't even tell what it is." Indeed, the fact that it lacked a new paint job, fancy wheels, and a booming stereo made it nameless.

The parking lot at many of these festivals in the park serves as a liminal space that regulates the division between the party within the park grounds and the outside. Those out for the *joling*[9] will go back and forth to their vehicles throughout the evening. At the beginning of the celebration, the parking lot will serve as one last opportunity to make an entrance. Since everyone must pass by, it is a good opportunity to meet and greet, determine who is and who is not in attendance, and to draw attention to oneself through a combination of the music being played, sartorial style, and the perception that one has prepared well for the party by having a large, well-stocked cooler box and snack kit. The latter aspect will be particularly important in gaining credibility and respect as a serious partier, for those who are less prepared (or less financially well-off) will eventually seek out the better prepared. A set of negotiations will then ensue. For example, boys will use a well-stocked cooler box to attract girls. The same group of boys may calculate that it is better to use any extra stash to attract other groups of guys, who may then return the favor at a later function. Or, conversely, a group of girls may want to be seen at the party with a particular well-liked or popular girl and may be willing to part with a few of their provisions for her and her friends to join their group.

Individuals will leave their groups either in ones or twos to see what is happening around the grounds. I noticed this as my group began to dwindle from five to three and finally to two. It would then shoot back up to four or five as people who knew us would stop to chat. A really good song, or an anticipated performance by one of the kwaito or hip-hop stars, would also stop movement from group to group. In that moment, the essence of what makes a festival is revealed. The first strains of the popular house song would begin to amplify from the speakers and would be followed by a scream of recognition that reverberates through the crowd and bounces off the trees. At this moment the sound from the crowd, an undecipherable cheer of joy, would be more significant than the actual music itself, for a split second made inaudible by the sound emanating from the crowd. Then as the crowd dies down, the business at hand begins: serious dancing. The track's initial melody comes in, and the pulsating beat takes over. Groups of girls writhe their bodies to the beat of the music, braids flying from their faces, jackets and jerseys tied around their waists. Groups of boys are involved in variations of pantsula-style dances. Couples enmeshed dance in ways that are beyond sexual suggestion. Slowly, they move into the realm of sexual simulation. The senses of the body are overloaded at this moment, in some cases enhanced by the alcohol, tobacco, and dagga. The pounding bass of the music can literally be felt in the body. The sense of touch is stimulated by the autoeroticism of self-touch, or by the grinding pelvis of a dance partner. Each dancer appears out of control of his or her movements, under the power, instead, of the DJ, who now dictates the pace and ferocity of the movements with each selection of a popular track. From house, to hip-hop, to kwaito, bodies are contorted in a frenzied state of joy and arousal. The best dancers occupy center stage. Inside the circle, movements are punctuated by the unregulated flow of dancers from the edge to the center. The latest dances are shown off. When attention is turned to the stage, the dancers shout out the lyrics.

By 4 a.m., I am exhausted and ready to go. At this moment, the boys in my car are negotiating with a group of girls about who is going home with whom. Apparently the couple that we came with has found alternative transportation, leaving room in my vehicle for us to pick up additional passengers. So I find myself with two new passengers in my car, who have somehow been talked into joining my two friends for the after party. After dropping them off, I give a fairly paternal warning about the importance of safe sex and head home to digest the evening.

Conclusion

During the apartheid era, the horn at Turbine Hall reminded blacks that they had to be outside the city unless they had special permission. Today, Johannesburg is witnessing an amazing moment of rewriting space. Turbine Hall has become one of the sites of new musical expression, hosting hip-hop and kwaito parties and being the location of hip-hop group Skwatta Kamp's "The Clap Song" video.

Since 1994, the government has been committed to restoring the black body to both the nation and the city. The city of Jozi has become a place of possibility for many young, upwardly mobile blacks—those black young bodies that were so perpetually excluded. However, what I hope emerges is an understanding that the right to the city is not simply a one-way process. The examination of space, sound, and the body in this essay reveals a city that is traversed from township spaces to predominantly white suburbs by increasingly assertive young black people. At the same time, a number of whites, Coloureds, and Indians no longer regard every black township as a no-go zone. While new musical cultures highlight the push of township into town, they also highlight the push of town into township. Those who have moved out do not simply sever ties and may choose to enter township sonic arenas for both the music played and the atmosphere provided. Likewise, those in the township, seeking out new and different experiences, enter into the havens of the (black) bourgeois party scene. The city that is made anew is one where the connections between the city itself—town and its outlying areas—and the township are increasingly revealed. The tropes that consistently mark these areas as completely separate in experience—town as white and wealthy, township as black and poor, are no longer valid, if they ever were so in the stark binaries that structured the ideology of separateness. Kwaito is the music of this new black mobility, the growing black middle class, signaling the incorporation of blackness into the city—the space from which it was once hidden or even denied—creating spaces of integration and equality, and the creation of a blackness that engages the city on its own terms. Johannesburg displays the residues of apartheid while also creating a space for the radical reimagination and obliteration of the apartheid logic.

Notes

1 *Rhythmanalysis* was Lefebvre's term for a general theory of "the relation of the townsman to his city." Such a relation "does not consist only of a sociological relationship of the individual with a group. It is on the one hand a relationship of the human being with his own body, with his tongue and speech, with his gestures, in a certain place and with a gestural whole, and on the other hand, a relationship with the largest public space, with the entire society and beyond it, the universe" (1996: 235). I borrow the term to suggest the importance of paying attention to the everyday patterns that characterize city life and to examine the ways in which these patterns develop sonically and the relationship to the body and the use of space. I link the term *rhythmanalysis* with a series of moments that I call situations that allow the reader to enter directly into the sonic patterns of the everyday (12).

2 Kwaito is a hybridized new music that has been described by Maria McCloy (the editor of the youth culture Web site www.rage.co.za) as follows: "Let's begin with the basic ingredients (of kwaito): South African disco music, hip hop, rhythm and blues, reggae and a mega dose of American and British house music. Mix it up, add loads of local spice and attitude and you've got kwaito." Kwaito has been variously described as a South African version of hip-hop and house; however, in recent years, local practitioners of both types of music (hip-hop and house) have taken great pains to define their local versions of hip-hop and house in distinction to kwaito.

3 For more information on Iscamtho, check out the excellent youth culture Web site www.sowetorocks.com, and see Ntshangase 1993. On similar urban linguistic forms outside Johannesburg, see Cook 1999.

4 *Mzansi* is another black urban vernacular term popular with the youth and standing for South Africa.

5 Oddly enough, the popularity of mixing traditional or neo-traditional music with techno-house sounds into a blend of African house was spurred by the popularity of this trend among French house DJs in the mid-1990s. Local DJs felt that if European DJs could remix mbaqanga tunes into international hits, why couldn't they? The sonic textures of various musics that were popular in the past (particularly those of the 1960s and 1970s) were important in fashioning contemporary South African house.

6 On debates, see Peterson 2000 and Singer 1993. All of the major international and local music companies, such as Sony, EMI, BMG, Universal/Polygram, and Gallo,

are based in the city, and their studios have the most advanced technology. Most artists in a wide array of genres therefore do their recording in town. Much of the production of new musical genres nevertheless occurs in smaller studios or is driven by independent labels headed by young black South Africans during the early 1990s. The same applies to performance venues. A great number of performances generally take place in parks and small clubs, or in areas easily accessible to the fan base of the music. This practice is so entrenched that long after they have become successful, many kwaito artists will continue to perform at these venues since they are still lucrative, particularly in creating publicity around a new release. The independent nature of music production is therefore an important facet of Johannesburg's musical cultures. Equally noteworthy is Johannesburg's place as the arbiter of cultural styles from abroad. New musical genres in particular flow initially into the space of the city and may, for months, undergo a process of vernacularization. It is only after they have been reconfigured as local style in Johannesburg that they reach other urban centers of South Africa.

7 See www.sowetorocks.com for more information regarding nightlife and entertainment venues in Soweto.

8 I am aware that this state is in constant flux, and it is possible that the private car as social model that I am proposing here may not hold as cars become more accessible to additional individuals.

9 The Afrikaans term *jol* means to frolic, have fun, or to have a great time, and I am using it in this sense here. However, the term has been adopted into Iscamtho and has come to mean to date, particularly in a nonserious sense.

Nocturnal Johannesburg

JULIA HORNBERGER

From the flat roof of Helvetia Court, eye to eye with the wrought-iron water tower, I have a 360-degree view over the city. Up on the fifth floor, in a building perched on top of Yeoville's ridge, there are few obstacles to obstruct the view. It is five past six in the evening, that time of the day when the city of Johannesburg switches on its streetlights, though they do not yet have an effect. Hardly a cone of light can be seen. At early dawn, it is as if the light does not really diminish but that it is the eyesight that is weakening. Then, by twenty past six, the daily wrestle between night and day seems to be decided. Lights inside houses and apartments are being switched on. Curtains are still pulled close, but warm light seeps through the fabric. Going forward into the night is like going backward in time. Chipped corners on balconies heal, cracks in the plastering disappear, and patches of flaked-off paint grow fainter. The texture of trees and bushes becomes flat. The sky soars into its final act, gushing out pink and yellow and then indigo, as if sucking the colors from the world as the final darkness creeps up from the far edges of the horizon where sky and city meet. Streetlights, no longer just light dots without purpose, spread their cones of light.

Of course, it is not just in Yeoville that all these lights emerge. On the ridge to the south, two parallel strings of narrow beaded lights appear, drawing into focus a street invisible and fused into the surroundings of the hills during the day. A different reading of the city is enabled, as if underscoring that the city at night is a different place and deserves its own reading. The prominence of the lights in the darkness of the evening neglects everything that lies in between them, like the spaces in drawing by numbers. It contracts distance so that lights accumulate and move into the foreground and with them bring horizons closer by.

In the far south it is especially obvious how a dimension of the city that was not visible during the day becomes sharply apparent during the night. A multiplicity of orange lights, accumulated on the horizon, is the lights of Soweto. In Soweto, it is not just main arteries that are marked by cheap orange lights but ordinary streets. Hardly any white lights can be seen there. Further to the east, by contrast, a wealth of white lights spill out, marking some of the comfortable middle-class suburbs. Tiny white lights also adorn the top line of the Kensington ridge. Below the ridge is Bez Valley, which flows over into the city bowl, whose beginning is marked by two sports stadia. A game is on that night, and the floodlights illuminating the fields are refracted in the moist of the evening air and glow behind the Yeoville water reservoir as if the moon has dropped into the city bowl.

As I turn my head further clockwise, the iconic, fifty-story apartment tower Ponte, crowned with its eternally flashing green, blue, and white Vodacom advertisement, absorbs my view. It is hypnotic watching the repetitive illumination of the commercial logo. While from the roof it is as if I only have to stretch out my hand to touch it, Ponte can also be seen from as far as fifty kilometers outside the city when coming from the south. Then there are the untended multistory flats of Hillbrow, honeycombed with lights, which stand huddled together as if they are a group of shipwrecked passengers on a shaky raft holding tightly onto each other to avert dropping into the sea. The sea in this case is the north of Johannesburg, where houses hardly rise above two stories and where street lighting cannot be seen from above because it is sheltered beneath an umbrella of thousands of trees, as if hiding a good secret.

Coming full circle, my gaze returns to Yeoville's multistory flats. The children who were vying for the most daring acrobatic act between the washing lines on the top of the neighboring roof have long disappeared.

A Short History of Johannesburg's Illumination

Johannesburg could easily dispute Paris's title as the city of lights—not because of its man-made illumination but because of weather conditions that provide the South African Highveld, on which Johannesburg is built, with a "lightning ground flash density of 6 to 9 flashes/km²/year," one of the highest in the world (Blumenthal 2005).[1] In the summer months, afternoon thunderstorms provide a daily spectacle of lightning. Ironically, this drama of illumination quite regularly leads to blackouts in the city and constitutes an economic threat because of service disruption as well as damage to electronic equipment.[2] In addition, Johannesburg's electric infrastructure and power stations suffer from lack of maintenance and obsolescence, which also sometimes leaves Johannesburg in the dark (*News24* 2004a and 2004b; and Swart and la Grange 2004). The blackouts bring with them a realization of how lighting has become integral to the practice and imagining of city life as well as an awareness of the contingency and fragility of this modern condition.

Johannesburg's electricity circuits are inextricably linked to its history of mining—once again proving how Johannesburg's original raison d'être as a city of gold seeps through so many facets of its becoming. Kimberley, where electricity was readily available because of diamond mining, was the first place in South Africa to have electric street lighting, in 1882. In Johannesburg, following the same rationale, the need for deep-shaft mining had, early on, made it an absolute necessity to have an unrestricted supply of electricity available. As a byproduct of industrialization, Johannesburg received its first electric street lighting in 1891. However, the primacy of electric supply for industrial use also meant that, with the exception of the street lighting, electricity supply was short when it came to general domestic use. Electricity was initially supplied only to some privileged white households (Veck 2000: 71–72). It was only with the Power Act of 1910, at the advent of the Union, and the political climate of national assertion, that the state became the main regulator of electricity supply (previously in private hands) and the provision of electricity was inscribed as a public service.[3] At this time, too, attempts were made to electrify the (white) countryside following the electrification of the railway lines. By 1982 Johannesburg had 61,681 streetlights. And as recorded in Johannesburg's annual report by the city electrical engineer, there was still a steady increase to come of an additional average of 1,000 a year until 1993.[4]

In the same report, the paragraphs on the annual Festive Illumination equal in length the one on street lighting. Considerable importance was given to decking out the city with lights, especially during the Christmas period and around special celebrations such as the city's centenary.[5] While these lights had an enchanting effect on children and spoke to a human fascination for brilliance and light, they also served to lure the white population from surrounding suburbs and towns into the inner city and to increase the consumption of goods offered in the city's shops. It was also a way to evoke the city's metropolitan character and its ability to compete with cities of the north.

This electric exuberance accentuated the lack of lighting in the black urban townships. For until the 1970s vast areas of Soweto remained without household electrification. Township facilities were discussed only in terms of building houses and the provision of sewage and mainly communal water taps.[6] Soweto and other urban townships in the country had received their own particular kind of street lighting. High mast lights had been installed to serve as cheap compensation for domestic lighting (Mandy 1984: 209–11). This had a prison-camp effect, illuminating everything from far above and sneaking into backstreets and backyards. Additional floodlights using halogen light were brought in during the insurrection in 1985–86—adding to the effect of glaring light pervading unashamedly into the houses.[7] Only after the Soweto uprising of 1976 did the electrification of Soweto for domestic use and as a means to pacify the population become a priority (Veck 2000: 163–91). Proper streetlights were installed, especially along the main roads. But streetlights remained a marker of the difference between township and city. While the city had made a conscious decision to use only white lights for public lighting, Soweto was supplied with sodium lights instead. Sodium lighting emits an orange light and is generally used for motorways because of its low shadow-producing quality. Such lighting is low in terms of electricity consumption and maintenance and has a luminous effect. Because of its monochromatic nature, it does not allow for color rendering and dips everything within its reach into an abnormal atmosphere. By contrast, mercury street lighting, as it is used in most Johannesburg streets, allows for good color rendering. It bathes roads in a white light and evokes an environment closer to daylight.[8] To have a less distorted nightlight became the privilege of the city.

The city reserved the use of orange light mainly for its highways. When the M1 and M2, the inner-city highway, with its overpasses that traverse the inner city from east to west and from south to north, was completed in 1974, it was illuminated with orange lights. The rest of the main arteries that stretch across the northern city still resemble white ways, broad lanes bathed in uninterrupted white light. However, nowadays the once stark contrast between Soweto and the city is blurred. Notorious Hillbrow streets such as

Quartz have received orange lights, conducive to surveillance because of the lack of shadows, while certain areas in Soweto that are of national interest, such as Kliptown, the cradle of the freedom charter, receives state-of-the-art French-designed streetlights. From the roof of Helvetia Court, this two-color landscape of white and orange lights is painted in rough strokes.

Turning into the suburban residential roads leading off the white ways is a dip into darkness. While many of the gardens and driveways are provided with movement-sensitive floodlights, the high walls prevent light from houses and gardens from supplementing street lighting. In addition, lush greenery and huge trees intercept, filter, and defer the light of the streetlamps.[9] This darkness allows for the emergence of red-light areas. The suburban twilight is conducive to prostitution, which has become a permanent business at some of the northern suburban main intersections, where enough light prevails for the women to display themselves, and enough shadow remains to keep pimps and clients in discreet darkness.

The darkness of the suburb is easily outdone by places such as Orange Farm, one of the most far-flung townships of Johannesburg, of which huge parts even today still have no electricity and no street lighting and where nighttime simply means impenetrable darkness. In other areas, particularly in Soweto, where street lighting is now—although partly orange—as common as in the rest of Johannesburg, a difference is reinforced through the introduction of prepaid electricity meters. This is often presented by local government as the remedy to a so-called culture of nonpayment through the introduction of—to use the neo-liberal euphemism—responsible citizenship. Together with issues around the provision of water, this has provoked fierce contestation and politicization of a trend where electricity, despite all the affirmation to the opposite by local and national government, is being administered as a private rather than public good. While these are presented as necessary local economic measures, Eskom, South Africa's monopolistic electricity company, is out to electrify and light up Africa and manifest itself as an electric African multinational and to cash in on South Africa as—literally—the powerhouse of Africa (see Chalmers 2001). In one of their advertisements, Eskom used an imaginary night satellite image of Africa where Africa was fully lit up so that it resembled Japan and the East Coast of the United States. By evoking this illusion of development, the advertisement squarely mobilizes the questionable dichotomy of the dark continent on the one hand and the notion of the inextricable link between illumination and modernity on the other.

City lights create a topography of illumination—a drawing of place through light in its different qualities. Reading this topography, its contours and shadings, its elevations and slopes, constitutes a comment on Johannesburg as metropolis, its terrains of access and exclusion, inequality and transformation, security and insecurity, consumerism and scarcity, its township and suburban living, and its raison d'être as mining city.

Back in Yeoville

Coming down from this overview in time and space, I leave my aloof position on the top of the Yeoville apartment block and plunge back to the street level of the suburb to explore one of the cultural meanings of city lights: nightlife. Nightlife is, however, not simply a figurative extension of city lights. It is rather the actual transformation of city spaces at night through the materiality and physical effect of lights.[10]

If one looks at the newspaper, such as the Friday section of the *Mail and Guardian,* for the traces of Johannesburg's nightlife, then one easily gets the impression that nightlife is something that takes place within closed and inside spaces. This seems natural and appropriate for a city where night and its darkness stand for the heightened danger of becoming a victim of crime. But then, as we dig deeper into the different parts of town, we find single streets, often at the heart of an otherwise residential area, which speak of a different form of nightlife.[11] Here the illumination of streets and the light of bars and music pouring out onto the pavement dissolve the boundaries between the inside and the outside of a street and create inner spaces contrasting in light and life with the rest of the city (Schlör 1998). These are pockets seemingly isolated from each other where senses are differently employed in the reenchantment of the night and where the city comes alive. There is Grand Street in Norwood, Seventh Street in Melville, Hendrik Verwoerd Drive in Randburg, and then there is Rockey Street (which is partly called Raleigh Street) just here at the heart of Yeoville, where we begin our evening.

We drive down Cavendish, which runs perpendicular to Rockey Street, through the grid of streets where single-story high Victorian houses with their typical verandas and corrugated iron roofs alternate with medium-size apartment buildings dating from the 1930s to the 1970s. We can't help noticing the steady flow of people who, despite the darkness, walk the pavements of the streets. Groups of five, six, sometimes two or three are chatting away, in no hurry but clearly on their way from somewhere or to somewhere, at least until early evening. (After 9 p.m. the flow becomes thin, and by 11 p.m. to walk home alone becomes a dangerous undertaking.) Some of these people might just be on their way to the next corner, where at a little shed the use of telephones is offered. A paraffin lamp is burning, and about three other people are queuing right after the one who is on the phone, willingly or unwillingly becoming witness to his or her conversation. But it is mainly toward or away from Rockey Street that people stride.

As we reach Rockey Street, we pass by a street-side vendor who has his sweets, single cigarettes, some batteries, and grandpa headache-powder sachets neatly spread out over a wooden panel balancing on some plastic crates. He is sitting next to his stall on another crate, and the little paraffin lamp is illuminating his head from one side while the other half is in darkness, the contrast drawing rough contours around the features of his face. At the stop sign of the intersection, a youngish man is crouching by a little fire on which he is preparing some chicken kebabs. A customer is waiting for the meat to cook, watching him while he attentively brushes some marinade or oil on it. Nightlife means the gathering of nightly economies that serve those who are drawn to turning the night into day.

We then come to a precinct called Times Square, which is a multitude of buildings grouped in a U-shape around a courtyard that opens up onto Rockey Street. The fountain in the middle of the courtyard of Times Square has long stopped functioning. However, the light-blue mosaic with which it is decorated and the couple of palm trees that slightly arch across the yard give it a leisurely urban outdoor, even slightly tropical, feeling. Several bars extend out into the courtyard. The bar that has opened most recently is the busiest. The name LA CRÈCHE—CHEZ NELLY has been painted in big red and blue letters over the entire house front and flanked with some expressive faces wearing sunglasses. Inside the bar, the murals become even more abundant, with a tropical beach and palm-tree scene on the one side and an oversized plate with an equally oversized steaming roasted chicken on the other. The gate erected between the street and the courtyard in the times when Yeoville plunged into crime like the rest of the inner city of Johannesburg has been opened up again and now allows for an uncontrolled flow of people between the yard and the street. It is as if some kind of relaxation has taken place where people can see a gate again as an obstacle rather than a safety measure.

On the street a variety of black middle-aged men and women hang out. Young people are conspicuously absent from this part of the street. There are trendy figures with their neat designer-label denims, tight-fitting T-shirts, and straight-cut black leather jackets; or the odd eccentric, like a man wearing a white linen suit and a black hat, 1950s style. They are moving along the street, hanging out in front of bars, shaking hands, snipping fingers, or leaning over the bar's balustrade to chat with some women who are sipping a glass of white wine and holding on preciously to their pastel leather handbags. Two other, more mature women, with pinned-up artificial hair, promenade along the pavement without much attention to those around them. After a while they return, as if they really just went for a stroll and to have an undisturbed moment for a personal update. Their movements along and across the illuminated and lively street convey a sense of tenure of the street and a sense of insouciance that only leisure time can offer.

Yeoville has always been a center of nightlife, but it has mutated and transmogrified substantially over time. Gone are the multiracial bohemian days. It has now evolved as a place of pan-African, particularly francophone, nightlife. And it is particularly through nightlife that it has inscribed itself visibly into Johannesburg as the place of francophone migrancy. Bar names, like the above-mentioned Chez Nelly, and Café Joie Patisserie and Coffee Shoppe,[12] reveal such unmistakable inscription on the visual level. Opposite Times Square there is a bar/pool place/restaurant called Kin Malebo, offering Congolese cuisine such as cassava bread or smoked chicken with peanut sauce. Its precinct wall is marked with the words *Amitié, Retrovaille,* and *Gaeité.* On the stoep, where men are lingering with some bottles of imported beer in their hands, there is another mural displaying a huge African map. While the use of the shape of the African continent commonly appears in shop signs, advertisements, or logos, this map is peculiar. It resembles a proper political map where the different countries are set up against each other by the use of contrasting colors and clear delimitation in black of the national boundaries. The name of each country is written with black or white letters in its colored field. The map, in a very direct and self-conscious way, seems to want to inscribe Yeoville into Africa and Africa into Yeoville.

The street is a microcosm of social and spatial aspirations expressed through and in nightlife. Here at the upper end of Rockey, where in fact it is still called Raleigh, several bars and restaurants mark a space that wants to be seen as respectable. This is achieved, for example, through age restriction and dress code, and by being the target of prolific J&B Whiskey marketing campaigns. An oversize illuminated J&B billboard in red and yellow towers above the street, keeping out the brandy drinker and the broke male youngster. Inside Kin Malebo, intricate interior decoration makes its statement in this regard in a twofold way.

Lumumba, shaking hands with Martin Luther King, is looking down on us from a black-and-white photo hanging at the same height as the television. The rest of the walls are purposefully decorated with memorabilia from Congo and a mix of local crafts that clearly reveal the aim of distinguishing this restaurant from a simple beer hall. It has a signal function in terms of delimiting the respectable space—as captured in the etymological affinity between decoration and decorum. This is underlined by the fact that even the waitresses are wearing uniform, vulgarity-forestalling, simple black blouses and all of them have their straightened or braided hair pinned up in the same fashion. But there is more to this space. There is a real passion to how the place has been designed, and it clearly shows the signature of a person who has put a lot of thought and idiosyncratic planning into it. It is as if the restaurant has been given a theme. The assemblage of paraphernalia relating to music such as a shelf with a collection of music DVDs is just the beginning. Then there is a room, something like a cigar lounge (however strictly nonsmoking) or a VIP lounge. With a couch arrangement, a fireplace, and a wall of fame dedicated to LPs and laminated music posters from Kwassa Kwassa and Soukous artists ranging from Koffi Olomide and Papa Wemba to Kanda Bongo Man, J. B. Mpiana, and Zaiko, it also comes across as a shrine to music. There is a collage of photos capturing festive events, Christmas and New Year's dinner parties, that have taken place at Kin Malebo, featuring special and regular guests. It emerges that this place already has established a history in Yeoville and has become a familiar feature, and with this assertion of continuity and its upmarket aspiration it is there to stay. In the midst of the rapid flux of Yeoville, it has established and conveyed an invariable presence and consistency. It is as if through their nightlife, these places offer a sense of stable, everyday life and citizenship to Yeoville and to the country.

Moving down Rockey Street toward Piccadilly Corner, the leisurely and established atmosphere gives away to rougher territory. While there is no shortage of bars, places are more hidden, as if they do not want to give away too much of what is going on inside. The glass of windows has been blinded with paint and does not let the light from the inside shine onto the pavement—nor does it let the curious look in from the outside.

Here the main phenomenon is the butcher and braai places. With the little bit of extra money available from the week's end, salarymen (there are few women around at these places) treat themselves here to a piece of raw red meat which they can immediately braai with gusto on a braai place in the dusty backyard of the butchery. Then they can sit at rickety plastic tables with universal white plastic chairs under a glaring neon lamp throughout the night and get up only to fetch another liter of beer from the counter, which with its parallel burglar bars looks like the counter of an old-fashioned bank. Some bars are implicitly men-only bars, where when you enter as a woman you automatically compromise yourself with regard to sexual availability. Pleasure and sexuality are, of course, inextricably linked with nightlife. And the parading on the street or the encounters in bars are a huge part of its attraction and seduction.

Rockey Street itself seems as busy as its establishments, if not more. Much of the time, the street itself becomes the venue. In the lights of the Victorian arcades, men are grouped together around some dice players. Their forward-crouched positions speak of the absorption in the game and form an impenetrable and protective wall around the gamblers. Further back, although the market has already closed, hawkers are selling vegetables until late into the night. They have built elaborate steplike rising counters from cardboard boxes on which vegetables and fruit have been artfully mounted into shaky pyramids. Just around the corner, three old women are sitting next to each other, each with a small stall with sweets and cigarettes in front of them. In fact, I see them sitting there every evening on my way home—no matter how late I pass their spot. They seem good company to each other, since often I see them chatting. It must give them a feeling of protection, as they look out for each other and each other's goods and meager income.

Our last stop on Rockey Street is Tandoor. While before Tandoor also had a dance floor downstairs, recently only the roof terrace is open. Sitting up there on the ledge of the roof, one has a good view down onto the street. The smell of dagga hangs in the air, and even if the sound system is not too clear, the relaxed Rasta atmosphere along with the reggae music sets the place apart from many of the other rougher places that we have just passed further down the street, as well as the rather classy places further up the street. There are also many more women around, who confidently frequent the place, playing pool without men seemingly importunely coming on to them.

A young man is sitting next to us and we get to chat a bit. Much later in the evening, when we move on to Seventh Street Melville, I bump into him again. Seventh Street is much more of a middle-class space, with more of a tendency and aspiration to evoke European-style street life. Its side streets, because of its closeness to the headquarters of the South African Broadcast Co-operation (SABC), are home to what somebody called the genteel broadcasting coterie. It offers a different feeling of the city of the night. But I realize that it is not just I who out of explicit research curiosity moves from bar to bar, from street to street, and from one part of town to another. To move from pocket to pocket, transcending a lot of different settings and traversing the empty white ways, dark suburban alleys, and nightly deserted spaces between those pockets, is a form of living the nightlife in Johannesburg. While these pockets seem isolated from each other, those living the night create faint pathways between them. This is not to say that an absolutely unrestricted social traffic exists between those different places; surely there are social markers related to race, gender, class, and age that regulate the motion between these spaces through making one feel more at ease and welcome in one space rather than the other. But that people are actually determined to go to only particular spaces according to those markers—something that is often assumed when talking about the difference between Seventh Street and Rockey Street, is equally misrepresentative. Instead, to move from place to place, even within Rockey Street, allows for a certain way of taking on different nightlife identities, from the trendy to the hardboiled, from the bohemian to the aspiring, from the corporate to the leisurely. It is partly about a sense of freedom of choosing who to be. And the city's nightlife spaces allow for this more than any other spaces in the city.

Notes

1 In the Highveld countryside, lightning forms a threat, with high numbers of lightning related death (38 victims for the period 1987–2000).

2 See Sinetech's "Facts about Lightning in South Africa," available at www .sinetech.co.za/lightning4.htm.

3 Under the Power Act of 1910, the Electricity Supply Commission (Eskom in Afrikaans and Escom in English) was set up. It later became the parastatal Eskom, the South African main electricity company (Veck 2000: 40–42).

4 See the Johannesburg Electricity Department, *Annual Report of the City Electrical Engineer*, 1982/83–1992/93 (Johannesburg: Greater Johannesburg Transitional Metropolitan Council).

5 A book published on the occasion of Johannesburg's centenary (Fick and Venter 1986) proudly showcases the idea of Johannesburg as the modern metropolis on

the front cover by juxtaposing a photo taken at the end of the nineteenth century showing a settler's camp beside one showing a Johannesburg illuminated skyline at night.

6 An interesting exception to this were the townships of Benoni, where streetlights were installed as early as 1914. Audrey Cowley and James Mathewson (1968: 95, 126–28) explain that later, when the township of Daveyton was erected, "the old conception of supplying only communal amenities for the Bantu was completely discarded, each house in Daveyton was supplied with water, electricity, and waterborne sewerage." While this generous supply of amenities did not undo the aspect of the spatial racial discrimination, people both living in Daveyton and visiting it experienced it as a very different kind of place compared to Johannesburg's townships. It allowed for the evocation of an imaginary of *participating* in modernity instead of just being in the underbelly of it.

7 Today the issue of floodlights (besides their use in sports stadiums) has transmuted into one of security and protection against crime. While searching the Internet for information on Soweto's floodlights of the 1970s, I hit a multitude of advertisements by security companies offering as part of their product and service range the installment of floodlights with movement sensitive mechanisms.

8 It has to be added that the mercury lights do not perfectly recreate daylight. They emit a lot of blue light, which makes people look rather pale and slightly unhealthy (by my own observation). On the different kinds of street lighting and their physical and visual qualities, see www.lamptech.co.uk and www.eskimo.com/~jrterry/lampspage.html.

9 Thus, in an ironic twist, often those areas considered rather safe in terms of crime are actually the darkest and most deserted areas at night.

10 A purely figurative meaning of lights would be its spiritual or religious association with life or its philosophical association with reason, as in *enlightenment*.

11 Joachim Schlör (1998) makes a similar point with regard to city guides in the late nineteenth century. They directed the tourists toward the inside of special establishments but would underplay the nightlife that happens in the street and which did not need a special venue.

12 While the name might point to something else, the place is very much a bar that serves alcohol.

Megamalls, Generic City

FRED DE VRIES

It's impossible not to panic when you're about to lose your megamall virginity
to Sandton City. The multifunctional complex, which comprises shops, hotels,
offices, conference centers and squares, rises like a massive, impenetrable for-
tress of cement, steel, and glass, encircled by freeways. Miss the right off ramp,
and you're back in the lush but aggressively walled-in northern suburbs of Johannesburg. Forget where you've parked your car, and you'll search for hours.
Come with the idea of some swift shopping, and you'll end up in tears.

To penetrate Sandton's innards, a carefully planned attack is a prerequisite. A good approach is to take Sandton Drive and ignore the first parking
signs. Then, just before you hit Rivonia Road, you turn left where it says
"roof parking." That's the tactic I use when I take a Dutch visitor along, in
order to introduce her to Joburg's biggest mall.

We take that left turn and find ourselves in a Ballardian landscape[1] of concrete and cars, with several small pyramid-like structures signaling entrances
to the heart of the mall. A small red car with the sign CRIME PREVENTION
races past us, ostensibly on its way to a danger spot, ready to act. Young black
guys with STOP WASH signs on their backs ask us if they can wash our car.
Security guys—also black—with walkie-talkies stand at strategic places to
make sure all our goods and belongings will still be in our cars when we
come back. In the near distance, builders are working on a giant tower that
forms part of the latest addition to the complex. Elsewhere, work is going on
on yet another extension. Sandton knows no limits.

We make a mental note of where we've parked the car and pick entrance 17 (this is my friend's lucky number, hence we will not forget). This turns out to be a good choice. Escalators run up and down, taking visitors to the various levels of the center. Staring into the depths of the mall with the moving steps working against each other causes a mild form of vertigo. We descend one floor and find ourselves in shopping heaven: a dazzling display of lights, marble, glass, and goods.

Sandton City certainly deserves the tag *city*. In the 1990s, when downtown Joburg became synonymous with crime, degradation, and despair, Sandton became more than a mall. Together with the surrounding area, it developed into a sanctuary for offices and hotels. Newspapers, the stock exchange, everything moved to Sandton. It's a development that has made Johannesburg one of the few cities in the world with two versions of the Central Business District (CBD).[2]

With 127,380 square meters and growing, Sandton City is the biggest mall in South Africa. It qualifies as a super-regional shopping center, exceeding 80,000 square meters. The South African consumer spends on average 168 minutes in the super-regional mall. He or she is prepared to drive 150 kilometers to reach the destination.

The megalopolis Johannesburg-Midrand-Pretoria has six of these mega-malls, with names like Eastgate, Northgate, Westgate, and Southgate. They are late-capitalist versions of the old city gates, a continuation of the original mall idea that was based on the layout of a cathedral: a large central passage that leads to the altar (the "anchor," usually a megasupermarket), with wings (for the other, less important anchors) and alcoves (the smaller shops that the customer has to pass to reach the altar). The anchor, which functions as the main magnet, pays about twenty times less per square meter than the small specialist shop.

The main pleasure of the mall is that you can walk around without any worries. Security guards and cameras protect us from the thugs and thieves who have made the Joburg CBD such an unnerving place. In this shell-like space the lure is to loiter and to get pleasantly lost—which turns out to be harder than expected. As soon as we check the Sandton City information map, a worried guardian with the word SECURITY emblazoned on his arm rushes over to ask us what we are looking for and points us in the right direction. Once in the mall, one doesn't need to think for oneself.

We flow through corridors and wander into a huge space that turns out to be the lobby of the Sandton Sun, part of the InterContinental Group. Mall and hotel have merged seamlessly into one another. *Lobby* is not the right word for the area where we find ourselves. This is a vast, beguiling space where you find the hotel reception, comfortable leather seats, and a chic café. Huge umbrella-shaped chrome structures give the café a plazalike appearance. From the tables, sipping a sundowner, you can watch golden elevators endlessly moving up and down a tower that resembles a basilica, with a star-shaped window in the high ceiling.

We explore the roof terrace, look out over Johannesburg's leafy suburbs, and turn around, searching for what used to be called Sandton Square but has been rechristened as Nelson Mandela Square. Back past the jeweler's. Past the curio shops. Past an eatery called Ciao Baby Cucine, which rubs shoulders with a restaurant called Cape Town Fish Market. One of the passages is decorated with a set of reproductions of scenes from a European town circa the Renaissance. We try to figure out which town. The churches, domes, and columns suggest it must be a Mediterranean place. Venice? Rome? Who cares. It's the suggestion of ancient grandeur that matters.

We stop for a while at the shop window of the Pharmor pharmacy, an anomaly among the other full-to-the-brim, state-of-the-art stores, which advertises only three products. If you are female and want to "fan the flames of your desire," you must use a herbal product called Utejna. If you happen to be a man and want "the power to love better," Indiaga is the natural product you've been looking for. And if you feel like Dorian Gray, the specialists of Solal Technologies are there to make your antiaging dream come true. Oh, and then there's a fourth product, slightly hidden: KGB antihangover pills.

We note that the Hypermarket has thirty-five tellers, which is a tad disappointing since Sandton City's Pretoria competitor, Menlyn Park (155,000 square meters), has a Hypermarket with no fewer than fifty-four tellers. We have tea in the Walnut Grove, an entresol coffee shop that begs for blurbs like "classic, sumptuous, and comfortable." Below us, we see a cross section of affluent post-apartheid South Africa passing by. It is a boxed-in version of the Mediterranean late afternoon stroll along the main boulevard.

What's striking is how similar they all look: hardly anyone is overweight, and virtually everyone is dressed in casual designer clothes. Only very few people carry shopping bags. Obviously visiting Sandton City is a proper outing, much more than just a trip to buy essentials. Interestingly, although it is more than ten years after apartheid, the old racial categorization still applies. Whereas in general terms the mall is a heady mix of all previous groups and categories (white, Coloured, Indian, and black), these subgroups mostly stick to themselves. A few mixed couples are to be seen, but more often it is schoolchildren, particularly teenagers, who moved around in cross-racial packs—especially on weekends.

Sandton City is classier than most other malls. No market stalls in the middle of the passage here that sell T-shirts with quasi-funny Afrikaans slogans like "Hey wil jy vry" ("Hey, you wanna make love?") or "Randy Lover" in the Land Rover logo. What it does have in common with other malls is the concept of microspaces. Each shop, each restaurant tries to create its own sound and concept. CD Warehouse has the sensitive-young-men-sound of Coldplay. Elsewhere it's classical music, or pounding techno.

Sandton City offers all the entertainment one could wish for. There's a cinema with eleven screens. There's a theater. There are special events. There are conference centers. There's even a library. And there are tons of restaurants, cafés, and specialized food stores. Want a particular kind of bread? Check out the Bread Basket.

Finally we stroll into Nelson Mandela Square. For this central plaza, the developers have copied the idea of the old European city square, with fountains and outdoor terraces and a place for performances—but without the chaos, the vagabonds, the bums, the punks, the shitting pigeons, or the scooter gangs that liven up European squares. It's safe, secure, and dull.

The square is dominated by a large statue of Mandela. A present from donors who wanted to remain anonymous, it's six meters high, made out of bronze, and shows Mandela doing one of his slightly clumsy but endearing dances, the Madiba jive. It's so hideous it makes you chuckle with embarrassment. It's completely out of proportion. The legs are too long, the arms too short, and, most awkward, the head is way too small. Every bit of dignity that characterizes Madiba has been deleted. He looks comical in an unfunny way. Or as *Sunday Times* columnist David Bullard put it: "It looks as though Madiba is off to the fridge for a midnight snack" (June 9, 2005).

We sit down in one of the sidewalk cafés, Wine on the Square. It's a place where one is expected to lounge in soft leather chairs with a cigar and a glass of best red. Prices are stunning, at least triple of what you pay in an upmarket Joburg restaurant. The clientele is mixed. A white couple sits down to have a small meal. Three black women are busy killing a bottle of chardonnay. They are brash and confident. Sandton City, they implicitly demonstrate, is no longer the playground for the wealthy white.

After finishing our Alto Cabernet and Graham Beck Shiraz, we've had enough and decide to walk back. But it's only then, around 8 p.m., that the real Nelson Mandela Square spectacle reveals itself. First we think that there must be some rock event in the theater on the square. Or maybe a famous pop star is staying in the Michelangelo Hotel. But none of that. The huge groups of teenagers who have amassed on the square are there purely for the fun of the square. It's their version of hanging out. They stand in little groups of five or six, boys and girls separate. The girls, some not older than thirteen, have all plastered their faces with layers of makeup, to look like Britney or Angelina. Despite the winter's cold, they show enough belly, cleavage, and leg to make people stop and stare. Long hair, tight bleached jeans, and pink tops are compulsory. Quite a few girls seem to have serious eating disorders.

The boys try to look cool, with their torn jeans and carefully tussled, gelled hair or David Beckham–inspired semi-mohawks. The black boys, who form a minority, have 50 Cent and Tupac as role models. All of them stand in small circles, chatting and flirting. Every once in a while they walk up and down, giving each other the eye. Dozens of them shuffle in and out of the entrance. It's the South African rich kids' version of the game of attraction.

The kids have nowhere else to go. Their houses have been turned into fortresses, with alarms, electric fences, and spikes to keep the other out. They are taken to school by their moms or dads in a car. The streets are forbidden territory. Downtown is out of the question. Even parks do not function as meeting places for those full of raging hormones. The only area where they feel free to walk, flirt, and flaunt is the mall. And out of all the malls available, Sandton City is unmistakably number one. As someone once remarked: in Johannesburg you don't say in which neighborhood you live, you say which mall you frequent.

It's the miracle of Sandton City, of any luxury mall. You stroll, you look, and you buy—things you don't really need, like disappointing CDs, clothes you'll wear only once, or books you'll never read. You're away from the rain and the sun. It's safe and secure. The choice is endless. You can spend hours, days without getting bored. There are no annoying beggars or hawkers. The only smells are those of perfume and food. Everything African has been reduced to veneer. The Dark Africa curio shop is as African as it'll ever get here.

Everyone, white, brown, black, looks smart, lean, clean, and beautiful. The kids love it. Every shop, every corner has its own concept, its own sound, its own biosphere. This is not a shopping center, this is not a shopping mall. This is what the American architect Jon Jerde called an Urban Entertainment Center, a place where the sense of community is defined by shopping and relaxation, where the customer is feted and entertained.[3] It's a place that makes no distinction between skin color or gender, a place where happiness is for sale, or at least can be marveled at.

If the Apartheid Museum is the yin of the new era, then the shopping mall is the yang. The success of Sandton City over the past ten years is an unplanned example of the rainbow nation. It works as a reversed prism: all colors are reduced to one bright light. Origin, race, and gender are of secondary importance. Money does the magic trick. "We had a congress some years ago," recalls Andre Viljoen, editor of *Shopping SA*. "The American visitors who were taken around said it was amazing that there was no problem with blacks shopping in white malls. That doesn't happen in the States. I said: we're more pragmatic here; a rand is a rand."

The mall works like a Pandora's box of aspirations. One would assume that those who don't have a car or a credit card have little interest in a mall. The architecture of the malls and the goods for sale exclude those who depend on public transport and small cash. But even that is not true. Ask around, and you'll hear stories about black domestic workers in white suburbia who have their rural family over for a visit. Those visitors love to spend their days in the malls, gazing at the people, the goods, the restaurants—without spending a penny.

"Yes, malls are very democratic," says Lone Poulsen of the faculty of architecture of the University of Witwatersrand. She points out that these days Joburg even has black *kugels,* particularly in trendy malls like the Zone in Rosebank. In the past the word *kugel* was used for spoiled, affected Jewish girls. These days anyone can be a *kugel.* "But [black kugels] are still only a tiny minority," she adds with a touch of venom. Poulsen argues that megamalls have undermined and ruined the inner cities by luring shops, restaurants, and customers away from the CBD. Minimalls have had a similar effect on the old suburban high streets. Malls have turned interesting and idiosyncratic bits of the old South Africa into decay. "I loathe malls," says the Johannesburg architect Henry Paine, who as a matter of principle has refused to have anything to do with mall designs. "They make me angry. I get lost. They charge five rand for five minutes parking. They use machines. They don't contribute to our society. They are senseless, soulless. We have a lovely climate, why then have that artificial environment? People must return to the CBD. They must discover African culture. I know Joburg people who have never been downtown." Certainly, Paine agrees, he can see how the mall is an antidote to apartheid, a place where people blend and can forget about the past and their current anxieties. "Absolutely. I agree with that theory. No, it's not a conscious government policy. That would be very Machiavellian. It's a natural development. It's escapism, based on the idea that people are equal."[4]

Constructed in 1972, Sandton City was the first American-styled mall. It was built some fifteen kilometers away from the CBD, on what used to be farmland. Cunning businessmen and speculators foresaw that this specific spot, where various freeways merge, would be ideal for building a new hub. Initially they had a regional center in mind, so the wealthy wouldn't have to leave the northern suburbs for their shopping and entertainment. With the help of Canadian experts, they constructed a monolithic block, which resembled a colossal container. "It has very hard surfaces, but it became a bloody sensation," says Clive Chipkin, author of the book *Johannesburg Style* (1993), which covers urban development between 1880 and 1970. "The developers understood very well where the money was: housewives with credit cards."[5] Since then Sandton City has grown so big and multifarious that it causes panic attacks in new visitors. "The first time I went there, I cried," says journalist Sonja Loots. "I didn't have a clue where to go for the few things I needed."

A shopping center, wrote the political philosopher Hannah Arendt in 1958 in her book *The Human Condition,* has the power to bring people together, to create a bond, and to separate them. That's exactly what happened in South Africa. Initially, the mall catered only to the white, English-speaking elite. Next, under president P. W. Botha, the Afrikaner boss-class emerged and occupied large parts of western Johannesburg. Cresta Mall (92,740 square meters) started out serving the needs and desires of this new bourgeoisie. After the Afrikaners came the emancipation of the Coloureds and the Indians. Finally, after the elections of 1994, a black middle class took off. The consuming masses grew in huge numbers. Even after deducting the staggering proportion of have nots, there are at least 10 million potential mallers, eager to spend and to be seen spending. "There's a huge new middle class, which is consuming beyond its means. We suffer from the American disease: living on credit," says Chipkin.[6]

A stroll through the current Cresta Mall feels like submerging into a futuristic version of the new South Africa. Over twenty years, it has changed from a dull container for Afrikaners to a palacelike labyrinth with wings and domes in the great Victorian tradition. Afrikaners pass Indians, who pass blacks, who pass Coloureds. Just like in Sandton City, this happens without communicating or socializing. The superficiality of this blend is not necessarily negative. Perhaps a heavily scarred country like South Africa does need a mild form of amnesia, with consuming as a healing power, the way West Germany and Japan lost themselves in the Economic Miracle after World War II. "Now all the people who never had a chance come to the surface," observes the architect Paul Whitehead, designer of two malls. "They make sure there's growth. For them, visiting a mall is a sign of progression. It's both entertainment and an outing."[7]

The South African mall is an offshoot of what the Dutch architect Rem Koolhaas in his influential book *S, M, L, XL* (Koolhaas and Mau 1996: 1255) introduced as the "Generic City." He describes it as an urban center that has liberated itself from the old city center after that had become too small, too congested, and too hectic to properly function. Since the Generic City doesn't need an identity, history and tradition become irrelevant, argues Koolhaas. It's all about here and now. Hence, the mall goes so well with the flighty post-apartheid spirit. It is adaptable. If it becomes too small, it extends; if it becomes too old, it rejuvenates. Effortlessly it can assume a new identity. It can also go wrong and become a dead mall—sad, empty cement blocks like Northcliff Corner Shopping Centre or the Bruma Lake Mall, which hasn't recovered from the setback it suffered after two serial killers murdered eight people in the area.

But malls also have to deal with a certain amount of unpredictability in consumer behavior. The shopping center expert Andre Viljoen cites the example of Brightwater Commons, in western Johannesburg. Some ten years ago, this was meant to be the Joburg answer to the Cape Town Waterfront, complete with an artificial lake that was surrounded by restaurants and shops. The public came, saw, and left. Something was wrong, and the people didn't like it. The complex quickly developed into a place for bored youngsters and drug dealers to hang around. The lake has since been replaced with grass. A small stream and some fake rocks are reminders of those liquid days. But the center is still craving success. "Look," points Viljoen, "half of the shops stand empty."[8]

The Generic City, says Koolhaas, doesn't follow laws. Every hypothesis can be confirmed or rejected. Malls lead to alienation. Sure. Malls bring people together. Indeed. The mall is at the same time antihistoric and nostalgic. It offers a re-created past, working as a time machine. It molds a synthetic, optimistic version of the past: the double-decker bus, the healthy farm, the cozy village. It's that kind of lost innocence that we long for in these chaotic, disturbing times.

It's a strange paradox that ten years after apartheid, in a country where more than three-quarters of the population are black, it's still a huge risk to come up with a proper "black" or "African" mall.[9] "Sandton City is seen as a white mall, but most of the money comes from black pockets," says *Shopping SA* editor Viljoen. "Simply because of sheer numbers. But if you cater purely for blacks, you chase away the whites—and the blacks even more. It all boils down to new aspirations." He cites the example of Southgate, which for a while started focusing on the nearby Soweto, with its estimated 1.5 million inhabitants. The results were disastrous. The white Southgate crowd went elsewhere, and so did the blacks. Soweto itself has always lacked a prestigious mall. The diminutive Dobsonville Shopping Centre (17,320 square meters) houses some of the main chain stores, but comes nowhere near Cresta, Rosebank, or Sandton City. Township dwellers perceive the local mall as second-rate or inferior and prefer to take a taxi to the nearest regional mall. Given its population, Soweto should have forty malls, calculates Viljoen. "But no one is mad enough to do that. Even one Sandton City in Soweto would be a waste of time and money."[10]

He may be proven wrong. In July 2005, work started on Soweto's first mega–shopping mall, an initiative of Soweto businessman Richard Maponya. Costs for this 60,000-square-meter complex will be 450 million rand. Maponya promised it would be the heartbeat of Soweto and would try to attract all the big names: Woolworths, Edgars, Pick 'n Pay, Ackermans, Jet, Sportscene, and cinema company Ster Kinekor. "This mall," predicts Maponya on the Web site of Finance24.com, "is going to be a mall just like any modern mall you see in the city, there will be no compromise in design and quality, and we will have all the best retailers. For the first time, people in Soweto will be able to wake up and walk to a shopping mall."[11] Viljoen is sceptical about such projects. "You have the people, but a crappy environment. They want to be seen with wealthy whites, rubbing shoulders with that version of South Africa. It's all about aspirations. Malls symbolize the new South Africa."

But the shopping-center world is undergoing fast changes. While mega-malls still flourish thanks to the entertainment factor, the medium-sized regional malls are starting to suffer. "I have the feeling that their sell-by date has passed," says Viljoen. "People avoid them for their daily shopping, they're too big. You keep pushing your trolley forever. Now Woolworths are building lots of little shops in small centres. Pick 'n Pay as well. They laughed at Spar when they did that." Examples of successful small-scale strips in Johannesburg are plenty. The arrival of Woolworths turned Greenside into a lively area. Parkhurst is booming. Parkview's Tyrone Avenue has become a local magnet, with a heady mix of restaurants, supermarkets, and old-fashioned shops. It portrays itself cheekily as "a village."

Charming as this "back to small" may seem, it also has a hypothetical downside. What if this retreat of the white elite, away from the mall, back to the village idyll, is a desire to move away from the multicultural society? What if it is (subconsciously) fueled by racism? The development of the mall will remain the perfect barometer for the new South Africa.

Notes

1 British writer J. G. Ballard has a preference for setting his novels in the dehumanized environments of gated communities, industrial estates, and airport surroundings.

2 In 1994, of the just over 600 businesses listed on the Johannesburg Stock Exchange (JSE), 63 had Sandton as their base. By 2000, out of the 654 JSE-listed companies, 133 had their headquarters in Sandton, including the JSE itself, which made its move in 1998.

3 Interview with Jon Jerde by Anna Tilroe in Tilroe 2002, 31–38.

4 Interview with author, Johannesburg, January 27, 2004.

5 Interview with author, Johannesburg, February 6, 2004.

6 Ibid.

7 Interview with author, Johannesburg, February 3, 2004.

8 Interview with author, Johannesburg, February 3, 2004.

9 There is a successful Indian mall, the Oriental Plaza, which has developed despite its ugly appearance and apartheid-dictated location.

10 Interview with author, Johannesburg, February 3, 2004.

11 See www.fin24.co.za/articles/default/display_article.aspx?NAV=ns&ArticleID =1518–1786_1733108, July 6, 2005.

✛   ✛   ✛

Yeoville Confidential

ACHAL PRABHALA

"You know what Hillbrow and Yeoville are like," says a resident of Katlehong, glibly summarizing the moral character of an inner city he must have visited about twice in the last decade: "Full of criminals." But naturally: mainstream Joburg circles—the Melville café, the Soweto shebeen—have turned both names into abuses, conjoining them to a list of African cities similarly revered. So Time Square is apparently in Kinshasa; and Ponte Tower—rumored host of the Miss Transvestite Africa Contest circa 1996—is Little Lagos, with garbage piled up to the seventh floor in its central hollow. (The standing joke with Ponte is that the authorities wanted to turn it into a prison, when someone suggested that all they would have to do is lock the gates.)

Other times, you'll hear tender evocations of the days gone by, from good people—living in good suburbs with good security and not a Nigerian in sight—unable to forget an era when the House of Tandoor actually served tandoori food and cappuccino abounded in swish European patisseries. All very quaint, but frankly, the stories bore me. They're the memories of people with golden-age syndrome. My own Yeoville memories are exactly one year old. I'm not haunted by the ghosts of cappuccinos past—and I like that just fine.

When I moved to Yeoville, I knew nothing of its cosmopolitanism and its vivacious bustling streets. I moved because I happened to find a friendly housemate and cheap accommodation there. My motivations, I discovered, were widely shared. After six months of sitting on food stains from the last century, I tried to reupholster my housemate's furniture while he was away.

A snooty Mozambican tailor from the neighborhood suggested leather—"Then you can take it with you when you move to Sandton." I asked for something cheaper and told him I wasn't planning on moving to that hallowed outpost of exclusivity anytime soon. "Ah, but you will," he said. "Never give up hope."

In Mughal India, *Sarai* denoted a space, in a town or along a road, where travelers from all walks of life and social classes could find refuge and company. It signified a location of cultural exchange. The Sarai was thus at once a destination and a point of departure, as is Yeoville.

If all departures need a getaway vehicle, then the bed in Yeoville is a rented car. Precisely, an early 1980s Japanese model with moldy seats, a reliable engine, and a radio that catches pure static. Hillbrow is a borrowed v w Beetle—lots of character, malfunctioning taillights, and frequent engine breakdowns. Berea, with its giant blocks of concrete, is a bit like that Trabant you inherited from your East German aunt: presumably functional, but entirely mysterious. As much as this seems to be leading up to some trite explanation for the inner city's aesthetic degradation—such as "No one in the history of the world has ever washed a rented car"—it isn't. One visit to Kin Malebo, the Congolese restaurant on Raleigh Street, and a sense of its casually glamorous ambience, would correct any misconceptions about aesthetic standards in itinerant Africa.

Yet it's likely that no one in the history of the world has aspired to grow old driving a 1980 Mazda. Beer-soaked conversations in Time Square inevitably invoke the escape plan—to a better suburb, country, or continent. For the real people who live in Yeoville, there are real fears. It's not a nice place for the walking classes at any time of day, especially after dark. Women fear they'll be parted from their cell phones, and grown men prefer to walk in groups. The streets are poorly lit, and it's not because the lamps are being stolen—suspended at a height of twenty feet off the ground, it's hard to imagine how they could be.

Long-time residents who've never dialed beyond Durban suddenly discover their monthly phone bill is at R99,000: someone has tapped into their line and leased it out to people homesick for Douala, Lagos, and Kinshasa. This actually happened to our phone, and though I began the lengthy reconnection process with Telkom a whole year ago, things have stalled. We will have our phone back only once the background checks and the police clearance certificates come through clean, which—judging by the progress so far—is never. "You see," a tired official explains, "it is a high-risk area."

Residentially speaking, *high-risk* mainly applies to people living in houses. Flats are considered safe, though in some buildings, you have to watch out for the other residents. At the hardware shop on Raleigh Street, I get my first lesson in the etiquette of loot and pillage. "People come in here to buy big beams of plywood," the man at the counter explains. "The next day some house has been broken into and the owners come in to buy reinforcements. But as soon as we've sold that plywood, we know that someone's in trouble."

Weeks after I moved in, I was determined to show off my neighborhood. When you have to watch your friends' faces contort in alarm on telling them you live in Yeoville, you begin to take all those insults against the African Diaspora very personally. It was October, the jacarandas were in bloom, and I cooked lunch for a few friends. We took coffee on the balcony and gazed down at lazy Saturday afternoon street life: women stopping to look at the latest Nollywood offering; groups of men sprawled out on the grassy sidewalk, playing cards and drinking beer. My friends were suitably impressed (and suitably chastened). Later in the afternoon, one straggler remained. As I triumphantly concluded my "Yeoville is a normal place" lesson, a gunshot rang out. Below us, people ran screaming onto the main road. After the street had cleared, two shirtless gentlemen sauntered down the road, their heads and torsos covered with blood, broken beer bottles in hand. My friend the straggler, leaning over the balcony, thought he heard them speak French. "Now this," he said, with a smug grin, "is what we call the Inter-Congolese dialogue."

Civilians have done me no harm in Yeoville, or indeed, anywhere else in South Africa. I realize that I owe this happy existence—in different ways—to owning a car that isn't posh (in fact, a borrowed vw Beetle that doesn't lock), to living in a building that is strict about security, and to being a dark-skinned male. Friends in similar circumstances, but crucially lacking their own transport, have not had it quite so good. Michael, an Ndebele-speaker from Zimbabwe, lost a finger last year in an incident involving some thugs, one cell phone, and a lot of knives. Isha, a Lingala-speaker from the DRC, had his head bashed in with a beer bottle outside Tandoor and lost sensation on one side of his face for weeks. None of this has stopped them—or me—from continuing to explore inner-city nightlife.

In part, this is because the walking classes have their own ways of making nightlife safe. When, for instance, people need to get back home—after working the kitchens and tables in Midrand, Melville, and Norwood, or just enjoying a good night out—they take South Africa's safest form of late-night transport: the Armed Response Taxi. Security company employees, driven to boredom on their late-night patrols and eager for a quick buck, will pick you up and take you home for the same price as a taxi.

On Wednesday, Friday, Saturday—even Sunday, when much of the service class finally gets a chance to relax—Yeoville's bars are buzzing and Hillbrow's clubs are packed. In staid old Berea, the bootleg Kilimanjaro—an unlicensed "house party"—is swinging to the beat of an urban Africa. Whoever told you that Rockey Street was dead is lying.

Food (of the dining-out kind) is not exactly the inner city's forte. Good food, however, exists: it's the only place on this latitude where you can eat *fufu* and stew on the streets. Then there's Kin Malebo on Raleigh Street, which serves excellent fish with ginger and "oignon," or smoked chicken with peanut sauce and pap, in an atmosphere that pays just tribute to the sâpeur—with patrons to match. There are comfortable couches, a fireplace, a clientele decked out in black jeans and leather, and walls dedicated to images of Congolese music legends like Papa Wemba and Zaiko Langa Langa. Across the road is the legendary Charro's—a remnant of old Yeoville—which until very recently continued to roll out Durban Indian food (and the occasional Durban Indian version of Middle Eastern food) to a clientele that has no idea who Brenda Fassie was—as the owner will tell you, in between explaining that though he's adjusted to the new Yeoville, he's moving himself, his wife, and their kid to Melrose—"A more suitable place for a family." A couple of shebeens around Times Square, and one well-known house in neighboring Bertram's, serve unbelievably good Ethiopian food at unbelievably low Ethiopian prices.

The other establishments on Raleigh and Rockey Streets cater mainly to liquid diets, though quick fixes like meat and chips are always at hand. La Congolaise, Rockafellas, and the Zone seem to attract far more male clients than female, and a recently advertised Miss Rockafellas pageant might have been designed to change that. If there's one consistent performer in the Yeoville club circuit, it has to be the House of Tandoor. The original home of Johannesburg's Caribbean fan club, Tandoor was—and is—something of a philosophy, even if Horror Café in Newtown has lured the trustafarians away.

A reality of Johannesburg is that good African food is rare. This is not a political statement, merely a matter of taste. I am from South India, and over there, we like it hot. Moyo's is like going on a particularly tedious safari:

many native curiosities and everything priced for Swiss pensioners. To eat the food of Ethiopia, the DRC, and the "Monde Arabe," then, one follows the passports. Wherever in Johannesburg an immigrant working-class community exists, so does a cuisine.

But wherever a working class community exists, according to South African folklore, so does crime. The connection is perplexing. Throw a party, and people will assume that BYOB stands for "Bring your own bodyguard." I once got a response from an acquaintance, to an invite for drinks, saying he'd love to come except that Yeoville was "like Fallujah, bro!"—this from a man who grew up in KwaMashu. One friend claps every time he leaves Yeoville on the occasion that he has to drive through it; another takes a taxi though she owns a car. "You don't understand," she says, "If I drive myself, there's a 90 percent chance I will be hijacked." *Ninety percent?*

Most of the people I know have been broken in (so to speak), and apart from the obligatory jokes about the safety of their precious Teutonic automobiles, they're quite comfortable coming to visit me. My obligatory rejoinder is an offer to personally mug any visitor who feels he's missing out on the inner-city experience. Not that I understand the perception of this experience. In India, people generally fear lonely high-income neighborhoods—logically, they assume that it's where the crime is. Twelve months of Johannesburg, and I'm convinced that there would be a huge market for two very useful manuals: "How to Tell Working-Class neighborhoods from Battlefields" and its companion volume, "Not All Poor People Are Criminals."

Actually, I can think of at least two more: "Nigerians Are Human Beings, Too" and "Frail Old Ladies Who Sell Small Bags of Potatoes on the Road Should Not Be Put in Jail."

When I first moved to Yeoville, I had no office, though I had plenty to do. I needed a place to work and a good Internet connection. I found both down the road from home. The "Best Yeoville" Internet café cost all of R5 an hour. It was run by a Nigerian. Now, before this story goes any further, I must explain that the Nigerian world has generally treated me very well. Except for that time when we were walking back from the Nigeria–Bafana Bafana soccer match at Ellis Park, and certain Nigerian residents of Yeoville, in a spectacular fit of patriotism, decided to urinate from their balconies onto the road (Nigeria lost).

Ephraim, the owner of the café, let me know immediately that he also repaired and sold televisions, VCRS, computer printers, and almost anything else, and that he was interested in new business opportunities of almost any kind. The first few weeks, I walked to the café and back, spending all day there. A little later, I was the temporary owner of the aforementioned vw Beetle, so I drove (this allowed me to work late into the night). Still later, the Beetle had packed up, and my housemate, away on a trip, kindly lent me his car. It was a gleaming new Toyota Corolla. Ephraim watched my apparent upward mobility with growing interest—and growing respect. One day he took me aside and conspiratorially whispered, "I want to do your kind of business."

I explained that I worked for a nonprofit organization, and that I was being paid only living costs. Unfortunately, critical investigations of intellectual property—which is what I work on—mean nothing to most people (and not just because they're from Nigeria), so it was all a bit hazy. But Ephraim remained convinced that I was the man to know. As a preferred customer, albeit one who was soon going to move to a real office, I was given special treatment—like being allowed to keep my time (if I didn't use the whole hour in one sitting) or, embarrassingly, having someone tossed out to accommodate me when the café was full.

It was frequently full. Initially, I was surprised at the number of people who needed to constantly send e-mails throughout the day. Peering over into the next computer, I noticed a letter being composed in the name of Mrs. Stella Sigcau. Now either the honorable South African minister for public works (official hobbies: "Reading and Tapestry") was wandering around Yeoville incognito, sporting snakeskin boots, considerable shoulder muscles, and a trim beard, or I had somehow landed myself in scam central.

I discovered that I was surrounded by a group of rather distinguished people: other than Mrs. Sigcau, there was Albert Chissama, Esq. (writing from his own chambers in the High Court of Lagos, no less), Olusegun Abacha (General Abacha's second son by his third wife, who had to go into hiding at an early age because Abacha's first wives were jealous and spiteful, you understand), even the secret male lover of Colonel "Khadafi." And they were all writing, with "a deep sense of purpose and the utmost sincerity," to inform you of vast sums of money hidden in secret Swiss banks that could be yours, in exchange for some consequential personal information or a little hard cash.

Nigerian 419 scam letters (named after the section of the Nigerian penal code that describes the fraud) had long intrigued me. Douglas Cruickshank, writing in Salon.com, suggests that Nigerian scammers have invented a whole new literary genre: "The truth is I've fallen for them, too—not for the scam part, but for the writing, the plots (fragmented as they are), the characters, the earnest, alluring evocations of dark deeds and urgent needs, Lebanese mistresses, governments spun out of control, people abruptly 'sacked' for 'official misdemeanours' and all manner of other imaginative details all delivered in a prose style that is as awkward and archaic as it is enchanting" (2001).

Cavendish Street suddenly became a lot more exciting. Forced to relocate by crackdowns at home, my neighborhood in South Africa had become the Grub Street of this Nigerian literary movement. The scamsters came in at dawn and left at dusk. All day, they would sit before their computers with software that trawled the Internet for intact e-mail addresses; then, with the flick of a wrist, Barrister Momoh Sanni Momoh's dark deeds and urgent needs would be broadcast to thousands of unwilling recipients. They had it down pat. They knew exactly how many e-mail addresses to append to each outgoing mail (Yahoo and Hotmail impose limits on the number of people you can e-mail in one go), and their cell phones were always switched on, just in case someone needed to contact the offices of Sierra Leone Diamond Mines, currently represented by a Vodacom pay-as-you-go number in Johannesburg.

There's a whole moral element to these scams, of course, but I can't say I feel sorry for the victims. The letters make it plain that it's a scam within a scam: the illegality of the entire enterprise is laid out right from the word go. How do you feel sorry for someone who thinks he didn't get his fair share of a burglary? I tried to push this further with Ephraim, but he clammed up. All he said was this: "Me, I don't do it. But what they get from these e-mails, it is what allows so many people to leave Nigeria and come here, to begin new lives."

There are other people who hope to begin new lives in Yeoville. Some of them are frail old ladies who have traveled from Sebokeng and Soweto to sell vegetables on Raleigh Street. They pitch up each day, squat on the road, and offer a small quantity of fresh produce. Since everyone knows that selling vegetables on the road is the number-one reason for crime in South Africa, the police swoop down on them regularly. They come in with sirens blazing, put on their bulletproof vests, and fearlessly confiscate anything they can lay their hands on. The contraband is then taken away, presumably to that well-known national storehouse of illegal vegetables.

Perhaps the ladies need a giant corporation to represent them. Across the road from where they sit is a brightly colored Cell-C phone booth. I went there once to call my parents in India and dialed without asking the rates. I was alarmed to find that Cell-C charges exactly double the Telkom rate for international calls—as they do in similar booths set up in low-income areas all around Johannesburg. It's an infallible business plan: charge the poor people twice as much.

Six months ago, I was driving home late from work. It was a Sunday night, and I was finishing up a paper due to be presented at a conference. At about 12:30 a.m., I approached the intersection between Berea and Yeoville, when I was ordered to stop by police officers. They asked for my license. I showed it to them. They asked me where I was from; I told them. They asked to see my passport. I explained that I had left it in my office in Newtown—but that they were welcome to come with me and see it. After years of dealing with the Indian law enforcement, I know my police manners: always admit you're wrong, grovel for sympathy, and appeal to the greatness of the human spirit. Fresh from an intensive beginner's course in Zulu, I even spoke as much of it as I could recall. It didn't impress: the officer whose face rested on my window only seemed to speak Sotho. It was another matter that he was armed and extremely drunk.

He thought I was being impertinent. I was a foreigner driving late at night through the inner city; therefore, I was a criminal. Officer One (no name badge) took my car keys and hauled me off to the back of a police van. Inside were two frightened Nigerians and one Cameroonian. None of them had any money to bribe the police with—hence their confinement. Meanwhile, officers Two, Three, Four, and Five commandeered the road, threatening passersby to stop or be shot at. Four hours later, after the night's collections were in, I was let out. Just for good measure, my wallet was "confiscated." And in case I didn't understand the severity of my misdemeanor, I was told that they would be "watching me."

I tried to lodge a complaint with the Independent Complaints Directorate (ICD) of South Africa. The ICD has an ostensibly simple complaint process. Its Web site provides two useful services to the public. One is "lodging a complaint against a member of SAPS." The other is "complimenting a member of SAPS." Funnily enough, only one service actually works.

I carefully went through the categories of complaint on offer. I decided that mine was Type III, a category that includes offenses as precise as "Sodomy" and as poetic as "Defeating the ends of justice." But hit on the link to take you to the complaints form, and you are confronted with a blank page. Call the ICD in Pretoria, and they will tell you that though they would like to e-mail you the complaint form, procedure bars them from doing so. Ask in frustration, after several months of trying to register a complaint, as to what you are expected to do, and you will be told to come to Pretoria during working hours and lodge the complaint there.

But the ends of justice had finally defeated me, and I never got around to it. I didn't know the names of the officers who assaulted me that night, I was too scared to note the registration number of the police van we were in, and frankly, I was just sick and tired of the whole thing. These little love-ins with the police happen to everyone who lives where I do. The most bizarre event I have heard of is the police throwing an ID-less man from Durban in jail overnight—all because he couldn't recite the numbers one to ten in Afrikaans (irrefutable proof of his foreignness, never mind that he spoke chaste Zulu). I'm still frequently asked for my papers. But I'm wiser now: I tell them that my passport is at home, show them a photocopy, and, if they persist, offer to call the Commissioner of Police to clarify matters—not that I know him, or have his number.

Last week, a friend picked me up from home. It was a Friday night, and driving out, we noticed the enormous police presence in the area. There were patrol cars everywhere. "What a safe area this is," he said, approvingly. Rot. As long as the upstanding citizens of Sandton believe that the police are keeping their 2.3 bedrooms safe from inner-city thugs, the men in blue are free to do their thing. Residents of Yeoville are not confused by flashing lights. Armed Response wants passengers, and policemen want cash. Try driving through the intersection of Rockey and Raymond Streets *without* being pestered to buy some kind of narcotic, regardless of how many police officers are around. Try it.

Even as I whine about the self-appointed immigration squads of Yeoville, Berea, and Hillbrow, the truth is, they are but cogs in a vast machine. My indignation at being treated like an illegal immigrant arises mainly from the fact that I am not. This is not a situation that applies to many of my neighbors. If police corruption is the problem, as seems the case, is an efficient process the answer? Faced with the prospect of an indefinite holiday in Lindela (a detention center for illegal immigrants), most people I know would prefer to part with some loose change.

Perhaps the real problem is too big for this essay, or for the residents of Yeoville, who—for the most part—seem to be quite happy to endure occasional police torture in exchange for residence in Johannesburg. The politics of nationhood and South Africa's peculiar relationship with the third world deserve a better examination elsewhere. As for now, we're happy to go about doing our thing and enjoying the salubrious delights of the inner city while we can.

For it is hard not to appreciate a place where you can have your sandals stitched up—after you played soccer in them—for less than R5, or a place where you can haggle over the price of fresh plantains with people who then become your friends. It's hard not to feel thankful for being alive when you wander about an open-air market to pounding rhythms from five countries and three continents. And it's hard not to love the fact that you can always find someone to repair your microwave oven after it blew up when you hard-boiled eggs for thirty minutes instead of ten, in the course of surprising your housemate with breakfast.

In fact, it's a place just like home: except so very excitingly foreign.

From the Ruins: The Constitution Hill Project

MARK GEVISSER

Between the University of the Witwatersrand and the inner-city neighborhood of Hillbrow (the densest square kilometer of urban space in Africa) is a giant building that emerges from rubble and ruins. To watch it rise is to see a city and a democracy heaving itself from the debris, carrying with it the physical markers and the tangible echoes of an iniquitous political system but also of a history stretching back long before apartheid. The building is the new Constitutional Court, and it is being erected on the site of the Old Fort, Johannesburg's notorious prison complex. On this 95,000-square-meter site, the municipal and provincial governments are developing a major urban regeneration project and mixed-use heritage precinct: Constitution Hill. Constitution Hill will house the new court, symbol and guardian of the South African Constitution, one of the most democratic public declarations in the world; it is also being developed as a "campus for human rights" that will house many statutory bodies and non-governmental organizations whose job it is to protect and interpret the Constitution. Constitution Hill will bear the mantle of this new order—understood, always, within the context of the past. Prominent in the precinct are the three derelict prisons, left mostly to rot since 1983 when they were closed down and the prison was moved to Soweto. Each prison has its own legacies and ghostly presences; each will fulfill separate roles in the new public space being wrought from the heart of the city.

As the court rises, its every shape is etched against the high-rise apartment blocks of Hillbrow, a neighborhood of 100,000 people, most of whom are immigrants from other parts of Africa. From the ramparts of the Old Fort, you look down into the neighborhood and see right into its mass of humanity. Church song rises from the neighborhood, mingling with the sounds of children playing in the park directly below. The disparities of Johannesburg, and of South Africa more generally, are immediately evident: in one glance, you can take in both the inner city with all its social problems and the leafy green forest of Johannesburg's affluent northern suburbs. The ramparts provide perspective over not only space but also time. On one side of the site are the colonial prisons; on the other side is the maximum-security prison of a later era, doors to the cells now ajar, yellow highveld grass rising in the cracks of the courtyard. The first phase of the five-year Constitution Hill development was completed and opened to the public in March 2004. It is a site in formation, its future uncertain but as full of promise and as vulnerable to implosion as the history of South Africa always has been. It's a city site, reaching far beyond itself. The only way to get to know the site and to fully understand the scale of the project is to walk it.

The text below is the result of a walking conversation that took place in late 2003 between me and Mark Gevisser, content adviser to Constitution Hill's Heritage, Education, and Tourism team. The accompanying images were taken during the course of the walk and were part of the process of making sense of the place in its incarnations of the past, the present, and the future. S. N.

SARAH NUTTALL: Mark, this is an evocative site for any of us who grew up in this city. You can feel its presences as we walk here now, but it was always powerful from the outside too, as we walked and drove past it but didn't quite know what it was. . . .

MARK GEVISSER: Like so many kids who grew up in Johannesburg, I remember being driven down Kotze Street and seeing what appeared to be a gash in the landscape, this hole in the hill, and knowing that something bad was on the other side, but, yes, not knowing what it was. It was actually the entry through the ramparts of the Old Fort into the Johannesburg Prison. So the Old Fort and its prisons were some kind of absent center, a place that was literally overlooked—in two senses: they were neglected or ignored, but also, quite strangely for a place of incarceration, they were right in the middle of the city. So if you lived in those then rather stylish modernist Hillbrow apartment blocks, you could sit there on your balcony doing whatever it was you did on a Saturday afternoon and look down at the prisoners doing their exercises or having to dance the *tauza* without actually seeing them.[1] In both these senses, it was overlooked.

sn: What about people on the inside—what could they see?

mg: There's a story I love about a man called Cecil Williams, a white gay communist theater director who was detained here during the 1960 state of emergency, with a whole lot of others. He recalls one evening being in one of the recreation courtyards of the Old Fort and looking up at the flats above him and seeing, on one balcony, a party in full swing. He actually recognized some of the people hanging off the balcony and drinking *parfait d'amour* and having a gay old party on a beautiful Johannesburg evening. But they couldn't see him. Or they wouldn't see him. It's a metaphor, I think, for how whites dealt with apartheid: it was under their very noses, but it was invisible to them.

And if the Old Fort has that kind of metaphorical power for whites, it has another, even stronger one for blacks, as this place of darkness in the middle of the city to which they'd be taken if their passes were out of order, or they had broken the curfew regulations, or any one of a number of other petty apartheid laws that criminalized their very existence. Given that all pass offenders in Johannesburg were brought here, there's barely a black family in the city that doesn't have some memory of what it was like inside. In black popular culture, the Old Fort is still known as Number Four because the black male section was section four, and those two words still send shivers down people's spines. Yvonne Chaka Chaka wrote a song in which she uses "number four" as a kind of code for apartheid repression, because she was a gospel singer who played her hits on Radio Bantu so she had to talk in a signifying way. Even now, people from all over the country know nothing about the fort, but they do know about Number Four. They don't locate it, root it, in this site, but they know that it exists. And it's fearsome [see figure 1].

sn: This site has so many earlier incarnations as well, multiple histories of the changing faces of carceral space. How did the British and the Boers imagine and use the site differently?

mg: The Old Fort actually was built originally as a military garrison, by Paul Kruger's Boer Republic in the late 1890s, as a way of keeping watch over the restive uitlanders—the foreign miners—in the village of Johannesburg below. The uitlanders were believed to be plotting to overthrow Kruger and hand the precious gold reef over to the British. So it was a place of surveillance, and of control, and of defiance: a way of saying to the British, "Fuck you, we're not scared of your imperial designs!" There was one howitzer cannon on the southwest corner of the ramparts trained

1 View of Number Four prison from the Old Fort ramparts, 2004.
Photo by Mark Gevisser

on the village below and another on the northeast, protecting the road to
Pretoria, the republic's capital. But the Boers were also not entirely comfortable with their identity, so they did a bizarre thing: they camouflaged
the outside of the fort as a hill and built their facade with its grand Zuid-
Afrikaansche Republiek coat of arms on the inside. It's such a strong image of the laager! The Boers never really liked Johannesburg, they saw it as
Gomorrah, and so when the Brits marched in, in 1900, they gave it away
without much fuss. The fort became a British bastion and a place where
Afrikaners were humiliated, forced to surrender their precious muskets.
In fact, a few Cape Rebels—British subjects who had fought on the side
of the Boers—were executed here, the only executions that ever happened
on the site. Then, once the war was over, the fort reverted to being a prison
(there was originally a prison on the site, built in 1892), and that's what it
remained until 1983—Johannesburg's main place of incarceration—when
the prison was moved to Diepkloof, outside Soweto. Since then it has been
largely derelict and neglected, until the Constitutional Court came along
in the late 1990s and said, "We want our permanent home here."

SN: Why do you think they chose this site, given the heaviness of its history and its proximity to one of the least safe and, in some senses, one of the most traumatic parts of the city?

MG: They explicitly liked the symbolism of building the home of the Constitution atop or within this place of oppression—to put the Constitution into a historical context, to show that it was a consequence of a long and difficult struggle. And second, the current court is both activist and evangelical: they want to be of the people, with the people, and in the people. That's important to them, given the constitutional values of transparency and accountability. So they wanted to be right here, slap bang in the middle of Hillbrow, with all its social problems, rather than in, say, rarefied Sandton. An international competition was held for the design of the court and won by an exceptional, a truly exceptional team of young South African architects. And then we were brought in to try to figure out how to give this place meaning; how to interpret it as a heritage site, a tourist site, a place of education, as a place that people could use.

SN: How will you give the site meaning as public space?

MG: It was clear that the first thing we had to do was shine some light on it. We interviewed people in Hillbrow, people who live in the buildings that overlook it. They are no longer trendy gay men drinking *parfaits d'amour* but abject illegal immigrants, often twelve to a one-bedroom flat. They hang their washing on their balconies watching the construction of the court, but not one of them stopped to think, hey, what's going on there? It says something about the way Johannesburg's inner-city residents are alienated from their environment and about how daunting our task is, which is to create safe and meaningful public space in the middle of the city.

Constitution Hill, in fact, is actually built on one of the highest points of the Witwatersrand, on a watershed, and there is this sense of it being on a cusp between two things. We were really struck by what happens when you stand on the rampart and you walk along toward Hillbrow: on one side, you see the Old Fort falling down, and on the other side, you see the new court coming up, and there's this sort of balance of forces or energy, the promise of the Constitutional Court rising up out of the ruins of the past. It seemed as if, as we were walking along the rampart, we were suspended between the past and the future, the past derelict and misunderstood and the future still very much under construction—a utopian dream of what we might be able to achieve in this country but is nowhere near being built yet. This society is still very much in transition and the values of the Constitution remain an ideal rather than something that has been realized. That's what walking on the ramparts evokes, and that's the way we want the site to work interpretatively: to be used as a place where you find yourself between the past and the future, and where you understand that the only way the future can happen, resting on the past, is through your agency as someone in the present. So you pull from the past and put into the future. That's the energy that we want to drive this site: you are in the imperfect present, and you can make the future happen by understanding the past. There's nothing triumphalist about it. Like South Africa itself, it's a work in progress. A place where you watch, and participate in, democracy at work.

sn: Is the Constitution so very important in the life of a society, or are we only imagining that it is? Should we attach such significance to it? Won't its symbolic, material, and living power fade? Have you remained convinced as you work on the site that it will continue to be an important document?

mg: I think the whole point of this development is to make sure that it doesn't fade, that it remains relevant and alive in people's minds. Most South Africans *are* aware of the Constitution and know that it gives them rights, even though they don't necessarily know what those rights are. They know that the Constitution is the fruit of the liberation struggle and of their suffering. Our American consultants who've been here have been struck by the way South Africans say *my* Constitution or *our* Constitution, whereas Americans would say *the* Constitution. So I do have a sense of the Constitution being not just a document or a set of ideas but a place of refuge, a place of possibility. It is that architecture that drives the development of this site: it will be a place that embodies the Constitution and its possibilities—and perhaps also its frailties.

It is very difficult to know what the Constitution will mean in one or two generations' time. But if this place is constructed in such a way that it is dynamic, that it responds to what's happened to its society around it, rather than ossifying this grand moment, the "Mandela magic moment" of the late nineties, then it will remain relevant. It has to be looking at the society around it and measuring that society against the values of the Constitution.

sn: What are the stories that these prisons tell? They are each so different, they seem to carry quite different senses of the past; even as one thinks of the bodies that were confined in each, one imagines those bodies—the way they move and lay and sat and suffered—quite differently. Much of this is suggested by the architecture of each, which signals, in particular ways, what it means to be imprisoned and what kinds of humiliation the prisoner ought to suffer.

MG: Almost immediately, an apartheid developed in terms of the spatial design of the fort, and this existed up until its closure. The whites were kept within the ramparts, and new prisons were built outside of the ramparts for black men and women. These were sections four and five, which contained the native jail, the venereal section, the awaiting-trial block (which has been demolished to make way for the Court), and the Women's Gaol. It's very interesting to compare the buildings. The Old Fort was built by the Boers, and it has a kind of ramshackle inefficiency to its logic. The Women's Gaol was built by the people who perfected the building of jails—the British, the empire—and it's built as a panopticon. You really see how it works. It's an extraordinarily handsome building with its redbrick courtyards and its oval double-volume atrium in the center. It's very British in that it is beauty with a purpose. It's not just aesthetic; its beauty masks a function that is brutal, efficiently so. Fatima Meer, who was imprisoned here with Winnie Mandela after the 1976 Soweto student uprising, tells a story in her memoirs that really brings this home. She talks about how she was led into the oval atrium, with its perfect neoclassical proportions and columns and its finely wrought iron balustrades along the gallery above, and she imagined that she might see women in Victorian ball gowns sweeping down the staircase. Then, as her eyes accustomed to the darkness, she saw what was really going on in there—naked African women, new intakes, having their vaginas searched for contraband.

In contrast is the experience of going into sections four and five: you really do feel when you walk into them that you're entering the dark heart of apartheid, that you're treading on bones. I don't know why that is. I don't know if it's because this part's derelict, because it's falling apart and nature is pushing through and taking over. Unlike the Old Fort and the Women's Gaol, it wasn't reused after the prison closed in 1983 (the Old Fort was taken over by the Rand Light Infantry and the Women's Gaol by the Metropolitan Police). So it was just left to rot, abandoned. I've been thinking about why that is. Maybe it's because it resisted reuse; that's its power. The way it was built—which says a lot about the attitude to black prisoners—was to relegate all communal activity to the outside. So the very architecture didn't lend itself to being interpreted in any other way—and still doesn't. This is clear. We'll reuse the other buildings: the Commission on Gender Equality is moving into the Women's Gaol, and an educational center will be set up in the Old Fort. But we can't do anything with sections four and five. They will be a place of interpretation only—where you enter and you understand what happened in the past.

Because the fort and the Women's Gaol were reused, they were repainted. Which means that we lost, forever, the most potent prison records available: the graffiti. There are two kinds of prison record—the story from above, the official documents, and the story from below, the graffiti. In section four, you walk under an observation bridge (which I have to say makes me feel like I'm in a Nazi concentration camp) and down into what really is the darkest place in the darkness of the prison: the solitary punishment cells. Like everywhere else in section four it is built around an outdoor courtyard. But in this punishment section, the outdoor courtyard has wire mesh between you and the sky. So you're outside but you're caged. Coming off this courtyard are the cell doors, and on the back of them, a hundred years of records. And what's fascinating about them is that most of the people who were kept there were violent or dangerous criminals, which is why they were kept there, and we know some Soweto kids were kept there—yet the discourse on the doors is a discourse of liberation: "Viva ANC," et cetera. The liberation struggle became a metaphor for freedom. You're incarcerated, you're oppressed by white warders, you identify with the liberation struggle [see figure 2].

SN: The other major national and international political heritage site in this country is Robben Island. This site seems utterly different from the symbolic political symmetry of the island. It seems to offer quite different imaginative force from the particular drama and undiluted majesty and therefore the perfect horror—the clear juxtaposition of beauty and ugliness—of the island. This site is more messy, ambiguous, less clear-cut in terms of the psychic and political terrains it seems to take us into, even as we walk here this afternoon. I can feel right now, for instance, its banality and brilliance (perhaps it's the proximity of the everyday life of the city—just over there, so close one can hear it, even smell it) that demystifies the site and makes its history seem, on the one hand, ethereal and untouchable; and then suddenly, as we walk through a particular entrance or find objects we can't identify still lying around, we're back to the full force of its violence, in the midst of this sunny Saturday afternoon.

2 Graffiti on the door of an isolation cell in Number Four prison, 2004.
Photo by Mark Gevisser

MG: What's really important about these prisons is that we cannot claim
them as a Robben Island, a place where political prisoners exclusively were
sent and incarcerated for decades, a place of heroes and martyrs. The fort
was a busy, bustling urban prison holding all sorts of people. Certainly
there were political prisoners who were brought in here while they were
awaiting trial—Mandela himself was kept in here for two sessions of a
few weeks each, one during the treason trial of 1956 and one after his final arrest in 1962; Gandhi was in and out of here at the beginning of the
twentieth century; virtually any political activist, anyone who opposed the
state, throughout the century, spent time here. But the bulk of the people
here were common criminals, among them violent murderers, rapists, so-
ciopaths, *bad* people—and one's got to deal with that legacy: the people
who were imprisoned here were not necessarily noble and one can't iconize
them. But the zone of interpretation we're most interested in when we look
at the site is that most of the people held here were criminalized because
of the colonial and apartheid race laws; they were pass offenders, curfew

breakers, people arrested under the Immorality Act, beer brewers—all people who in a just society would never have been imprisoned. Understanding that particular prisoner profile is very important in interpreting this site, for it sets the scene for the constitutional rights that the court now upholds. If there's a constitutional clause that says, "Everyone has the right to freedom of movement," this has to be interpreted within the context that tens of thousands of people were held here for breaking the pass laws, which denied them that freedom.

SN: Over here was the awaiting-trial block. What's happened to it? And where has the visitors' block gone?

MG: The awaiting-trial block was demolished to make way for the court, in one of those terrible trade-offs between urban regeneration and conservation. For an inexplicable and quite frankly unforgivable reason, the heritage consultants who originally advised the Constitutional Court said the building had to be demolished to make space for the new buildings, so the court made it a precondition of moving onto the site. The South African Heritage Resources Agency gave permission for it to be demolished, because they understood that by giving up this building you could save the rest—by bringing the court onto the site and creating a heritage precinct around it. But the rub is that in terms of heritage significance, the awaiting-trial block was far and away the most important site in the complex, because it was where most of the political prisoners were kept—including the 1956 treason trialists and the kids of the Soweto uprising—and also where the visitors' block was, where "outside" met "inside." Luckily, the very innovative architects have found ways of commemorating the building. All its red bricks have been carefully preserved and are used both to build the walls of the court chamber and to mark the footprint of the original building. Its four stairwells have been kept and have been built into the design of the court and the square. You'll be able to see them from all over Johannesburg: they'll be glazed, and images will be projected onto them. They'll be seven stories tall, spires of the cathedral, built on the ruins of the past. They've also kept the visitors' block, which has been demolished brick by brick and kept in containers. Part of our brief is to figure out where and how it will be rebuilt. All this says something about the terrible compromises made in urban development.

SN: We're walking here today as we have many times before, because the site means a great deal to us as participants in the city, as two people who grew up here and care about the future of our city. But how can the site be made to speak to the tourist, both the local tourist and the international tourist—and in what kind of language? Why would people most want to come here, in the name of what kind of vision, do you think? We walk here now, in the red soil and the piles of rubble. In a few months' time, this will be a paved concourse, a shortcut from Hillbrow through to Braamfontein, or a place to linger—even play soccer or watch the court in session. What visiting rites will be conjured from this high city terrain, and for whom?

MG: There's an essential contradiction to the site that is also the core of its energy: it needs to be both sacred space and living, vibrant space. Sacred because of the ghosts who inhabit the prisons and the (hopefully!) Solomonic wisdom taking place inside the court chamber; vibrant because it is the place where the Constitution becomes a living, breathing document, a place where democracy is both at work and at play, where we perform the values of the Constitution into being. So one of our jobs is to harness the energy created by the juxtaposition—the clash—of these two personalities, to understand that the one defines the other, just as a medieval cathedral opens out onto a bustling town square.

One of the reasons tourism is limited to the extent that it is, especially in Johannesburg, is that there is an assumption that locals aren't tourists. Think of Washington, D.C.: if you are American, it's a journey you have to take, your pilgrimage to the shrine of democracy. So our first question is, can we make Constitution Hill a place of pilgrimage for South Africans, a place you have to visit at least once in your lifetime? It's also in the middle of a city—a very underresourced city, a city that has negative public space. It is so clear to us from our research in Hillbrow that people are not interested in the values of the Constitution but in how those values are going to improve their lives. One shocking figure about Hillbrow is that it has a population of 100,000 people and yet there's currently only one library with twenty seats in it. So much for freedom of access to information! So much for the right to education! A lot of people come to live in Hillbrow because it's close to places of study. The need for study places is huge, as is the need for safe spaces for children. This is articulated by residents all the time. And safety is important, because what is the Constitution if not a place of refuge for those in our society who are vulnerable? So just as the Constitution is a place of refuge, this place has to be a space of refuge, too.

There's a lesson that comes out of rural ecotourism that we'll be trying to apply here: the way you ensure the sustainability of a tourism project like this is that you make sure that the host community owns it. So there are lots of ideas about how the residents of Hillbrow are going to own this site in terms of the economic value they're going to be able to draw from it, the fact that it's going to be a place of pride for them, and so forth. Whether that can happen or not remains to be seen, because there are a lot of balancing acts that have to happen, because our imperative—our *constitutional* imperative—is to be open and accessible and transparent. The court site has to function as a series of city blocks—it has to be a thoroughfare as well as a destination with no physical access control to the site. People have to be able to walk through, hang out, and do what they do. But it's right next to Hillbrow—and we know what people do in Hillbrow: on the one hand it's a community of schools and churches, but a whole lot of bad stuff goes down here too. The site has to function as part of the city. It's a huge issue, the issue at the center of Johannesburg's battle for survival. In a place like inner-city Johannesburg, can public space be secure and accessible at the same time? Can it be attractive to tourists without being removed from the city by security booms and white-gloved officials, like Melrose Arch, or reachable only through a shopping mall and a parking garage, like Sandton Square? This is Constitution Hill's real challenge.

Because, let's face it, the reason the city authorities are supporting this project is not so much because they believe in the power of heritage, but because they are interested in inner-city regeneration, and they see a heritage precinct as a means toward that end. Which means one thing more than anything else: foreign tourists, who bring resources in quantum leaps. If this site is going to work for international tourists, it has to serve two functions: it has to be a place of pilgrimage, the place where you touch the holy stone of the "South African miracle." Then, in that contradictory way, it also has to be a place where you can experience the buzz and tension of Johannesburg and South Africa in action. Johannesburg could be marketed as a very exciting Afropolitan city: as a place where you can eat fufu or Swahili curry or *pap en vleis*. It's all there at the moment, but it's inaccessible to foreigners. Research also shows that even continental Africans, who come here to shop, stay in their hotels—they fear xenophobia and mugging.

There's a very interesting theory of urban design, advanced by Christine Boyer of Princeton in her book *The City of Collective Memory* [2001], about how modern cities create simulacra of democratic public space.

These spaces are all civic or nationalist projects to create the sense of an eternal value that is embedded in their cobblestones, contrived and often anachronistic—built to look older than they are—because their purpose is to represent the ethos out of which the city was developed. Constitution Hill would need to be that kind of place, in the best possible way; the place to which you would come to experience the essence of Johannesburg and of South Africa; just like you go to the Potzdamerplatz to experience the essence of Berlin, or the Plaza Mayor to experience the essence of Madrid, or Red Square to experience the essence of Moscow, or the Mall to experience the essence of, well, not just of Washington but of the American democracy. Right now we go to another kind of mall to experience the essence of Johannesburg. Hopefully, in the future, you're going to come to Constitution Square, at the middle of Constitution Hill, to see the South African democracy embedded in its stones and represented on its surfaces. But because the South African foundation myth is such a dynamic one—the negotiated settlement, the nation that talked itself out of war and into democracy—it won't be, it can't be, a project of ossification or memorialization. What needs to be embedded into Constitution Hill's surfaces is a process rather than ideology: the belief that debate, reason, interaction, negotiation, and reconciliation will make the future happen. That's why we are using the Sesotho word *lekgotla* so much—a "meeting place." It follows the concept at the core of the Constitutional Court and its new building: "justice under a tree."

Postscript

SN: Mark, the conversation above took place in 2003, before the Court had been completed and the site was in full use by the public. How does Constitution Hill look now, as a site and as an idea, and how does it compare to what you envisaged in 2003?

MG: The first month that the site opened—March 2004—there were 3,500 visitors. From August 2004 onward, once the public programs began, there have been between 8,000 and 10,000 a month. With the opening of the Women's Gaol [see figure 3] in August 2005, there were a record of 15,000. This works out to an average of 5,000 a day. This is extraordinary. The most exciting thing about these numbers is that a large percentage of the visitors to the site are locals. When we first did our research, we noted,

3 Women's Gaol atrium, 2006. Courtesy of Constitution Hill

as one of our major risks, the fact that South Africans do not tradition-ally go to museums and heritage sites. Yet Constitution Hill appears to be reaching the apparently unreachable.

Obviously, once visitors and users start populating a site—start making it their own—it begins to develop a life of its own. It really is no longer a black hole in the middle of Johannesburg. It is used, visited, crossed, discussed, criticized, even loved! It has become what we wanted it to be: a must-see, a pilgrimage site, for anyone who wants to touch base with what the South African democracy means, and few things move me more than watching visitors—international tourists or schoolkids, or ex-prisoners—engaging with our permanent exhibition in Number Four, which tells the story of how criminality was racialized—and race was criminalized, of course—in apartheid South Africa. It was an article of faith that our interventions be substantial enough to draw people in, yet light enough to let the buildings talk for themselves, and to allow visitors to make their own sense of them. And I do think we have succeeded.

Also in our interactive approach: if our philosophy is that each visitor adds to the development of Constitution Hill by leaving his or her story or memory or response, then we have to capture those responses, archive them, and integrate them into future exhibitions. It's an immensely com-plicated process, particularly if one is working in a low-tech, low-budget environment, and it is an area of trial and error. But there is one clear and powerful proof of Constitution Hill's effect: our visitors are not passive. They want to engage, and respond, and leave their traces.

SN: It is a place I go to often, for lectures and debates and exhibitions. It's become part of *my* Johannesburg. . . .

MG: Something we have learned from studying other projects is being vali-dated: if you want locals to visit your heritage site, you have to offer them a real smorgasbord of programs—events and attractions that will bring them back again and again, so that it doesn't function just as a destination site, but as the context for a whole lot of other activities—the "campus for human rights" we envisaged in our business plan; the place where people come together to explore and expand, or maybe just enjoy, the rights en-trenched in the Constitution.

Something that I personally find very gratifying is that Constitution Hill is now the launch pad for the annual Lesbian and Gay Pride March, and the venue of a whole week of activities around pride. I was involved in organizing the first of these marches in 1990, which took place in the city, but since then, they've moved to the suburbs and become purely commercial ventures. Now Constitution Hill—the home of the document that entrenches gay and lesbian equality—not only enables pride to come back to the inner city, but provides it with a very important political context.

SN: How are the activities chosen? You spoke earlier about balancing "the cathedral" with the "town square." Have you succeeded?

MG: Quite soon after the Hill opened [see figure 4], a hip young party promoter, Politburo Sessions, approached the programmers to hold a party in the Old Fort. There's a long history of parties and raves in the building since its closure as a jail, but now that it was formally Constitution Hill, was a party appropriate? "We, the People, have the right to party?" Well, yes, of course. But if so, where? Are there some spaces that are sacred? And does it make a difference if the Politburo Sessions brand their events with political consciousness—fabulous video montages of South African struggle and redemption? Or that their target market are young politically savvy urbanites of all colors, a key target market for animating Constitution Hill? In the end the party took place, but no food or drink (or smoke!) was allowed inside the spaces of the Old Fort. Albie Sachs, one of the justices of the Constitutional Court, likes to talk about how outraged he was when he heard that permission was given for the party to happen, but then how his mind was changed by his son, a political activist himself, who spoke of the necessity for celebration, and the importance of letting Constitution Hill grow, and develop its own identity. I mean, after all, a big fat party filled with people of all races in the middle of the Old Fort could be seen as the ultimate act of reappropriation. Imagine Paul Kruger and H. F. Verwoerd turning in their graves!

But what if Joe Slovo and Mahatma Gandhi are turning in their graves, too? And while I personally might relish Oom Paul turning in his grave, Constitution Hill—like the document it embodies—belongs to everyone. There should be a protocol as to what events can happen where in the precinct—just as there should be a protocol about who can and can't be tenants in all the new office space. And Constitution Hill should be run by a nonprofit institution that sets such protocols, an institution governed in public trust by a board of highly respected individuals. This is what we proposed in the business plan, and it unfortunately has not yet happened, or even begun to happen, which is a pity, for as soon as such an institution is established, there is a clear line of authority and accountability. In the meanwhile, the Constitution Hill heritage, education, and tourism team

4 Entrance to the Constitutional Court, 2007. Courtesy of Constitution Hill

[HET] continues to function under the guidance of the Johannesburg De-velopment Agency, and does, I think, an excellent job following the prin-ciples for programs set out in the business plan and carefully reviewing everything on offer.

SN: These issues are particularly intense at the Women's Gaol, right?

MG: Yes, because—unlike Number Four—it is designated as a mixed-use space. So the South African Commission for Gender Equality, a statutory body, and other organizations have their offices in new buildings that have been erected on the original courtyard of the jail, a place of great trauma and suffering for the women who were once kept there. This is dif-ficult, and it has upset several of the ex-prisoners, who did not even have a chance to reclaim their memories of this section of the jail before it was turned into an office block. Personally, it is not a decision I would have made myself: we in HET inherited it and had to make the best of it—but there it is. We have to work with it—and accept that the development model of Constitution Hill is such that the commercial activities not only fund the heritage ones but have the potential to give them their life, their currency. And it does give the Women's Gaol a very special energy—this interplay of past and present, so beautifully articulated by Joyce Seroke, the head of the Gender Commission, who tells the story of how she gets

5 Foyer, Constitutional Court, 2007. Courtesy of Constitution Hill

up every morning and goes to work, to *help* women, in the very place where she was once imprisoned.

I was in Brazil recently, in the city of Recife, and there, the extraordinary old jail—a multistory panopticon—has been turned into a craft market, with each entrepreneur given an old cell to peddle his or her wares. The only sign that it was once a prison is a little information panel in the central lobby [see figure 5]. It's a highly successful tourism and local empowerment project, but is that enough? These are difficult questions, and one of the things I love about Constitution Hill's model is that it allows us to examine them as the development is taking place. And that its mixed-use approach is trying, creatively, to resolve the dilemma about funding heritage in the developing world.

SN: What was it like working with women ex-prisoners?

MG: To prepare the exhibition in the Women's Gaol, which is now up and open to the public, we expanded on the process we had begun in Number Four: unearthing the site, if you will, through a series of workshops with ex-prisoners, to enable them to share their experiences with us, but also to take ownership of the place for themselves. I did not attend any of the workshops but I have seen the footage, and it is extraordinary how these women responded—not just political prisoners, but ordinary women, beer brewers, immorality act offenders, pass offenders, so-called common criminals, women who had given birth in jail. The trauma that they experienced reentering the site was devastating. It got us thinking about how, no matter how difficult jail is for men, it is—well it *was,* at least, in apartheid South Africa—something expected; almost a rite of passage. For women it is so different—something totally unnatural, against the correct order of things; the source of deep and enduring wounds. In what we do at the Women's Gaol, we need to respect this and honor this but also create and support dynamic institutions and programs that remedy it.

The opening of the Women's Gaol, which took place in August 2005, was certainly the most powerful event I have ever attended on the site. There was a very moving lamp-lit procession, led by ex-prisoners, from Constitution Square up to the jail, and the women themselves—once more, running the spread from formidable icons of struggle to aging gangsters—took ownership of the event and the place through a Women's Forum, which they set up and which is now actively involved in the further development of the site. But then, during a tedious official ceremony of speechifying before a formal sit-down dinner, one of the women stood up and started to protest: "Who are these people speaking?" she cried. "What do they know about this place? This is *my* place! I was here eleven years! Who are *you?*" I'm paraphrasing, but that was the sense of it. It was very embarrassing, very uncomfortable, but it contained, in a cross-section, all the dilemmas and difficulties of developing this site, and I hope it is something that all of us who were there will remember as we move forward with it.

SN: What next?

MG: Number Four and the Women's Gaol are up and running and fully functional, as, of course, is the Court itself. The awaiting-trial block visitors' center is about to be reconstructed on the Hillbrow side of the Court. We will also start activating the Old Fort more fully, while the developers complete the western commercial side of the precinct, with its office blocks, retail facilities, and—most exciting—its visitors' center. This will also be the home of the Nelson Mandela Centre for Memory and Commemoration, a South African version of the grand presidential libraries that dot the United States. We have already started working with the Nelson Mandela Foundation on this, and it promises to be one of the Hill's greatest drawcards.

Note

1 The *tauza* was a "dance" that prisoners had to perform, naked, to show the guards that they had nothing concealed in their anuses.

Reframing Township Space: The Kliptown Project

LINDSAY BREMNER

In 1955, the African National Congress (ANC) held its historic Congress of the People to ratify its liberation manifesto, the Freedom Charter. This event took place in Kliptown, on the outskirts of Soweto, at a site that came to be called Freedom Square in honor of the occasion. Today Freedom Square is an open, windswept tract of land, lying between a shack settlement, a railway line, and a taxi rank and bounded by the back facades of warehouses and wholesale stores. The trees that once lined its edges, providing shade for local traders and commuters, have mostly died, and the farm that once cultivated the land around it has long been abandoned. Remarkable today only for the tapestry of footpaths marking its surface, tracing the movement of people who traverse it in the course of their daily lives, Freedom Square has an auspicious history.

This site in Kliptown was chosen for a meeting of what became known as the Congress of the People simply because it lay outside of municipal jurisdiction, was big enough to accommodate the expected 10,000 attendees, and had functioned many times before as the site of civic gatherings—religious services, political and trade union meetings, and cultural and sporting events.

On June 25–26, 1955, nearly 3,000 delegates and 7,000 spectators from all over South Africa assembled on the site and, surrounded by members of the South African Police, ratified a document that had taken two years to prepare. This process had been inaugurated by Z. K. Matthews of the ANC, not yet a banned organization. His vision was to gather, from across the country, popular demands for a free society. Volunteers from the ANC and its alliance partners collected statements and petitions in church halls, at political rallies, on buses, and in trains. Shortly before the historic meetings, a committee crafted these into a draft charter. This was presented to the delegates at the Congress of the People, amendments were proposed, and delegates voted on its wording, clause by clause. A year later, after it had circulated through the branches of the ANC and its partners, this document was signed by Chief Albert Luthuli, chairperson of the ANC. The Freedom Charter became the manifesto of the liberation movement, symbolizing its vision and dreams of a free South Africa.

Today Kliptown is home to approximately 30,000 people, many from neighboring Soweto or Eldorado Park but also from the rural hinterlands of southern Africa, Lesotho, and Mozambique. These multiple geographies are mapped via the names given to its component neighborhoods—Charter Square, Mandelaville, Chris Hani, Swaziland, Tamatievlei (Tomato Marsh), Geel Kamers (Yellow Rooms)—its superimposed spatial stories about political affiliations, kinship networks, places of origin, and landscape features. Kliptown is a virtually invisible place, folded into and through the myriad of geographies its residents occupy and the stories they tell.

The singularity of this place called Kliptown lies in this seeming invisibility, in this unlocatedness or, rather, in this condition of being located in many places simultaneously. Kliptown is not singular but rather multiple: a locale of teeming, undisciplined practices and trajectories of people who, for all intents and purposes, have been excluded from or by the regulatory discourses of spatial planning and social administration. Kliptown is a community of surplus people living in a leftover space.

Kliptown's history is indistinguishable from this condition of being unincorporated, leftover, or outside of. Its origins lie in the eradication of a Johannesburg inner-city slum yard in the early 1900s. When pneumonic plague broke out in 1904 in the downtown neighborhood known as Coolie Location, its entire population was relocated to a site on the Klipspruit River outside the city limits, close to where Kliptown now lies. The former mixed, slum-yard population—destabilizing to notions of fixed identity and status, of modernity and civilization—was rendered, in effect, invisible and inconsequential. Remaining outside the boundaries of any municipality until 1970, Kliptown survived as a neglected, hybrid space, not least due to the confusing and often mutually contradictory, overlapping bureaucracies under whose jurisdiction it fell under apartheid law—the Peri-Urban Areas Health Board, the Group Areas Board, the Department of Community Development, the House of Representatives, the South West Management Committee, and so on. It was one of the few places in the city where "non-Europeans" could engage in trade or own their own businesses, where couples in racially mixed marriages could live with impunity, or where pass-law offenders could hide. In short, Kliptown was a place where people experimented, through undisciplined, hybridized, and frequently illegal encounters, with change, exchange, and fusion. For authorities, the way to deal with Kliptown—site of activities marginal and illicit—was to simply ignore it.

Kliptown still does not exist, at least not officially. On maps, it appears as a loose grouping of portions of the Klipriviersoog farm. Freedom Square is a collection of small, vacant properties owned by both public authorities and private individuals. The people of Kliptown live in shacks or in dilapidated houses, many without electricity, and with only rudimentary services—portable chemical toilets, communal standpipes, and refuse collection from designated communal sites in the area. Kliptown has a police station but no schools, clinics, or other public services (e.g., a library or community center). The spaces that anchor its social practices, however, are rich and multiple. People live overlapping associational lives between the shebeen, the church, the *stokvel* (collective savings society), the funeral society (mutual aid organization for the bereaved), the youth club, the street, the home. During the day, everyone is out. To stay at home is to miss the life of the street. Private space is small and cramped; things spill out. The prized vantage point is the street—a place to watch, view, greet, sell, and drink, to produce and reproduce the life of the collective.

Since 1999, Kliptown has been targeted for redevelopment by the Gauteng provincial government, under whose jurisdiction it now falls. While this initiative includes the rehabilitation of the adjacent Klipspruit River, improved bulk infrastructure, the building of 7,000 new houses, and the provision of services to its shack yards, the fulcrum of this project—which absorbs more than 33 percent of its budget—is the commemoration of the signing of the Freedom Charter through the redevelopment of Freedom Square.

In 2000, the provincial government decided to include the development of Kliptown on its list of high-priority economic development projects (others include such megaprojects as a rapid rail link between Johannesburg and its airport and the development of the Cradle of Humankind paleoanthropological site as a UNESCO-recognized World Heritage site). This reawakened interest in the neighborhood owed little to a sense of benevolence, responsibility, or redistributive justice on the part of the provincial government but much to a new conception of tourism's significance for economic development.

Gauteng is an inland province with few exploitable natural resources. It is urban and industrialized, with a landscape shaped historically by the booms and slumps of the gold mining industry and by the banality of apartheid's spatial planning. Tourism strategies, in this context, have focused on two areas—shopping (malls, hotels, restaurants) and the township. The township has been reconceptualized as one of the province's few tourist attractions—as an image of apartheid's legacies of racial segregation and poverty, a site of ethnic and cultural identity, and the locus of idealized or aestheticized political struggle. The Hector Peterson Museum in Soweto, erected on the site of the shooting of thirteen-year-old Peterson during the student uprising of 1976, has drawn thousands of local and international tourists since its opening in 2002.

The idea of an architectural competition for the redesign of Freedom Square was conceptualized within this imaginary. In commemorating the events that took place in Freedom Square, the redesigned space was meant to resonate with the "visions and dreams of a free South Africa" (Johannesburg Development Agency 2001: 9); to represent the ideals of the Freedom Charter to an international community so that it would "support struggles for freedom and human rights wherever this is required" (11); and, at the same time, to deal with a range of specific community needs—housing, retail space, library, meeting rooms, local government offices, sports hall, taxi rank, bus stops, and so forth. In other words, architects were asked to mediate between, on the one hand, the "near order" (Lefebvre 1996: 101), that is, direct relations between people and groups interacting in a space, producing and reproducing themselves, and, on the other hand, the "far order"—society's significant ensembles and institutions of power, propelled, in this instance, by notions of freedom, democracy, and human rights. They were asked to imagine how a democracy of populist origins, represented in the Freedom Charter, could be transformed into a spatial or, rather, an urban democracy.

What follows is a discussion of several entries to the competition, chosen from the thirty-three submissions, that can be seen to "dramatiz[e] . . . possibilities for a different urban form" (Minkley 1998: 218) and, in so doing, expand the architectural terrain.

For architects and urban designers from StudioMAS, the competition presented an opportunity to completely re-vision not only Freedom Square and

1 Clothes sellers on the perimeter of the Walter Sisulu Square of Dedication
(formerly Freedom Square), 2005. Photo by Lindsay Bremner

Kliptown but also the entire greater Soweto area and to position it at the
heart of the nation. They constructed a metanarrative for the space, transforming an apartheid buffer strip (including and extending a portion of
Freedom Square itself) into a three-kilometer-long public boulevard lined
with a three-story colonnaded megastructure that connected the wetlands
of the Klipspruit River to the west with the city's sewer works and the Orland
Dam to the east. This nineteenth-century beaux-arts set piece formed the
backdrop to a series of squares: from Freedom Square to the west, patterned
with a giant replica of local artist Willem Boshoff's artwork, to a forecourt to
the national houses of Parliament, relocated from Cape Town, to the east.

The scheme appropriated a number of easily recognizable symbols of
power: the conical towers of the ruins of Great Zimbabwe, the colonnades
of ancient Rome, the light columns of Hitler's Nuremberg stadium, and the
underground vault of the Voortrekker Monument in Pretoria. The Freedom
Charter itself would be laid to rest inside a truncated cone, in which, at mid-

2 View across the Walter Sisulu Square of Dedication, 2005. Designed by
Studiomas, the winners of the architectural competition.
Photo by Lindsay Bremner

3 Papers pinned to the podium at the Congress of the People, 1955. African National Congress Archive, University of Fort Hare, South Africa

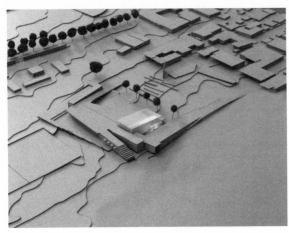

4 Competition model, Mashabane Rose Architects in association with Lindsay Bremner, architect. Photo by Lindsay Bremner

day on June 26 each year, observers would be able to watch the sun briefly light up its surface, before it receded once more into the shadows of history (see figures 1 and 2).

By contrast, though also broad in its scope, Kate Otten and Charles van Breda's entry connected the shack yards to the west with the stretch of open ground to the east using a strategy that deferred the making of form almost entirely. Otten and van Breda simply created platforms of intention, or precincts of activity, based on spatial practices observed at the site. These included a place of gathering or celebration (what they called a "platform of endeavor"), bridging the railway line and increasing the access of shack dwellers to the site; a marketplace; a transport plaza; a community square; and an urban park. Within this civic framework, unforeseen subjectivities, both individual and collective, would shape or appropriate spaces of significance.

My own proposal, formulated together with Mashabane Rose Architects, made use of an analogous relationship between memory, as portrayed by an image of the crumpled papers pinned to the podium at the Congress of the People (see figure 3), and contemporary social practice—the manner in which secondhand clothes are daily laid out for sale in Freedom Square, effectively clothing the earth. The inclusive populism of the Freedom Charter was connected with current modes of economic and associational life and spatial practice. We crumpled and folded the earth to contain an oral history museum and archive, while allowing the micronarratives of everyday life in Kliptown to carry on undisturbed. The events of the Congress of the People were minimally reenacted—a single cable of electric lights, a raised podium, and rows of benches served as a series of mute and almost invisible markers at the intersection of history and lived spatial practice. Space was thus suspended between past and present, a site of negotiation between a multiplicity of times and uses (see figure 4).

Hannah le Roux's response to Kliptown read it as a fragmented web of spatial relationships. Foregoing the temptation to order, unify, or tidy these up, she chose, instead, to create resources at points of potential intersection between tourism and local need. So, for instance, she transformed one of the existing buildings backing Freedom Square through a coupling of the programmatic requirements of a museum and a movie house; she constructed a new connection between Freedom Square and the shack settlements to its west and marked this movement route with a monumental linear scaffold for exhibiting posters, one of the most effective and popular mediums of mobilization during the antiapartheid struggle. In a similar, though more abstract reference, Ivan Kadey, David Barkham, Wilhelm Hahn, and Harold Poliak (American architects, two of whom are formerly from Johannesburg) drew on the modernist (in this case working-class) imagery of industrial space—steel girders, electricity pylons, sports stadia, and billboards—in their reframing of Freedom Square as a site for ongoing political dialogue. Their scheme makes no claims on the wider urban field, constructing instead a single figure around which the fragmented space of the township is clustered.

Other approaches to the space of the township saw its incorporation into the market system as a guarantee of freedom. During the apartheid period, township space existed outside of this logic; it belonged to the state. For Gadija Bux (who submitted jointly with MGB Draughting and Design) and

Feral Gathoo, two nonarchitect participants in the competition, the generalization of exchange across the space of freedom would lift the burden of constraint and misery under which residents had lived for so long and would allow them to participate in contemporary urban (conceived of as economic) life. A trading space bearing the names of liberation heroes Oliver Tambo, Dr. Dadoo, and Lilian Ngoyi and a hotel named after Nelson Mandela would distinguish this place of commerce from any other.

Thus we see a number of approaches to the reframing of township space, responses to the admission of the township into the arena of post-apartheid architectural discourse. These range from refusal, eradication, and displacement to incorporation and an unsettling of disciplinary boundaries.

StudioMAS, which won the competition, saw the township as a not-yet-urban, incoherent, dependent periphery. Marked by poverty and a lack of resources, its space is impoverished and urban life is experienced as no more than a burden of constraints (Lefebvre 1996: 79). For StudioMAS, the commemoration of a founding myth of the new democracy, the Freedom Charter, enabled the investment of resources in monumental urban spaces as stage for celebration and spectacle. Dramatic and exaggerated forms created the image of a possible new city, a new morphology for urban life.

Yet, argues Henri Lefebvre (1996: 114), in the construction of the urban, the formal morphology of the city cannot be separated from social practice. By whom, one wonders, can this formal morphology be construed a city? For, in a single gesture, all traces of the existing site and its peoples have been erased. Mannequins—beautiful, happy, young, and black—have instantaneously populated the newly formed spaces. Kliptown's motley, creolized community of outsiders and their meandering narratives have, yet again, been displaced. They have been rendered invisible by an architecture anxious to redeem a space that has been shaped historically by its outsider status, its dislocation, its fluidity.

Otten and van Breda's work, on the other hand, admitted the social and spatial practices of Kliptown into architectural discourse as potentially unsettling to its procedures and received forms. For them, architecture's role in this space is to establish new connectivities—an inclined plane bridging a railway line, an underpass under a road—to facilitate movement and human interaction. Apartheid planning segregated, fragmented, and dispersed; post-apartheid planning connects, stitches, and centralizes. Otten and van Breda sought to defer to residents and to refrain from overdesigning the space (not always successfully)—to facilitate rather than dictate. The users of the space, would, in time, construct places of identity and value—through singing, dancing, drinking. The architect, displaced from the center, opened architecture to its outside and admitted a less colonizing, less binary set of questions, positions, and procedures.

My own work with Mashabane Rose, like that of Otten and van Breda, conceived of the space of Kliptown not as one of eradicated urbanity but as a unique and open-ended "place of the possible" (Lefebvre 1996: 156) that, having evaded the modernist social project, exists as a place of simultaneity, gathering, and convergence, a place of encounters and multiple narratives. In addition to the specter of the Congress of the People, a new figure—that of the tourist—was about to make its presence felt. Our approach was to fold this new presence into the field of Kliptown through a modification of the ground—through layering, digging, burying, pushing, shifting, raising, encircling, and extending, thereby reterritorializing its space. Building became not landscape but topography—a continuous, folded surface of experience (Deleuze 1993). An oral history museum was inserted under the surface of Freedom Square, the micronarratives that traverse it thereby reformulated. Our approach to architecture was anthropological. We attempted to observe spatial practices from an ethnographic, not a panoptic point of view (the position usually assumed by the architect) and to admit other spaces (the spaces of the other) into the discourse, but we nevertheless reserved for architecture the prerogative of poetic interpretation.

Le Roux sought to realize ideas articulated in a previous theoretical piece, "Undisciplined Practices: Architecture in the Context of Freedom" (1998). In this, she had begun to map emerging tendencies in post-apartheid architectural practice. In her work, space is hybridized, becoming a site of negotiation among a multiplicity of users. She argues that, in environments such as Kliptown, "the construction of a community of users takes priority over the construction of form," and given that "communities may be simultaneously unified and dispersed . . . the appropriate architectural responses may be fragmented and arranged across a broad territory, contrary to the conception of architecture as form enclosing discrete spaces" (355).

While in other contexts, Kadey, Barkham, Hahn, and Poliak's modernism might appear nostalgic, it has specific resonances for the South African township. Jo Noero (1999), winner of a previous competition for the design of an apartheid museum in Red Location, a township outside Port Elizabeth, explains his choice of an industrial aesthetic based on the significance of the factory as the only truly "civic" space during the apartheid years. The factory, through the trade union movement, was one of the few spaces in which visions of an alternative society were mobilized and lived.

Finally, the designs by Bux and MGB Draughting and Design and by Gathoo, like that by StudioMAS, began from a reading and possibly the experience of Kliptown as a space configured within an economy of lack. By reprogramming it with fast-food outlets, fitness centers, sports shops, movie houses, cell-phone suppliers, banks, and other accoutrements of consumer society, its incorporation into an economy of plenty would be signaled to the world.

This representative sample of plans submitted to the competition indicates some of the ways that architects and designers gave shape to the idea of an architecture of freedom in Kliptown—a place, like many others in the country, still bearing the marks of apartheid neglect. All claimed to both represent the ideals of the Freedom Charter and, at the same time, contribute to the development of local people's lives. All interpreted township space and proposed alternative modalities for architecture within it. In doing so, in constructing new imaginaries for the space of the township, they introduced some difficult and unresolved questions: What are architecture's conditions and possibilities in a place like this? What are its purposes and procedures? To whom is it accountable? Who are its subjects? What are its references? If architecture is to have a role in constructing a new urban democracy in South Africa, these are some of the questions it will be required to address.

Afterword: The Risk of Johannesburg

ARJUN APPADURAI AND CAROL A. BRECKENRIDGE

The edited book *Johannesburg, the Elusive Metropolis* is a bold effort to write *the* city. And it is also an effort to write a particular city, a post-apartheid city. This dual effort exemplifies the sort of risk that informed the beginnings of the journal *Public Culture*, where a slimmer version of this book first appeared in the year 2004. With the founding of *Public Culture* in 1988, we proposed that the study of emerging sites of media, consumption, spectacle, and self-making, especially outside the Euro-American world, were no longer understudies in the theater of modernity, waiting for some imagined Western place or actor to fall ill so that an eager aspirant could take her place. The places and people we sought to discuss were, like Johannesburg, different in a common way. And like Johannesburg, they forced us to think of ways to combine comparison, observation, and prognostication, ever alert to the twin dangers of social science flatlining on the one hand, and thickening our stories with new exoticisms—spitting in New Guinea, cybernationalism in Sri Lanka, nostalgia in Jakarta—on the other.

What we have all learned since then is a hard lesson about criticism as a culture of risk. The lesson is this: all that one risk does is to lead you to another one. If you succeed with a risky subject, author, or space, you are compelled to raise the stakes. And if you fail, as we periodically did in *Public Culture*, you are seduced to return to the scene of the crime, to make the return a better remake. So it is with the road that led to this remarkable book on Johannesburg, as one more in the risks that the *Public Culture* project has made compulsory for some of us.

So what are these risks? The first is the risk of self-criticism in regard to the representation of Africa. We have been acutely aware of the longstanding racialisms that have characterized all sorts of work on Africa. We have been sensitive to the images of Africa as the land of weak states, amputated limbs, corrupt dictators, and reckless sexuality. We have been caught, like others, between joyless developmentalism and tasteless Afrocentrism as opposed ways to write of Africa, or to write off Africa. We have been aware that the Conradian journey continues to be seductive as new forms of writing and reportage discover new hearts and new darkness in Africa. And we have puzzled over the challenges of writing about the politics of hope in Africa without losing sight of its severe sufferings. We have worried about the dangers of splitting Africa into its minute sufferings or of lumping it into its continental availability as a chronotope for our own worries about race, poverty, corruption, and disease. After years sustained by friendships, reflections, and conversations over long distances, we have found a way through and beyond these dilemmas, by engaging Africa through the lens of the city.

One risk sets up the next. In "Afropolis," their brilliant introduction to this volume, Achille Mbembe and Sarah Nuttall lay out some of the big ones, starting with the rejection of the default sense of Africa itself, as a land of savannahs and tribes, of gold and slavery, of great migrations and brutal occupations, of untold wealth and fabulous art, of everything that cities are not. The city is an impossible place in Africa, conceived as a land of farmers, hunters, kings, and adventurers. Yet this is not quite true, as Africa is also, especially in one strand of Western adventure literature and anthropology, the land of great entrepôts and trading centers, and of many smaller places that are nothing if not sites of commerce and of city life. Yet these cities were not generally available to us as anything other than the scenes of promiscuous traffic, empty of their own special lives, nodes in a great world of rural and ethnic movements, mining and migrations.

Johannesburg takes the risk of placing the idea of the city at the center of an Africa that has heretofore been composed of kingdoms, villages, tribes and peoples, Nature's Ethnos. This choice leads the editors to assemble many fabulous studies: Mbembe's on superfluity, Nuttall's on self-making and the literary city, Simone's on the infrastructure of improvisation, and Le Marcis's on the suffering body, not to speak of the nuanced and suggestive readings in the section called "voice lines." Each contribution moves us to consider a continent in which crisis has been made the everyday, thus leading those who produce the everyday to improvise practices of self-construction suited to large-scale uncertainty. Everywhere, we are invited to observe how ordinary people in Johannesburg make lives in the shadow of large questions. Yet this is not an ethnography of bare life.

There is a related risk that *The Elusive Metropolis* takes with and through Johannesburg. This risk is at the heart of the debate between the editors and geographer Michael Watts in a subsequent issue of *Public Culture*. Does this project somehow evade, elude, or cheat the real of money and power, of inequality and suffering? Does it somehow forsake the obligation we all have to that Africa which fills the bottom ranks of the *Human Development Report?* We are not about to referee the passionate exchange of voices in this debate. Suffice it to say that *Johannesburg* is filled with instances that show how an aesthetics of the everyday is fully compatible with life on the margins, life under severe uncertainty, and life as a terrain of danger and suffering. There is a subtler issue here, of course, than the tired debates between "culture" and "political economy" or even between critique and curiosity or between seeing like a state and staring like a fool. The issue is whether Africa can be asked any more to defer its encounter with beauty, desire, commodities, and style, while the world decides how to forgive its debt or witness the truth of its reconciliations.

The editors and the contributors to *Johannesburg* have a position on this debate, and it is clear. We will not wait, they argue, and we cannot afford to wait, to defer the writing of Africa until that day (perhaps some sort of Day of Judgment from the Hague, Geneva, or Davos), when the world shall declare that Africa has now officially been allowed the privilege of having an everyday, of having an urban life, of having lives worth studying and styles worth emulating. Presumably that declaration will come when Africa becomes our New Jerusalem, free of warfare, ethnic violence, debt, misery, and forced migration. We understand, as the founding editors of *Public Culture*, why such patience is misplaced. For it requires that Africa bear the special burden of solving the problems of the world. Jesus may have died for our sins, but we cannot ask Africa to do the same.

So we are indebted to Achille Mbembe and Sarah Nuttall for bringing *Johannesburg* to us now, for their refusal to wait until the last product comes out of the last satanic mill in the continent. They show us a city whose very fabric is a statement about the impatience and the insistence of all sorts of people that they will claim an everyday now, and that they will do so with style, conscience, cunning, and confidence. Johannesburg gives us hope as a city, because it shows us that no amount of brutality can quite stop the insistence of ordinary people that they will not postpone their exercise of "the capacity to aspire" (Appadurai 2004).

Johannesburg also gives us hope that the acts of writing and representation (about which the editors speak most eloquently) can be part of the refusal to allow the harder places on this planet to be chained to the fables of breakdown, malfunction, disrepair, and degradation. It is not that these deficits do not exist. But this book, and the longer *Public Culture* project it so brilliantly embodies and inspires, are committed to putting these deficits into a more nuanced account of how people in cities—and others too—nevertheless lead lives of judgment, taste, deliberation, and action, all marks of human life, life that refuses to be entirely bare.

Bibliography

Abbas, Ackbar. 2000. "Cosmopolitan De-scriptions: Shanghai and Hong Kong." *Public Culture* 12, no. 3: 769–86.

Abrahams, Peter. 1957. *Tell Freedom*. London: Faber and Faber.

Addison, Catherine. 2002. "Dangerous but Irrepressible: Cars and Driving in Post-Apartheid South Africa." In *Autopia: Cars and Culture*, ed. Peter Wollen and Joe Kerr, 219–26. London: Reaktion Books.

Amin, Ash, and Nigel Thrift. 2002. *Cities: Reimagining the Urban*. Cambridge: Polity.

Amisi, Baruti, and Richard Ballard. 2005. *In the Absence of Citizenship: Congolese Refugee Struggle and Organisation in South Africa*. Forced Migration Studies Working Papers Series, no. 6. Johannesburg: University of the Witwatersrand.

Anagnost, Ann. 2004. "The Corporeal Politics of Quality (*Suzhi*)." *Public Culture* 16, no. 2: 189–208.

Anderson, David M., and Richard Rathbone. 2000. "Urban Africa: Histories in the Making." In *Africa's Urban Past*, ed. David M. Anderson and Richard Rathbone, 1–17. Oxford: James Currey.

Andersson, Muff. 2002. *Bite of the Banshee*. Johannesburg: STE.

Appadurai, Arjun. 1996. *Modernity at Large: Cultural Dimensions of Globalization*. Minneapolis: University of Minnesota Press.

———. 2000. "Spectral Housing and Urban Cleansing: Notes on Millennial Mumbai." *Public Culture* 12, no. 3: 627–51.

———. 2002. "Deep Democracy: Urban Governmentality and the Horizon of Politics." *Public Culture* 14, no. 1: 21–47.

———. 2004. "The Capacity to Aspire: Culture and the Terms of Recognition." In *Culture and Public Actions*, ed. Vijayendra Rao and Michael Walton, 59–84. Stanford, Calif.: Stanford University Press.

Arendt, Hannah. 1958. *The Human Condition*. New York: Doubleday Anchor.

———. 1966. *The Origins of Totalitarianism*. New York: Harcourt.

Barnes, Leonard. 1930. *Caliban in Africa: An Impression of Colour-Madness.* London: Victor Gollancz.

Barry, Margaret, and Nimmo Law. 1985. *Magnates and Mansions: Johannesburg, 1886–1914.* Johannesburg: Lowry.

Barta, Peter I., Paul Allen Miller, Charles Platter, and David Shepherd, eds. 2001. *Carnivalizing Difference: Bakhtin and the Other.* New York: Routledge.

Bataille, Georges. 1988. *The Accursed Share: An Essay on General Economy,* vol. 1. New York: Zone.

Baudelaire, Charles. 1968. *Œuvres complètes,* ed. Y.-G. Le Dantec and Claude Pichois. Paris: Gallimard.

Bauman, Zygmunt. 1996. "From Pilgrim to Tourist—or a Short History of Identity." In *Questions of Cultural Identity,* ed. S. Hall and P. du Gay, 18–36. London: Sage.

———. 2000. *Liquid Modernity.* Cambridge: Polity.

Bayat, Asef. 1997. "Un-civil Society: The Politics of the 'Informal People.'" *Third World Quarterly* 18, no. 1: 53–72.

Beall, Jo. 2002. *The People behind the Walls: Insecurity, Identity and Gate Communities in Johannesburg.* Working Paper no. 10. Crisis States Programme.

Beall, Jo, Owen Crankshaw, and Susan Parnell. 2002. *Uniting a Divided City: Governance and Social Exclusion in Johannesburg.* London: Earthscan.

Beavon, Keith. 2000. "Northern Johannesburg: Part of the 'Rainbow' or Neo-Apartheid City in the Making?" *Mots pluriels,* no. 13. Available at www.arts.uwa.edu.au/MotsPluriels/MP1300kb.html.

———. 2004. *Johannesburg: The Making and Shaping of the City.* Pretoria: Unisa.

Beinart, William, et al. 1986. *Putting a Plough to the Ground: Accumulation and Dispossession in Rural South Africa, 1850–1930.* Johannesburg: Ravan.

Bender, Thomas. 2002. *The Unfinished City: New York and the Metropolitan Idea.* New York: New York Press.

Benjamin, Walter. [1982] 2002. *The Arcades Project.* Trans. H. Eiland and K. McLaughlin. Cambridge, Mass.: Belknap.

———. 2002. *Paris, capitale du XIXe siècle: Le livre des passages.* Trans. Jean Lacoste. 3rd ed. Paris: Editions du Cerf.

Berlant, Laurent. 1997. *The Queen of America Goes to Washington City: Essays on Sex and Citizenship.* Durham, N.C.: Duke University Press.

Berman, Marshall. 1982. *All That Is Solid Melts into Air: The Experience of Modernity.* New York: Simon and Schuster.

Bertelsen, Eve. 1998. "Ads and Amnesia: Black Advertising in the New South Africa." In *Negotiating the Past: The Making of Memory in South Africa,* ed. S. Nuttall and C. Coetzee, 221–41. Cape Town: Oxford University Press.

Best, Stephen M. 2004. *The Fugitive's Properties: Law and the Poetics of Possession.* Chicago: University of Chicago Press.

Bester, Rory. 2001. "City and Citizenship." In *The Short Century: Independence and Liberation Movements in South Africa, 1945–1994,* ed. Okwui Enwezor. Munich: Prestel.

Bhabha, Homi. 1998. "On the Irremovable Strangeness of Being Different." *PMLA* 113, no. 1: 34–39.

Bishop, Ryan, John Philipps, and Wei-Wei Yeo, eds. 2003. *Postcolonial Urbanism: Southeast Asian Cities and Global Processes.* New York: Routledge.

Blumenthal, Ryan. 2005. "Lightning Fatalities on the South African Highveld: A Retrospective Descriptive Study for the Period 1997 to 2000." *American Journal of Forensic Medicine and Pathology* 26: 66–69.

Boehmer, Elleke, and Gaitskell, Deborah. 2004. "Editorial: Writing the New, Or Now, in South Africa." *Journal of Southern African Studies* 30, no. 4: 725–29.

Bogatsu, Mpolokeng. 2003. "Loxion Kulcha: Cultural Hybridism and Appropriation in Contemporary Black Youth Popular Culture." Honors research paper, University of the Witwatersrand, Johannesburg.

Boloka, Gibson. 2003. "Cultural Studies and the Transformation of the Music Industry: Some Reflections on Kwaito." In *Shifting Selves: Post Apartheid Essays on Mass Media, Culture and Society,* ed. Herman Wasserman and Sean Jacobs, 97–108. Cape Town: Kwela Books.

Bond, Patrick. 2000. *Cities of Gold, Townships of Coal: Essays on South Africa's New Urban Crisis.* Asmara: Africa World.

Bonner, Phil. 1982. "The Transvaal Native Congress 1917–1921: The Radicalisation of the Black Petty Bourgeoisie on the Rand." In *Industrialization and Social Change in South Africa: African Class Formation, Culture, and Consciousness, 1870–1930,* ed. Shula Marks and Richard Rathbone, 270–313. London: Longmans.

———. 1988. "Family, Crime and Political Consciousness on the East Rand, 1939–1955," *Journal of Southern African Studies* 14, no. 3: 87–106.

———, ed. 1989. *Holding Their Ground: Class, Locality and Culture in 19th and 20th Century South Africa.* Johannesburg: Wits University Press.

Bonner, Phil, Peter Delius, and Deborah Posel, eds. 1993. *Apartheid's Genesis, 1935–1962.* Johannesburg: Wits University Press.

Boraine, Andrew. 1989. "Managing the Urban Crisis, 1986–1989: The Role of the National Management System." *South African Review* 5:106–18.

Bosman, Herman Charles. 1994. "Johannesburg Riots." In *The Collected Works of Herman Charles Bosman,* ed. Lionel Abrahams. Johannesburg: Halfway House.

Bourgois, Philippe. 1995. *In Search of Respect: Selling Crack in El Barrio.* Cambridge, U.K.: Cambridge University Press.

Bourriaud, Nicolas. 2002. *Relational Aesthetics.* Trans. Simon Pleasance and Fronza Woods. Dijon-Quetigny, France: Le presse du réel.

Boyer, M. Christine. 2001. *The City of Collective Memory: Its Historical Imagery and Architectural Entertainments.* Cambridge, Mass.: MIT Press.

Boym, Svetlana. 2001. *The Future of Nostalgia.* New York: Basic Books.

Bozzoli, Belinda, ed. 1983. *Town and Countryside in the Transvaal: Capitalist Penetration and Popular Response.* Johannesburg: Ravan.

Bozzoli, Belinda. 2000. "Why Were the 1980s 'Millenarian'? Style, Repertoire, Space and Authority in South Africa's Black Cities." *Journal of Historical Sociology* 13:78–110.

Bozzoli, Belinda, and Peter Delius. 1990. "Radical History and South African Society." *Radical History Review,* no. 46–47: 13–45.

Bradford, Helen. 1990. "Highways, Byways, and Culs-de-Sacs: The Transition to Agrarian Capitalism in Revisionist South African History." *Radical History Review,* no. 46–47: 59–88.

Braithwaite, Edward Kamau. 1973. *The Arrivants.* Oxford: Oxford University Press.

Braudel Fernand. 1981. *Civilization and Capitalism, Fifteenth–Eighteenth Century.* Vol. 1. *The Structures of Everyday Life.* London: Collins.

Braudel, Fernand. 1982. *Civilization and Capitalism, Fifteenth–Eighteenth Century.* Vol. 2. *The Wheels of Commerce.* London: Collins.

Bremner, Lindsay. 1998. "Crime and the Emerging Landscape of Post-Apartheid Johannesburg." In Judin and Vladislavić 1998, 48–63.

———. 2000. "Reinventing the Johannesburg Inner City." *Cities* 17, no. 3: 185–93.

———. 2002. "Closure, Simulation and Making-Do in the Contemporary Johannesburg Landscape." In *Under Siege: Four African Cities,* ed. Okui Enwezor, 153–72. Ostfildern-Ruit: Hatje Cantz.

———. 2004. *Johannesburg: One City, Colliding Worlds.* Johannesburg: STE.

Brenner, Robert. 1977. "The Origins of Capitalist Development: A Critique of Neo-Smithian Marxism," *New Left Review* 1, no. 104 (July–August): 21–46.

Brown, Bill. 2003. *A Sense of Things: The Object Matter of American Literature.* Chicago: University of Chicago Press.

Buck-Morss, Susan. 1989. *The Dialectics of Seeing: Walter Benjamin and the Arcades Project.* Cambridge: MIT Press.

Buhle, Paul. 1987. *Marxism in the USA: Remapping the History of the American Left.* London: Verso.

Bull, Michael. 2001. "Soundscapes of the Car: A Critical Study of Automobile Habitation." In *Car Cultures,* ed. Daniel Miller. New York: Berg.

Burke, Timothy. 1996. *Lifebuoy Men, Lux Women: Commodification, Consumption, and Cleanliness in Modern Zimbabwe.* Durham, N.C.: Duke University Press.

Butler, Judith. 1993. *Bodies That Matter: On the Discursive Limits of "Sex."* New York: Routledge.

———. 1999. *Gender Trouble: Feminism and the Subversion of Identity.* New York: Routledge.

———. 2004. *Precarious Life: The Powers of Mourning and Violence.* London: Verso.

Cacciari, Massimo. 1993. *Architecture and Nihilism: On the Philosophy of Modern Architecture.* New Haven, Conn.: Yale University Press.

Caldeira, Teresa. 2001. *City of Walls.* Berkeley: University of California Press.

Callinicos, Alex. March 1986. "Marxism and Revolution in South Africa." *International Socialism Journal* 31, no. 3: 3–66.

Cameron, Dan, William Kentridge, and Carolyn Christov-Bakargiev. 1999. *William Kentridge*. London: Phaidon.

Cameron, Robert. 1991. *Democratisation of South African Local Government: A Tale of Three Cities*. Pretoria: J. L. van Schaik.

Campbell, Ross. 1999. Review of "Thievery Corporation." *SL*, February: 105.

Canclini, Nestor. 2001. *Consumers and Citizens: Globalization and Multicultural Conflicts*. Minneapolis: University of Minnesota Press.

Chakrabarty, Dipesh. 2000. *Provincializing Europe: Postcolonial Thought and Historical Difference*. Princeton, N.J.: Princeton University Press.

———. n.d. *Historical Difference and the Logic of Capital: Towards a Different Marxism*. Manuscript.

Chalmers, Robyn. 2001. "Eskom Enters Africa, Mideast." *Business Day,* November 8. Available at http://www.businessday.co.za/Articles/TarkArticle.aspx?ID= 467952.

Chaterjee, Margaret. 1992. *Gandhi and His Jewish Friends*. London: Macmillan.

Chipkin, Clive. 1993. *Johannesburg Style: Architecture and Society, 1880s–1960s*. Cape Town: David Philip.

Christopher, A. J. 1994. *The Atlas of Apartheid*. London: Routledge.

Clarke, Simon. 1978. "Capital, Fractions of Capital and the State: Neo-Marxian Analyses of the South African State." *Capital and Class* 5:32–77.

Clingman, Stephen. 2000. "Surviving Murder: Oscillation and Triangulation in Nadine Gordimer's *The House Gun.*" *Modern Fiction Studies* 46:139–58.

Cock, Jaclyn. 1980. *Maids and Madams: A Study in the Politics of Exploitation*. Johannesburg: Ravan.

Cock, Jaclyn, and Laurie Nathan, eds. 1989. *War and Society: The Militarisation of South Africa*. Cape Town: David Philip.

Comaroff, John, and Jean Comaroff. 1992. *Ethnography and the Historical Imagination*. Boulder, Colo.: Westview.

———. 1999. "Occult Economies and the Violence of Abstraction: Notes on the South African Postcolony." *American Ethnologist* 26, no. 2: 279–303.

———. 2001. "Millennial Capitalism: First Thoughts on a Second Coming." In *Millennial Capitalism and the Culture of Neo-liberalism,* ed. John Comaroff and Jean Comaroff, 1–56. Durham, N.C.: Duke University Press.

———. 2005. "Naturing the Nation: Aliens, Apocalypse and the Postcolonial State." In *Sovereign Bodies: Citizens, Migrants and States in the Postcolonial World,* ed. T. Blom Hansen and F. Stepputat, 120–47. Princeton, N.J.: Princeton University Press.

Connor, Steven. 2004. *The Book of Skin*. London: Reakton.

Cook, Sue. 1999. "Street Setswana: Language, Identity and Ideology in Post-Post-Apartheid South Africa." PhD diss., Yale University.

Coplan, David. 2002. "Nkosi ukurocka iAfrika: Some Thoughts on Politics in Popular Music in South Africa." Paper presented to the Symposium on Ethnomusicology, International Library of African Music, Rhodes University, September 14.

Couzens, Tim. 1983. *The New African: A Study of the Life and Work of HIE Dhlomo.* Johannesburg: Ravan.

Cowley, Audrey M., and James E. Mathewson. 1968. *Benoni: Son of My Sorrows. The Social, Political, and Economic History of a South African Gold Mining Town.* Cape Town: Cape and Transvaal.

Crankshaw, Owen, and Sue Parnell. 2000. "Johannesburg: World City in a Poor Country." Paper presented at Urban Futures, University of the Witwatersrand, Johannesburg, July 10.

Crewe, Louise. 2000. "Geographies of Retailing and Consumption." *Progress in Human Geography* 24:275–90.

Cruickshank, Douglas. 2001. "I Crave Your Distinguished Indulgence (and All Your Cash)." *Salon.com,* August 7. Available at http://dir.salon.com/story/people/feature/2001/08/07/419scams/.

Crush, Jonathan, Alen Jeeves, and David Yudelman. 1991. *South Africa's Labor Empire: A History of Black Migrancy to the Gold Mines.* Boulder, Colo.: Westview.

Damisch, Hubert. 2001. *Skyline: The Narcissistic City.* Trans. John Goodman. Stanford, Calif.: Stanford University Press.

Davies, R., D. Kaplan, M. Morris, and D. O'Meara. 1976. "Class Struggle and the Periodisation of the South African State." *Review of African Political Economy* 3, no. 7: 4–30.

Davis, A. 2000. Review of "Magnum Chic," by Harper Engler. *Y Magazine,* November: 30.

Dawson, Ashley. 2004. "Squatters, Space and Belonging in the Underdeveloped City," *Social Text* 22, no. 4: 17–34.

Dawson, Ashley, and Brent Hayes Edwards. 2004. "Introduction: Global Cities of the South." *Social Text* 22, no. 4: 1–7.

de Boeck, Filip, and Marie-Françoise Plissart. 2006. *Kinshasa: Tales of the Invisible City.* Ghent: Ludion.

de Certeau, Michel. 1984. *The Practice of Everyday Life.* Berkeley: University of California Press.

———. 1990. *L'invention du quotidien 1: Arts de faire.* Paris: Gallimard.

Deleuze, Gilles. 1993. *The Fold: Leibniz and the Baroque.* Trans. Tom Conley. Minneapolis: University of Minnesota Press.

Deleuze, Gilles, and Félix Guattari. 1987. *Anti-Oedipus: Capitalism and Schizophrenia.* Minneapolis: University of Minnesota Press.

Derrida, Jacques. 1991. *The Work of Mourning.* Chicago: University of Chicago Press.

De Kiewiet, Cornelius William. 1957. *A History of South Africa, Social and Economic.* London: Oxford University Press.

———. 1965. *The Imperial Factor in South Africa: A Study in Politics and Economics.* London: Cass.

de Kock, Eugene, and Jeremy Gordin. 1998. *A Long Night's Damage: Working for the Apartheid State.* Saxonwold, South Africa: Contra.

de Sousa, Noémia. 2001. *Sangue Negro.* Maputo: Associação dos Escritores Moçambicanos.

de Villers, Gauthier, Bogumil Jewsiewicki, and Laurent Monnier, eds. 2002. *Manières de vivre: Economie de la "débrouille" dans les villes du Congo/Zaïre, Cahiers africains* 49–50. Tervuren, Belgium: Institut Africain-CEDAF.

Dolby, Nadine. 2000. *Constructing Race.* New York: State University of New York.

Dong, Stella. 2001. *Shanghai: The Rise and Fall of a Decadent City.* New York: Perennial.

Drew, Allison. 2002. *Discordant Comrades: Identities and Loyalties on the South African Left.* Pretoria: Unisa.

Edgar, Robert. 1992. "Prologue." In *An African-American in South Africa: The Travel Notes of Ralph J. Bunche, 28 September 1937–1 January 1938,* ed. R. Edgar, 1–42. Johannesburg: Wits University Press and Ohio University Press.

Eksteen, Paul. 2000. "Ethno-kitsch Isn't Enough for African Casino." *IOL,* December 20. Available at www.iol.co.za/index.php?art_id=ct20001220142502400T132704.

Elder, Glen S. 2003. *Hostels, Sexuality, and the Apartheid Legacy: Malevolent Geographies.* Athens: Ohio University Press.

Elphick, Richard, and Hermann Giliomee, eds. 1979. *The Shaping of South African Society, 1652–1840.* Middletown, Conn.: Wesleyan University Press.

Evian, Clive. 2000. *Primary AIDS Care: A Practical Guide for Primary Health Care Personnel in the Clinical and Supportive Care of People with HIV/AIDS.* 3rd ed. Houghton, South Africa: Jacana Education.

Fanon, Frantz. 1963. *The Wretched of the Earth.* New York: Grove.

Farber, Tanya. 2002. "Loaded with Labels: The Meanings of Clothing amongst Urban Black Youth in Rosebank, Johannesburg." MA thesis, University of the Witwatersrand.

Farrell, James J. 2003. *One Nation under Goods: Malls and the Seductions of American Shopping.* Washington, D.C.: Smithsonian Institution Press.

Fassin, Didier. 2002. "Le sida comme cause politique." *Les temps modernes,* no. 620–21: 429–48.

———. 2003. "Anatomie politique d'une controverse: La démocratie sud-africaine à l'épreuve du sida." *Critique internationale* 20:93–112.

Fassin, Didier, and Helen Schneider. 2003. "The Politics of AIDS in South Africa: Beyond the Controversies." *British Medical Journal,* no. 326: 495–97.

Favero, Paolo. 2003. "Phantasms in a 'Starry' Place: Space and Identification in a Central New Delhi Market." *Cultural Anthropology* 18, no. 4: 551–84.

Featherstone, Mike. 2004. "Automobilities: An Introduction." *Theory, Culture and Society* 21, no. 4–5: 1–24.

Ferguson, James. 1999. *Expectations of Modernity: Myths and Meanings of Urban Life on the Zambian Copperbelt.* Berkeley: University of California Press.

———. 2006. *Global Shadows: Essays on Africa in the Neoliberal World Order.* Durham, N.C.: Duke University Press.

Fick, J. C., and H. S. Venter. 1986. *Johannesburg: One Hundred Years.* Melville: Chris van Rensburg.

Forman, Murray. 2002. *The 'Hood Comes First: Race, Space, and Place in Rap and Hip-Hop.* Middletown, Conn.: Wesleyan University Press.

Foucault, Michel. 2001. *Herméneutique du sujet.* Paris: Gallimard.

———. 2003. *"Society Must Be Defended": Lectures at the Collège de France, 1975–1976.* New York: Picador.

Frisby, David. 2001. *Cityscapes of Modernity.* Oxford: Polity.

Gandhi, Mohandas K. 1957. *An Autobiography: The Story of My Experiments with Truth.* Boston: Beacon.

Gaonkar, Dilip, and Elizabeth Povinelli. 2003. "Technologies of Public Forms: Circulation, Transfiguration, Recognition." *Public Culture* 15, no. 3: 385–97.

Gibbal, Jean-Marie, Émile Le Bris, Alain Marie, Annik Osmont, and Gérard Salem. 1981. "Situations urbaines et pratiques sociales en Afrique." *Cahiers d'études africaines* 21:7–10.

Giliomee, Hermann. 1985. "The Changing Political Functions of the Homelands." In *Up against the Fences: Poverty, Passes, and Privilege in South Africa,* ed. Hermann Giliomee and Lawrence Schlemmer, 47–62. Cape Town: David Philip.

———. 2003. *The Afrikaners: Biography of a People.* Cape Town: Tafelberg.

Gilroy, Paul. 1993. *The Black Atlantic: Modernity and Double Consciousness.* Cambridge, Mass.: Harvard University Press.

———. 2000. *Between Camps: Nations, Cultures and the Allure of Race.* London: Penguin.

———. 2001. "Driving While Black." In *Car Cultures,* ed. Daniel Miller, 81–104. New York: Berg.

———. 2005. *Postcolonial Melancholia.* New York: Columbia University Press.

Gordimer, Nadine. 1999. *The House Gun.* London: Bloomsbury.

Gordon, Robert J. 1977. *Mines, Masters and Migrants: Life in a Namibian Mine Compound.* Johannesburg: Ravan.

Grant, George, and Taffy Flinn. 1992. *Watershed Town: The History of the Johannesburg City Engineers's Department.* Johannesburg: City Council.

Gray, Stephen. 2005. *Life Sentence: A Biography of Herman Charles Bosman.* Cape Town: Human and Rousseau.

Gready, Paul 2002. "The Sophiatown Writers of the Fifties: The Unreal Reality of Their World." In *Readings in African Popular Fiction,* ed. Stephanie Newell, 144–55. Oxford: James Curry and Bloomington: Indiana University Press.

Green, Nick, and Reg Lascaris. 1988. *Third World Destiny: Recognizing and Seizing the Opportunities Offered by a Changing South Africa.* Tafelberg: Human and Rousseau.

Guffin, Bascom. 2002. Series of interviews conducted by Bascom Guffin with staff of the Johannesburg Development Agency and the Central Johannesburg Partnership. July 8–10.

Gule, Phindi. 2000. Review of "Yesterday I Cried," by Iyanla Vazant. *Y Magazine,* October: 89.

Gunner, Liz. 2003. "Writing the City: Four Post-Apartheid Texts." Paper presented at Advanced Research Seminar, WISER, University of the Witwatersrand, Johannesburg, February 24.

Guyer, Jane I. 2004. *Marginal Gains: Monetary Transactions in Atlantic Africa.* Chicago: University of Chicago Press.

Guyer, Jane I., LaRay Denzer, and Adigun Agbaje, eds. 2002. *Money Struggles and City Life: Devaluation in Ibadan and Other Urban Centers in Southern Nigeria, 1986–1996.* Portsmouth, N.H.: Heinemann.

Halliwell, Stephen. 2002. *The Aesthetics of Mimesis: Ancient Texts and Modern Problems.* Princeton, N.J.: Princeton University Press.

Hanak, Peter. 1999. *The Garden and the Workshop. Essays on the Cultural History of Vienna and Budapest.* Princeton, N.J.: Princeton University Press.

Hannerz, Ulf. 1980. *Exploring the City: Inquiries Toward an Urban Anthropology.* New York: Columbia University Press.

Hansen, Miriam. 1999. "Benjamin and Cinema: Not a One-Way Street." *Critical Inquiry* 25, no. 2: 306–43.

Hart, Deborah M., and Gordon H. Pirie. 1984. "The Sight and Soul of Sophiatown." *Geographical Review* 74, no. 1: 38–47.

Harvey, David. 1989. *The Condition of Postmodernity: An Enquiry into the Origins of Cultural Change.* Oxford: Blackwell.

———. 2001. *Spaces of Capital: Towards a Critical Geography.* New York: Routledge.

———. 2003. *Paris, Capital of Modernity.* New York: Routledge.

Haughton, Sidney Henry. 1964. *The Geology of Some Ore Deposits in Southern Africa.* Johannesburg: The Geological Society of South Africa.

Hayden, Dolores. 2003. *Building Suburbia: Green Fields and Urban Growth, 1820–2000.* New York: Pantheon Books.

Helgesson, Stefan. 2004. "'Minor Disorders': Ivan Vladislavić and the Devolution of South African English." *Journal of Southern African Studies* 30, no. 4: 777–87.

———. 2006. "Johannesburg as Africa: A Postcolonial Reading of *The Exploded View* by Ivan Vladislavić." *Scrutiny2* 11, no. 2: 27–35.

Hoad, Neville. 2004. "Welcome to Our Hillbrow: An Elegy for African Cosmopolitanism." In *Urbanization and African Cultures,* ed. T. Falola and Steve Salm, 267–78. Durham, N.C.: Carolina Academic Press.

Holquist, Michael, ed. 1981. *The Dialogic Imagination: Four Essays by M. M. Bakhtin.* Austin: University of Texas Press.

Horrell, Muriel. 1973. *The African Homelands of South Africa.* Johannesburg: South African Institute of Race Relations.

Hutcheon, Linda. 1985. *A Theory of Parody: The Teaching of Twentieth Century Art Forms.* New York: Methuen.

Hyslop, Jon. 2003. "Global Imagination before Globalization: The Worlds of International Labour Activists on the Witwatersrand, 1886–1914," unpublished. Seminar paper presented at Wits Institute for Social and Economic Research, University of the Witwatersrand, Johannesburg. June 24.

———. 2005. "Shopping During a Revolution: Entrepreneurs, Retailers and 'White' Identity in the Democratic Transition." *Historia* 50:173–90.

Itzkin, Eric. 2001. *Gandhi's Johannesburg: Birthplace of Satyagraha.* Johannesburg: Wits University Press.

Iyer, Pico. 2000. *The Global Soul: Jet-Lag, Shopping Malls and the Search for Home.* London: Bloomsbury.

Jacobsen, Karen. 2004. "Just Enough for the City." World Refugee Survey.

Jameson, Fredric. 1991. *Postmodernism, or The Cultural Logic of Late Capitalism.* Durham, N.C.: Duke University Press.

Johannesburg Development Agency. 2001. Freedom Square Precinct Architectural Competition Brief. Johannesburg.

Johnstone, Frederick. 1970. "White Prosperity and White Supremacy in South Africa Today." *African Affairs* 69, no. 2: 124–40.

———. 1976. *Class, Race, and Gold: A Study of Class Relations and Racial Discrimination in South Africa.* London: Routledge and Kegan Paul.

Jones, Peris Sean. 2000. "The Basic Assumptions as Regards the Nature and Requirements of a Capital City: Identity, Modernization and Urban Form at Mafikeng's Margins." *International Journal of Urban and Regional Research* 24:25–26.

Judin, Hilton, and Ivan Vladislavić, eds. 1998. *Blank__: Architecture, Apartheid and After.* Rotterdam: NAi Publishers.

Kallaway, Peter, and Patrick Pearson. 1986. *Johannesburg: Images and Continuities. A History of Working Class Life through Pictures, 1885–1935.* Johannesburg: Ravan.

Kaplan, Mendel and Marian Robertson. 1986. *Jewish Roots in the South African Economy.* Cape Town: C. Struik.

Kinda, Akihiro. 2001. "The Concept of 'Townships' in Britain and the British Colonies in the Seventeenth and Eighteenth Centuries." *Journal of Historical Geography* 27, no. 2: 137–52.

King, Charles William. 1867. *The Natural History of Precious Stones and of the Precious Metals.* London: Bell and Daldy.

Klandermans, Bert, Marlene Roefs, and Johan Olivier. 2001. *The State of the People: Citizens, Civils Society and Governance in South Africa, 1994–2000.* Pretoria: Human Sciences Research Council.

Klennerman, Fanny. n.d. Transcripts of Fanny Klennerman interviews by Ruth Sack. Fanny Klennerman papers, Historical Papers, University of the Witwatersrand, Johannesburg, A 2031/A.

Knopfli, Rui. 1959. *O País dos Outros*. Lourenço Marques: Minerva Central.

———. 1962. *Reino Submarino*. Lourenço Marques: Minerva Central.

———. 1968. "Kwela for Tomorrow." *Ophir* 6:2–3.

———. 1972. *Mangas Verdes com Sal*. 2nd ed. Lourenço Marques: Minerva Central.

———. 2001. "In Paris." Trans. Suzette Macedo. *Modern Poetry in Translation* 17:192–93.

Koch, Eddie. 1983. "Without Visible Means of Subsistence: Slumyard Culture in Johannesburg, 1918–1940." In *Town and Countryside in the Transvaal*, ed. Belinda Bozzoli, 151–75. Johannesburg: Ravan.

Koolhaas, Rem. N.d. "Lagos: How It Works." Unpublished draft, copy in the personal collection of Achille Mbembe.

———. 1978. *Delirious New York: A Retroactive Manifesto for Manhattan*. London: Thames and Hudson, 1978.

Koolhaas, Rem, and Bruce Mau. 1996. *S, M, L, XL*. New York: Monacelli.

Koolhaas, Rem, and Sanford Kwinter. 1996. *Rem Koolhaas: Conversations with Students*. New York: Princeton Architectural.

Kracauer, Siegfried. 1995. *The Mass Ornament: Weimar Essays*. Cambridge, Mass.: Harvard University Press.

Krause, Linda, and Patrice Petro, eds. 2003. *Global Cities: Cinema, Architecture, and Urbanism in a Digital Age*. New Brunswick, N.J.: Rutgers University Press.

Kruger, Louise. 2001. "Theatre, Crime, and the Edgy City in Post-apartheid Johannesburg." *Theatre Journal* 53, no. 2: 223–52.

Kurgan, Terry, and Jo Ractliffe. 2005. *Johannesburg circa Now*. Johannesburg: Paul Emmanuel.

Landau, Loren, and Karen Jacobsen. 2003. *Forced Migrants in the New Johannesburg*. Forced Migration Studies Working Paper Series no. 6. Johannesburg: University of the Witwatersrand.

Lane, Richard J. 2000. *Jean Baudrillard*. London: Routledge.

Larkin, Brian. 2004. "Bandini Music, Globalization, and Urban Experience in Nigeria." *Social Text* 22, no. 4: 91–112.

Lee, Leo Ou-fan. 1999. "Shanghai Modern: Reflections on Urban Culture in China in the 1930s." *Public Culture* 11, no. 1: 75–107.

Lefebvre, Henri. 1976. "Reflections on the Politics of Space." Trans. Michael Enders. *Antipode* 8:30–37.

———. 1991. *The Production of Space*. Oxford: Blackwell.

———. 1996. *Writings on Cities*. Trans. Eleonore Kofman and Elizabeth Lebas. London: Blackwell.

Legassick, Martin. 1974. "South Africa: Capital Accumulation and Violence." *Economy and Society* 3:425–58.

Le Page, David. 2001. "Gauteng's Newest Citadel of Sin." *Economist,* January 5, 16.

Le Roux, Hannah. 1998. "Undisciplined Practices: Architecture in the Context of Freedom." In Judin and Vladislavić 1998, F9.

Lipsitz, George. 1994. *Dangerous Crossroads: Popular Music, Postmodernism and the Poetics of Place.* London: Verso.

LiPuma, Edward, and Thomas Koelbe. 2004. "Cultures of Circulation and the Urban Imaginary: Miami as Example and Exemplar." *Public Culture* 17, no. 1: 153–80.

Lodge, David. 2005. *Scenes of Academic Life.* Penguin. London.

Lodge, Tom. 1983. *Black Politics in South Africa since 1945.* Johannesburg: Ravan.

Lu, Hanchao, ed. 1999. *Beyond the Neon Lights: Everyday Shanghai in the Early Twentieth Century.* Berkeley: University of California Press.

Mabin, Alan. 1995. "On the Problems and Prospects of Overcoming Segregation, Fragmentation and Surveillance in Southern Africa's Cities in the Post-Modern Era." In *Postmodern Cities and Spaces,* ed. S. Watson and K. Gibson, 187–98. Oxford: Blackwell.

———. 2003. "Suburbs on the Veld, Modern and Postmodern." Unpublished paper.

Mabin, Alan, and Dan Smit. 1997. "Reconstructing South Africa's Cities: Aspects of Urban Planning, 1900–2000." *Planning Perspectives* 12:193–223.

Mabogunje, Akin. 2000. "Global Urban Futures: An African Perspective." *Urban Forum* 11:165–83.

MacCrone, I. D. 1937. *Race Attitudes in South Africa: Historical, Experimental and Psychological Studies.* London: Oxford University Press.

MacGaffey, Janet, and Rémy Bazenguissa-Ganga. 2000. *Congo-Paris: Transnational Traders on the Margins of the Law.* Oxford: James Curry.

Madondo, Bongani. 2004. "Beemer Me Up." *Sunday Times Lifestyle,* April 4.

Malaquais, Dominique. 2005. "Introduction." *Politique Africaine,* no. 100: 7–11.

Mandela, Nelson. 1995. *Long Walk to Freedom.* Johannesburg: Macdonald Purnell.

Mandy, Nigel. 1984. *A City Divided: Johannesburg and Soweto.* Johannesburg: Macmillan.

Marcuse, Peter. 1988. "Space over Time: The Changing Position of the Black Ghetto in the United States." *Netherlands Journal of Housing and the Built Environment* 13:7–24.

Marder, Elissa. 2001. *Dead Time: Temporal Disorders in the Wake of Modernity (Baudelaire and Flaubert).* Stanford, Calif.: Stanford University Press.

Markovits, Claude. 2003. *The Un-Gandhian Gandhi: The Life and Afterlife of the Mahatma.* Delhi: Permanent Black.

Marx, Karl. 1973. *Grundrisse: Foundations of the Critique of Political Economy.* Trans. Martin Nicolaus. Harmondsworth, U.K.: Penguin.

———. 1977. *Capital.* Vol. 1. Trans. Ben Fowkes. New York: Vintage.

Masekela, Hugh and D. Michael Cheers. 2004. *Still Grazing: The Musical Journey of Hugh Masekela.* New York: Crown.

Masemola, Thami. 2000. "Dlala Mapantsula." *Y Magazine,* June–July, 47.

Maud, John P. R. 1938. *City Government: The Johannesburg Experiment.* Oxford: Clarendon.

Mayekiso, Mzwanele. 1996. *Township Politics: Civic Struggles for a New South Africa.* New York: Monthly Review.

Mazarella, William. 2003. *Shoveling Smoke: Advertising and Globalization in Contemporary India.* Durham, N.C.: Duke University Press.

Mbembe, Achille. 2001. *On the Postcolony.* Berkeley: University of California Press.

———. 2002a. "African Modes of Self-Writing." *Public Culture* 14, no. 1: 239–73.

———. 2002b. "On the Power of the False." *Public Culture* 14, no. 3: 629–41.

Mbembe, Achille, Nsizwa Dlamini, and Grace Khunou. 2004. "Soweto Now." *Public Culture* 16, no. 3: 499–506.

Mbembe, Achille, and Sarah Nuttall. 2004. "Writing the World from an African Metropolis." *Public Culture* 16, no. 3: 347–72.

McGregor, Liz. 2005. *Khabzela.* Johannesburg: Jacana Books.

McIntyre, Pat. 2007. "(More or Less) Democratic Forms: Relational Aesthetics and the Rhetoric of Globalization." *Anamesa* 5, no. 1: 35–45.

Mda, Zakes. 1995. *Ways of Dying.* Cape Town: Oxford University Press.

Merrifield, Andy. 2002. *Metromarxism: A Marxist Tale of the City.* New York: Routledge.

Mhlongo, Niq. 2004. *Dog Eat Dog.* Cape Town: Kwela Books.

Millin, Sarah Gertrude. 1926. *The South Africans.* London: Constable.

Minkley, Gary. 1998. "'Corpses Behind Screens': Native Space in the City." In Judin and Vladislavić, 203–19.

Molamu, Louis. 2003. *Tsotsitaal: A Dictionary of the Language of Sophiatown.* Pretoria: UNISA.

Momplé, Lília. 2001. *Neighbours: The Story of a Murder.* Trans. Richard Bartlett and Isaura de Oliveira. London: Heinemann.

Moodie, T. Dunbar, with Vivienne Ndatshe. 1994. *Going for Gold.* Johannesburg: Witwatersrand University Press.

Morphet, Tony. 2005. "A Comic Eye and Oblique Take Presents New-Century Jo'burg." Review of *The Exploded View. Sunday Independent,* January 30.

Morris, Alan. 1999a. *Bleakness and Light: Inner City Transition in Hillbrow, Johannesburg.* Johannesburg: Wits University Press.

———. 1999b. "Race Relations and Racism in a Racially Diverse Inner City Neighbourhood: A Case Study of Hillbrow, Johannesburg." *Journal of Southern African Studies* 25:667–94.

Morris, Mike. 1976. "The Development of Capitalism in South African Agriculture: Class Struggle in the Countryside." *Economy and Society* 5, no. 3: 292–354.

Morris, Rosalind. 2004. "Apparitions of Desire: Clive van den Berg and the Art of Historical Knowability." *Gender and History* 16:813–24.

Motsemme, Nthabiseng. 2002. "YFreedom—Nthabiseng on Blackness in Post-Apartheid South Africa." *WISER In Brief* 1, no. 2: 6.

Motsepe, Fanuel. 2004. Roundtable Discussion on Cultural Creativity in and Representation of "the Township" at the Townships Now Symposium, WISER, University of the Witwatersrand, Johannesburg, June 9–11.

Mpe, Phaswane. 2001. *Welcome to Our Hillbrow*. Pietermaritzburg: University of Natal Press.

Mstali, Bulelwa. 2000. "Street Couture," *Y Magazine*, May, 61.

Mstali, Bulelwa, T. Masemola, and T. Gule. 2000. "Manga-Manga." *Y Magazine*, June–July, 19.

Mudimbe, Valentin.Y. 1988. *The Invention of Africa: Gnosis, Philosophy, and the Order of Knowledge*. Bloomington: Indiana University Press.

Nancy, Jean-Luc. 1997. *The Sense of the World*. Minneapolis: University of Minnesota Press.

Nappy Head. 1998. "Into Yam, Bongo Maffin." *Y Magazine*, October–November, 46.

News24. 2004a. "Blackout: DA Wants Answer," November 25. Available at www .news24.com/News24/South_Africa/Politics/0,6119,2-7-12_1626600,00.html.

News24. 2004b. "Power Outage in Joburg," December 25. Available at www.news24 .com/News24/South_Africa/News/0,,2-7-1441_1640076,00.html.

Nicholls, George H. 1923. *Bayete! "Hail to the King!"* London: Allen and Unwin.

Nixon, Rob. 1994. *Homelands, Harlem and Hollywood: South African Culture and the World Beyond*. New York: Routledge.

Nkosi, Lewis. 1983. *Home and Exile and Other Selections*. London: Longman.

Noero, Jo. 1999. "Red Location: A Cultural Experience." *South African Architect*, June 19.

Ntshangase, D. K. 1993. "The Social History of Iscamtho." MA thesis, Witwatersrand University.

Nuttall, Sarah. 2004a. "City Forms and Writing the 'Now' in South Africa." *Journal of Southern African Studies* 30:731–48.

———. 2004b. "Stylizing the Self: The Y Generation in Rosebank, Johannesburg." *Public Culture* 16, no. 3: 430–52.

———. 2005. "The Shock of Beauty: Penny Siopis' Pinky Pinky and Shame Series." In *Penny Siopis*, ed. Kathryn Smith. Johannesburg: Goodman, 2005.

Nuttall, Sarah, and Cheryl-Ann Michael. 2000. "Introduction: Imagining the Present." In *Senses of Culture: South African Culture Studies*, ed. Sarah Nuttall and Cheryl-Ann Michael, 1–23. Cape Town: Oxford University Press.

O'Loughlin, John, and Jürgen Friedrichs. 1996. *Social Polarization in Post-Industrial Metropolises*. Berlin: Walter de Gruyter.

Olsson, Gunnar. 2000. "From a = b to a = a." *Environment and Planning A* 32, no. 7: 1235–44.

Packard, Randall M. 1989. *White Plague, Black Labor: Tuberculosis and the Political Economy of Health and Disease in South Africa*. Berkeley: University of California Press.

Parnell, Susan. 1988. "Racial Segregation in Johannesburg: The Slums Act, 1934–1939." *South African Geographical Journal* 70:112–26.

———. 1991. "Sanitation, Segregation and the Natives (Urban Areas) Act: African Exclusion from Johannesburg's Malay Location, 1897–1925." *Journal of Historical Geography* 17:271–88.

———. 1992. "Slums, Segregation and Poor Whites in Johannesburg, 1920–1934." In *White but Poor: Essays on the History of Poor Whites in Southern Africa, 1880–1940*, ed. R. Morrell. Pretoria: University of South Africa.

Parnell, Susan, Mark Swilling, Edgar Pieterse, Dominique Woolridge. 2002. *Democratising Local Government: The South African Experiment.* Cape Town: Juta Academic Press.

Peffer, John. 2003. "Strange Utopia: John Peffer in Conversation with Minnette Vári." *Art South Africa* 2:44–49.

Peterson, Bhekizizwe. 2000. "Kwaito, 'Dawgs' and The Antimonies of Hustling." *African Identities* 1:198–213.

Phillips, William and Phillip Rahv, eds. 1946. *The Partisan Reader: Ten Years of Partisan Review.* New York: Dial.

Pike, David L. 2005. *Subterranean Cities: The World Beneath Paris and London, 1800–1945.* Ithaca, N.Y.: Cornell University Press.

Pirie, G. H. 1992. "Traveling under Apartheid." In *The Apartheid City and Beyond: Urbanization and Social Change in South Africa,* ed. David Smith, 172–81. London: Routledge.

Plaatje, Sol. 1921. *The Mote and the Beam: An Epic of Sex Relationship 'twixt White and Black in South Africa.* New York: Young.

Place, Rodney and Sarah Nuttall. 2004. "A Laboratory of Uncertainty." *Public Culture* 16, no. 3: 532–47.

Poovey, Mary. 1998. *A History of the Modern Fact: Problems of Knowledge in the Sciences of Wealth and Society.* Chicago: University of Chicago Press.

Posel, Deborah. 1991. *The Making of Apartheid, 1948–1961: Conflict and Compromise.* Oxford: Clarendon.

———. 2000. "A Mania for Measurement: Statistics and Statecraft in the Transition to Apartheid." In *Science and Society in Southern Africa,* ed. Saul Dubow, 116–42. Manchester: Manchester University Press.

———. 2001. "Race as Common Sense: Racial Classification in Twentieth-Century South Africa." *African Studies Review* 44:87–114.

———. 2003. "'Getting the Nation to Talk about Sex': Reflections on the Politics of Sexuality and 'Nation-Building' in Post-Apartheid South Africa." Paper presented at the On the Subject of Sex seminar series at the Wits Institute for Social and Economic Research, University of the Witwatersrand, Johannesburg, February 25. Available at www.wiserweb.wits.ac.za/PDF%20Files/sex%20-%20poosel.PDF.

———. 2005. "Sex, Death, and the Fate of the Nation: Reflections on the Politicization of Sexuality in Post-Apartheid South Africa." *Africa* 75, no. 2: 123–53.

Povinelli, Elizabeth A. 2001. "Consuming *Geist:* Popontology and the Spirit of Capital in Indigenous Australia." In *Millennial Capitalism and the Culture of Neo-liberalism,* ed. John Comaroff and Jean Comaroff, 241–70. Durham, N.C.: Duke University Press.

Rajchman, John. 1998. *Constructions.* Cambridge, Mass.: MIT Press.

———. 2000. *The Deleuze Connections.* Cambridge, Mass.: MIT Press.

Raman, Parvathi. 2004. "Yusuf Dadoo: Transnational Politics, South African Belonging." *South African Historical Journal* 50: 72–91.

Rampolokeng, L. 2004. "Johannesburg." *The Half Rantology.* Johannesburg: Shifting Music.

Retort [Iain Boal, T. J. Clark, Joseph Matthews, and Michael Watts]. 2005. *Afflicted Powers: Capital and Spectacle in a New Age of War.* New York: Verso.

Richards, Colin. 2005. *Sandile Zulu.* Johannesburg: David Krut.

Robinson, Jennifer. 1998. "(Im)mobilising Space—Dreaming of Change." In Judin and Vladislavić, D7.

Rogerson, Chris. 1989. "The Deregulation of Hawking: Rhetoric and Reform." *South African Review* 5:136–48.

Rose, Tricia. 1994. *Black Noise: Rap Music and Black Culture in Contemporary America.* Middletown, Conn.: Wesleyan University Press.

Rosenthal, Eric. 1970. *Gold! Gold! Gold! The Johannesburg Gold Rush.* Johannesburg: Ad Donker.

Ross, Fiona. 1996. "Diffusing Domesticity: Domestic Fluidity in Die Bos." *Social Dynamics* 22, no. 1: 55–71.

Sampson, Anthony. 2003. *Mandela: The Authorised Biography.* Johannesburg: Jonathan Ball.

Sansone, Livio. 2003. *Blackness without Ethnicity.* New York: Palgrave Macmillan.

Santa Rita, Maria Tereza. October 1948. "Coisas que eu vi." *Itinerário* 8:10.

Sassen, Saskia. 1991. *The Global City: New York, London, Tokyo.* Princeton, N.J.: Princeton University Press.

———. 2002. *Global Networks, Linked Cities.* New York: Routledge.

Saúte, Nelson. 2003. *A Viagem Profana.* Maputo: Marimbique.

Schelling, Vivian, ed. 2000. *Through the Kaleidoscope: The Experience of Modernity in Latin America.* New York: Verso.

Schlemmer, Lawrence. 1985. "Squatter Communities: Safety Valves in the Rural-Urban Nexus." In *Up against the Fences: Poverty, Passes, and Privilege in South Africa,* ed. Hermann Giliomee and Lawrence Schlemmer. Cape Town: David Philip.

Schlör, Joachim. 1998. *Nights in the Big City.* London: Reaction Books.

Scott, Allen J. 1988. *Metropolis: From the Division of Labor to Urban Form.* Berkeley: University of California Press.

Scribner, Charity. 2003. *Requiem for Communism.* Cambridge, Mass.: MIT Press.

Seekings, Jeremy. 2003. "Are South Africa's Cities Changing? Indications from the Mid-1990s." *International Journal of Urban and Regional Research* 27, no. 1: 197–202.

Sepamla, Sipho. 1975. *Hurry Up To It!* Johannesburg: Ad Donker.

Serote, Mongone Wally. 1982. "City Johannesburg." In *Mongone Wally Serote: Selected Poems*, ed. Mbulelo Mzamane, 22. Johannesburg: Ad Donker.

Shisana, Olive, and Leickness Simbayi. 2002. Nelson Mandela/HSRC Study of HIV/AIDS: South African National HIV Prevalence, Behavioural Risks, and Mass Media: Household Survey 2002. Cape Town: Human Science Research Council.

Silverman, Melinda, and Msizi Myeza. 2005. "Four Spaces." In Kurgan and Ractliffe 2005.

Simmel, Georg. 1950a. "The Metropolis and Mental Life." In *On Individuality and Social Forms: Selected Writings*, ed. Donald N. Levine. Chicago: University of Chicago Press.

————. 1950b. *The Stranger.* In *The Sociology of Georg Simmel*, ed. Kurt H. Wolff. New York: Free Press.

————. 1971. *On Individuality and Social Forms.* Chicago: University of Chicago Press.

Simone, AbdouMaliq. 2004a. *For the City Yet to Come: Changing African Life in Four Cities.* Durham, N.C.: Duke University Press.

————. 2004b. "People as Infrastructure: Intersecting Fragments in Johannesburg." *Public Culture* 16, no. 3: 407–29.

Simons, Jack, and Ray Simons. 1983. *Class and Colour in South Africa, 1850–1950.* London: IDAF.

Singer, Linda. 1993. *Erotic Welfare: Sexual Theory and Politics in the Age of Epidemic.* New York: Routledge.

Sisulu, Elinor. 2002. *Walter and Albertina Sisulu: In Our Lifetime.* Johannesburg: David Philip.

Smith, Charlene, and Aaron Nicodemus. 1999. "More Human Guinea Pigs for Virodene." *Johannesburg Mail and Guardian*, March 19. Available at www.aegis.com/news/dmg/1999/MG990305.html.

Solnit, R. 2000. *Wanderlust: A History of Walking.* New York: Viking.

"South Africa's 'Discarded People': Survival, Adaptation, and Current Challenges." 1998. *CDE Research: Policy in the Making* 9.

Spit, T. 1976. *Johannesburg Tramways: A History of the Tramways of the City of Johannesburg.* London: The Light Railway Transport League.

Stein, Pippa, and Ruth Jacobson. 1986. *Sophiatown Speaks.* Johannesburg: Junction Avenue.

Stephens, Simon. 2000. "Kwaito." In *Senses of Culture*, ed. Sarah Nuttall and Cheryl-Ann Michael, 256–73. Cape Town: Oxford University Press.

Stobart, Jon. 2002. "Culture versus Commerce: Societies and Spaces for Elites in Eighteenth-Century Liverpool." *Journal of Historical Geography* 28:471–85.

Sunday Times. 2000. "AIDS: Mbeki Versus Leon." *Johannesburg Mail and Guardian*, July 9. Available at www.suntimes.co.za/2000/07/09/news/news13.htm.

Swan, Maureen. 1985. *Gandhi: The South African Experience.* Johannesburg: Ravan.

Swart, Lucia, and Borrie la Grange. 2004. "Joburg Blackout 'might linger.'" *News24*, November 23. Available at www.news24.com/News24/South_Africa/News/ 0,,2-7-1442_1625733,00.html.

Tang, Xiaobing. 2000. *Chinese Modern: The Heroic and the Quotidian*. Durham, N.C.: Duke University Press.

Thomas, Deborah. 2004. *Modern Blackness: Nationalism, Globalization, and the Politics of Culture*. Durham, N.C.: Duke University Press.

Thomas, Jeremy. 2000a. "Montecasino Complex to Open End—November." *Business Day*, September 27. Available at http://www.businessday.co.za/Articles/ TarkArticle.aspx?ID=364594.

————. 2000b. "'Shoppertainment' Comes to Fourways." *Business Day Johannesburg*, May 31, http://www.businessday.co.za/Articles/TarkArticle.aspx?ID=380544.

Thrift, Nigel. 2004. "Driving in the City." *Theory, Culture and Society* 21, no. 4–5: 41–59.

Tilroe, Anna. 2002. *Het Blinkende Stof: Op zoek naar een nieuw visioen*. Amsterdam: Querido.

Titlestad, Michael. 2004. *Making the Changes: Jazz in South African Literature and Reportage*. Pretoria: UNISA Press.

Tomlinson, Richard, Robert A. Beauregard, Lindsay Bremner, and Xolela Mangcu. 2003. *Emerging Johannesburg: Perspectives on the Postapartheid City*. New York: Routledge.

Trend Youth. 2005. Produced by University of Cape Town Unilever Institute of Strategic Marketing, in partnership with the youth marketing consultancies Youth Dynamix and Instant Grass.

Trump, Martin. 1979. "The Clearance of the Doornfontein Yards and Racial Segregation." *Africa Perspective* 12:40–56.

Truth and Reconciliation Commission in South Africa Report. 2003. vol. 6. Cape Town: Juta and Co.

Turok, Ivan. 1994. "Urban Planning in the Transition from Apartheid: Part 2—Towards Reconstruction." *Town Planning Review* 65:355–74.

"A Tuscan Village in South Africa." 2001. *Economist*, April 5. Available at www .economist.com/cities/displaystory.cfm?story_id=561883.

Urry, John. 2004. "The System of Automobility." *Theory, Culture and Society* 21, no. 4–5: 25–39.

van Alphen, Ernst. 1998. *Francis Bacon and the Loss of Self*. London: Reaktion Books.

Van der Veer, Peter. 1994. *Religious Nationalism: Hindus and Muslims in India*. Berkeley: University of California Press.

————. 2001. *Imperial Encounters: Religion and Modernity in Britain and India*. Delhi: Permanent Black.

van Niekerk, Philip. 1989. "The Bus Stop Republic." In *The Transported of Kwandebele: A South African Odyssey*, ed. David Goldblatt. New York: Aperture Foundation; Durham, N.C.: Center for Documentary Studies, Duke University.

van Onselen, Charles. 1982. *Studies in the Social and Economic History of the Witwatersrand, 1886–1914.* Johannesburg: Ravan.

———. 2001. *New Babylon, New Niniveh: Everyday Life on the Witwatersrand, 1886–1914.* Johannesburg: Jonathan Ball.

van Tonder, D. 1993. "'First Win the War, Then Clear the Slums': The Genesis of the Western Areas Removal Scheme, 1940–1949." In *Apartheid's Genesis, 1935–1962,* ed. Philip Bonner, Peter Delius, and Deborah Posel, 316–40. Johannesburg: Raven.

Veck, Griffith. 2000. *The Politics of Power in an Economy of Transition: Eskom and the Electrification of South Africa 1980–1995.* PhD thesis, University of the Witwatersrand.

Venuti, Lawrence, ed. 2000. *The Translation Studies Reader.* London: Routledge.

Vincenzo, Ruggiero. 2000. *Movements in the City: Conflict in the European Metropolis.* Harlow: Prentice Hall.

Vladislavić, Ivan. 2001. *The Restless Supermarket.* Cape Town: David Philip.

———. 2004. *The Exploded View.* Johannesburg: Random House.

Von Mucke, Dorothea E. 2003. *The Seduction of the Occult and the Rise of the Fantastic Tale.* Stanford, Calif.: Stanford University Press.

Ward, Janet. 2001. *Weimar Surfaces: Urban Visual Culture in 1920s Germany.* Berkeley: University of California Press.

Watts, Michael. 2005. "Baudelaire over Berea, Simmel over Sandton?" *Public Culture* 17, no. 1: 181–92.

Webster, David, and Maggie Friedman. 1989. "Repression and the State of Emergency: June 1987–March 1989." *South African Review* 5:16–41.

Wheatcroft, Geoffrey. 1985. *The Randlords.* New York: Simon and Schuster.

Wilson, William Julius. 1996. *When Work Disappears: The World of the New Urban Poor.* New York: Alfred A. Knopf.

Wolfe, Cary. 1998. *Critical Environments: Postmodern Theory and the Pragmatics of the Outside.* Minneapolis: University of Minnesota Press.

Wolpe, Harold. 1972. "Capitalism and Cheap Labour Power: From Segregation to Apartheid." *Economy and Society* 1:425–58.

Worger, William H. 1987. *South Africa's City of Diamonds: Mine Workers and Monopoly Capitalism in Kimberley, 1867–1895.* New Haven, Conn.: Yale University Press.

Yeh, Wen-Hsien, ed. 2000. *Becoming Chinese: Passages to Modernity and Beyond.* Berkeley: University of California Press.

Yudelman, David. 1984. *The Emergence of Modern South Africa: State, Capital, and the Incorporation of Organized Labour on the South African Gold Fields, 1902–1939.* Cape Town: David Philip.

Žižek, Slavoj. 1989. *The Sublime Object of Ideology.* London: Verso.

Contributors

ARJUN APPADURAI is a professor of anthropology at the New School University. His most recent book is *The Fear of Small Numbers* (2006).

CAROL A. BRECKENRIDGE is the founding editor of *Public Culture* and teaches at the New School University.

LINDSAY BREMNER is a former chair of architecture at the School of Architecture and Planning at the University of the Witwatersrand, and she is now the Chair of Architecture at Temple University in Philadelphia. A practicing architect, she has published widely on Johannesburg, including the book *Johannesburg: One City, Colliding Worlds* (2004), and was cocurator of the exhibition "Johannesburg Emerging/Diverging Metropolis" at the Università della Svizzera Italiana in Mendrisio in 2007.

DAVID BUNN has published widely on contemporary South African literature and culture, visual theory, and the politics of space. He holds a chair in art history and was until recently Head of the Wits School of Arts at the University of the Witwatersrand in Johannesburg. He is coeditor of *From South Africa* (1987) and a former editor of the journal *Social Dynamics*. He has also worked for many years on projects relating to land claims, development, migrancy, and the politics of national parks.

FRED DE VRIES is a freelance journalist and writer based in Johannesburg where he writes about travel, culture, and politics for the *Weekender* and the Dutch publications *de Volkskrant, Elsevier Magazine,* and *Trouw.* He is the author of *Club Risiko* (2006), a book about the 1980s underground, and is currently working on a book about the South African beat poet Sinclair Beilis.

NSIZWA DLAMINI is a doctoral fellow at the Wits Institute for Social and Economic Research (WISER). He has studied heritage and identity in KwaZulu-Natal and is a curator at the Natal Museum.

MARK GEVISSER is a journalist, biographer, consultant, and filmmaker who has written extensively for publications both in South Africa and abroad. His books include *Portraits of Power: Profiles in a Changing South Africa* (1996) and a biography of Thabo Mbeki titled *Thabo Mbeki: The Dream Deferred* (2007).

STEFAN HELGESSON is an essayist and literary researcher with a PhD from Uppsala University, where he is currently based. He has published *Writing in Crisis: Ethics and History in Gordimer, Ndebele and Coetzee* (2004) and *Efter västerlandet: texter om kulturell förändring* (2004). He is completing a comparative study of print culture and transnationalism in anglophone and lusophone literature from southern Africa.

JULIA HORNBERGER is a researcher at the Wits Institute for Social and Economic Research (WISER). She recently completed her PhD thesis, "Human Rights in Everyday Practice: An Ethnography of Police Transformation in Johannesburg." Her articles on policing in Johannesburg have been published in *African Studies* and *Politique Africaine.*

JONATHAN HYSLOP is the deputy director of the Wits Institute for Social and Economic Research (WISER) at the University of the Witwatersrand in Johannesburg. He has published many articles on nineteenth- and twentieth-century South African social history. His most recent book is *The Notorious Syndicalist: JT Bain—A Scottish Rebel in Colonial South Africa* (2004).

GRACE KHUNOU completed her PhD at the Wits Institute for Social and Economic Research (WISER) in 2006, writing a dissertation titled "Maintenance and Changing Masculinities as Sources of Household Conflict." She has published several journal articles and book chapters and is currently a social policy analyst in the South African Department of Social Development.

FRÉDÉRIC LE MARCIS is an assistant professor in the department of social anthropology at Université Victor Segalen–Bordeaux 2 in France. He spent three years researching the experience of AIDS in South Africa. He has recently developed an interest in the migration of Bulgarian people to France, looking at the interactions between migrants and institutions in the context of Bulgaria's integration into Europe.

XAVIER LIVERMON is currently a postdoctoral researcher at the University of North Carolina, Chapel Hill. His dissertation is titled "Kwaito: Exploring the Politics of Post-Apartheid Sound in the Public Sphere."

JOHN MATSHIKIZA is an accomplished actor, playwright, and director. He is currently a columnist for the *Weekender,* a newspaper in Johannesburg, and is completing a biography of his father, Todd Matshikiza.

ACHILLE MBEMBE is a research professor in history and politics at the University of the Witwatersrand and a senior researcher at the Wits Institute for Social and Economic Research (WISER). He is the author of many books in French, including *Afriques Indociles* (1988) and *La naissance du maquis dans le Sud-Cameroun, 1920–1960* (1996). His most recent book in English is *On the Postcolony* (2001).

ROBERT MUPONDE is a senior lecturer in the English Department at the University of the Witwatersrand. His research explores concepts of childhood, the politics of nationhood, and history in Zimbabwean fiction. His publications include *Sign and Taboo: Perspectives on the Poetic Fiction of Yvonne Vera* (2002), coedited with M. Taruvinga, and his most recent book, *Versions of Zimbabwe: New Approaches to Literature and Culture* (2005), coedited with R. Primorac.

SARAH NUTTALL is an associate professor of literature and cultural studies at the Wits Institute for Social and Economic Research (WISER). She is the author of *Entanglement: Literary and Cultural Reflections on Post-Apartheid* (2007). She is also the editor of *Beautiful/Ugly: African and Diaspora Aesthetics* (2006) and *Sense of Culture: South African Culture Studies* (2000), and coeditor of, among other works, *At Risk: Writing On and Over the Edge of South Africa* (2007).

TOM ODHIAMBO was recently a researcher at the Wits Institute for Social and Economic Research (WISER). His general research interests are in African studies, specifically African popular media, literatures, and cultures. He has published essays on Kenyan popular literature and is currently researching transnationalism in African popular media with special reference to *Drum* magazine. He recently moved to Nairobi.

ACHAL PRABHALA is a researcher and writer based in Bangalore, India. He recently relocated from Johannesburg, where he worked for a year and a half on the consequences of intellectual property regulation on access to learning materials and access to medicines. He is writing a novel.

ABDOUMALIQ SIMONE is a professor of sociology at Goldsmiths College, University of London. He is the author of *In Whose Image: Political Islam and Urban Practices in Sudan* (1994) and *For the City Yet to Come: Urban Change in Four African Cities* (2004).

Additional Illustration Credits

Index

as protection from, 288–89, 296n7,
296n9; in townships, 241–47; whistle
brigades and, 157, 169n17; in Yeoville,
308–16
cross-racial identity, 110–14
Cultural Arc project, 160
cultural theory: creation of Johannesburg and role of, 18–24; economic activity and, 32n3; impact of apartheid
on, 58–64; in Johannesburg, 25–26;
retail malls in Johannesburg and,
298–306; Y Culture and, 93. *See also*
Y Culture (youth culture)
"culture of things": Afropolitanism
and, 24–26; urban studies of Johannesburg and, 17

Dadoo, Yusuf, 134
Dakar, Senegal, 226–29
Dakar Biennale, 161
Damisch, Hubert, 63, 67n28
"Darkies and Ecstasy: Is It the New
Zol?" (*Y Magazine*), 104, 117n14
Daveyton Township, 296n6
Davies, R. D., 139
Dawson, Ashley, 3–4
de Boeck, Filip, 6–7
de Certeau, Michel, 29, 70, 171–72, 198,
201, 274
De Kiewiet, C. W., 43
Deleuze, Gilles, 47–48, 150, 168n11,
218n17
Democratic Republic of Congo, 77,
90n4
Derrida, Jacques, 150, 152, 162
de Sousa, Noémia, 260–62
de Valera, Eamon, 125
de Vries, Fred, 31
Dewey, John, 120
diamond industry: gang control of,
77–78, 90n4; racialized labor organization in, 42–43, 66n12

Diepkloof: clinic in, 180–81, 242; prison
in, 320
disability grants: for AIDS patients,
188–89; urban mobility and importance of, 172–73
Dlamini, Nsizwa, 31; oral ethnography
by, 239–47
Dobsonville Shopping Centre, 305
Docked in a Field of Lights (van den
Berg), 145
Dog Eat Dog (Mhlongo), 96, 212–14,
217n15
Dolby, Nadine, 98–99
Dong, Stella, 11
Dr. Seuss, 153
drug trafficking: inner-city spaces and,
73–75, 77–78, 90n4; Nigerian dominance in Johannesburg of, 81
Drum magazine, 99, 113, 116n4, 120,
195–96, 216n1; as political forum,
225–26
Du Bois, W. E. B., 133

Eckstein, Soho, 141
economic activity: AIDS epidemic as
opportunity for, 180–87; drug trafficking as, 80–84; global cities as loci
of, 2–3, 32n3; in inner-city Johannesburg, 72–79; in Kliptown, 339–50;
in Mozambique, 259–70; people as
infrastructure for, 68–89; race and,
42–48, 58–64; Sandton City as center
of, 298, 306n2
Economist magazine, 56–57
Edenvale Hospital, 174–77
edge cities, 14–15
education system, post-apartheid, 97
"Egoli" (Zulu name for Johannesburg),
187–88, 194n16
electricity infrastructure, 285–95, 295n3
Electricity Supply Commission
(Eskom), 289, 295n3

human immunodeficiency virus (HIV). *See* acquired immunodeficiency syndrome (AIDS)

Human Sciences Research Council, 110

Hurston, Zora Neale, 228

Hutcheon, Linda, 213–14

Hutchinson, Alf, 225

Hyslop, Jon, 15, 28, 65n4

hysteria, architecture of: post-apartheid development and, 62–64

Igoli (City of Gold), 22

immigrants: in Hillbrow, 76–77; Indian, 127–28; Malawian, 76–79; Nigerian, 73–75, 79–80, 90n3; nightlife and food of, 310–16; Senegalese, 76–79; xenophobia towards, 235–37; in Yeoville, 311–16; Zimbabwean, 74–79. *See also* migrant workers

Immorality Act Amendment Act, 45–48

immune-system boosters, 186–87

Independent Complaints Directorate (ICD) of South Africa, 314–15

India: immigrants in South Africa from, 127, 303–4, 306n9, 307–16; politics and Gandhi's legacy in, 135–36

Indian National Congress, 127

indigenous medical practices, 183–87

indunas, 140, 168n6

industrial capitalism: electrical system in Johannesburg and, 287–95; evolution of Johannesburg and, 18–24; Gandhi's critique of, 129

"industrial quarantine line," 173

informality: African cities and role of, 4–8

informalization, economic, 9, 23–24, 32n3

information technology: globalization and, 2, 32n1

infrastructure: absence of, in inner-city Johannesburg, 86–89; apartheid and segmentation of, 21–24; boundaries of Johannesburg and, 27; decay in African cities of, 7–8; literary images of, 200; operating infrastructures, 79–84; "people as infrastructure" concept, 68–89, 154; of street lighting in Johannesburg, 285–95

Inkatha Freedom Party, 168n14

inner-city Johannesburg: art in, 159–67; Constitution Hill Project and, 320–36; drug trafficking as economic activity in, 80–84; ethnic and national identity groups in, 75–79; post-apartheid restructuring of, 72–75; preparedness paradigm in, 85–89; urban Africa and, 84–88

Insanitary Area Improvement Scheme, 20–21

instrumentalist theory: post-apartheid studies of Johannesburg and, 14–15; race and, 43–48

InterContinental Group, 298–99

international culture, 122

investment patterns, fragmentation of, 78–79

irony, in advertising, 107–14

Iscamtho dialect, 272, 282n3

Itinerário (Santa Rita), 262

Jameson, Fredric, 32n1, 147, 149

Jameson Raid, 121–22

Jammeh, Yaya, 77, 90n4

Jerde, Jon, 301–2

Jinnah, M. A., 130–31

"Joanesburgo" (Saúte), 269–70

Johannesburg: anthropological view of, 8–10; as instant city, 221–38; literary images of, 234–35; negative images of, 11–12, 33n6; survey of research on, 10–15

Johannesburg Art Gallery, 156, 158

Johannesburg Biennale, 143

Johannesburg Development Agency, 78, 159–60
Johannesburg General Hospital, 177–80
Johannesburg Stock Exchange (JSE), 306n2
Johannesburg Style (Chipkin), 303
Johnstone, R. W., 139
joling, 280–83, 284n9
Jones, LeRoi, 228
Joubert Park: artistic activity in, 153–59; inner-city infrastructure in, 80; spatial characteristics of, 72–76
Joubert Park (Tshabangu), 154–55
Joubert Park Public Art Project, 158–59
Joyce, James, 119–20, 124–26, 135–36

Kabila, Laurent, 90n4
Kadali, Clemens, 224
Kadey, Ivan, 344, 346–47
Kallenbach, Hermann, 129
kasi ("township boy"), 97
Kaunda, Kenneth, 226
kaw Mai Mai trading center, 162
Kentridge, William, 66n18, 141–43
Kenyan immigrants, ethnographic study of, 248–58
Kenyatta, Jomo, 225–26
Kgobe, David, 224
Khama, Seretse, 223
Khunou, Grace, 31, 239–47
Kinshasa, 7
Klennerman, Fanny, 119–20, 123
Kliptown Project, 289, 337–50
Knopfli, Rui, 262–70
Koelbe, Thomas, 3–4
Koloane, David, 156–57
Koolhaas, Rem, 4, 6–8, 304–5
Kracauer, Siegfried, 17, 60
Krause, Linda, 3
Kreutzfeldt, Dorothee, 158
Kruger, Paul, 221–22, 237

K-Swiss shoes, 107–14
kugel, 302
Kurgan, Terry, 158–59, 164
kwaito music, 33n4, 94, 96–97; media coverage of, 101–7; in townships, 273–74; urban images in, 272–83, 283n2
"Kwela for Tomorrow" (Knopfli), 263

labor theory: art in Johannesburg and, 138–40; disjunctive inclusions and, 49–54; instrumentality of labor and capital production, 37–38; race and, 42–48, 66n13; urban planning in Johannesburg and role of, 19–24; urban studies of Johannesburg and, 15
"Lagos: How It Works" (Koolhaas), 4, 7–8
land acts, biopolitics of, 51–54
language, as literary metaphor, 208, 211–12
Lascaris, Reg, 113
Lee, Leo Ou-fan, 16
Lefebvre, Henri, 70, 89n2, 198, 214–15, 271, 283n1, 345
Legassick, Martin, 139
Le Marcis, Frédéric, 29, 352–53
Lembede, Anton, 131, 134
Leon, Tony, 193n7
Le Page, David, 56–57
Le Roux, Hannah, 344, 346
liberal frontier thesis, 139
Lifebuoy Men, Lux Women (Burke), 103–4
lightning strikes, 287, 295n1
Lipsitz, George, 273
LiPuma, Edward, 3–4
Lissouba, Pascal, 77, 90n4
literature: African modernity and, 119–20; apartheid in, 66n18; images of Johannesburg in, 29–30, 195–216; mining industry depicted in, 140–41;

regressive forgetting: post-apartheid development and, 62–64

regularity: urbanization and, 68–72

Reino Submarino (Knopfli), 263

religion: Gandhi's movement and, 129–31

representation, in Johannesburg, 91–93; literary images of, 198; in Y Culture advertisements, 107–14

repression: art in Johannesburg and, 137

research methodology, 9–10

"reserves," territory, 49–54

Restless Supermarket, The (Vladislavić), 204–7

retail development, 25–26; megamalls and, 297–306; Melrose Arch complex and, 55–64; Y Culture and, 94–97, 116n6

Revolutionary United Front (Sierra Leone), 77–78, 90n4

Rhema Church Service Foundation, 174–76

Rhodes, Cecil John, 222

"rhythmanalysis" (Lefebvre), 283n1

risk: African urban studies and concept of, 351–54

Riverrun (Vári), 166

Road to Ghana (Hutchinson), 225

Robben Island, 324–25

Robeson, Paul, 133

Robinson, Jennifer, 33n7, 197–98, 200, 214–15

Rosebank development: retail business in, 305; Y Culture in, 95, 98

Ross, Fiona, 157

Ruskin, John, 129–30

Sachs, Albie, 332

sacred space: Constitution Hill Project and, 327–36

Sandton City shopping mall, 31, 297–306

Santa Rita, Maria Tereza, 262

Sassen, Saskia, 3

Sassou-Nguesso, Daniel, 77, 90n4

satyagraha, 128, 130

Saúte, Nelson, 268–70

Schlemmer, Lawrence, 49

Schlesin, Sonia, 129

Schlör, Joachim, 290, 296n11

security systems: electricity as tool for, 288, 296n7; homegrown industry of, 80–84; in Johannesburg retail developments, 57–58; at Sandton City, 297–99; Y Culture and use of, 95, 116n6

segregation: urban planning in Johannesburg and, 138–40. *See also* apartheid

Selassie, Haile, 226

self-criticism, risk of, 351–54

self-determination and self identity: in advertisements, 107–14; African nationalism and, 133–35; visual representation as tool for, 92–93; Y Culture and, 101–4

Senegal: artistic images inspired by, 161, 226–29; immigrants in Johannesburg from, 76–79

Sentinel (Vári), 166–67

Sentinel Mining Industry Retirement Fund, 54

Sepamla, Sipho, 216n3

Seroke, Joyce, 333

Serote, Mongane Wally, 196–98

sewer systems, 287–89, 296n6

sexuality: art in Johannesburg and images of, 152–53; nightlife in Johannesburg and, 293–94; post-apartheid erotic performance venues and, 245–47; racism and, 45–48; in South African literature, 234–35

Shanghai, urban studies research on, 11, 16, 33n5

Sharpeville demonstration, 116n8, 2265

Shopping SA magazine, 302
sibondas, 140, 168n6
Sigcau, Stella, 312
Silverman, Melinda, 169n17
Simmel, Georg, 17, 24, 26, 58, 121–22
Simone, AbdouMaliq, 6–7, 27, 154, 200
Simons, Jack, 52–54
Simons, Ray, 52–54
Siopis, Penny, 148–53, 167
Sisulu, Albertina, 131
Sisulu, Walter, 21–22, 131, 133, 225
skin, images of, 148–53
Skwatta Kamp, 104, 282
"Skwatta Kamp: Hard to the Core Hip-Hop" (Y Magazine), 104
slavery: apartheid vs., 117n17
SL magazine, 106, 117n18
slums: African cities and images of, 5–8
Slums Clearance Act, 21
Small World (Lodge), 217n16
Smith, Kathryn, 159
S, M, L, XL (Koolhaas), 304–5
sobel military personnel, 77–78, 90n4
social interaction: Constitution Hill Project as symbol of, 322–36; nightlife in Johannesburg and, 290–95; reworking of, in post-apartheid Johannesburg, 75–79; urbanization and, 6–8, 32n3, 68–72, 89n2
sodium lighting in townships, 288
Sophiatown: as counterculture location, 99, 224–26; literary culture of, 195–96, 269–70
Souls of Black Folk, The (Du Bois), 133
South African Broadcasting Corporation (SABC), 94, 295
South African Commission for Gender Equality, 333
South African Communist Party, 168n3
South African Heritage Resources Agency, 326

South African Medicines Control Council, 185–87
South African Police, 337–38
South African Students Organisation (SASO), 116n10
Southgate shopping mall, 305
Soweto Township: electricity and street lighting in, 288–89; health care systems in, 177–78; historical public space in, 31; kinship and neighborhood relations in, 76; Kliptown Project and, 304–50; literary images of, 232–34; music culture in, 276–78; nocturnal images of, 286; oral ethnography on, 239–47; retail mall development near, 305; urban studies of Johannesburg and role of, 13–15
spatial restructuring: anatomopolitcs and, 52–54; apartheid policies and, 16, 20–24; car culture in Johannesburg and, 274–76; Constitution Hill Project as example of, 317–36; of inner-city Johannesburg, 72–75; Kliptown Project and, 289, 337–50; moral order and, 47–48; nightlife in Johannesburg and, 290–95; in post-apartheid Johannesburg, 14–15, 54–64; race and, 42–48; reworked intersections and, 75–79; urbanization and, 68–72; Y Culture and, 95–97
spectrality: African cities and role of, 4–8
spiritualism, 129
squatters: AIDS epidemic among, 170; in inner-city Johannesburg, 74–75; townships vs. camps for, 240; urban planning in rights of, 21–24; Y Culture images of, 104–7
state heritage programs, 163–64
Stoned Cherrie brand, 95–96, 99, 116n4
Story of My Experiments with Truth, The (Gandhi), 127

SARAH NUTTALL is an associate professor of literature and cultural studies at the Wits Institute for Social and Economic Research (WISER). She is the author of *Entanglement: Literary and Cultural Reflections on Post-Apartheid* (2007). She is also the editor of *Beautiful/Ugly: African and Diaspora Aesthetics* (2006) and *Sense of Culture: South African Culture Studies* (2000), and coeditor of, among other works, *At Risk: Writing On and Over the Edge of South Africa* (2007).

ACHILLE MBEMBE is a research professor in history and politics at the University of the Witwatersrand and a senior researcher at the Wits Institute for Social and Economic Research (WISER). He is the author of many books in French, including *Afriques Indociles* (1988) and *La naissance du maquis dans le Sud-Cameroun, 1920–1960* (1996). His most recent book in English is *On the Postcolony* (2001).